Sami Beydeda · Volker Gruhn (Eds.)

Testing Commercial-off-the-Shelf Components and Systems

Sami Beydeda · Volker Gruhn (Eds.)

Testing Commercial-off-the-Shelf Components and Systems

With 115 Figures and 38 Tables

 Springer

Sami Beydeda
Federal Finance Office (Bundesamt für Finanzen)
Friedhofstraße 1
53225 Bonn, Germany
e-mail: sami.beydeda@bff.bund.de

Volker Gruhn
University of Leipzig
Applied Telematics / e-Business
Klostergasse 3
04109 Leipzig, Germany
e-mail: gruhn@ebus.informatik.uni-leipzig.de

ACM Computing Classification (1998): D.2.4, D.2.5

ISBN 978-3-642-06009-0   e-ISBN 978-3-540-27071-3

Springer is a part of Springer Science+Business Media

springeronline.com

© Springer-Verlag Berlin Heidelberg 2010
Printed in Germany

Cover design: KünkelLopka, Heidelberg

Printed on acid-free paper 45/3142/YL - 5 4 3 2 1 0

Preface

Component-based development has an intuitive underlying idea. Instead of developing a system by programming it entirely from scratch, develop it by using preexisting building blocks, *components*, and plug them together as required to the target system. The benefits are obvious. Parts of a system which do not have to be programmed do not entail costs and do not face the project manager with the risks typically encountered in software projects. It was expected that using components will also contribute to an increase in system quality. However, this expectation is fulfilled only holds in certain circumstances; quality assurance techniques, particularly testing, are still required.

The topic of this book is quality assurance and testing in component-based development in particular. In software construction using preexisting components, various subjects of testing can be distinguished; we also have several roles, each of which is concerned with quality assurance. Each subject of testing and each role has its own requirements of testing techniques. The chapters of this book present testing techniques which can be applied in the various situations.

In component-based development, testing can firstly be classified according to the subject under test. The subject under test can on the one hand be a component and on the other hand be a system consisting of components. We do not consider in this book the testing of component frameworks, such as application servers, or technologies for specific purposes, such as middleware. The testing of components can be further distinguished according to the assumptions made and information available. When testing a component, tests can be carried out without assuming an explicit context in which the component will be embedded. Such type of testing is usually conducted by the component provider, who does not necessarily know the specific environment in which the component will later operate. Tests can also be carried out within a specific system, particularly for integration testing purposes. Such type of testing is often employed by the component user prior to integration into a certain system. As discussed before, the significant difference of these two types of testing is generally the availability of information, particularly source code.

This book consists of three parts, each reflects one of the above types of testing in component-based development.

Part I: Testing Components Context-Independently

This part of the book contains chapters covering the testing of components without assuming an explicit context in which the component will be embedded. This form of testing is usually conducted by the component provider.

Testing Polymorphic Behavior of Framework Components. The first chapter in this part deals with a specific type of component. Tyler and Soundarajan describe the testing of framework components with particular consideration to problems resulting due to polymorphism used for customization.

COTS Component Testing through Built-In Test. Barbier presents in this chapter an approach which employs the strategy of enhancing a component with the purpose of increasing testability. In particular, Barbier proposes to augment a component with metadata constructed on the basis of relevant aspects and present a technical class structure.

COTS Component Testing through Aspect-based Metadata. Cechich and Polo employ a similar approach. They explore aspect-based categorization of information for testing and augmenting a component with metadata for the generation of aspect-dependent test cases.

Automatic Testing of Exception Handling Code. In contrast to all approaches in this part, the approach of Fetzer, Högstedt, and Felber requires access to the source of the component under test. They describe a possibility of testing exception handling code vital, for instance, for recovery during runtime after a failure.

Part II: Testing Components in the Context of a System

This part of the book considers the testing of components, in contrast with the first part, in the context of the system in which the components will be integrated. This form of testing corresponds to that carried out by the component user and includes integration testing in particular.

A Process and Role-based Taxonomy of Techniques to Make Testable COTS Components. In this chapter, a survey of approaches and strategies for component user's testing is given by Memon.

Evaluating the integrability of COTS components – software product family viewpoint. Taulavuori, Niemelä, and Matinlassi address issues of component integrability with emphasis on integration aspects specific to software product families.

A User Oriented Framework for Component Deployment Testing. In this chapter Polini and Bertolino describe the generation of test cases from a system architecture specification for assessing suitability of components to a given environment.

Modeling and Implementation of Built-in Contract Tests. Gross, Schieferdecker, and Din also employ the strategy of enhancing a component for increasing testability. They explain how built-in testing can be used to enable components to test their environments.

Using a specification approach to facilitate component testing. Hybertson describes an approach to specification of components and system architectures for facilitating tests by the component user.

A Methodology of Component Integration Testing. Zhu and He consider integration testing formally; they propose a formal model for integration testing and a hierarchy of behavior observation schemes.

Part III: Testing Component-based Systems

This part shows the testing of entire component-based systems. Component-based systems possess certain properties, particularly at the architectural level, which other types of systems do not possess. This part shows how testing can be conducted when assuming such properties.

Modeling and Validation of Publish/Subscribe Architecture. Baresi, Ghezzi, and Zanolin focus on a specific type of architecture and show how a component-based system having such an architecture can be tested.

Performance Testing of Distributed Component Architectures. Denaro, Polini, and Emmerich show the use of testing techniques for performance analysis in early stages of development once the architectural decisions have been made.

A Generic Environment for COTS Testing and Quality Prediction. An approach for predicting quality of components, and thus a system consisting of these components, is presented by Cai, Lyu, and Wong.

Automatic Testing for Robustness Violations. Fetzer and Xiao explain an approach for detecting faults and security problems in third-party libraries without having access to their source codes with the application of fault injection techniques.

Testing Component-Based System Using FSMs. Beydeda and Gruhn present in this chapter an approach to black-box testing of component-based systems once the single constituents' specifications are given as finite state machines.

Acknowledgments

In July 2003, we invited the leading researchers in the area of testing components and component-based system to summarize their research results in the format of chapters. Fortunately, most of them accepted our invitation and contributed chapters to specific aspects of testing in component-based development. We are very grateful for this and would like to thank all authors for their effort.

Inviting the leading researchers guaranteed a high quality of the individual chapters and thus of the book. We, however, decided to conduct a review to further improve the chapters. The review was conducted with the support of a committee. The committee members reviewed the individual contributions and gave valuable remarks to revise and improve them. We want to thank the committee members for their support; without them the book would not have its quality.

The committee members were:

Franck Barbier
LIUPPA, Université de Pau
BP 1155
64013 Pau CEDEX, France

Luciano Baresi
Politecnico di Milano – Dipartimento di Elettronica e Informazione
Piazza L. da Vinci, 32 – I20133
Milano, Italy

Fevzi Belli
Universität Paderborn
Fakultät V (EIM-I)
Pohlweg 47-49 / Postfach 16 21
D-33095 Paderborn, Germany

Antonia Bertolino
Istituto di Scienza e Tecnologie dell'Informazione - "Alessandro Faedo"
Area di Ricerca del CNR di Pisa, Via Moruzzi 1
I-56124 Pisa, Italy

Jean-Michel Bruel
LIUPPA, Université de Pau
BP 1155
64013 Pau CEDEX, France

Teresa Cai
Dept. of Computer Science and Engineering, The Chinese University of
Hong Kong
Hong Kong, China

Xinyu Chen
Dept. of Computer Science and Engineering, The Chinese University of
Hong Kong
Hong Kong, China

Giovanni Denaro
Università di Milano-Bicocca, Dipartimento di Informatica Sistemistica e
Comunicazione
via Bicocca degli Arcimboldi 8, I-20126
Milano, Italy

Anne Eerola
Department of Computer Science and Applied Mathematics
University of Kuopio P.O.Box 1627
70211 Kuopio, Finnland

Wolfgang Emmerich
University College London, Department of Computer Science
Gower Street
WC1E 6BT London, UK

Christof Fetzer
Dresden University of Technology
Dresden, Germany

Carlo Ghezzi
Politecnico di Milano – Dipartimento di Elettronica e Informazione
Piazza L. da Vinci, 32 – I20133
Milano, Italy

Engin Kirda
Distributed Systems Group, Technical University of Vienna
Argentinierstr. 8/184-I 1040
Vienna, Austria

Michael Lyu
Dept. of Computer Science and Engineering, The Chinese University of
Hong Kong
Hong Kong, China

Atif Memon
Department of Computer Science and Institute for Advanced Computer
Studies
University of Maryland
College Park, MD 20742, USA

Andrea Polini
Istituto di Scienza e Tecnologie dell'Informazione - "Alessandro Faedo"
Area di Ricerca del CNR di Pisa, Via Moruzzi 1
I-56124 Pisa, Italy

Neelam Soundarajan
Computer Science and Engineering
Ohio State University
Columbus, OH 43210, USA

Benjamin Tyler
Computer Science and Engineering
Ohio State University
Columbus, OH 43210, USA

Hong Zhu
Department of Computing
Oxford Brookes University
Wheatley campus
Oxford OX33 1HX, UK

Again, we want to thank all authors and committee members.

Leipzig,
April 2004

Sami Beydeda
Volker Gruhn

Contents

Basic Concepts and Terms 1

Context of the Book 15

Part I Testing Components Context-Independently

Testing Polymorphic Behavior of Framework Components
Benjamin Tyler, Neelam Soundarajan 33

COTS Component Testing through Built-In Test
Franck Barbier 55

COTS Component Testing through Aspect-Based Metadata
Alejandra Cechich, Macario Polo 71

Automatic Testing of Exception Handling Code
Christof Fetzer, Karin Högstedt, Pascal Felber 89

Part II Testing Components in the Context of a System

A Process and Role-Based Taxonomy of Techniques to Make
Testable COTS Components
Atif M. Memon 109

Evaluating the Integrability of COTS Components – Software
Product Family Viewpoint
Anne Immonen, Eila Niemelä, Mari Matinlassi 141

A User-Oriented Framework for Component Deployment
Testing
Andrea Polini, Antonia Bertolino 169

Modeling and Implementation of Built-In Contract Tests
Hans-Gerhard Gross, Ina Schieferdecker, George Din 195

Using a Specification Approach to Facilitate Component Testing
Duane Hybertson 213

A Methodology of Component Integration Testing
Hong Zhu, Xudong He 239

Part III Testing Component-Based Systems

Modeling and Validation of Publish/Subscribe Architectures
Luciano Baresi, Carlo Ghezzi, Luca Zanolin 273

Performance Testing of Distributed Component Architectures
Giovanni Denaro, Andrea Polini, Wolfgang Emmerich 293

A Generic Environment for COTS Testing and Quality Prediction
Xia Cai, Michael R. Lyu, Kam-Fai Wong 315

Automatic Testing for Robustness Violations
Christof Fetzer, Zhen Xiao 349

Testing Component-Based Systems Using FSMs
Sami Beydeda, Volker Gruhn 363

References 381

Index 407

Basic Concepts and Terms

1 Software Development in the Large

1.1 Software Reuse

Industrial development of software systems, often called *software development in the large*, generally needs to be guided by engineering principles similar to those in mature engineering disciplines. Informal methods, which might be appropriate for the development of simple software, cannot be employed for the development of software systems with high inherent complexity. This is one of the lessons learnt from the software crisis. The software crisis lead to the creation of the term *software engineering* to make clear that software development is an engineering discipline. A characteristic of an engineering discipline is the use of systematic, disciplined, and quantifiable methods [194]. One such a method in mature engineering disciplines is that of *reuse*: the development of a new product is based, particularly for cost-effectiveness, on prefabricated components which are tried and tested in previous projects.

Reuse can increase cost-effectiveness of software projects. Considering reusable software units as assets, cost-effectiveness can be increased by using these assets in a number of projects and sharing their development costs. Improved cost-effectiveness, however, is only one of the possible benefits motivating reuse in software projects. According to [369], other possible benefits are:

> *Increased reliability.* Reuse is supposed to have a positive effect on the quality of the software entity reused. A frequently reused software entity is expected to improve in quality and, in particular, to become more reliable, since frequent reuse is expected to reveal failures and other adverse behaviors which maybe otherwise would not be revealed when the entity is developed and tested. Even if this effect can be observed for some software entities, it cannot be generally expected, as shown in the next chapter.

Reduced process risk. Software reuse can reduce risks inherent in software projects. For instance, the cost of reusing existing software entities can usually be estimated with less uncertainty than that of developing the same software entities from scratch.

Effective use of specialists. Software reuse can also contribute to an effective use of specialists. Often, specialists are assigned within one project to development tasks that need also to be conducted within other projects. Reusable software entities can encapsulate the knowledge and experience of specialists and be reused within many projects.

Standards compliance. Reusing software in the development of a software system can also improve its standards compliance, which in turn can have other benefits, such as improved quality. For instance, usability of a software system can be increased by reusing software entities implementing a user interface that users are already familiar with.

Accelerated development. Finally, software reuse can accelerate development. A software project can be completed in less time, and development time can be saved using prefabricated software entities. The reused entities do not have to be developed from scratch, which obviously would take more development time and effort than reusing existing ones.

The potential benefits of software reuse outlined above depend on several factors. One of these factors is the size of the reused software entities in relation to the size of the system to be developed. Risks inherent in software projects, for instance, can be significantly decreased when reusing large software units. Cost estimation in the development of large software systems is more complex and thus associated with more uncertainty than in the development of small software units, whereas reuse costs estimation in both cases requires similar effort and is associated with comparable risk. Reuse of software can be classified into three categories , according to the size of the reused software entities [369]:

Application system reuse. The first category is application system reuse, which can be encountered mainly in two distinct forms. The subject of reuse can be either a complete, unchanged software system or an application family, also called *product line*, which can be adapted to certain platforms and needs.

Component reuse. The second category is component reuse. The term *component* again refers to arbitrary constituents of a system in this context. Single entities of a software system can be reused for the development of a new software system. The reused entities can range in size from single classes to whole subsystems.

Function reuse. Finally, the third category is function reuse. In contrast with application system reuse at one end of the spectrum, software entities consisting of single functions can also be subject for reuse. Mathematical functions, for instance, have been successfully used in such a form for decades [78].

Another factor determining the extent to which software development can benefit is through the reuse of artifacts other than binary software entities. Artifacts, such as the design of a software system, can also be reused from former projects instead of being reproduced from scratch. In the case of design reuse, the design of software can be based on *design patterns* [135] which represent abstract solutions to problems encountered often in the design phase.

1.2 Abstraction Principle

Besides reuse, another method for managing complexity in software development in the large is abstraction. The abstraction principle aims at separating the essential from the non essential. In the context of software development, the essential generally refers to business logic, whereas the non essential refers to technical details. According to [158], a problem often encountered in software projects is that the development of business logic is dominated by technical details. Development of technical details can dominate the development of business logic in three distinct ways:

Firstly, a significant amount of effort is often spent on technical issues which do not contribute to the functionality of the software system. Such a technical issue is, for instance, transactions handling.

Secondly, software is often overloaded with technical details, which hinders analysis of the implemented business logic, for instance for reengineering purposes, and thus complicates its further development and maintenance.

Thirdly, separation of business logic and technical details allows their development and maintenance to be conducted by separate specialists who can contribute to quality improvements.

Various levels of abstraction can be identified in software development. Figure 1 shows some of the typical levels [158]:

Binary values. At the lowest level of abstraction are binary values, which are grouped into binary words. At the lowest level of abstraction, instructions and data are represented by binary words. For instance, the binary word 000100101010 can be an instruction to add two values.

Assembler languages. Assembler languages are at the next level of abstraction. In assembler languages, each instruction is represented by a statement instead of a binary word. For instance, adding two values can be represented as the statement ADD A,B instead of the binary word 000100101010.

High-level languages. High-level programming languages are at another abstraction level. High-level programming languages provide complex

4

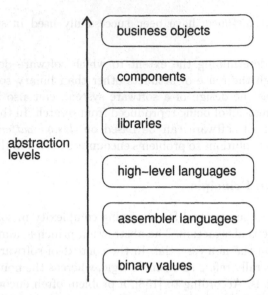

abstraction
levels

- business objects
- components
- libraries
- high–level languages
- assembler languages
- binary values

Fig. 1. Typical abstraction levels in software development

statements which are not mapped to single instructions of the underlying machine. At this level of abstraction, the underlying machine is usually completely transparent to the developer, who can thereby concentrate on the functionality of the software system to be implemented.

Libraries. Above the abstraction level of high-level programming languages are the libraries. Libraries contain solutions, either binary or source code, to problems often encountered during development. The developer of a certain system therefore does not need to implement such solutions from scratch and can instead focus on the functionality of the software system. A library can, for instance, provide solutions for data storage in the form of appropriate data structures.

Components. Components can be considered as forming the next level of abstraction. They further separate business logic from technical details.

Business objects. Finally, business objects can be found at the top level of abstraction. A business object is developed according to a business concept. Business objects represent entities in real-world such as employees, products, invoices, or payments.

2 Components as Building Blocks

In recent years, components and component-based development received much attention due to the explicit support for software reuse and the abstraction principle, two methods of software development in the large. A large number of scientific articles have been published on the subjects of components and component-based development and several component models have been released for development of component-based systems. The subjects of components and component-based development, however, are still not mature, as definitions of basic terms, such as that of a component, did not converge. The various definitions are not discussed here. According to [385], it is assumed that:

Definition 1. *A software component is a unit of composition with contractually specified interfaces and explicit context dependencies only. A software component can be deployed independently and is subject to composition by third parties.*

A similarity between component-based and object-oriented development is the distinction between components and classes, respectively, and their instances. A component is a static description of its instances, while a class is a static description of corresponding objects. Component instances are sometimes assumed to be stateless, such as in [385], which has various consequences. One of the important consequences is that instances of a component cannot differ with respect to their output and behavior, which depend solely on the input. A component-based system thus needs to maintain a single instance of a component, which does not mean that it cannot be multithreaded. In practice, however, instances are often implemented statefully and the instances of a component are distinguished from each other with regard to their state. In some applications, it might be necessary to make an instance persistent, for example, by storing its state in a database. Such an instance exists beyond the termination of the creating process and can be identified by its state.

The type of a component is often defined in terms of the interface implemented by that component. The component type names all operations of the corresponding interface, the number and types of parameters, and the types of values returned by each operation [385]. As a component can implement several interfaces, it can also be of several types. The operations of a component are accessed through its interfaces and are implemented by its methods. Figure 2 shows a meta-model of the basic terms [158]. Note that the meta-model in Fig. 2 also indicates that a component can be implemented according to the object-oriented paradigm, which is, however, not an obligation [385].

In [158], a list of technical properties is given characterizing a component. Some of these technical properties are a direct implication of Definition 1. This list, however, also includes technical properties that do not follow from the definition but are nevertheless explained for completeness. A component is characterized by the following technical properties:

Well-defined purpose. A component needs to have a well-defined purpose. The purpose of a component is typically more comprehensive and more abstract than that of a class. A component, however, does not usually implement the entire functionality of an application, and thus needs to be embedded in an application context.

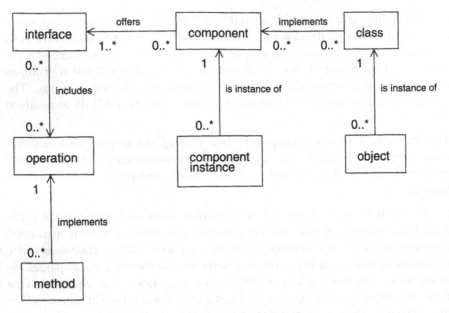

Fig. 2. Meta-model of basic terms

Context independence. A further technical property of a component is its context independence. Even though a component needs to be embedded in an application context, it should remain separated from its technical issues. Separation from technical issues of the application context concerns, for instance, issues of communication.

Portability and programming language independence. Portability and programming language independence means that a component can be implemented in an arbitrary programming language as long as the resulting binary code is compatible with the intended technical environment. Consequently, a component does not necessarily have to be implemented using object-oriented languages. Instead, a component can also be implemented using procedural or functional languages [385].

Location transparency. An important property, at least in the case of distributed applications, is that of location transparency. The quality of services provided by a component should be independent of the component's technical environment. Specifically, aspects of the component's physical location, such as whether a component is executing as a separate process or on a separate host, should be transparent to clients.

Separation of interface and implementation. The property of separation of interface and implementation requires that a component interact with its clients solely through its interfaces and that its implementation be encapsulated. The implementation of a component should be transparent to clients, which should not be able to access internal features of the component. Separation of interface and implementation leads to explicit dependencies between a component and its context, and this in turn simplifies its reuse.

Introspection. Introspection refers to the ability of a component to provide clients meta-information describing its interfaces and functionality. In contrast to *reflection*, which also allows clients to obtain meta-information, the meta-information is usually assembled by the component developer and can thus be focused on certain composition-related aspects [151]. The meta-information provided can be explored by clients at runtime, allowing thereby, for instance, dynamic reconfiguration of a component-based system.

Plug-and-play. Furthermore, a component should possess plug-and-play capability. Installation of a component should be automatic as far as possible, and supported by the component itself. Installation tasks which can be automated are, for instance, registration of the component in naming services.

Integration and composition. A component should support integration and composition as typical properties. Component integration and composition can be distinguished in *static* and *dynamic*, where static refers to integration and composition during the development of a component-based system, and dynamic to those during runtime. A component should support both types of integration and composition.

Reuse. A component needs to support techniques allowing its reuse. One of the two methods for software development in the large is reuse as explained before. Usability of a component in software development in the large thus strongly depends on its support for techniques allowing its reuse, particularly in the application context for which it was developed.

Configuration. Closely related to the property of reuse is that of configuration. Configuration of a component can be necessary for its reuse in the development of a new system. Thus, a component needs to support configuration techniques, particularly those based on parameterization.

Approval. One of the possible benefits of reuse is that of increased reliability and thereby approval. Frequently reused software units are expected to be more reliable than newly developed ones, as they have been tried and tested in other projects. It was thus expected that reuse would make testing obsolete. Contrary to expectations, however, reuse does not generally obviate testing, as explained in the next chapter.

Binary form. Finally, components are often available in binary form only. The developer of a component often does not disclose the source code and other detailed information in order to protect intellectual property. Furthermore, disclosing such information can give competitors advantages over the developer, which is obviously undesirable, and not only in the case of commercial components.

The technical properties illustrate the close relation between components and software development in the large. On the one hand, use of components pays off in terms of cost and time savings only if the system to be developed possesses a certain critical size, since the use of components involves a certain overhead. On the other hand, software development in large makes use of two specific methods: reuse and abstraction. Both methods are supported by components, as the above explanation of technical properties shows.

3 Component Models and Frameworks

3.1 Basic Concepts

Software development in the large in general and component-based development in particular typically involve several parties, something which requires technical standards for cooperation. In the context of component-based development, such standards and conventions are specified by component models. As with other terms in this context, the term *component model* is not defined uniquely. According to [14], it is assumed here that:

Definition 2. *A* component model *is the set of component types, their interfaces, and, additionally, a specification of the allowable patterns of interaction among component types.*

A component model can require that components of that model implement certain interfaces, and can thereby impose certain component types. Furthermore, a component model can define how components have to interact with each other in the form of allowed interaction patterns that can cover aspects such as which component types can be clients of which other component types.

The standards and conventions specified by a component model are necessary for component-based development due to the following reasons [14]:

Uniform composition. Information describing the required and provided services of each component is a necessary condition for correct interaction of two components. This information usually needs to address aspects such as the functionality of each component, how each component is located, how control flow is synchronized, which communication protocol is used, and how data is encoded.

Appropriate quality attributes. The quality of a component-based system obviously depends on the quality of its constituent individual components. The component model can specify interaction patterns necessary to set those characteristics to certain values and states that affect the quality of the component-based system to achieve a certain system quality.

Deployment of components and applications. Besides composition of components, another critical success factor for component-based development is deployment of individual components and the resulting component-based system. Specifically, standards and conventions need to be specified allowing deployment of individual components into the development environment and deployment of the resulting system into the end user environment.

The standards and conventions specified by a component model are technically supported by a *component framework* implementing the necessary technical infrastructure and providing the necessary services. A component framework thus establishes the environmental conditions for the components following a certain component model. Typical services implemented by a component framework are the following [14]:

Management of resources shared by components. One of the main services implemented by a component framework is the management of resources. For instance, component frameworks often provide load balancing services for distributing available processing capacity among components according to certain scheduling criteria.

Communication among components. Another important service provided by a component framework is facilitating communication among components. Usually, the service provided allows component communication without requiring close coupling of components, something which encapsulates technical details within components.

Management of component life cycle. A service implemented, for instance, by component frameworks for the Enterprise JavaBeans component model is management of the component life cycle. A component framework can directly work with a component and change the states of its instances according to certain criteria.

A component framework can be implemented according to various paradigms. It can be implemented as an autonomous system existing at runtime independently from the components supported, such as the component frameworks for the Enterprise JavaBeans component model. Such a component framework can be regarded as an operating system with a special purpose. A component framework, however, can also be implemented as a non-autonomous system which can be instantiated by components. An example of a non-autonomous component framework can be found in [233]. As a third alternative, a component framework can also itself be implemented as a component, which allows the composition of component frameworks [385]. In such an approach, a high order component framework might regulate the interaction of other component frameworks and might provide them with the necessary technical services. Such high order component frameworks, however, are currently not available.

3.2 Enterprise JavaBeans Component Model and Framework

One of the component models widely used in practice is the one following the Enterprise JavaBeans specification released by Sun Microsystems. The Enterprise JavaBeans specification defines the *Enterprise JavaBeans architecture* for the development of distributed, component-based client/server systems. The initial specification of the Enterprise JavaBeans was released in 1998. Since then, the specification was developed further, and several extensions were made to the initial release. In this subsection, the Enterprise JavaBeans component model and framework are explained with respect to release 2.1 of the specification, which can be found in [92]. Other examples of component models are the CORBA Component Model proposed by the Object Management Group [312] and the Component Object Model and related technologies proposed by Microsoft Corporation [283].

Component Types

One of the component types defined by the Enterprise JavaBeans specification is the *session bean*. The primary purpose of a session bean is to encapsulate business logic. A session bean is usually non-persistent, i.e., its data is not stored in a database and is lost after the session is terminated. Furthermore, a session bean cannot be accessed simultaneously by multiple clients. A session bean provides its services through specific interfaces, depending on the type of client and service. Clients that can access a session bean can be either local or remote, and the services provided can be classified as being related either to the life cycle of a particular session bean or to the business logic implemented. In this context, the main distinction between a local and a remote client is that local clients execute in the same Java virtual machine, and that the location of the session bean is not transparent for local clients, whereas a remote client can execute in a different Java virtual machine and thus on a different host, so the location of the session bean is transparent.

Figure 3 shows two session beans embedded in the component framework as specified by the Enterprise JavaBeans specification, which defines a component framework consisting of *servers* and *containers* to support the component model. A server is generally responsible for providing technical services such as persistence, transactions, and security, whereas a container provides services related to management of the component life cycle. An enterprise bean is encapsulated in a container, which is in turn embedded in a server. The Enterprise JavaBeans specification, however, does not clearly separate containers from servers, and the terms are often used interchangeably. The component framework consisting of a server and a container is transparent to the user of an enterprise bean. Initially, a client intending to access the business logic implemented by a certain session bean needs to create a reference to it. The appropriate methods can be invoked through the *home interface* of the session bean, which in Fig. 3 is called EJBLocalHome and EJBHome for the local and the remote session bean, respectively. Note that, technically, a

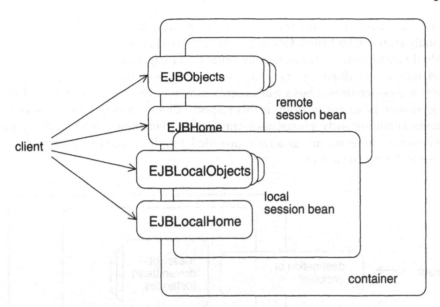

Fig. 3. Client view of session beans deployed in a container

session bean can implement both types of interfaces; however, this is rarely the case. Having obtained a reference to the session bean, methods implementing the business logic can be invoked through the *local interface* and the *remote interface*. In Fig. 3, these interfaces are called `EJBLocalObjects` and `EJBObjects`.

The second component type defined by the Enterprise JavaBeans specification is the *entity bean*. An entity bean represents a business object. In contrast to session beans, an entity bean can be persistent, i.e. data encapsulated in an entity bean can be stored in a database and can thus exist beyond the termination of the component-based system and the component framework. Database entries are mapped to entity beans through *primary keys*, which are unique identifiers of entity beans. Another distinction to session beans is that an entity bean can be accessed by several clients. As several clients might intend to modify data simultaneously, transaction techniques might be required to ensure the consistency of the data. Such techniques, however, are implemented by the server hosting the container of the corresponding entity bean, and do not need to be implemented by the entity bean itself. An entity bean provides similar interfaces as a session bean; thus, Fig. 3 is also valid, with minor changes, for entity beans.

One of the new features in release 2.0 of the Enterprise JavaBeans specification is a third component type called *message-driven bean*. Its main differences with the other component types is that it allows asynchronous computations: a message-driven bean is invoked by the container when a messages arrives. A direct consequence is that a message-driven bean is not accessed through interfaces similar to session and entity beans. Instead, a client intending to access a message-driven bean needs to generate a message. A message-driven bean is usually stateless and thus does not need to be persistent. Consequently, individual message-driven beans usually cannot be distinguished from each other and unique identifiers are not required, as opposed to entity beans. However, a message-driven bean can process messages from several beans; thus, it is similar to an entity bean in this respect. The capability to serve several clients simultaneously necessitates transaction techniques. Such underlying techniques, however, are generally provided by the component framework, specifically, by the server.

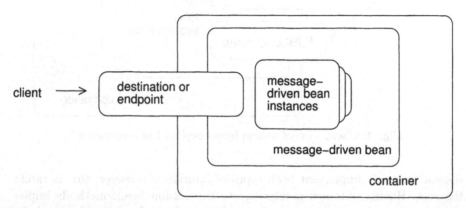

Fig. 4. Client view of message-driven beans deployed in a container

Figure 4 shows a message-driven bean embedded in the component framework. As in the case with the other two component types, the component framework consists of servers and containers. They have the same objectives, namely providing basic technical services in the case of the server and managing the life cycle of the enterprise bean, i.e., the message-driven bean.

Roles in Component-based Development

The Enterprise JavaBeans specification defines six roles that are responsible for the various tasks in the life cycle of a component-based system. The specification particularly defines contracts between the various roles, for instance, the products to be delivered by one role to another. In the Enterprise JavaBeans specification, these roles are defined as follows :

Enterprise bean provider. The enterprise bean provider is responsible for the development of beans. Tasks which particularly need to be conducted by the enterprise bean provider are the definition of the bean interfaces, development of classes implementing business logic, and composition of the bean deployment descriptor making external dependencies explicit.

Application assembler. The application assembler is responsible for packaging EJB components to larger deployable entities. The task assigned to the application assembler is to generate files containing EJB components and information, stored in the corresponding deployment descriptors, on various technical aspects of the EJB components.

Deployer. The deployer is responsible for the deployment of the files produced by the application assembler into a specific operational environment. The operational environment is in such a case a specific component framework, i.e., an Enterprise JavaBeans server and container. The deployer needs to take into account the external dependencies of each bean, specified in the corresponding deployment descriptor by the bean provider, and also application assembly information provided by the application assembler.

EJB server provider. The main responsibility of the EJB server provider is to deliver the EJB server in which EJB containers can be embedded. The server implements technical services such as transaction management and encapsulates the implementation of the technical services from the container.

EJB container provider. In a manner to the EJB server provider, the EJB container provider is responsible for delivering the EJB container in which single beans can be embedded. Furthermore, the EJB container provider is also in charge of developing tools necessary for beans deployment and for providing runtime support for deployed beans.

System administrator. Finally, the system administrator is responsible for the configuration and administration of the operational environment including the component framework. The system administrator is usually also in charge of monitoring the deployed EJB components to avoid problems at runtime.

The Enterprise JavaBeans component model and frameworks explicitly support reuse and abstraction, two methods of software development in the large. Software reuse, on the one hand, is facilitated, for instance, by the deployment descriptor associated with each EJB component specifying its context dependencies. The abstraction principle, on the other hand, is facilitated, for instance, by the roles defined in the Enterprise JavaBeans specification. Specifically, the development of business logic is assigned to a single role, and corresponding tasks have to be carried out solely by that role. Technical and administrative tasks are assigned to other roles. The definition of the six roles contributes to an abstraction of business logic development from technical and administrative tasks during component-based development. An abstraction of business logic from technical details in the architecture of a component-based system is achieved by the component framework. An EJB component solely implements the intended business logic, whereas techniques necessary, for instance, for distribution and persistence are implemented by the component framework.

4 Commercial-off-the-Shelf (COTS) Components

In comparison to other reusable software entities, one of the distinguishing features of components, particularly those referred to as *commercial-off-the-shelf* (COTS) components, are their market-related aspects. According to [20], a COTS component has the following characteristics:

> *The buyer has no access to the source code,*
>
> *the vendor controls its development,*
>
> *and it has a nontrivial installed base.*

The term *COTS component*, however, is not uniquely defined, as a discussion of the various definitions in [291] shows, and the above characteristics do not exist to the same degree for each commercially available component. Among other factors, the existence of the above characteristics depends on the organizational relationship between the vendor of the component and its buyer. The organizational relations between the component provider and component user can be manifold, and a component can be associated with one of following categories [58]:

> *Independent commercial item.* A component can be an independent commercial item that can be purchased from a possibly anonymous component market. This category of components is referred to as *COTS components.*
>
> *Special version of commercial item.* A component can also be a special version of a commercial component. The component user might contract with the component provider to produce a customized version of a commercially available component.
>
> *Component produced by contract.* Depending on the organizational relation, a component can also be produced by contract. The component user can ask the component provider to develop a component for an agreed-upon fee.
>
> *Existing component from external sources.* A component can originate from an external source without being commercial. The component provider and component user might reside in different organizations, but the component could be one developed under a joint contract.
>
> *Component produced in-house.* Finally, a component can also be developed for a specific project. The component provider and component user might be involved in the same project or the roles of the component provider and component user can even be played by the same person.

This book focuses on COTS components. If not otherwise noted, components are assumed to have the above characteristics of COTS components, and the two terms *component* and *COTS component* are used interchangeably.

Context of the Book

1 Lack of information in development of and with components

1.1 Misperceptions in quality assurance of components

It is often argued that the quality of components will improve under certain conditions and less quality assurance will be required in the development of a component-based system to satisfy given quality requirements. The conditions under which the quality of components will improve according to this argument include [385]:

Frequent reuse. Reuse is generally supposed to have a positive effect on the quality of the software entity reused. A frequently reused component is expected to improve in quality, since frequent reuse is expected to reveal failures and other adverse behavior which possibly would not be revealed when, instead of being reused, the component would be redeveloped and tested from scratch.

Competitive markets. Competitive markets are also supposed to contribute to improvements of component quality, since quality is expected to become a success factor in such markets.

One of the implications of this argument described in the literature is that quality assurance actions are considered less important in component-based development than in software development in general. Components are supposed to possess a certain degree of quality obsoleting further quality assurance actions, and component-based systems are expected to inherit the quality of their individual constituents. However, these arguments do not take into account the following:

Firstly, the quality of an entity, in this context a component, is defined according to common definitions, such as that in [200], with regard to stated or implied needs. In this context, these needs are those of a particular component user. The needs of one component user might contradict those of another, and might also change after some time. Thus, even if the quality of a component might be sufficient according to the needs of a particular component user, additional quality assurance action might nevertheless be necessary prior to its use either by the same component user due to a change in requirements or by another component user due to a difference in the needs.

Secondly, competitive markets do not necessarily relieve the component user from conducting quality assurance actions. The needs of the component users might not be entirely known to the component provider so that the step taken by the component provider in order to increase quality might not be successful. Such problems are particularly caused by a limited exchange of information between the component provider and component user.

Limited exchange of information between the roles of the component provider and component user does not only limit the positive effect of competitive markets on component quality. It also relates several other issues in developing components and component-based systems and can be considered the primary factor distinguishing testing components from testing software in general.

1.2 Examples of Information Exchanged

The component provider and component user generally need to exchange information during the various phases of developing a component and a component-based system. The development of a component, if the component is not component-based and is thus not itself a component-based system, usually consists of the typical phases of software development. Software development usually comprises the phases *requirements analysis and definition, system and software design, implementation and unit testing, integration and system testing,* and *operation and maintenance* if it is conducted according to the waterfall model or a derivative of it [369]. The single phases might be named differently depending on the actual software process model; however, that does not affect the following explanations. During some of the phases, the component provider needs to exchange information with the component user. Such phases, for instance, are:

Requirements analysis and definition. The requirements analysis and definition phase obviously necessitates information concerning the capabilities and conditions the component needs to satisfy according to the component user's expectations.

Operation and maintenance. The operation and maintenance phase necessitates information enabling the component user to work with the component and information required for its maintenance by the component provider.

Even though a waterfall model-based software process has been assumed so far, similar patterns of information exchange can also be identified for other software process models and the results obtained also apply to them.

Information flow between component provider and component user does not occur only during the development of a component. Information often also needs to be exchanged during the development of a component-based system using the component. Even though the following explanations assume a concrete process model for component-based development, as described in [369], they are also valid for other process models for component-based development, since the phases in which information is exchanged between the two roles usually also have their counterparts in those models. The process model for reuse-oriented software development with components includes six phases, as described in [369]. These phases are *requirements specification, component analysis, requirements modification, system design with reuse, development and integration*, and *system validation*. During some of these phases, information flow between the component provider and component user can be observed. Examples of these phases are:

Component analysis. The component analysis phase requires information supporting identification of components available from the various sources, their analysis with respect to certain criteria, and finally selection of the component most suitable for the component-based system to be developed.

Development and integration. The phase of development and integration can also require technical information that the component user needs to obtain from the component provider. Such technical information might concern the interfaces of the component or the required middleware.

System validation. Information often needs to be exchanged between the two roles in the system validation phase. Such an exchange of information might concern program-based test cases generated by the component provider or meta-information supporting the component user in testing.

The above list of phases in component-based development that require exchange of information between the component provider and component user is not necessarily comprehensive. Other process models of component-based development might include other phases that also require information flow between the two roles. For instance, the process model proposed in [289, 290] for COTS-based software development defines an activity called *write glueware and interfaces* within the coding phase. This activity encompasses the development of auxiliary code necessary for integrating the various components, requiring detailed technical information which the component user might need from the component provider. However, the aim of the above list is only to show that interaction between the two roles takes place throughout the life cycles of components and component-based systems, and the flow of information is not merely one way [289, 290]. Furthermore, the various phases of component-based development generally also encompass information exchange with roles other than the two mentioned above, such as with the end user of the component-based system. While the previous explanations focused only on communication between the component provider and component user and omitted other types of communication, it does not mean that they do not exist.

1.3 Organization Relation as an Obstacle for Information Exchange

Various factors impact the exchange of information between the component provider and the component user. The information requested by one role and delivered by the other can differ in various ways, if it is delivered at all. It can differ syntactically insofar that it is, for instance, delivered in the wrong representation, and it can also differ semantically in that it is, for instance, not on the abstraction level required. The differences might be due to various factors, one of them being the organizational relation between the two roles. With respect to the organizational relation, a component can be associated with one of the following categories: *independent commercial item*, *special version of commercial item*, *component produced by contract*, *existing component from external sources*, and *component produced in-house*. Information exchange between the component provider and the component user depends, among other factors, on the organizational relationship between them.

At one end of the spectrum, the component can be a commercial item. In this case, the quality of information exchange between component provider and component user is then often the worst in comparison to the other cases. There are various reasons for this, such as the fact that the component provider might not know the component user due to an anonymous market. In such a case, the component provider can base development of the component on assumptions and deliver only that information to the component user which is supposedly needed. Furthermore, the component might be used by several component users and the component provider might decide to consider only the needs of the majority. The specific needs of a single component user might then be ignored. Finally, the component provider might not disclose detailed technical information even if needed by the component user to prevent another component provider from receiving this information. The component provider might decide to make only that information available which respects intellectual property and retains a competitive advantage.

At the other end of the spectrum, the component can be produced in-house. The quality of information exchange between component provider and component user is then often the best in comparison to the other cases. One of the reasons for this can be the fact that the component is developed in the same project in which it is assembled. The exchange of information in both directions, from the component provider to the component user and the reverse, can take place without any incompatibility in the requested and delivered information. Furthermore, the component provider and component user are roles, so they can even be played by the same person if the component is used in the same project in which it is developed. Information exchange would not even be necessary in that case.

1.4 Problems Due to a Lack of Information

According to [169, 170], quality assurance actions, particularly testing, that are applied to a component can be viewed from two distinct perspectives: *Component provider perspective* and *component user perspective*. Quality assurance of a component usually needs to be conducted by both the component provider and the component user. The corresponding tasks, however, differ insofar as the component provider generally needs to conduct them independently from the application context, whereas the component user of a component can concentrate on a certain application context while carrying out such tasks. The two distinct views on quality assurance of components underline this difference.

Context-Dependent Testing of a Component

One type of information required for the development of a component is an indication of the application context in which it will be used later. Such information, however, might not be available, so the component provider might develop the component on the basis of assumptions concerning the application context. The component is then explicitly designed and developed for the needs of the assumed application context, which, however, might not be the one in which it will actually be used. Even if the component is not tailored to a certain application context, but constructed for the broader market, the component provider might assume a certain application context and its development might again become context-dependent. A consequence of context-dependent development of a component can be that testing is also conducted with context dependency. A component might work well in a certain application context while exhibiting failures in another [406, 423].

The results of a case study given in [423] show the problem of context-dependent testing in practice. A component was considered a part of two different component-based systems. The component-based systems mainly provided the same functionality, but differed in the operations profiles associated with them. The operational profile of a system is a probability distribution which assigns a probability to each element in the input domain, giving the likelihood that this element is entered as input during operation, e.g., [131]. A set of test cases was generated for the first component-based system with a 98% confidence interval. The probability that an arbitrary input is tested was 98%, and both the component-based system as well as the component in its context were considered to be adequately tested. However, the fact that a component is adequately tested in the context of one system does not generally imply that it is also adequately tested in the context of another. In the case study, the set of test cases corresponded only to a 24% confidence interval of the second system's operation profile, so occurrence of an untested input during the second system's operation was much more likely.

Observations such as those made during the case study are captured by a formal model of test case adequacy given in [350], an extension of that in [422], encompassing components and component-based systems. The formal model of test suite adequacy also considers that a component tested with a certain test suite might be sufficiently, i.e., adequately, tested in a certain application context, but not adequately covered by the same test suite in another application context. In the terminology introduced, the test suite is C-adequate-on-P_1, with C being the test criterion used to measure test suite adequacy and P_1 being the former application context, but not C-adequate-on-P_2, with P_2 being the latter application context. An exact definition of the formal framework and theoretical investigations on test suite adequacy in case of components and component-based software can be found in [350].

One of the reasons for context-dependent development of a component is often the component provider's lack of information concerning the possible application contexts in which the component might be used later. Tests conducted by the component provider might also be context-dependent, so a change of application context, which might be due to reuse of the component, generally requires additional tests in order to give sufficient confidence that instances of the component will behave as intended in the new context. Additional tests are required despite contrary claims, such as in [385], that frequently reused components need less testing. Moreover, a component that is reused in a new application context needs to be tested irrespective of its source. A component produced in-house does not necessarily need less testing for reuse than a component that is an independent commercial item [423].

Insufficient Documentation of a Component

Development of a component-based system generally requires detailed documentation of the components that are to be assembled. Such documentation is usually delivered together with the respective components, and each of them needs to include three types of information:

Functionality. The specification of the component functionality describes the functions of that component, i.e., its objectives and characteristic actions, to support a user in solving a problem or achieving an objective.

Quality. The specification of component quality can address, for instance, the quality assurance actions applied, particularly testing techniques, and the metrics used to measure quality characteristics and their values.

Technical requirements. The specification of the technical requirements of a component needs to address issues such as the resources required, the architectural style assumed, and the middleware used.

Documentation delivered together with a component and supposed to include the above specifications might, however, be insufficient for development of a component-based system. The various types of information provided by the documentation can deviate from those expected both syntactically and semantically, and may even be incomplete. This problem can be viewed from two different perspectives. On the one hand, it can be considered a problem due to lack of information. The component provider might be lacking information and might therefore not provide the information that is actually needed by the component user in the form of documentation. On the other hand, it can be considered a reification of a lack of information. Instead of assuming that the component provider is lacking information while developing the component and assembling its documentation, the component user is assumed to be lacking information while developing a component-based system using the component. According to the latter perspective, insufficient documentation is not the effect of a lack of information but its reification. However, the subtle differences of these perspectives are not further explored here.

A case study found in [139] reports several problems encountered during the integration of four components into a component-based system. The problems encountered are assumed to be caused by assumptions made during the development of the individual components. The assumptions, even those concerning the same technical aspects of the components and the component-based system, were incompatible with each other, which was the reason for what the authors call an *architectural mismatch*. As one of the solutions to tackle the architectural mismatch problem, the authors propose to make architectural assumptions explicit. These assumptions need to be documented using the appropriate terminology and structuring techniques. Another solution to problems such as those in the case study is proposed in [371]. Here, the author suggests prototyping during component-based development in order to detect potential problems.

In [289, 290], the authors propose a process model for COTS-based development that includes a specific activity to tackle problems due to insufficient documentation. The process model encompasses an activity called *COTS components familiarization*, in which components selected earlier are used to gain a better understanding of their functionality, quality, and architectural assumptions. The importance of such an activity obviously depends on the quality of the component documentation already available.

Both prototyping and familiarization require that the component under consideration is executed, which is also the main intrinsic property of testing. In fact, both can be considered testing if the term *testing* is defined more generally. The objectives of both are not necessarily related to quality assurance, but aim to obtain information which is not delivered as part of the documentation. Furthermore, components delivered with insufficient documentation might also require testing in its original sense, particularly if the documentation does not include information concerning the quality assurance actions taken.

Component User's Dependence on the Component Provider

Context-dependent development and insufficient documentation of a component are two problems resulting from a lack of information that often obligate the component user to test a component before its use and the system in which the component is embedded. The component user can encounter other problems after tests are finished, particularly if the tests revealed failures. The problem which the component user can encounter is dependence on the component provider. A fault often cannot be removed by the component user, since the component user might not have the software artifacts required for isolating and removing the fault. Such artifacts include documentation, test plans, and source code of the component. Even if the required artifacts are available to the component user, debugging might be difficult or even impossible due to lack of expertise. Lack of expertise and insight of the component user might entail significant debugging costs, which can offset the benefits gained by using the component. Thus, the component user often has to rely on the component provider for maintenance and support, which the component user might not be able to influence. This can obviously entail risks in the life cycle of the developed component-based system.

The problem of dependence on the component provider can be aggravated if the component is not maintained as demanded by the component user, or if the component provider decides to discontinue support and maintenance or goes bankrupt [406, 423]. The possible financial effects of such an event is shown in [406] using a simple example. It was suggested that escrow agreements and protective licensing options be considered for the relevant artifacts of a component in order to avoid these problems. Even if the component provider accepts such an agreement, missing expertise can still hinder the component user from carrying out the corresponding tasks.

Difficulties faced by the component user because of a dependence on the component provider are not necessarily restricted to maintenance and support. Generally, several of the decisions taken by the component provider during the life cycle of the component also impact its use as part of a component-based system. Other problems which can occur due to dependence on the component provider can be [289, 290, 406]:

- Deadlines might be missed because of delays in the release of a component version,
- functionality promised might never be implemented in the component,
- modifications might have adverse effects, such as incompatibilities or even faults,

- some functionality of the component might be altered inconsistently,
- documentation might be incomplete or might not sufficiently cover modifications,
- technical support might not be sufficient.

As with context-dependent component development, the problem of component user dependence on the provider varies with the quality of information exchanged. The more the information about the component available to its user, the less dependent the user on the provider, as some maintenance and support tasks can be carried out by the user. Specifically, dependence on the component provider affects reputation of the component user. In the case of a problem, the component user's reputation will suffer even if the problem is caused by a component for which not the component user, but the provider, is responsible [423].

2 Issues in Testing Components and Component-based Systems

2.1 Objective of Testing

The intrinsic property of testing is execution of the software under test. The basic procedure of testing is to execute the software to be validated and to compare the behavior and output observed with that expected according to the specification. Although the basic procedure is clear, a common definition of the term *testing* does not exist. Several definitions can be found in the literature, all emphasizing different aspects. The definition assumed in the following is the one according to [194]:

Definition 3. [Testing *is*] *The process of operating a system or component under specified conditions, observing or recording the results, and making an evaluation of some aspect of the system or component.*

Testing for Quality Assurance

Even though Def. 3 does not explicitly state its objective, testing is an action of quality assurance. A definition of the general term *quality* can be found, for instance, in [200]:

Definition 4. [Quality *is*] *The totality of characteristics of an entity that bear on its ability to satisfy stated and implied needs.*

In our case, the entity referred to in the above definition is software, a component, or a component-based system, together with its documentation and data. The characteristics determining quality of software products are further refined in [208]. The quality model described is not restricted to a specific

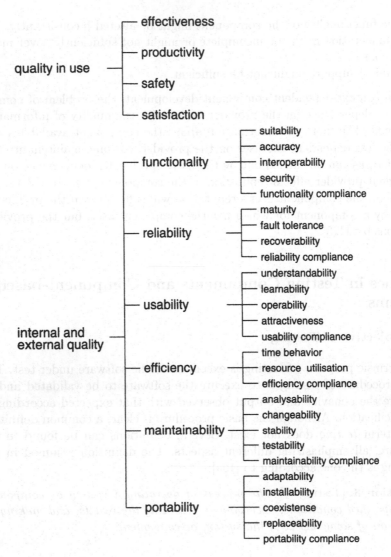

Fig. 5. A two-part quality model for software

type of software. It applies rather to software in general, to components, and to component-based systems. The general software quality model is defined according to [208] a model consisting of two parts, also shown in Fig. 5:

Internal and external quality. Internal and external quality consider software quality from the perspective of the developer. Internal quality consists of characteristics which can be observed in an internal view of the software and can thus be measured by static properties of the code, such as path length. In contrast with internal quality, external quality consists of characteristics which are observable in an external view of the software and can be measured by dynamic properties, such as response time, during runtime of the software.

Quality in use. Quality in use considers software quality from the perspective of the user. Quality in use consists of characteristics, such as productivity, describing the extent to which software supports users in achieving their goals in a certain application context. Quality in use thus assumes an external view of software.

Specification and evaluation of software quality, for instance by testing, require that the various characteristics defining the internal and external quality and quality in use be measurable. To allow measurability, a characteristic is either further decomposed into *attributes*, which are measurable using metrics, or its measure is induced based on the measures of other characteristics. In the latter case, a characteristic used to induce the measure of another is called *indicator*. A detailed explanation of the various characteristics constituting software quality, together with the corresponding metrics, can be found in [208]. A software quality evaluation process based on the quality model described is given in [202–207]. A COTS components-specific quality model can be found in [26].

An example of a quality assurance action is that of testing. The assessment by testing typically includes executing the software, observing and measuring a characteristic or subcharacteristic using specific metrics, and comparing the observed values with those expected. Testing, however, can assess only some of the quality characteristics of the quality model introduced, mainly due to the fact that the others cannot be measured by executing the software considered. The characteristics of the quality in use model part can generally not be measured by testing, as these characteristics are subjective and depend on the application context. Similarly, the characteristics of maintainability and portability, both affecting internal and external quality, can generally also not be validated by testing, since, for instance, maintainability depends particularly on the availability of design documents which obviously cannot be assessed by an execution of the corresponding software [346]. However, efficiency of software, according to [346], can be validated by testing only if corresponding targets are specified. Similarly, usability of software can be tested only if corresponding targets are given, such as ergonomic guidelines. Functionality and reliability, however, can be validated thoroughly by testing, as explained briefly as follows [346]:

Functionality. The quality characteristic of functionality is further decomposed into the subcharacteristics of suitability, accuracy, interoperability, security, and functionality compliance, as shown in Fig. 5. Each of these subcharacteristics can be assessed by testing. For instance, suitability of software can generally be shown in the context of system testing, accuracy by determining deviations between observed and expected results, and interoperability in the context of integration testing.

Reliability. The quality characteristic of reliability is also further decomposed into subcharacteristics, as indicated in Fig. 5. These characteristics maturity, fault tolerance, recoverability, and reliability compliance can also be assessed by testing. For instance, maturity can be tested or measured by counting the number of failures within a certain time period, fault tolerance by observing the behavior in the case of failures, recoverability by measuring the effort required to recover after failures. In all of these cases, the failures which might occur and the behavior which is expected in the case of a failure need to be specified beforehand.

Testing for COTS Components Evaluation

In component-based development, testing can also have an objective other than that of quality assurance. It can aim at reducing the risks inherent in software development, which can originate from inaccurate or incomplete information concerning the individual components used. Even if reuse as one of the strategies of software development in the large, supported by component-based development, has the potential of decreasing risks inherent in software development, the use of components might introduce new risks. The process of risk management in software development encompasses several stages according to [369]:

Risk identification. The stage of risk identification includes listing the possible risks affecting the project, product, and business.

Risk analysis. The stage of risk analysis encompasses assessment of the likelihood and consequences of the risks identified.

Risk planning. The stage of risk planning involves identifying the means by which the risks identified can be tackled.

Risk monitoring. The stage of risk monitoring consists of assessing the risks and revising plans for risk mitigation as more information becomes available.

One of the difficulties the component user needs to tackle when using components is lack of information. The information which the component user needs in the risk identification and risk analysis stages of risk management can be inaccurate or incomplete. The component user might therefore not be able to appropriately carry out the successor stages. To avoid this problem, the component to be used can be evaluated by building a prototype system, as in explorative prototyping [129]. The evaluation of a component mainly aims to gain information not delivered together with the component by the component provider and to confirm the validity of the available information. Other reasons can be [90, 295] to

- identify undocumented features, e.g., hidden interfaces,
- confirm or deny the published information and specifications,

- determine how well a component fits within the system environment,
- determine possibility to mask out unwanted features and faults, e.g., with wrappers,
- ensure that unwanted features and faults do not interfere with the system's operations.

According to [61], the testing techniques often used for the purpose of evaluation are binary reverse engineering and interface probing. The former is a technique enabling the component user to derive the design structure of a component from its binary code, i.e., the component as delivered, without source code. The latter allows the component user to gain insight into functionality and limitations of a component which might not be explicitly documented.

2.2 Test Case Generation

Test case generation in the context of testing a component or a component-based system generally needs to follow the same principles as test case generation in general. One of them is to avoid input inconsistencies. A principle of test case generation is that test cases have to comprise information that avoids input inconsistencies, which means that tests carried out using the same test case must always result in the same output and behavior to ensure reproduceability. However, the information that needs to be included in a test case might be difficult to determine, particularly in the context of testing components, due to various reasons.

Firstly, the relation between input and output might not be explicit. A method of a component might compute its output using not only its arguments, but also other data, something which might not be known to the component user. The component user can suffer from a lack of information insofar that specification might be incomplete and source code not available, so the component user might not be able to determine exactly the information which must be part of the test cases.

Secondly, the behavior of a component instance and its computation of output can also depend on factors that are external to the component. For example, behavior of a component instance is often affected by the component framework in which it is embedded. The component user might not know how the component framework can impact component instance behavior, and might not be able to identify the information required to control it.

Test case generation has to be conducted, except possibly in the case of very simple software, with regard to an adequacy criterion, which can be considered another principle. An *adequacy criterion* gives for a set of test cases the degree of adequacy of that test case set, depending on the software under test and its specification [440]. A set of test cases can be considered to be adequate, and testing on the basis of this test case set to be sufficient, if the adequacy of the test case set exceeds a predefined value. However, some problems related to adequacy criteria can be encountered in test case generation for components and component-based systems that hinder their application.

Firstly, one of the classifications of adequacy criteria provided distinguishes them with regard to the source of the information used to measure adequacy. The component user does not generally have full access to all types of information regarding a component. As a specific example, source code is often not available, and program-based adequacy criteria, which require such type of information, can generally not be computed. The problems due to a lack of information are not necessarily restricted to this category of adequacy criteria. The component user might encounter problems when trying to compute specification- or interface-based adequacy criteria if the respective information, such as unspecified functionality, is incomplete or even wrong or inaccurate, such as an operational profile assigning wrong probabilities to certain inputs.

Secondly, even with full access to the necessary information, the component user can still encounter problems in computing adequacy criteria due to their limited scalability, particularly when testing component-based systems [142]. Even if the testing of a component can in certain circumstances be considered as unit testing, adequacy criteria generally used in unit testing can only be employed to a limited extent. The adequacy criteria often used in unit testing, such as program-based and structural adequacy criteria, suffer from a lack of scalability. Such adequacy criteria can necessitate a large number of test cases for adequate testing, particularly if the methods of a component interact with each other and share global variables in the context of a component-based system.

2.3 Test Execution and Evaluation

Test execution, which is often also called testing in the narrow sense, and test evaluation are in principle conducted in the same way as for software in general. However, when testing components and systems consisting of components, difficulties can be encountered which do not exist in such a form when testing software in general. Such a difficulty is caused by the fact that some factors affecting a component's behavior might not be controllable by the tester. In this context, *controllability* of a factor refers to the tester's ability to set it to a specific value or ensuring that it satisfies a specific condition. Specifically, component-external factors, such as databases in distributed environments, might not be controllable by the tester due to access permissions, for instance.

As with testing of software in general, the output and behavior of a component instance or a system need to be observed and recorded together with all other relevant data describing the effects of the test execution. Generally, one possible way of obtaining the output and behavior is in the form of a trace. A *trace* is a record of the execution showing the sequence of instructions executed, the names and values of variables, or both [194]. The execution of a component can be observed and traces can be built using three basic approaches [136–138]:

Framework-based tracing. The capability necessary for producing traces can be added to a component by integrating it with a framework which implements the corresponding functionality. The integration of a component with a framework can obviously be conducted only by its developer, i.e., the component provider, since source code access is mandatory for such a task.

Automatic code insertion. The above integration of the component with the framework providing the necessary functionality can be automated by using automatic code insertion techniques. Such techniques can generally be used to automatically extend the source code of the component with arbitrary statements to support trace generation. Obviously, this approach can also only be conducted by the component provider due to the necessity of source code.

Automatic component wrapping. The externally visible effects of an execution can also be observed by embedding the component into a wrapper which is capable of producing the desired traces. Externally visible effects are, for instance, the returned output and the interactions with other components. This approach considers the component as a black-box insofar that information concerning internals of the component are not required. Thus, this approach to generating traces can also be conducted by the component user.

A comparison of the three approaches to generating traces can be found in [136–138]. Generally, the component user has very limited possibilities of observing the execution of the tests if appropriate provisions were not taken by the component provider, since several of the approaches to producing traces require source code access. Even if the components used in the context of a system provide capabilities to generate traces, the traces generated might be incompatible with each other syntactically and semantically, and missing configuration possibilities can hinder the removal of such incompatibilities.

The testing of software in general and of components and component-based systems in particular is usually continued after test execution, with an evaluation of the observations. For each test conducted, the observed output is validated by means of a test oracle. The problems which need to be tackled in this context for software in general, i.e., the oracle problem, may also be encountered when evaluating the observation of component tests. Another problem in the evaluation of component test observations can be that of *fault propagation* [288]. Faulty software does not necessarily exhibit a failure even if a faulty section is executed. A failure becomes visible, i.e., is identified by a test oracle based on the observations, only if a faulty section is executed, some variables are assigned wrong values (known as *infection*), and wrong values are propagated to an output. This problem can in principle also occur when testing software in general, but the problem that a fault is not propagated to an output can be harder to identify when testing components. The reason is that factors which hinder fault propagation might not be known to the component user due to missing insight and a lack of relevant information, such as source code.

Testing Components Context-Independently

Testing Polymorphic Behavior of Framework Components

Benjamin Tyler and Neelam Soundarajan

Computer Science and Engineering
Ohio State University
Columbus, OH 43210
{tyler, neelam}@cse.ohio-state.edu

Summary. An object-oriented framework is often the key component in building products for a given application area. Given such a framework, an application developer needs only to provide definitions suited to the needs of his or her product for the *hook* methods. With appropriate initializations, the calls to the hook methods made by the *template* methods defined in the framework will then be dispatched to the definitions provided by the developer, thus customizing the behavior of the template methods. Specifying and testing such a framework, in particular, specifying and testing its polymorphic behavior that enables such customization, presents some challenges. We discuss these and develop ways to address them.

1 Introduction

A well-designed object-oriented (OO) *framework* [44, 215] for a given application area can serve as the key component for applications built on it [70]. An early example was the MacApp framework [11] that provided many of the functionalities of applications for the Macintosh, thereby reducing the work involved in building a new application, and ensuring a uniform "look-and-feel" among the applications. But specifying and testing the framework component appropriately so that it can serve as a reliable foundation for building these applications presents special challenges. In this chapter, we discuss these challenges and investigate ways to address them.

An OO framework component is a class, or collection of classes, that implements basic functionalities that are common to several different applications. The framework component should provide only general behaviors; it is the application developers who are responsible for specializing these frameworks to meet their particular needs. The framework contains one or more *template* methods [135] that provide these general behaviors, something which often entails mediating the interactions between different objects in the system. Since the interaction patterns implemented in the template methods are often the most involved aspect of the total behavior required in the application, the framework component can considerably reduce the amount of effort required for developing a new application. Template methods are used "as-is" by the users of the final application; they are not supposed to be overridden by developers, and are generally final in the *Java* sense.

Now, how do application developers specialize the behavior of these frameworks? Template methods call, at the right points, appropriate *hook* methods of various classes of the system when they are executed. Although the code of the template methods are not to be overridden by the application developers, the code of the hook methods *can* and usually *should* be overridden by these developers. Hook methods are intended to be specialized to reflect the needs of the specific application that is to be built by the developer. Thus, by employing objects of the derived classes containing the redefined hooks in the final framework application, calls made by the template methods to the hook methods will be dispatched at runtime, via the mechanism of OO *polymorphism*, to their definitions in the derived classes. This ensures that the template methods defined in the framework exhibit behaviors customized to the needs of the application, even though the template methods' codes are not modified.

For the developer to exploit this fully, he or she needs a thorough understanding of how the framework behaves, in particular, which hooks the template methods invoke, in what order, under what conditions, etc., because only then can he or she precisely predict what behavior the template methods will exhibit for particular definitions of the hooks in the derived classes. In particular, a standard *Design by Contract* (DBC) [277] specification consisting of a pre- and post-condition on the state of the object (and the values of any other parameters of the method) that hold at the time of the call to and return from the template method is insufficient since it does not give us information about the hook method calls the template method makes during execution. In the next section, we present an example that will further illustrate the problem. We then show how a richer specification, which we will call an *interaction* specification to contrast it with the standard DBC-type specification, which we call *functional* specification, can be used to capture the relevant information. In essence, we will introduce a *trace* variable as an *auxiliary* variable; the trace will be a sequence on which we record, for each hook method call, such information as the name of the hook method, the argument values, the results returned, etc.; the post-condition of the interaction specification will give us, in addition to the usual information, information about the value of the trace, i.e., about the sequence of hook method calls the template method made during its execution. Given the interaction specification, the application developer will be able to plug in the behavior of the hooks, as redefined in the derived classes, to arrive at the resulting richer behavior that the template methods will have. Szyperski [385] considers a component to be a "unit of composition with contractually specified interfaces and explicit context dependencies;" for frameworks, in particular for their template methods, functional specifications are inadequate to capture this information fully; we need interaction specifications.

Specification is one part of the problem. The other has to do with how we *test* that the framework meets its interaction specification. If we had access to the source code of the framework, we could instrument it by inserting suitable instructions in the body of the template method to update the trace. Thus, prior to each call to a hook method, we would append information about the name of the hook method called, the parameter values passed, etc.; immediately after the return from the hook, we would append information about the result returned, etc. Then we could execute the template method and see whether the state of the object and any returned results when the method finishes, *and* the value of the trace at that point, satisfy the post-condition of the interaction specification. But such an approach, apart from being undesirable, since it depends on making changes to the code being tested, is clearly not feasible if we do not have the source code available as would likely be the case if it were a COTS framework. As Weyuker [420] notes, "as the reuse of software components and the use of COTS components become routine, we need testing approaches that are widely applicable regardless of the source code's availability, because ... typically only the object code is available."

If the goal was to check whether the *functional* specification of a template method was satisfied in a given test, we could certainly do that without accessing its source code: just execute the method and see whether the final state of the object (and any returned results) satisfy the (functional) post-condition. To test against the interaction specification, however, we clearly need to appropriately update the trace variable. It would seem we would have to insert the needed instructions, as described above, into the body of the template method at the points where it invokes the hook methods. This is the key challenge that we address in this chapter. We develop an approach that, by exploiting the same mechanism of polymorphism that template methods exploit, allows us to update the trace as needed without making any changes to the body of the template method. Here, we do not have to assume that our components already have this tracing capability built into them, as described in the chapter 'A Process and Role-based Taxonomy of Techniques to Make Testable COTS Components', or any built-in testing capabilities, such as those mentioned in the chapter 'COTS Component Testing through Built-In Test'.

One important question that has to be addressed as part of a complete testing methodology is the question of *coverage*. When testing against interaction specifications, appropriate coverage metrics might involve such considerations as whether all possible sequences of up to some appropriate length of hook method calls allowed by the interaction specification are covered in the test suite. But the focus of this chapter is on the question of how to determine, without access to the source code of the template methods, whether the interaction specification is satisfied during a given test, and not on questions of adequacy of coverage that a given test suite provides.

The main contributions of the chapter may be summarized as follows:

- It discusses the need, when specifying the behavior of template methods of frameworks, for interaction specifications providing critical information not included in the standard functional specifications.
- It develops an approach to testing frameworks to see if their template methods meet their interaction specifications without modifying or otherwise accessing the code of the methods.
- It illustrates the approach by applying it to a typical case study of a simple framework.

In this chapter, we use a diagram editor framework component as our running case study. We introduce this framework in the next section. In Sect. 3, we develop the interaction specifications for this framework. In Sect. 4, we turn to the key question of how to test template methods of the framework to see if they meet their interaction specifications without accessing their source code. We present our solution to this problem and apply it to the case study. Section 5 briefly describes a prototype tool that implements our approach to testing template methods. In Sect. 6, we discuss related work, and also briefly discuss possible criteria for adequacy of test coverage. In the final section, we reiterate the importance of testing interaction behavior of frameworks and of the need for being able to do so for COTS frameworks for which we may not have the source code. We also provide some pointers for future work, including our plans for improving our prototype testing tool.

2 A Diagram Editor Framework Component

"Node-and-edge" diagrams are common in a number of domains. Some examples are road maps where the nodes are cities, and edges, perhaps of varying thicknesses, represent highways; electrical circuit diagrams, where the nodes represent such devices as transistors, diodes, etc., and the edges represent wires and other types of connections between them; and control flowcharts, where the nodes represent different statements of a program, and the edges represent the possibility of control flowing from one node to another during execution. In each of these domains, a diagram editor that allows us to create and edit diagrams consisting of the appropriate types of nodes and edges is obviously very useful. While each of these diagram editors can be created from scratch, this is clearly wasteful since these diagrams, and hence also the diagram editors, have much in common with each other.

A much better approach is to build a framework component that contains all the common aspects, such as maintaining the collection of nodes and edges currently in the diagram, tracking mouse movements, identifying, based on mouse/keyboard input, the next operation to be performed, and then invoking the appropriate (hook method) operation provided by the appropriate Node or Edge class. A developer interested in building a diagram editor for one of these domains would then have to provide only the derived classes for **Node** and **Edge** appropriate to the particular domain. Thus, for example, to build a circuit diagram editor, we might define a **TransistorNode** class, a **DiodeNode** class, a **SimpleWireEdge** class, etc. Once this is done, the behavior of the template methods in the framework will become customized to editing circuit diagrams, since the calls in these methods will be dispatched to the definitions in the classes **DiodeNode**, **SimpleWireEdge**, etc.

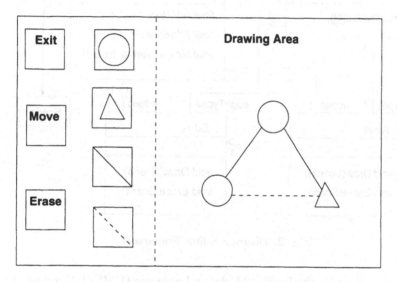

Fig. 1. A diagram editor in use.

Throughout this chapter, we will use a simple diagram editor framework, modeled on the one in [187], as our running case study. Figure 1 shows a diagram editor built on this framework component, in use. In this application, there are two **Node** (sub)types (represented by a triangle and a circle respectively) and two **Edge** (sub)types (the first, an unbroken, undirected line, the second a dashed line). The "canvas" is split into two parts, the left part consisting of a collection of action icons (Move, Erase, and Exit), and an icon corresponding to each possible **Node** type and each possible **Edge** type; the right part of the canvas displays the current diagram. The user can click the mouse on one of the **Node** icons in the left part, and the icon will be highlighted; if the user next clicks anywhere on the right part of the canvas, a new **Node** object of that particular type will be created and placed at that point. The **Edge** icons are similar, except that after highlighting an **Edge** icon, the user must *drag* the mouse pointer from one **Node** object to another to place the **Edge** connecting the two **Nodes**. Clicking on Move will highlight its action icon; if the user next clicks on a **Node** object in the current diagram and drags it, the **Node** will be moved to its new location; any **Edges** incident on that **Node** will be redrawn appropriately. **Edges** cannot be moved on their own. Clicking on **Erase** will highlight that action icon; if the user next clicks on a **Node** object in the diagram, that **Node** and all its incident **Edges** will be erased; clicking on an **Edge** will erase that **Edge**. Clicking on Exit will, of course, terminate the diagram editor program.

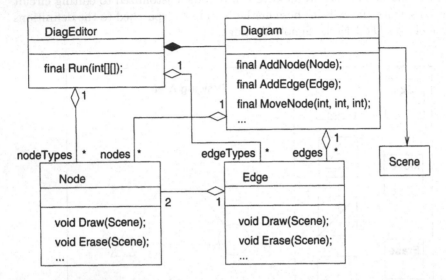

Fig. 2. Diagram Editor Framework.

Figure 2 contains the Unified Modeling Language (UML) [41] model of the framework. The **DiagEditor** provides most of the functionality corresponding to tracking mouse movements, determining which action, or **Node** or **Edge** type, has been highlighted. To achieve the actual display of the individual **Nodes** or **Edges**, the main template method **Run()** of the framework will invoke the appropriate hook methods defined in the appropriate individual derived classes, since the method of display depends on the particular **Node** or **Edge** type. Indeed, this is the key aspect that distinguishes the diagram editor for a given domain from that for another domain. "Hit-testing," i.e., given the current mouse location, whether it lies on a given **Node** or **Edge** object is also something that has to be determined by hook methods defined in the appropriate derived classes, since the shape and sizes of these objects is not known to the framework component. We use an auxiliary class **Diagram** that contains all the **Nodes** and **Edges** currently in the diagram being edited. The **Run()** method of **DiagEditor** will invoke the appropriate operation of **Diagram** along with information about the particular **Node** or **Edge** involved, and the **Diagram** class's methods will invoke the actual hook methods of **Node** and **Edge**.

One important practical question that the framework has to deal with is that although it doesn't know what the derived **Node** or **Edge** types are, nor even how many such types there are (since all this will be decided by the application developer when he or she customizes it for the particular application domain by providing the corresponding derived classes) the framework is still responsible for maintaining the corresponding icons. This is handled by requiring that at its start the diagram editor application "register" each type of Node and Edge specific to the application by using an instance of each of these types; these instances are represented by the nodeTypes and edgeTypes roles depicted in Fig. 2. These instances also serve as the prototypes for cloning when the user chooses to add a Node or Edge of a given type to the diagram.

Since our goal in this chapter is to focus on behavioral and testing issues, we have simplified the handling of the user commands by assuming that these commands will be represented as numerical values in the argument cmds to the Run() method, rather than having to obtain them by analyzing the mouse movements. The Scene in Fig. 2 represents the "graphics scene." In practice, this role would be played by a graphics window, or the screen buffer, or something else of this nature. In any case, the Scene contains information that represents an appropriate description of what is displayed by the diagram editor, for example, in Fig. 1. However, since our interest is not in the details of the graphics, we will represent the scene by means of a class containing a collection of strings describing the Nodes and Edges currently displayed.

In the next section we will consider segments of the code of some of the methods of the framework, including the main template method Run(). The key question we will consider is, how do we specify Run() so that an application developer can plug into this specification the behaviors of the hook methods of the Node and Edge classes, as defined in the application, to arrive at the corresponding customized behavior that Run() will exhibit.

3 Interaction Specification

Figure 3 contains (portions of) the Node and Edge classes as they may be defined in the framework. It may be worth noting that in an actual framework of this kind, it might be more appropriate to have these classes as abstract in the framework, with appropriate implementations in the applications. A Node contains its x and y coordinates, as well as a boolean variable, er, whose value will be set to true when the Node is erased. Edge is similar but instead of x- and y- coordinates, an Edge object has references to the "from" and "to" Nodes that it joins. The Name() method in each class gives us information, in the form of a string, of the corresponding Node or Edge object, which is then used by the Draw() method to add this information to the Scene. Node and Edge objects will also of course implicitly carry type information, since polymorphic dispatching to the appropriate hook method definitions in the appropriate derived classes depends on it; in the specification, therefore, our models of Node and Edge will include this information.

A portion of the DiagEditor class appears in Fig. 4. A DiagEditor object contains an array nodeTypes[] that contains an instance of each of the derived

```
class Node {
  protected int x = 0, y = 0; // center of Node
  protected bool er = false; // will be set to true if the Node is erased.
  protected String Name() {return new String("Node: ("+x+", "+y+")");}
  public final void Erase() { er = true;}
  public void Draw(Scene sc) {sc.AddToScene(Name());}
  public void UnDraw(Scene sc) {sc.RemoveFromScene(Name());}
  public final void Move(int xc, int yc) { x = xc; y = yc; } }

class Edge {
  protected Node fromN, toN; protected bool er = false;
  protected String Name() { return new String (
    "Edge: ("+fromN.x+", "+fromN.y+") → "+"("+toN.x+", "+toN.y+")" );}
  public final boolean IsAttached(Node n) { return (n==fromN || n==toN);}
  public final void Erase() { er = true;}
  public void Draw(Scene sc) {sc.AddToScene(Name());}
  public void UnDraw(Scene sc) {sc.RemoveFromScene(Name());}
  public final void Attach(Node f, Node t) { fromN = f; toN = t;} }
```

Fig. 3. Node, Edge classes.

types of Node (to be defined in the application); these serve as the prototypes used for cloning when the person using the application clicks on one of the Node icons on the left side of the canvas to create a new Node of that type. edgeTypes[] is a similar array of Edge objects. diag, of type Diagram (defined in Fig. 5), is the main component of the diagram and contains in diag.nodes[] all the Nodes and in diag.edges[] all the Edges that the user creates. diag.scene is the diagram as displayed (or, rather, is our string representation of the display).

As we saw in the last section, Run() is the main method of the framework; it analyzes the user input (encoded as numbers in the cmds[] array), and orchestrates the control flow among the hook methods of the appropriate Node and Edge classes. In order to simplify the structure of Run(), we have introduced another method, RunOne(), which Run() invokes to handle each user command in cmd[]. Thus, Run() checks the command value, and then passes the command on to RunOne() to actually carry it out by invoking the appropriate hook methods on the appropriate Node and/or Edge objects.

RunOne(cmd) works as follows: if cmd[0] is 1, it corresponds to adding a new Node. A clone n of the appropriate prototype Node is created, its x- and y-coordinates are assigned (by the Move() method), and AddNode() is invoked to add n to diag. AddNode() adds n to the nodes[] array, and "draws" the new Node by invoking the hook method Draw(); Draw(), as defined in our Node class, simply adds appropriate information in the form of a string to the scene component of the diagram. The case where cmd[0] is 2 corresponds to adding a new Edge, and is similar.

```
class DiagEditor {
  protected Diagram diag;
  protected Node [] nodeTypes; // these correspond to the Node/Edge icons and
  protected Edge [] edgeTypes;  //    are used in creating new diagram elements
  public final void Run(int[][] cmds) { int cmdNum = cmds.length;
    for(int i = 0; i < cmdNum; i++) { ... check cmds[i] for correctness... ;
    RunOne(cmds[i]); } }
  protected final void RunOne(int[] cmd) {
    switch(cmd[0]) {
      case 1: // Add Node
        Node n = nodeTypes[cmd[1]].Clone();
        n.Move(cmd[2], cmd[3]); diag.AddNode(n); break;
      case 2: // Add Edge
        Edge e = edgeTypes[cmd[1]].Clone();
        e.Attach(diag.nodes[cmd[2]], diag.nodes[cmd[3]]); diag.AddEdge(e); break;
      case 3: diag.EraseNode(cmd[1]); break;// Erase Node
      case 4: diag.EraseEdge(cmd[1]); break;// Erase Edge
      case 5: // Move Node
        diag.MoveNode(cmd[1], cmd[2], cmd[3]); break; } }
}
```

Fig. 4. The framework class.

```
class Diagram {
  protected Node [] nodes;   protected Edge [] edges;
  protected Scene scene;
  public final void AddNode(Node n) { ... add n to nodes[]... ; n.Draw(scene); }
  public final void AddEdge(Edge e) { ... add e to edges[]... ; e.Draw(scene); }
  public final void EraseNode(int i) {
    nodes[i].UnDraw(scene); nodes[i].Erase();
    ... for each Edge in edges[] attached to nodes[i], invoke EraseEdge() on it... }
  public final void EraseEdge(int i) { edges[i].UnDraw(scene); edges[i].Erase();}
  public final void MoveNode(int i, int x, int y) {
    ... UnDraw() nodes[i] and nodes[i]'s attached edges, nodes[i].Move() to move
    nodes[i] to new position, Draw() nodes[i] and its attached edges... }
}
```

Fig. 5. Diagram class.

The case where cmd[0] is 3 corresponds to erasing a Node and is more complex. Here, we first invoke the hook method UnDraw() on the Node in question, set its erased bit to true, and then, for each Edge in the edges[] array, check if it is attached to the Node in question; if it is, we invoke EraseEdge() on it (which in turn invokes the hook method UnDraw() on that Edge and sets its erased bit to true). The case where cmd[0] is 4 is simpler and corresponds to erasing a single Edge; Nodes are not affected. The last case corresponds to moving a Node. In this case, we first invoke the hook method UnDraw() on the Node, invoke UnDraw() on all the attached Edges, update the coordinates of the Node, and then invoke Draw() on the Node, and on the attached Edges.

Let us now consider how we may specify the framework, in particular the DiagEditor class. In standard Design by Contract, the specification of a class would consist of a conceptual model of the class and an invariant for the class, plus pre- and post-conditions for each method of the class, these assertions being in terms of the conceptual model. For DiagEditor, a suitable conceptual model is directly dictated by the member variables of the class; thus, our model will consist of three components, nodeTypes[], edgeTypes[], and diag, these being an array of Nodes, an array of Edges, and a Diagram object, respectively. diag, in turn, consists of three components, nodes[], edges[], and scene, these being the array of Nodes and Edges in the diagram, and our string-representation of the Nodes and Edges that are currently displayed, respectively. Further, as noted earlier, our model of Node consists of its actual (runtime) type, its x- and y- coordinates, and the er boolean denoting whether the Node has been erased; and our model of Edge consists of its actual type, its "from" and "to" Nodes, and the er variable.

$$\text{invariant} \equiv \tag{1}$$
$$[(\text{nodeTypes}[] = \text{nT0}[]) \wedge (\text{edgeTypes}[] = \text{eT0}[])] \wedge \tag{1.1}$$
$$[\text{diag.scene} = (\{\text{name}(n)|(n \in \text{diag.nodes}[] \wedge n.\text{er} = \text{false})\} \tag{1.2}$$
$$\cup \{\text{name}(e)|(e \in \text{diag.edges}[] \wedge e.\text{er} = \text{false})\})] \wedge$$
$$[(\text{diag.edges}[k].\text{from.er} = \text{true} \Rightarrow \text{diag.edges}[k].\text{er} = \text{true}) \wedge \ldots] \tag{1.3}$$

Fig. 6. Invariant for the framework.

Let us first consider the invariant, which is shown in Fig. 6. Once the initialization (which we have not shown in our DiagEditor code) is complete, nodeTypes[] and edgeTypes[] do not change; thus, we have clause (1.1), where nT0[] and eT0[] are the values to which these arrays are initialized. More interesting is the invariant relation between diag.scene on the one hand, and diag.nodes[] and diag.edges[] on the other, shown in (1.2). This asserts that the scene component is just made up of the Names of all the Nodes and Edges that exist in their respective arrays and that have not been erased. Another important clause of the invariant, (1.3), relates the "erase" status of Nodes and the associated Edges. That is, if the erased bit of either the from Node or the to Node of a given Edge is true, so will be the erased bit of that Edge. For the rest of the specification, we will, in the interest of simplicity, focus on the RunOne() method. Consider the specification that appears in Fig. 7.

The precondition simply requires that the argument cmd be "legal;" this means, for example, that no attempt be made to move a non-existent Node. The post-condition is organized into the same cases as the method. Thus, (2.1) corresponds to a command to create a new Node; in this case, edges[] remains pre.RunOne(cmd) ≡ (cmd is "legal")   (2)

post.RunOne(cmd) ≡
   cmd[0]=1: ((edges[]=edges'[]) ∧   (2.1)
                (nodes[]=nodes'[]+n where
                   (Type(n)=Type(nT0[cmd[1]]) ∧ n.x=cmd[2]
                    ∧ n.y=cmd[3] ∧ n.er=false)))
   cmd[0]=2: ((nodes[]=nodes'[]) ∧   (2.2)
                (edges[]=edges'[]+e where
                   (Type(e)=Type(eT0[cmd[1]]) ∧ e.from=nodes[cmd[2]]
                    ∧ e.to=nodes[cmd[3]] ∧ e.er=false)))
   cmd[0]=3: ((nodes[]=nodes'[][cmd[1]←nodes'[cmd[1]][er← true]]) ∧   (2.3)
                (edges[]=edges'[][k←edges'[k][er← true] |
                                         (edges'[k].from = nodes'[cmd[1]] ∨
                                          edges'[k].to = nodes'[cmd[1]])]))
   cmd[0]=4: ((nodes[]=nodes'[]) ∧   (2.4)
                (edges[]=edges'[][cmd[1]←edges'[cmd[1]][er← true]]))
   cmd[0]=5: ((edges[]=edges'[]) ∧   (2.5)
                (nodes[]=nodes'[][cmd[1]←nodes'[cmd[1]][x←cmd[2], y←cmd[3]]]))

Fig. 7. Functional specification of RunOne().

unchanged (note that x' denotes the value of the corresponding variable x at the *start* of the given method), and nodes[] will have a new element n that will have the appropriate type (the same as the type of the Node chosen from the nT0[] array), the appropriate coordinates, and its erased bit set to false. Note that we do not explicitly state that the scene is updated, since it is required by the invariant specified above. The case (2.2), where the value of cmd[0] is 2, which corresponds to creating a new Edge, is similar.

Case 3 is the most complex case and corresponds to erasing a Node. In this case, the er bit of the appropriate Node (the one numbered cmd[1] in the nodes[] array) is set to true, and also all the Edges that have either their from or to Node to be the Node being erased, have their er bit set to true. Note that we don't have to explicitly state that the scene component is updated appropriately, since that is ensured by the requirement of the invariant, in particular by (1.2) in Fig. 6. It may seem that (1.3) of the invariant would similarly ensure that the Edges are appropriately updated without our having to state it explicitly in the post-condition; while (1.3) would require that the er bit of any Edge whose from or to is set to true must itself be set to true, it would not by itself prevent other arbitrary changes to edges[], such as, for example, getting rid of one or more of the Edges; the post-condition states that the only changes resulting from processing this command are to modify the nodes[] and edges[] arrays only in the specified manner[1]. Similarly, in (2.4)

_____

[1]An alternative that is often used in specifications is to introduce a 'preserves' clause in the method definition asserting that the particular method does not in

for case 4, we need the first clause to ensure that no changes are made in the nodes[] array when processing this type of command, which corresponds to erasing a single Edge. The last case corresponds to moving a Node; in this case, the edges[] array is unaffected and nodes[] is modified only as far as changing the x- and y- coordinates of the specified Node; note again that (1.2) requires that the scene is updated appropriately to reflect the new coordinates of this Node.

While the specification in Fig. 7 gives us the behavior of RunOne() as implemented in the framework, there is an important aspect it ignores. Consider again the case when cmd[0] is 5, corresponding to moving a Node. As we just saw, according to (2.5) the effect of this is to change the x- and y- coordinates of the particular Node and, because of the invariant, to update the scene so the Node will be displayed at its new coordinates. Suppose now an application developer defines a derived class CNode of Node in which Draw() and UnDraw() are redefined so that not only do they add/remove information about the Node to/from diag.scene, but also update, say, a color variable that is maintained by the CNode class and that becomes progressively darker as the same given ·CNode is manipulated repeatedly. Thus, in this new application, as the commands in cmds[] are manipulated, some of the CNodes will get darker. However, this effect will not be evident from the specification (2.5), which states only that the effect of the MoveNode is to simply update diag.nodes[] and correspondingly diag.scene. Indeed, one could have a different implementation of DiagEditor and Diagram so that diag.nodes[] and diag.scene are updated *directly* without invoking Node.UnDraw(). If the framework did that, then the redefinition of Draw()/UnDraw() in CNode will indeed have no effect on the behavior of RunOne(). Thus, as we noted earlier, in order to enable the application developer to reason about the effects that his or her definition of various methods in the derived classes in the application will have on the behavior of the template methods of the framework, we must include information that, in this example, will tell us which hook methods will be invoked on which Node and Edge objects.

Let us introduce a *trace variable* τ which we will use to record information about the sequence of hook method calls that a given template method makes during its execution. Note that there is no need to record information about *non-hook* method calls since these cannot be redefined in the application; hence the effect of these calls will remain the same in the application as in the framework. At the start of the template method's execution, τ will be the empty sequence, since at that point it has not yet made any hook method calls. The post-condition of the template method will give us information about the value τ has when the method finishes, i.e., about the sequence of hook method calls the method made during its execution. We will call such a specification the *interaction* specification of the template method since it

---

any way modify the variables listed in the clause. If we did that, we could simplify portions of the post-condition of RunOne().

gives us information about the interactions between this method and methods that may be redefined in the application.

$$
\begin{aligned}
\text{Interaction.post.RunOne(cmd):} & \hspace{4cm} (3)\\
\text{cmd}[0]=5: \quad & [(\text{edges}[]=\text{edges}'[]) \wedge (\text{nodes}[]=\text{nodes}'[][\text{cmd}[1]\leftarrow \ldots]) \wedge \\
& (\tau[1].\text{obj}=\text{nodes}[\text{cmd}[1]]) \wedge (\tau[1].\text{hm}=\text{UnDraw}) \wedge \\
& (k=2..(\text{aEL}+1): \tau[k].\text{ob}=\text{aEdges}[k-1] \wedge \tau[k].\text{hm}=\text{UnDraw}) \wedge \\
& (\tau[\text{aEL}+2].\text{obj}=\text{nodes}[\text{cmd}[1]]) \wedge (\tau[\text{aEL}+2].\text{hm}=\text{Draw}) \wedge \\
& (k=(\text{aEL}+3)..(\text{aEL}+2+\text{aEL}): \\
& \hspace{2cm} \tau[k].\text{ob}=\text{aEdges}[k-\text{aEL}-2] \wedge \tau[k].\text{hm}=\text{Draw})]
\end{aligned}
$$

Fig. 8. Interaction specification of RunOne() (moving a Node).

A part of the interaction specification corresponding to the the MoveNode() command appears in Fig. 8. For convenience, we use aEdges[] to denote the 'affected Edges', i.e., the Edges that have the Node being moved as either their from or to Node; thus, aEdges[] is easily defined as a function of edges[] and nodes[cmd[1]], and we are using it just for notational convenience in the specification; further, let aEL denote the length of this array, i.e., the number of affected Edges. This specification may be read as follows: the first line simply repeats what we already saw in (2.5). The clauses in the second line state that the first element of the hook method trace τ represents a call to the UnDraw() method, and that the object involved is the appropriate Node from the nodes[] array. The next set of clauses state that the next aEL elements correspond to invoking UnDraw() on the various objects of aEdges[], i.e., the Edges that have nodes[cmd[1]] as their from or to Node. The following line states that the next element of τ corresponds to invoking Draw() on the same Node. The final line similarly states that the remaining elements apply Draw() on the various elements of aEdges[].

In effect, this specification gives the application developer information about the hook method calls that are made by the framework in processing a MoveNode command. Given this information, the application developer can plug in information about the behavior implemented in the hook methods, as defined in his or her application, to arrive at the behavior that RunOne() will exhibit in the application when processing this command. In [370] we propose a set of rules that the application developer can use for performing this plugging in operation. As an aside, it may be interesting to explore the possibilities of including such interaction information in component metadata, and using it as a basis for test case selection, similar to what is outlined in the chapter 'COTS Component Testing through Aspect-Based Metadata'. However, our focus is on *how* to test a framework to see if it meets its specification, in particular to see whether it meets interaction specifications such as (3). An important requirement, as we noted earlier, is that in carrying out such tests, we should not modify the source code of the framework's methods, or even access that source code. We turn to this problem and its solution in the next section.

4 Testing the Interaction Specifications

The key problem we face in testing the interaction specification of Run() is that we cannot wait until it finishes execution to try to record information about the calls made to the hook methods Draw() and UnDraw() on Node and Edge objects during its execution. What we need to do instead is to *intercept* these calls during the execution of RunOne() as they are made. How can this be done, though, if we are not allowed to modify the source code of the Diagram class at the points of these calls, or the source code of the Node and Edge classes themselves on which these hooks are invoked? The answer comes from the same mechanism that allows us to enrich the behavior of template methods such as RunOne() through the redefinition of hook methods, i.e., *polymorphism*. Rather than intercepting these calls by modifying already existing source code (which we may not have access to in the first place), we will redefine the hook methods so that *they* update the trace appropriately whenever they are invoked. Here, we define special "trace-saving" classes that accomplish this task, TS_Node (shown in Fig. 9) and TS_Edge (which is entirely similar to TS_Node).

```
class TS_Node extends Node {
  public Trace tau; // reference to the global Trace
  TS_Node(Trace t) { // allows us to bind tau to global Trace variable
    super.Node(); tau = t;}
  public Node Clone() {
    ...return a copy of the this object with tau bound to this.tau...}
  public void Draw(Scene sc) {
    traceRec tauel = ...info such as name of method called (Draw),
                    object value and identity, parameter value (sc) etc. ...;
    super.Draw(sc);    // call original hook method
    tauel = ...add info about current state etc. ...;
    tau.append(tauel); }
  public void UnDraw(Scene sc) {...similar to Draw above...}
}
```

Fig. 9. TS_Node class.

During testing, we use TS_Node and TS_Edge objects for our Nodes and Edges in the DiagEditor test case, so that whenever Draw() or UnDraw() is invoked on one of the diagram elements, the call is dispatched to those methods implemented in the trace-saving classes. In other words, when we create a DiagEditor test case object, we register a TS_Node object and a TS_Edge object to represent the types of Nodes and Edges that the diagram should use, as we would register, say, a DiodeNode, a TransistorNode, or a SimpleWireEdge when creating a circuit editor application. For this to work, TS_Node must be a derived class of Node (and TS_Edge a derived class of Edge). In TS_Node, Draw() and UnDraw() are both redefined so that they update the trace while still invoking the original methods. Here, tau is the trace variable (τ of specification (3)) and tauel will record information about one hook method call which will be appended to tau once the call to Node.Draw() has finished and returned.

If we are to test against interaction specs, all of the hook method calls from all of the trace-saving classes should be recorded on the *same* single trace object. To ensure that only one such trace is created during a test run, instead of each trace-saving class creating a new local Trace object for tau when a TS_Node is created, a *reference* to the single trace object is passed in to the constructor and bound to the local data member tau. Another concern is getting new Nodes and Edges a reference to this same tau. This is handled by redefining the Clone() method found in Node so that the new object returned is the same as the old, with its tau variable bound to the same trace object referred to by this.tau; no new Trace is created. Since the only way the DiagEditor creates new Nodes and Edges is via the AddNode and AddEdge commands, which in turn use the Clone operations on objects in nodeTypes and edgeTypes, no diagram elements of types other than TS_Node and TS_Edge are created and only a single trace is present during testing.

```
class Test_DiagEditor {
    public static void test_RunOne(DiagEditor tc, int[] cmd, Trace tau) {
        if (... tc and cmd satisfies RunOne's precond...) {
            DiagEditor tc_old = ... save tc's initial state... ;
            tau.Clear();
            tc.RunOne(cmd);
            assert(... trace-based postcond. of RunOne with appropriate subs....); };
    }
    public static void main(String[] args) {
        Trace tau = new Trace();
        TS_Node tsn = new TS_Node(tau); TS_Edge tse = new TS_Edge(tau);
        DiagEditor de = ... new DiagEditor with tsn and tse registered so that
                        de.nodeTypes = {tsn} and de.edgeTypes = {tse}... ;
        cmd = ... a valid command... ;
        test_RunOne(de, cmd, tau);
    }
}
```

Fig. 10. The testing class Test_DiagEditor.

Now let us look at the testing class, Test_DiagEditor (Fig. 10). Here, the main method first creates the Trace object tau that is to be used during the testing of RunOne(), and then passes a reference to tau to the constructors of the trace-saving classes. These trace-saving objects, tsn and tse, are then registered with the DiagEditor de that is to be used as our test case object. This allows us to track the calls made to Draw and UnDraw during execution, as we have already described. After cmds is initialized to a suitable sequence of commands, we are ready to test the method RunOne() by invoking test_RunOne(). test_RunOne() first checks to see if the object and parameters are a valid test case by checking the precondition of RunOne(). Since post-conditions often refer to values of objects and parameters when the method started execution, we need to save the incoming state. Thus, test_RunOne() saves the starting value of tc, the test case object. (The outgoing value of cmds is not mentioned in the post-condition, and thus does not need to be saved.) By invoking RunOne() on this test case object, the hook method calls made during its execution are recorded on tau, which is used in checking the trace-based post-condition when it is finished.

Let us see how Test_DiagEditor.test_RunOne() works using the *sequence diagram* [41] in Fig. 11. The first vertical line, labeled Test_DiagEditor represents the testing class; the second vertical line represents the DiagEditor test case object de; and the third vertical line represents the Diagram associated with de. The next two vertical lines grouped under the heading nodes[k] together represent the *k*th Node of the Diagram de. This object will be of type TS_Node. The two individual lines under the nodes[k] heading represent the two different aspects of this object: the base-class (Node) portion and the derived class (TS_Node) portion. We separate these two aspects to emphasize how the code in TS_Node and Node interact. The next two lines similarly represent the *j*th Edge of de. The final line represents the Scene. In the sequence diagram, the solid circles indicate where the trace is initialized or updated, and the dotted circles represent an update on an object's internal state.

To test that RunOne() satisfies its interaction specification, we first must create an appropriate instance of the DiagEditor as described above, where objects of type TS_Node and TS_Edge are registered with the DiagEditor, along with a command cmd. For this example, we will assume that cmd is an erase command to erase the *k*th Node which is adjacent to a single Edge, the *j*th Edge, in our DiagEditor object. Remember, the Nodes and Edges in the diagram should be of type TS_Node and TS_Edge here. To initiate testing, we invoke Test_DiagEditor.test_RunOne() with this test case, which is represented by the solid arrow at the top-left of the figure. The method starts by checking the precondition at the point labeled ◇ in the figure. Then, it initializes tau to ⟨ ⟩ and saves the initial state variable at (1t). Next, RunOne() is called on the test case object de, and when RunOne() processes the command, it invokes EraseNode() on the diag field object of the DiagEditor.

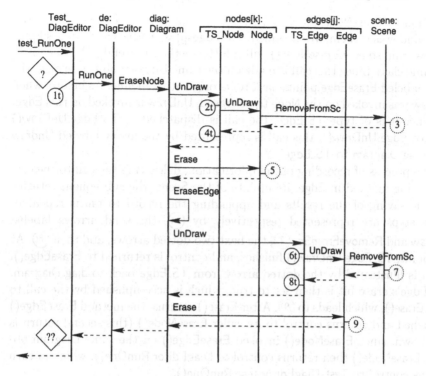

Fig. 11. Sequence Diagram for Test_DiagEditor.test_RunOne().s

Consider what happens when EraseNode executes. First, it invokes the method UnDraw(), which we *have* overridden in TS_Node. Since the Nodes of the Diagram object that RunOne() was applied to are of type TS_Nodes, this call is dispatched to TS_Node.UnDraw(). This dispatch is represented by the solid arrow labeled UnDraw from the lifeline of diag:Diagram to the vertical line labeled TS_Node under the heading nodes[k]. Now TS_Node.UnDraw() is simply going to delegate the call to Node.UnDraw() (represented by the next arrow from TS_Node to Node under the nodes[k] heading); but before it does so it records appropriate information about this call on the trace-record variable tauel at ②t in the figure. The code for UnDraw() found in the Node class calls RemoveFromScene() to update the Scene (this update is labeled ③), and after RemoveFromScene() and Node.UnDraw() return from execution, we are back at ④t. At this point, control is at TS_Node.UnDraw(), which now records appropriate additional information on tauel and appends this record to tau.

After TS_Node.UnDraw() finishes, control returns to the call to EraseNode() on diag. EraseNode() next calls Erase() on the Node (the code for Erase() is found in the Node class and is inherited by TS_Node), where the erase bit er is set to true, shown at ⑤. After Erase() is completed and control returns to

EraseNode(), EraseNode() looks for the Edges that were adjacent to the erased Node, and erases them. We assumed that edges[j] was adjacent to nodes[k] for this test run, so now EraseNode() will call the method EraseEdge(), which is in the same class. Since this call is made on the same Diagram object de.diag, the arrow labeled EraseEdge points back to its originating lifeline. As before, when UnDraw was invoked on the Node to be erased, UnDraw is invoked on this Edge; but since it is of type TS_Edge, the call is dispatched to TS_Edge.UnDraw() and not Edge.UnDraw(); this call is represented by the arrow labeled Undraw from diag:Diagram to TS_Edge.

The process of recording initial information, delegating the call to the corresponding method in Edge, its update of the Scene, the subsequent returns, and the saving of the results and appending the record to tau is repeated. These steps are represented respectively by ⑥t, the solid arrows labeled UnDraw and RemoveFromSc, ⑦, the next two dotted arrows, and then ⑧t. At this point, TS_Edge.UnDraw() finishes, and control is returned to EraseEdge(), which is illustrated by the dotted arrow from TS_Edge back to diag:Diagram. The Edge's erase bit is then set to true, which is accomplished by the call to Edge.Erase(), which leads to ⑨. After Erase() returns, the method EraseEdge() is finished and returns control to its caller EraseNode() (this second return is not shown, since EraseNode() invoked EraseEdge() on the same Diagram object). EraseNode() then returns control to DiagEditor.RunOne(), which in turn returns control to Test_DiagEditor.test_RunOne().

The final action, the one that we have been building up toward, is to check if the post-condition specified in the interaction specification for RunOne() (with tau substituting for τ, using the fields of tc_old in place of the primed values of the diagram editor's fields, etc.), is satisfied. This check is done at point ⟨n⟩ in the figure.

By defining TS_Node and TS_Edge as derived classes of Node and Edge, by overriding the hook methods Draw and UnDraw in them, and by using these derived classes in constructing the Diagram test case object, we are able to exploit polymorphism to intercept the calls made to the hook methods during execution of template methods such as RunOne(). These redefinitions allow us to record information about these calls (and returns) without having to make any changes to the framework code being tested, indeed without having any access to the source code of the framework. This allows us to achieve our goal of black-box testing of the interaction behavior of template methods.

This methodology is applicable to OO frameworks in general, where we would like to test template methods against their interaction specifications. By plugging in suitable trace-saving classes in place of the derived classes that would normally be built by application developers, we can intercept all of the necessary calls made to hook methods. If a method call cannot be intercepted in this way, then the call would necessarily be made to a method body implemented in the original framework code. Because this call is internal relative to the framework (as opposed to external calls, which are dispatched to the application code) this behavior should already be accounted for in the interaction specification, and the fact that such an internal call is made should be opaque to those using the framework component. In this way, the interaction specification can be viewed as a description of how the framework component interacts with the application code. For a formal discussion on observability, and how it can be used as a basis for integration testing, the interested reader can look through the chapter 'A Methodology of Component Integration Testing'.

5 Prototype Implementation

We have implemented a prototype testing system[2]. The system inputs the trace-based specifications for template methods of the class C under test and the black-box specifications for the non-template methods. The system then creates the source code for the test class, along with other adjunct classes needed for the testing process, in particular those used in constructing traces when testing the template methods of C. The methods to be treated as hooks must be explicitly identified so that they are redefined in the necessary classes. An alternative approach would have been to treat *all* non-final methods as hooks; however, our approach allows greater flexibility. Each redefined hook method that the tool produces can also check its pre- and post-condition before and after the dispatched call is made. This helps pinpoint problems if a template method fails to satisfy its post-condition.

Currently, our system does not generate test cases, but creates skeleton calls to the test methods, where the user is required to construct test values by hand. The user is also required to create suitable cloning methods by hand, due to the possibility of intended aliasing in data structures. To do the actual testing, the generated classes are compiled, and the test class executed. An example of the system's output is reproduced in Fig. 12.

To help illustrate what is going on in this example, the Show() method for the Scene which prints out its contents is invoked in the last line of RunOne(). Before invoking the test_RunOne() method, we see that the Scene contains three Nodes and three Edges. The command that was invoked by RunOne for the test case was to delete the third Node at $(7, -4)$. From the resulting Scene, the proper Node was deleted, along with its adjacent Edges; however, it was not done properly according to the trace-based post-condition. Looking at the resulting trace, we see that UnDraw was invoked for the Node, but not for each adjacent Edge. The actual error in the code was that EraseNode directly updated the Scene and called Erase on the very last adjacent Edge instead of calling UnDraw. We see that although the black-box specification of RunOne() was satisfied, its interaction specification was not.

---

[2]Available at: `http://www.cis.ohio-state.edu/~tyler`

```
Node: (9, 8)
Node: (7, -4)
Edge: (7, -4) → (9, 8)
Node: (-2, -6)
Edge: (-2, -6) → (7, -4)
Edge: (9, 8) → (7, -4)

Test number 1: testing Run.
    Method UnDraw called.
    Method UnDraw called.
    Method UnDraw called.
Node: (9, 8)
Node: (-2, -6)

Postcondition of Run not met!
tau =
    (("UnDraw", (7, -4, false), (7, -4, false), Scene@6b97fd, Scene@6b97fd),
     ("UnDraw", (Test_Node@c78e57, Test_Node@5224ee, false),
      (Test_Node@c78e57, Test_Node@5224ee, false), Scene@6b97fd, Scene@6b97fd),
     ("UnDraw", (Test_Node@f6a746, Test_Node@c78e57, false),
      (Test_Node@f6a746, Test_Node@c78e57, false), Scene@6b97fd, Scene@6b97fd))
Test number 1 failed!

* * * RESULTS * * *

Number of tests run: 1
Number of tests successful: 0
```

Fig. 12. Output from sample run.

6 Related Work

In Sect. 3, we had shown that arriving at the application-level behavior requires us to include, in our specification of the template methods, information about the calls to the hook methods. Helm et al. [177] introduce the notion of *contracts* to impose conditions on what calls to certain hook methods must do and under what conditions. Froehlich et al. [133] generalize the idea of *hook* to denote any aspect of the framework, not just single hook methods, that can be used to tailor it to the application's needs. They introduce a syntactic notation for these generalized hooks but do not consider specification of behavior or testing. Buchi and Weck [51] use traces, similar to ours, to specify information about hook method calls; they focus on developing special notations to simplify trace-based specifications. Kirani and Tsai [228] discuss the importance of specifying the sequence of calls a method $t()$ makes during its execution and testing against this specification; they are, however, interested in *all* calls, not just hook method calls. While the sequence of all calls $t()$ makes is useful in understanding how the body of $t()$ works, the calls that a template method makes to non-hook methods are of no interest to an application developer, since the effect of these calls are the same across all applications built on this framework.

A number of authors have addressed problems related to testing of polymorphic interactions [8, 260, 353]. In most of this work, the approach is to test a template method t() by using objects of many different derived classes to check whether t() behaves appropriately in each case, given the different hook method definitions to which its calls are dispatched, depending on the derived class that the object is an instance of. By contrast, our goal was to test the framework independently of the derived classes. The other key difference is our focus on testing the methods of the framework without the source code. Wu et al. [426] also consider the question of testing OO components in the absence of source code, but they do not focus on frameworks or template methods; and they use enriched UML diagrams, rather than formal specifications, to express the interactions between components. In the chapter 'Modeling and Implementation of Built-In Contract Tests', Gross et al. use testing classes that extend the components under test, which is similar to how we build our trace-saving classes. However, they use such classes to help facilitate testing standard DBC-style contracts, and not for capturing trace information for testing interaction specifications.

Let us now briefly consider test coverage. Typical coverage criteria [8, 353] for testing polymorphic code have been concerned with measuring the extent to which, for example, every hook method call is dispatched, in some test run, to each definition of the hook method. Such a criterion would be inappropriate for us since our goal is to test the framework methods independently of any derived classes. What we should aim for is to have as many as possible of the sequences of hook method calls to appear in the test runs. One approach, often used with specification-based testing, is based on partitioning of the input space. It may be useful to investigate whether there is an analogous approach for testing against interaction specifications, but partition-based testing is known to suffer from some important problems [101, 163]. The question of coverage and that of automating generation of test cases are the two main questions that we hope to tackle in future work.

7 Conclusions and Future Work

In this chapter, we have examined issues relating to the specification and testing of OO framework components. Framework components provide general behaviors that can be useful across a variety of applications. These behaviors can often be characterized by the patterns of hook method calls made by the template methods of the framework, and are precisely captured in interaction specifications. Because such components are often provided without source code, testing against such specifications would seem difficult, if not impossible. However, we have shown how to do so by exploiting polymorphism, and without having to rely on special testing code built into the component, or circumventing the language or runtime system entirely.

We have constructed a prototype testing tool that allows us to test using the methodology presented in this chapter. The tool, however, currently is in a rather primitive state, and there are several important respects in which we plan to improve it. First, we plan to investigate ways for the tool to automatically construct reasonable test cases, possibly with minimal user input. We are also looking into making the tool produce testing classes that are more compatible with the JUnit [23] testing framework, similar to the testing tool presented in the chapter 'A User-Oriented Framework for Component Deployment Testing'. Also, the assertion language we currently use for our interaction specifications is difficult to use in practice; we intend to investigate special notations, perhaps using formalisms such as regular expressions, to simplify these specifications. We will then revise the tool to work with these special notations. In Fig. 12, we see that outputs in the form of internal addresses for the objects makes it difficult to interpret the resulting output. We are planning on developing ways to identify objects in a manner that is easier for the application developer to comprehend.

COTS Component Testing through Built-In Test

Franck Barbier

LIUPPA, Université de Pau
BP 1155
64013 Pau CEDEX, France
Franck.Barbier@univ-pau.fr

Summary. Commercial software components have a typical characteristic, which is that they admit no variation. As a result, a component user has to cope with closed, even rigid, software units. In the case of interfaces, this is a sound characteristic because client/server coupling is well-defined, stabilized, and as low as possible. For implementation, this raises the problem of trustworthiness about a component's actual behavior, its quality of service and its integration capability. In the spirit of a component marketplace, the key actions are choosing and replacing components, upgrading individual components and resultant COTS-based systems, and some inevitable customization. Taking competition into account, vendors may gain much credit by offering technical support for the building of slightly amended versions that permit evaluation, tuning, and more. The ability to endow Commercial Off-The-Shelf (COTS) components with Built-In Test (BIT) material to increase component testability and configurability is the major theme of this chapter. At deployment time, we may thus have new releases called BIT components. Moreover, error correction, functional enhancement, and Quality of Service (QoS) improvement, are also considered in this chapter through the fact that BIT components are relevant software artifacts to organize and instrument a software quality circle between reusers and providers: users' feedbacks are BIT outputs that help and guide vendors in the construction of new versions.

1 Introduction

In this chapter, we introduce a software technology named Built-In Test or BIT. The BIT technology, developed within the IST 1999-20162 Component+ European project, has three major facets: contract testing (see the chapter 'Modeling and Implementation of Built-in Contract Tests'), QoS testing, and COTS component testing. The third facet is orthogonal to the first two. Testing outputs have impacts on COTS component evolution and COTS-based product evolution. At the time of requirements' evolution, software components *cannot* evolve concurrently due to the fact that they are, for the reusers, closed systems. Even if they support well-defined entry points (interfaces), their inside (implementation) is by definition encapsulated and, for safety reasons, not accessible to client components.

From a supplier point of view, evolution normally occurs due to market demands. This includes the emergence or the change of component standards, platforms, languages, and development environments. In such a coercive context, reusers benefit from the fact that they build more flexible and open applications by abandoning odd and tailor-made software parts that are not composable. In contrast, integration is more difficult because components have not been constructed for the reusers' own needs. In practice and in the best case, some component tuning is mandatory. In the worst case, the question is how to find and integrate, if they exist, the "good" COTS components? These components have to meet functional and nonfunctional (QoS) expectations, to be readily composable, and to be substitutable with regard to application evolution.

To partially rule such a process, we propose the BIT technology. We stress single component evolution to assess component appropriateness in users' runtime systems. Repairing, improvement, and even extension of components must however be envisaged by agreement with providers, since market-based harmonization is called for. If we now view applications as component assemblies, maintenance relies mainly on component replacement or adjunction. We think that component builders and vendors are therefore concerned with BIT in the sense that they may offer to potential purchasers, components *plus* customizable test material. To create confidence, reusers may develop unbiased test scenarios that help functional and behavioral component evaluation: does this component meet my functional requirements (contract testing) as well as my runtime constraints (e.g., reliability, performance)?

This chapter is organized as follows. Sect. 2 reviews general-purpose research trends concerning COTS components. In Sect. 3, component testability is discussed, as is more precisely, the current scope of the BIT technology. The Java BIT/J library is presented in order to explain how BIT may be exercised in the context of software distribution. Sect. 4 provides examples relating to three evolution scenarios that are illustrated with pedagogical case studies.

2 Components and COTS-based Products

Software components are recognized as one of the main issues of software engineering in the close future. Components are not ordinary software parts. "Components *are for* composition." [386]. There is a unanimously agreed *technical* meaning behind the word component: components are units of composability and, thus, reusable software assets, while all existing software parts may not be qualified as components. In our opinion, saying that a component is reusable is a pleonasm because it must in essence possess combination potential.

Despite considerable industry interest in components [21] and in computer science research, Wallnau et al. outline in their book [414] that "The challenges posed by systems that are constructed predominantly from *commercial off-the-shelf components* have yet to be addressed adequately. Indeed, the more general challenges posed by *large-scale reuse* of *existing* components, regardless of their origin, have yet to be addressed." In other words, the commercial facet of components creates specific problems ('further complexity' in [414]) that this chapter aims to address.

2.1 Deployment

Deployment is a new step in the Component-Based Development (CBD) process. It covers the phase when components become consumable computation resources. Launched in runtime environments, components aim to fit platform constraints. This mechanism is, for instance, supported by deployment descriptors in the Enterprise JavaBeans (EJB) component model. Nonfunctional properties may be set up in descriptors as, for example, access control or security.

In our opinion, there are two key problems that strongly relate to deployment. First, beyond component infrastructure standards such as EJB, component configuration is a great expectation and aims in general to set up extra functional properties [76]. This corresponds to a broader property spectrum than that of EJB: Fault tolerance and recovery, maximum response delay, worst-case execution time, and so forth have also to be controlled. Moreover, dynamic reconfiguration imposes the concept of configuration interface. Second, in [300], it is observed that, "However, this has led to design practices that assume components are 'compositional' in all other behaviors: specifically, that they can be integrated and still operate the same way in any environment. For many environments, this assumption does not hold." Hence, testing components and assemblies at development time raise strong restrictions. In the spirit of commercial components, developers cannot then ensure that coercive deployment conditions can be always and readily fulfilled.

2.2 Semantic Interoperability and Contracts

Component interfaces are in fact the basic, even unique, support for checking component compatibility, i.e., their real aptitude for collaborating at runtime. Within the scope of the client/server paradigm, a dual view of components is the separation between a provided interface (destined for clients) and a required interface that corresponds to what is required by components in order to properly function [386]. However, interfaces syntactically describe potential exchanges, as well as information processing through communication in general. This does not ensure that the provided and required interfaces of two different components either match in the semantic sense or that their full range of mutual collaboration possibilities is attainable. In this scope,

Heiler observes in [175] that, "*Semantic interoperability* ensures that these exchanges make sense - that the requester and the provider have a common understanding of 'the meanings' of the requested services and data."

The notion of contract is the most recognized support for checking, even certifying, that components behave in conformance with specifications or, more generally, with requirements. Assertions in the Eiffel programming language [277] provide a reputable native mechanism used to incorporate invariants, pre-conditions, and post-conditions into code. This leads to the expression Design by Contract that has gained a first-class status in Component-Based Software Engineering (CBSE).

2.3 Predictability

"Rapid engineering of high confidence systems requires a technology base of components with understood high confidence properties and a methodology for assembling those components in such a way that the properties of the resulting system can be understood, *reasoned about*, and validated." [76]. Prediction-enabled technology is often declared as a key research area of CBSE [413]. The question is, what distinguishes prediction from model checking if we look at the formal basis of verification and validation, or from testing if we stress the more empirical aspect of this important software engineering concern? Incomplete answers remain, but the introduction of executability in [168] is especially promising. This concept has been recently developed for the Unified Modeling Language (UML) [316] in the scope of the MDA (Model-Driven Architecture) initiative [269]. Within a discussion about validation in [76], it is written, "For example, automated validation technology is needed that can consider 'correct-by-construction' techniques" and, "As one example, methods might be explored that are analogous to *proof-carrying code* for certifying software." Executability aims to maintain a very strict functional mapping between specifications and implementations. Component and assembly model execution is simulation through graphical animation in Computer-Aided Software Engineering (CASE) tools. The main point is that all outputs and interpretations resulting from specification execution are considered to be true at runtime. Symmetrically, code testing amounts to model checking, provided that a certain assurance degree is stated.

Prediction mainly stresses component assemblies whose behaviors are hard to formalize and, thus, to anticipate, especially at deployment time and in the context of QoS assessment. In science, the sum of all of the properties of constitutive parts is never the set of properties of the whole to which these parts belong. Starting from this precept, component integration may indisputably benefit from adequate techniques that augment 'normal' component implementation with extra proof-carrying code.

2.4 Evolution

In their characterization of COTS components [280], Meyers and Oberndorf write, "A product that is

Sold, leased, or licensed to the general public
Offered by a vendor trying to profit it
Supported and *evolved by the vendor*, which retains the intellectual property rights
Available in multiple, identical copies
Used *without internal modification by a consumer*"

In this text, from a maintenance point of view, it clearly appears that COTS components are closed systems for end users. In other words, reusers are in essence not responsible for maintaining such entities. Szyperski et al. in [386] view components as units of extension, units of maintenance, and, more interestingly, units of management, but do not lay down a basis for controlling COTS-based application evolution. There is an implicit confirmation that maintainability and evolvability cannot be built in 'after the fact' but must be considered during component evaluation and selection, as well as during integration to make the component infrastructure flexible, and thus evolvable.

3 Component Testability, BIT

In this section, we present the fundamentals of BIT initially characterized in [39] as follows: "Built-in test refers to code added to an application that checks the application at runtime." As a rather recent software engineering notion, the idea of software component has fostered specific research tracks about test and testability. Gao et al. in [136], for example, point out that effort lacks in this research field and propose a specific testing framework for Java components. We, however, explore the impact of keeping test code once and for all in components. Testability is by definition a *potential* property of a component and is thus supposed to be assigned to components *at design time*. Since tests produce a lot of output, it is clear that this information first triggers and next enters into an improvement loop that controls component evolution. However, COTS components, due to their nature, raise a serious problem identified in [76]: "The dominant software testing theories and methods are based upon 'white box' testing that assumes the program code or other detailed representation of the software module to be available. (This is generally untrue of commercial, off-the-shelf (COTS) software and much legacy software.)" The inherent paradox is the need for investigating inner parts of components while preserving component integrity, confidentiality, and, particularly, security or intellectual property.

3.1 Contract Testing

Contracts benefit from being based on component states. For an object like a stack, for instance, a pre-condition (i.e., a contract) to 'pop' is 'not empty'. However, components are in most cases not fine-grained software entities but sizeable elements that own numerous states, as well as complex dependencies between them: concurrency, nesting, and elaborate event processing. States of components are thus partially composed of those of their subparts, i.e., subcomponents that are fully encapsulated (i.e., not shared) and that play a significant role in the implementation of the whole to which they belong. In other words, the whole is a component that is visible to clients. Client components ground their requests on the provided interface of the whole, which may in turn delegate jobs to subparts.

In this scope, BIT allows the prediction of component behavior as well as assembly behavior. Indeed, contracts may be violated in certain assembly patterns while they may work in other circumstances. Furthermore, contracts cannot be based only on states but have to take into account execution conditions that change from one operating environment to another. Our approach essentially makes some well-defined states of the component accessible to clients. This allows a client component to set an acquired component to a defined state, to invoke some services, and to verify that the expected result and state are reached before accepting the component as 'correct'.

A last point relates to the fact that CBD is increasingly organized around UML, in which dedicated modeling constructs exist. We single out Harel's Statecharts [167] in this chapter due to their inclusion in UML and their suitability for use as a backbone for contracts. In relation with this point, we also discuss the crucial need for the availability of *intuitive* component specifications for end users.

3.2 BIT and BIT/J Architectures

The BIT architecture is completely and rigorously defined in [402]. It is grounded on a consensual view of a component that owns a provided (or functional) interface, as well as a required interface. We add a testing interface and a configuration interface.

In Fig. 1, the purpose of the testing interface is essentially to recast the provided interface, to possibly make the inside of components accessible and create scenario-based test operations from scratch. Recasting means that the testing interface includes the same set of services as the provided interface, but implementation may vary for testing reasons, for instance, creating new variables in order to trace some paths of execution. The testing interface may also offer new operations to make visible hidden properties (in read and/or write modes), to establish *atomic* sequences of service calls, and so on. As for the configuration interface, it is strictly correlated to deployment and is not, by definition, used within client requests. Due to an implementation of the BIT

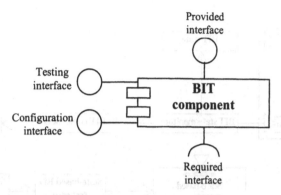

Fig. 1. Canonical organization of a BIT component.

architecture that conforms to a standard in the field of distributed systems, we are generally more interested in the idea of a manageable component that encompasses the idea of configurable and testable components.

The conceptual framework in [402] has generated a Java class library named BIT/J (Fig. 2) that is a partial implementation of the BIT architecture. The IBITQuery interface is a core element in the sense that it is the minimal and only way to transform COTS components into BIT components. In Fig. 2, we have a more complicated case study in which the State-based IBITQuery interface, which extends IBITQuery, offers additional services that together allow the derivation of BIT code and contracts from UML-based behavioral specifications (reuse of the *Statecharts* package, see the left hand side of Fig. 2) and the possible reconfiguration of components at runtime. The BIT state monitor plays a key role in reconfiguration since it monitors the overall component behavior through consistent setup or context recovery. Further explanation details about this approach appear in [18].

At this time, the BIT/J library does not include handlers, as advocated in the conceptual architecture, that are responsible for error processing. While testers capture and record computing results and/or failures through test case objects (*BIT component tester* and *BIT test case* classes in Fig. 2), handlers have to trigger actions in response to errors. Error handling is naturally application-specific and cannot be rigorously defined for the general case. Moreover, *State-based BIT component tester* and *State-based BIT test case* are two classes that are associated, respectively, with *BIT component tester* and *BIT test case* when *Statecharts* are used. An illustration of the BIT/J tool and the use of its key classes are given in Sect. 4.

3.3 Distributed System Concerns

Our Java implementation of the BIT technology is based on the Java Management Extensions (or JMX) technology [382] that supports the concept of a manageable component (or MBean). The basic principle that we adopt is

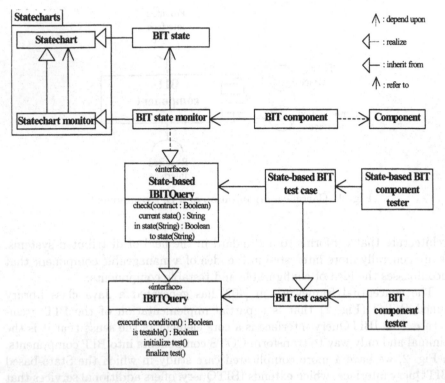

Fig. 2. BIT/J library, classes' relationships.

simply to implement BIT testers and State-based BIT testers (see Fig. 3) as MBeans.

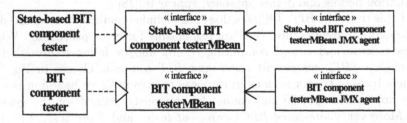

Fig. 3. BIT/J library and JMX.

The presentation of the overall JMX technology is beyond the scope of this chapter. So, Fig. 4 just sketches the final result. Tester methods can be activated within a Web browser. Compared to the conceptual framework in Fig. 1, all of the services constituting the testing and configuration interfaces of a BIT component may be made visible. In practice, as shown later, reconfiguration often occurs at a deeper level and, consequently, is obscure within the

Web browser. The overall mechanism delegates test execution to test cases that themselves handle BIT components within *generic* test protocols. In other words, the *BIT test case* and *State-based BIT test case* classes in Fig. 2 have a *test* method whose implementation is *fully independent* of BIT components. This *test* function imposes that BIT components implement either the *IBITQuery* or *State-based IBITQuery* interfaces.

Regarding the example of a *BIT_JGraph* component, further developed in Sect. 4.1, choices are such that no direct configuration is possible by means of the JMX Web browser and no extra test scenario has been written in addition to the original provided interface of *BIT_JGraph*. Only the read-only *trace* attribute has been added.

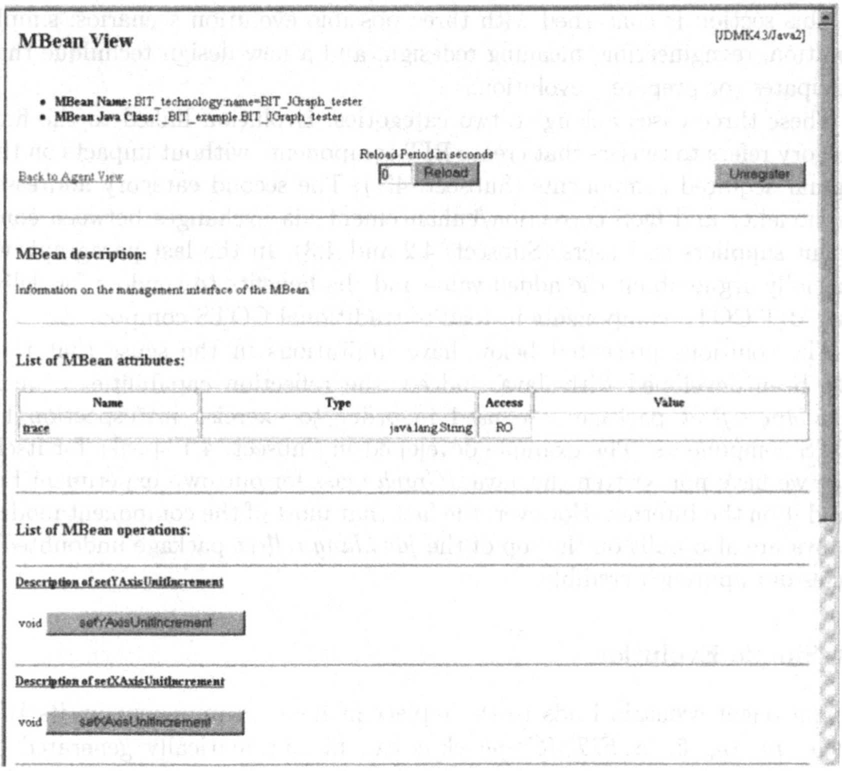

MBean View   [JDMK4.3/Java2]

 * **MBean Name:** BIT_technology:name=BIT_JGraph_tester
 * **MBean Java Class:** _BIT_example.BIT_JGraph_tester

                                      Reload Period in seconds
Back to Agent View   [0] [Reload]   [Unregister]

MBean description:

Information on the management interface of the MBean

List of MBean attributes:

Name	Type	Access	Value
trace	java.lang.String	RO	

List of MBean operations:

Description of setYAxisUnitIncrement

void   [setYAxisUnitIncrement]

Description of setXAxisUnitIncrement

void   [setXAxisUnitIncrement]

Fig. 4. JMX Web browser.

Numerous advantages follow from JMX, including conformance to component management standards and to component models (i.e., JMX may operate with EJB), and remote testing. Testers may indeed operate on deployment nodes distinct from those of BIT components in order to supervise behavior and quality of service without undesired side effects (e.g., local failure).

4 COTS Components and BIT-Based Application Evolution Scenarios

Since COTS components are *a priori* not subject to modification, requiring and generating new versions, even new releases that might make obsolete the originals is a nontrivial and, somehow, incongruous task for reusers. Normally, only COTS component authors and owners control evolution (the provided interface always falls within their competence). However, experience shows that outsourced components are rarely composable with others if they do not come from the same source. We discuss here substantial but nonfunctional change, i.e., the component's provided interface remains the same. Concomitantly, COTS components are equipped with testing and configuration interfaces and consequently with some inherent implementation.

This section is concerned with three possible evolution scenarios: simple evolution, reengineering, meaning redesign, and a new design technique that anticipates (or prepares) evolution.

These three cases belong to two categories. Evolution linked to the first category refers to reusers that create BIT components without impacts on the original acquired components (Subsect. 4.1). The second category addresses functionality and QoS correction/enhancement via exchanges between component suppliers and users (Subsect. 4.2 and 4.3). In the last paragraph we especially argue about the added value and the benefits to vendors for delivering BIT COTS components instead of traditional COTS components.

The solutions presented below have limitations in the sense that they have been developed with Java. Indeed, the reflection capabilities of Java (*java.lang.reflect* package) are used in order to exercise introspection for COTS components. The example developed in Subsect. 4.1 speaks for itself, since we have not written the Java *JGraph* class for our own experiment but found it on the Internet. However, the fact that most of the component models in Java are also built on the top of the *java.lang.reflect* package undoubtedly makes our approach credible.

4.1 Simple Evolution

A lightweight scenario leads to the replacement of a component by its BIT image. In Fig. 5., a *BIT_JGraph* class can be automatically generated by means of a tool under the condition that the original *JGraph* class be accessible through its source code (.java) *or* its binary form (.class and .jar), *or* be running and is attainable from a Java virtual machine, possibly remotely and under well-formalized security conditions. For the example in Fig. 5., we illustrate a replacement that leads to slight changes in code and imposes re-compilation.

Two advantages result from the incorporation of BIT code into application subcomponents: first, the possibility to discover, understand, and supervise the external (semantic interaction with clients) and internal behav-

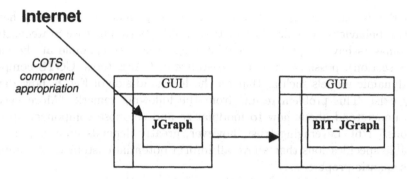

Fig. 5. Substitution of an equivalent BIT incarnation for the *JGraph* class.

iors of components. From a functional point of view, components may reveal shortcomings with regard to accurate computation expectations. From a QoS viewpoint, one may want to establish scores to be compared to strict acceptance/rejection thresholds. Endowed with dedicated code, the BIT_JGraph class offers the said testing and configuration interfaces that enable these investigations. Second, a systematic and rational approach emerges for instrumenting code and, as a result, for checking the behaviors of components via the addition of contracts.

In contrast, a drawback is that deployed BIT code may create resource burden, and overhead in general, that may be incompatible with real-time system constraints or similar concerns relating to critical software.

4.2 Reengineering

The approach presented in Sect. 4.1 may be viewed as a springboard. Indeed, progress expected from BIT use has to be more ambitious. Large-scale software systems and the need for a more open way of using the BIT technology call for more complex scenarios. In Fig. 6., an evolution path with optional directions is sketched for a COTS component.

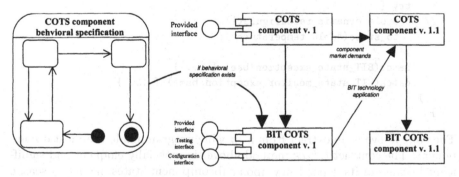

Fig. 6. BIT technology involving reengineering.

In Fig. 6., an assumption is that COTS component providers may have accurate behavioral specifications of their products (in our case Statecharts) or purchasers have to perform reengineering tasks (see example at the end of this section), possibly with the assistance of CASE tools. COTS component dynamic models such as that on the left hand side of Fig. 6, nowadays rarely exist. This problem results from the following remark: "More needs to be understood about how to modularize and compose component specifications." [76]. Leveraging trust, however, greatly depends upon supplying verifiable specifications that above all inform potential customers of component semantic properties.

The scenario posed here is the absence of a specification and, as a result, the existence of an abstruse set of services making up a COTS component's provided interface. In other words, we might imagine that we have to understand a given component's behavior without formal models. In such a context, the functionality offered by components is incomprehensible in the sense that it does not rigorously derive from intelligible models. Reengineering thus means the postponed modeling of component behaviors. This global task is sometimes unrealistic, even impossible, which may be due to complexity or the fact that components match with difficulty to state machines or to any similar formalism.

In Fig. 6., starting from a version 1 COTS component, we construct a version 1 BIT COTS component. Likewise, in the first scenario, the BIT image may be substituted for the initial COTS component and then deployed. A significant benefit is that contract expressions may be readily written by linking them to states:

```
public void season_switch_turned_off() {
  try {
// pre_condition:
    check(_season_switch.in(_season_switch.Is_heat)
     || _season_switch.in(_season_switch.Is_cool));
    super.season_switch_turned_off();
  }
  catch(BIT_contract_violation_exception bcve) {
    try {
// possible dynamic reconfiguration
      to_state("Hold temperature");
    }
    catch(BIT_state_exception bse) { ... }
    catch(BIT_state_monitor_exception bsme) { ... }
  }
}
```

The code above is an extract from a sizeable programmable thermostat component. The contract (*check* method above) is especially eloquent and significant because of its dependency upon subcomponent states, namely a season switch that may be set to a heat mode or a cool mode.

Applying the BIT/J library to a more ordinary Java COTS component in illustrating reengineering leads to the behavioral model in Fig. 7. This case study is such that the initial component (the Java *Stack* predefined class) has no statechart: it was not originally organized and delivered based on a comprehensive specification. We may thus abstract observable states according to what we want to test. In Fig. 7., for instance, one does not deal with a *Full* state since *Stack* does not reach such a state *a priori*. In contrast, one distinguishes two substates of a *Not empty* state, an *Empty* state, and, finally, associated transitions.

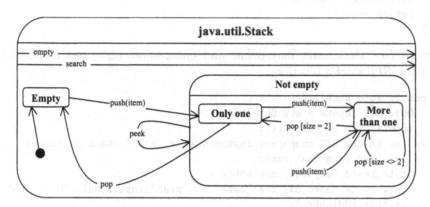

Fig. 7. Reengineering of the Java *Stack* COTS component.

The inside of a *BIT_stack* class can then be built, and properly maps to the statechart in Fig. 7 as follows:

```
// embedding of a common Java Stack instance:
private java.util.Stack _stack = new java.util.Stack();
// states:
protected BIT_state _Empty;
protected BIT_state _Only_one;
protected BIT_state _More_than_one;
protected BIT_state _Not_empty;
// state machine monitor:
protected BIT_state_monitor _BIT_stack;
private void init_behavior() throws Statechart_exception {
  _Empty = new BIT_state("Empty");
  _Only_one = new BIT_state("Only one");
  _More_than_one = new BIT_state("More than one");
// states are bound together:
  _Not_empty =
    (BIT_state)(_Only_one.xor(_More_than_one)).name("Not empty");
  _BIT_stack =
    new BIT_state_monitor(_Empty.xor(_Not_empty),"BIT stack");
  _Empty.inputState(); }
```

Now, each method may be reviewed in the context of reengineering; for instance, the *push* function:

```
public Object push(Object item) throws Statechart_exception {
   Object result = _stack.push(item);
// candidate transitions:
   _BIT_stack.fires(_Empty,_Only_one);
   _BIT_stack.fires(_Only_one,_More_than_one);
   _BIT_stack.fires(_More_than_one,_More_than_one);
// interpretation cycle:
   _BIT_stack.used_up();
   return result;
}
```

Next, a *BIT_stack_tester* may define and encapsulate test cases associated with the *BIT_stack*'s functions:

```
public void push() {
   Object[] inputs = new Object[1];
   inputs[0] = new Object();
// _bc is the BIT component instance (i.e. a BIT_stack instance)
// involved in a test case:
   State_based_BIT_test_case sbbtc =
      new State_based_BIT_test_case(_bc,"push",inputs,null,"Only one");
   _history.add(sbbtc);
   sbbtc.test();
}
```

Finally, a *BIT_stack_tester* instance can be plugged into JMX as follows:

```
public class BIT_stack_tester implements BIT_stack_testerMBean {...}
```

4.3 New Technique for COTS Component Design

The third and final scenario is grounded on the idea that the BIT software technology is an innovative development method for COTS components. COTS component vendors should have high interest in hearing from and exploiting customers' feedbacks. This is surely true when we consider component repairing. Equipping components with new functionality *cannot*, in essence, be peculiar to customer needs, with the exception of large adhesion, which, from a marketing point of view, justifies customer-oriented evolution. The question is how to organize and thus provide associated technical tools for such a business interaction. In other words, is it possible to implement in components some extra material that gathers and capitalizes on users' experience and consequently helps conduct of the evolution process for component holders?

In this line of reasoning, we view BIT as a support for component appropriation, from taking possession (component discovering, downloading, individual evaluation, etc.) to generalization, namely, the recurrent and intensive use in varied, even odd, applications that inevitably creates a strong dependence to vendors. Intermediate phases that occur in such an acquisition process appear in Fig. 8. Reaction goes beyond individual testing in order to assess component integration potential and facilities in the context of special constraints, for instance, the necessary collaboration with existing in-house components. Adoption is the act of qualification, even certification, when components are incorporated into highly critical systems, and leads to concomitant actions such as leasing or buying. Utilization precedes generalization and minimizes dependency. In other words, reusers stress the selection of units of functionality but also pay attention to component substitutability in anticipating and preparing application implementation alternatives that might, for various reasons, put aside any previously selected components. In contrast, generalization precludes reversing choices in the sense that the retained COTS components act as essential blocks in end user's products.

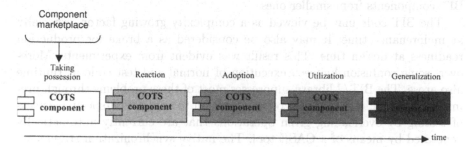

Fig. 8. Component appropriation cycle.

All of the stages in Fig. 8. naturally show that a key objective for vendors is to gain purchasers' trust. A significant barrier is that components hide implementation and offer only functional interface, something that may slow down, or otherwise restrict, such a COTS component acquisition process. As already observed, fostering confidence requires that reusers better predict component and assembly behaviors, as well as the resultant impact on QoS. To that extent, COTS components with BIT material allow in situ testing, create additional documentation ('best practices') and, more generally, facilitate inter-vendor comparison. Indeed, in a competing process, two BIT components that share an equivalent provided interface may produce distinct degrees of satisfaction at usage time.

5 Conclusion

The BIT technology has been developed for components that have to be built from scratch, as well as for COTS components. This chapter addresses the second aspect, showing in particular how BIT may be applied to fine-grained

Java components. In the scope of Java, it clearly and concretely appears that such software units may readily evolve with interesting inherent returns on investment. In the scope of the BIT technology, only bespoke components were previously examined. This chapter thus tries to fill a gap by dealing with *real* COTS components. Experience and assessment, however, demonstrate that some shortcomings remain.

Granularity is currently a central problem. COTS components are typically sizeable software subsystems. A theoretical BIT framework that properly addresses granularity issues must thus formalize composability, and consequently treat assembly QoS, assembly behavior prediction, and assembly evolution. Aggregation and composition of BIT components are under the spotlight: we investigate the Whole-Part theory in [17], especially in the context of UML since we want to have a design method that fundamentally relies on an agreed modeling language. We also start an experimental implementation based on the Relation Service of JMX that aims to formally lay out large BIT components from smaller ones.

The BIT code may be viewed as a complexity growing factor, especially at maintenance time. It may also be considered as a brake for production readiness at design time. This result was evident from experiments. Moreover, some confusion between execution of normal and test code at runtime also arose. The BIT/J library suppresses most of these problems through preimplementation: one only has to pay attention to application-specific aspects of testing by overloading given operations that are currently automatically generated by means of a CASE tool. The native synchronization statements of Java have naturally helped arbitration between normal and test code executions.

To close, one probably must insist on reflective component architectures. Allowing self-description of systems, reflection is an insufficiently explored paradigm that may be used for driving COTS-based product evolution. A key expectation is the close appearance of reflection standards for component frameworks. Even though reflection is intensively used in the Java world, this usage remains eclectic, i.e., not subject to agreed rules, or better, to normalized approaches.

Acknowledgments

This work has been partially funded by the European Union within the Component+ (IST 1999-20162) IST project.

COTS Component Testing through Aspect-Based Metadata

Alejandra Cechich[1] and Macario Polo[2]

[1] Departamento de Ciencias de la Computación
Universidad Nacional del Comahue, Buenos Aires 1400
Neuquén, Argentina
acechich@uncoma.edu.ar

[2] Grupo Alarcos, Escuela Superior de Informática
Universidad de Castilla-La Mancha, Paseo de la Universidad 4
Ciudad Real, España
Macario.Polo@uclm.es

Summary. Documentation is one of the key issues in Component-Based System Development that emphasizes the creation of models of testing information. Hence, testing based on these models might point out missing entities – such as methods – or inconsistencies in the treatment of entities for testing. Documentation influences component specification as well as specific information for testing. For example, Hybertson in the chapter 'Using a Specification Approach to Facilitate Component Testing' declares that more precise and complete specifications will enable and simplify component testing, and Memon in the chapter 'A Process and Role-Based Taxonomy of Techniques to Make Testable COTS Components' presents some examples in the use of meta-information applied to regression testing. There are many other examples of techniques that enrich documentation by structuring and classifying information. Along those lines, aspect information has been used to help implement better component interfaces and to encode knowledge of a component's capability.

In this chapter, we introduce an aspect-based categorization of information for testing. This information is added as a component's metadata to generate aspect-dependent test cases. We will illustrate the proposed technique and its supporting tool, which allows us to add testing metadata to Enterprise JavaBeans (EJB) components.

1 Introduction

One of the major steps toward achieving efficiency of COTS component testing lies in using testing techniques which support the identification and creation of test cases that are relevant for the component. Another is building up a sufficiently large and well-documented data of these test cases. Component-based systems introduce additional challenges to testing: components must fit into the new environment when they are reused, often requiring real-time detection, diagnosis, and handling of software faults.

The BIT-based COTS technology developed within the European project Component+ [102] makes it possible to reuse tests by applying BIT (Built-in Tests) to software components. A BIT-based COTS is a software component whose source code includes tests as special functions. This approach enables tests be embedded and reused as that of code in COTS and bespoke components, allowing the production of self-testable components so that dynamic faults may be detected at run time. This is a significant advance for improving software reliability and fault-tolerant capability in CBSD [153, 186, 415].

There are some variations on building BIT-based COTS. The approach in [415] includes the complete test suite inside the components, whereas [255] just puts a minimal number of tests, like assertions, inside the components. In both cases there are some pitfalls to consider: including all tests means occupying space while only few tests are used at deployment; and a minimal number of tests requires that specific software is used to transform the test specification into real tests. Besides, as Barbier argues in the chapter 'COTS Component Testing through Built-In Test',

> ... granularity is currently a central problem. A theoretical BIT framework that properly addresses granularity issues must thus formalize composability, and consequently treat assembly QoS, assembly behavior prediction, and assembly evolution.

However, built-in tests might be integrated by using flexible architectures without requiring additional software, and hence minimizing the time spent on testing [186]. As Gross et al. declare in the chapter 'Modeling and Implementation of Built-in Contract Tests', BIT technology might be integrated with automatic approaches to derive application testing from system models and generate executable tests from these models.

As a related approach, several authors add metadata to components to describe static and dynamic aspects of the component, useful for dealing with several software engineering tasks: in [374], annotations are used to perform dependence analysis over both the static and dynamic descriptions; in [171] and [319], metadata are added to components to provide generic usage information about a component (class and method names, for example), as well as information for testing. The common idea in these approaches is to add to the component a set of information to help the component user during its use, composition, testing, etc. Our proposal includes the addition of some aspect-based metadata to facilitate the component testing. So, in the following pages we identify what relevant information can fall into this metadata category, propose a formal specification for it, and present a tool to assist the component developer when adding this kind of metadata.

Metadata are also used in existing component models to provide generic usage information about a component (e.g., the name of its class, the name of its methods) as well as information for testing [171, 319], providing a general mechanism for aiding software engineering tasks. In the context of self-checking code, metadata needed to accomplish a task consists of invariants, and pre- and post-condition(s) for the different functions provided by the component. This information is used to implement a checking mechanism for calls to the component. As a result, developers have to identify many component properties recording which properties are in conflict with other expected properties. Metadata is used in the context of testing and analysis of distributed component systems. The metadata-based technique has also been extended and applied to regression test selection for component-based applications [171]. Details of this approach from the developer and composer viewpoints are further depicted by Memon in the chapter 'A Process and Role-Based Taxonomy of Techniques to Make Testable COTS Components'.

Moreover, component qualification is one of the major steps in the development of component-based applications [369], which includes performance testing, additional hardware and software requirements, and also functional testing to check the suitability of the component for the application where it will be integrated. In this sense, aspect-oriented component engineering uses the concept of different system capabilities to reason about component provided and required services. Aspect information is used to help implement better component interfaces and to encode knowledge of a component's capability [159, 160]. Each component aspect has a number of aspect details that are used to more precisely describe component characteristics relating to the aspect. Another benefit is that the aspect code can make decisions based on actual runtime values. Computational reflection enables a program to access its internal structure and behavior, and this is beneficial for testing by automating the execution of tests through the creation of instances of classes and the execution of different sequences of methods [332, 378]. Thus, in this way, the aspect code can dynamically decide how to instrument the running application and evolve based on runtime data.

In our approach [61], we have extended the notion of using metadata for testing COTS components by classifying testing information using aspects. A number of meta-procedures for black-box testing have been introduced to allow us to reason about completeness of data supplied for testing, and to eventually facilitate the use of test cases along with automated tools for the testing.

This chapter is organized as follows. The next section describes the basic principles of our approach for aspect-based testing along with a description that focuses on how this approach can add value to metadata for testing. Then, we present a Java environment that supports and automates our method. In the last section, we address some conclusion and topics for further research.

2 Aspects and Metadata for Testing

The concept of component aspects allows a better categorization of component capabilities according to a component's contribution to the component-based system's overall functions, and helps organize non-functional constraints. A key feature of this categorization of component characteristics is the idea that some components provide certain aspect-related services for other components (or end users) to use, while other components require certain aspect-related services from other components. Each component aspect has a number of aspect details that are used to describe component characteristics relating to the aspect. These details aim to increase developers' and end users' knowledge about components by providing a more effective categorization and codification mechanism for the component services.

When reasoning about operations of components, we analyze them in terms of particular aspects. For example, developers can describe interfaces in terms of a collaborative work aspect, persistency-related aspect, or user interface aspect. Note that some aspect categorizations may overlap (a service might be considered a user interface aspect as well as a collaborative work aspect). Figure 1 illustrates how some aspects map onto some services. The *Accounting View* component has services described only in terms of user interface aspects; meanwhile, the *Editing Balance* component has services described in terms of one aspect as well as overlaps between the user interface aspect and the collaborative work aspect, and the collaborative work aspect and the persistency aspect.

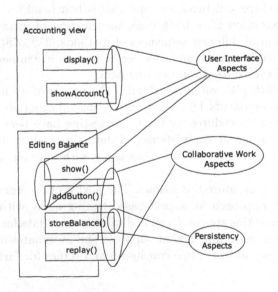

Fig. 1. An illustration of component's aspects.

The way a component developer can add metadata to his component can be accomplished by providing each component with two methods: one to query about the kinds of metadata available, and the other to retrieve a specific kind of metadata. In our approach [61], we have extended the notion of using metadata for testing COTS components by classifying testing information using aspects. A number of meta-procedures are introduced in the following section to eventually facilitate the generation of test cases.

2.1 Meta-Procedures for Aspect-Based Testing

Using metadata and aspects can extend the documentation of a component to define and validate its test cases. For example, in our approach, documentation to define test cases is grouped into a meta-object used as a descriptor of a base object. Documentation is extended to include an aspect-based analysis that allows reasoning about several properties of the test cases.

To introduce the approach, a number of concepts must be defined. We firstly define the notion of *aspect scope* of a method as the set of all aspects that influence a particular component's method. For the example introduced previously, the aspect scope of all the methods is the following:

$$ASc = \{(show(), \{User\ Interface,\ Collaborative\ Work\}), (addButton(), \{User\ Interface,\ Collaborative\ Work\}), (storeBalance(), \{Collaborative\ Work, Persistency\}), (replay(), \{Collaborative\ Work,\ Persistency\})\}$$

Identifying and creating test cases relevant for a component involve analyzing test cases for a single method as well as test cases for multiple methods. Defining test cases depends on several factors, such as the component's state, the invariants on the functionality associated to the component, and pre- and post-condition(s) of each method. These factors are extended when we consider aspects by including the aspect scope as we defined previously. Therefore, information for defining test cases of a particular method, or *Method Metadata (MM)*, can be summarized as the tuple *(M, S, ASc_M, M, Inv)*, where *M* represents the method to be tested, and implicitly includes its name and parameters, and its pre- and post-condition(s), *S* is the state of the component, *Inv* is the set of invariants that constrains the component's functionality, and ASc_M is the aspect scope related to the method *M*, that is, the set of aspects relevant to the method *M*. For example, $ASc_{show()}$ is the set {User Interface, Collaborative Work}.

More formally, let *AS* be an aspect set, and *ASR* be the set of relations between a particular method and its influencing aspects, $ASR = (Method \times AS)_{set}$; the aspect scope *ASc* can be expressed as a restricted subtype of *ASR* that satisfies the property *is_in_scope*, which certifies the existence of influencing aspects on the relationship

$ASc = \{asc : ASR \mid is\_in\_scope(asc)\}$
$is\_in\_scope : ASR \rightarrow Bool$
$is\_in\_scope(asr) \equiv \forall as : AS, m : Method \bullet$
$\quad (m, as) \in asr \Rightarrow influence(as, m)$

Hence, a meta-procedure for aspect-oriented generation of test cases can be enunciated based on the *MM* information, as Fig. 2 shows. For example, the method show() in Fig. 1 is affected by two aspects – User Interface and Collaborative Work. We first select the pre- and post-condition(s) relevant to the aspect User Interface and find test cases by using traditional techniques for black-box testing. After that, we proceed doing the same for the aspect Collaborative Work. Once all aspects have been considered, we analyze all test cases to identify incompatibility or inconsistency among them, generating a new set of test cases where tests are compatible. That is, values are selected from a consistent range of possibilities for every test case. Finally, several analyses of properties of test cases can be done. In particular, a completeness analysis that checks that all aspects have been considered, and hence all domains have been consolidated, could be useful for identifying a wider spectrum of test cases.

```
For each M
    For each aspect in the set ASC_M
        Specialise the pre/post conditions of M according
        to the considered aspect
        Select test cases for M
    Analyse the compatibility of all test cases
    Select compatible test cases and constraint domains
    Analyse completeness of selected test cases with respect
    to a combined domain for all aspects in ASC_M
```

Fig. 2. A meta-procedure (MP1) for aspect-oriented generation of test.

Again, *MP1* can be expressed more formally as a function definition. To do so, we need to express the information of a method as a type variable containing the method's name, its parameters and its pre- and post-condition(s) – *Method* = (name, param, pre, post). Let *Test* be a type variable containing information about a particular test case, such as its values passed as input, its expected results, and its actual results – *Test* = (obj, expectedRes, actualRes) – and *TestCase* a type variable representing a set of Test; *MP1* is defined as

$MP1 : ASc \times Inv \rightarrow TestCase$
$MP1(asc, i) \equiv$
$\quad \{ts \mid \forall as : AS, m : Method, a : Aspect \bullet (m, as) \in asc \land a \in as \land$
$\quad compatible(m.pre, m.pos, as) \Rightarrow$

$$\exists t : Test \bullet test\_m(a, m, t) \land is\_adequate(t, i) \land t \in ts\}$$
$$is\_adequate : Test \times Inv \rightarrow Bool$$
$$is\_adequate(t, i) \equiv adequate(t.expectedRes, t.actualRes) \land$$
$$satisfies\_invariants(state(t.obj), i)$$

Functions *compatible*, *test_m*, *adequate*, and *satisfies_invariants* are abstract function definitions, which should implement previously mentioned constraints in several ways. Particularly, compatibility of pre- and post-condition(s) relevant to the aspect should be verified by defining the function *compatible*; consistency of test values should be verified for every test case by defining the function *test_m*; and adequacy of test cases should be verified by analyzing its results and verifying the satisfaction of invariants previously stated.

A more complete selection of test cases also involves analyzing valid ranges from a combined view of methods, so aspects affecting methods can be used as a way of partitioning the testing space. Then, we have defined the notion of *relevant methods* (*RM*) as the set of all methods affected by a particular aspect. For the example, relevant methods of all the aspects are defined as follows:

RM = {(User Interface, {show(), addButton()}), (Collaborative Work, {show(), addButton(), storeBalance(), replay()}), (Persistency, {storeBalance()})}

RM_A is the relevant method set relating to the aspect A, that is, the set of all methods relevant to the aspect A. For example, $RM_{UserInterface}$ is the set {show(), addButton()}.

More formally, let ME be a method set and RMR be the set of relations between a particular aspect and the set of methods influenced by this aspect, that is, $RMR = (Aspect \times ME)_{set}$; the relevant methods RM can be expressed as a restricted subtype of RMR that satisfies the property *is_influenced_by*:

$$RM = \{rmr : RMR \mid is\_influenced\_by(rmr)\}$$
$$is\_influenced\_by : RMR \rightarrow Bool$$
$$is\_influenced\_by(rmr) \equiv$$
$$\forall me : ME, a : Aspect \bullet (a, me) \in rmr \Rightarrow is\_influenced(me, a)$$

Hence, another meta-procedure for aspect-oriented generation of multi-method test cases can be enunciated as Fig. 3 shows. For example, the method show() is related to the method addButton() by means of the aspect User Interface. After generating test cases for show(), we proceed by selecting the aspect – User Interface – that we want to consider.

Then, the method addButton() is analyzed, and we again select the pre- and post-condition(s) relevant to the aspect User Interface and find test cases

```
For each M
Select test cases for M /* applying the meta-procedure MP1 */
    For each aspect in the set RM
        For all other Mₖ  related by a particular aspect in
        the set RMₐ
            Specialise the pre/post conditions of Mₖ
            according to the considered aspect
            Select test cases for Mₖ
            /* applying the meta-procedure MP1  */
    Analyse the compatibility of all test cases
    for {M, Mₖ₁, Mₖ₂, ....}
    Select compatible combined test cases and constraint
    domains to the intersection
    Analyse completeness of selected test cases with
    respect to a combined domain for all interfaces in RMₐ
```

Fig. 3. A meta-procedure (MP2) for aspect-oriented generation of multi-method test cases.

by using traditional techniques for black-box testing. After that, we proceed by analyzing all test cases to identify incompatibility or inconsistency (between show()'s test cases and addButton()'s test cases). That is, values are selected from a consistent and common range of possibilities. Finally, a completeness analysis that checks that all ranges have been considered, and hence all domains have been consolidated, is done for all methods affected by the same aspect.

More formally,

$$MP2 : RM \times ASc \times Inv \rightarrow TestCase$$
$$MP2(rm, asc, i) \equiv$$
$$\{ts \mid \forall me : ME, m_1, m_2 : Method, a : Aspect, as_1, as_2 : AS \bullet$$
$$(m_1, as_1) \in asc \land (m_2, as_2) \in asc \land a \in as_1 \land$$
$$(a, me) \in rm \land m_1 \in me \land m_2 \in me \land$$
$$compatible\_pre(m_1.pre, m_2.pre, a) \land$$
$$compatible\_pos(m_1.pos, m_2.pos, a) \Rightarrow$$
$$\exists t_1, t_2, tc : Test \bullet test\_m(a, m_1, t_1) \land test\_m(a, m_2, t_2) \land$$
$$t_1 \in MP1((m_1, as_1), i) \land t_2 \in MP1((m_2, as_2), i) \land$$
$$is\_combination(t_1, t_2, tc) \land is\_valid(tc, i) \land tc \in ts\}$$

We should note that the procedure *MP2* does not explicitly mention the location of the methods M_k. This is particularly useful at this meta-level specification because the entire procedure can be adapted to black-box testing as well as to integration testing among components. If we consider the example detailed in the previous paragraph, the set of methods relevant to the aspect User Interface is calculated inside the component *Editing Balance*, which focuses on black-box techniques. However, the same procedure could be applied if we considered all methods in the model related to by the aspect User Interface, that is, methods in *Editing Balance* as well as methods in *Accounting View*. Therefore, integration testing is another possible implementation of the procedure *MP2*.

Finally, methods relate to each other by shearing a set of aspects that influence their behavior. This situation leads to an "aspect overlap", meaning that methods tested according to the procedure *MP2* are also influenced by compatibility of common ranges. To clarify this point, consider our example of Fig. 1. Procedure *MP1* has produced test cases for show() from the points of view of User Interface, addButton() from the point of view of User Interface, show() from the point of view of Collaborative Work, and so on. Procedure *MP2* has continued evaluating methods from the same point of view, such as show() and addButton() from the point of view of User Interface. But show() and addButton() should also be analyzed considering that both methods share different points of view or aspects (User Interface and Collaborative Work), which could constrain our test case domain.

Then, we have defined the notion of *common aspects* (*CA*) as the set of relations between all methods affected by a particular set of aspects, that is, a set of aspects affecting a set of methods, producing an intersection of relevant test cases for a particular domain. For the example, common aspects are defined as follows:

CA = { ({User Interface, Collaborative Work}, {show(), addButton()}), ({Persistency, Collaborative Work}, {storeBalance()}) },

where CA_k denotes an element of the set *CA* as the pair (a, m) where a is a particular set of aspects influencing the particular set of methods m. More formally, let *CAR* be the set of relations between a set of aspects and its influenced methods, that is, $CAR = (AS \times ME)_{set}$; the common aspects *CA* can be expressed as a restricted subtype of *CAR* that satisfies the property *is_influenced_by*:

$$CA = \{car : CAR \mid is\_influenced\_by(car)\}$$
$$is\_influenced\_by : CAR \rightarrow Bool$$
$$is\_influenced\_by(car) \equiv \forall me : ME, as : AS \bullet$$
$$(as, me) \in car \Rightarrow is\_influenced(me, as)$$

```
For each CAₖ = (a, m)
    For each method in the set CA.m
        Evaluate common ranges and compatibilities
        for test cases analysed in every CA.a
        /* applying the meta-procedure MP2 */
```

Fig. 4. A meta-procedure (MP3) for aspect-oriented generation of overlapping test cases.

Hence, the last meta-procedure for aspect-oriented generation of test cases can be enunciated as Fig. 4 shows. Every element of the set CA is evaluated to identify possible common test cases and/or inconsistencies among previously selected cases.

More formally,

$$MP3 : CA \times Inv \rightarrow TestCase$$
$$MP3(ca, i) \equiv \{ts \mid \forall me : ME, m : Method, a : Aspect, as : AS \bullet$$
$$(as, me) \in ca \wedge a \in as \wedge m \in me \Rightarrow$$
$$\exists t : Test \bullet t \in MP2((a, me), (as, m), i) \wedge$$
$$compatible(t, as, me) \wedge t \in ts\}$$

2.2 Modeling Metadata for Testing

As models mature from analysis into more detailed design models, more information will be available to examine. In particular, the existence of mismatches between the COTS product being integrated and the system is possible due to their different architectural assumptions and functional constraints. These mismatches must be overcome during integration. To allow for early fault identification, the viewpoint presented here is that testing goes beyond the execution of code. It is used here to indicate activities such as analysis of pre-requisites, comparisons, or any activity in which criteria are used to detect misconceptions, omissions, and mistakes and to provide feedback for improvement.

The importance of discussing COTS component integration shows up when considering that COTS products are developed to be generic; however, being integrated into a system, they are used in a specific context with certain dependencies. These products should be compatible with composition, avoid the inappropriate development-based goals of non-COTS-based solutions, support the declarative aspect of component integration, and be clearly distinct from the component- and system-level artifacts.

Interfaces are also central to our approach. However, a component is now characterized through metadata, not only by the required and provided services, but also by the operations of the interface in terms of its invariants, pre- and post-condition(s), and aspects.

Next, we introduce the example presented in [319] to motivate the need for aspects and metadata and to show a possible use of this information. The example consists of part of a distributed application for remote banking where one or more instances of an externally developed component are used to access a remote database containing account-related information. For the sake of this example we assume that the source code of BankingAccount is unavailable. We have extended the notation to include aspects as part of the component's metadata.

Figure 5 shows a subset of the BankingAccount component interface and a fragment of the component specification for invariants, pre- and post-condition(s), and aspects. Sets *ASc*, *RM*, and *CA* are easily calculated from metadata information. Particularly, *ASc* is part of the metadata, and *RM* and *CA* are extracted as

RM = {(User Interface, {withdraw(float amount), deposit(float amount)}),

(Collaborative Work, {open(), withdraw(float amount),

deposit(float amount)}), (Persistency, {withdraw(float amount),

deposit(float amount)})}

CA = { ({User Interface, Collaborative Work, Persistency}, {withdraw(float amount), deposit(float amount)})}

Black-box testing techniques develop test cases based on a functional description of the system. One such technique, the category-partition method, produces test frames that represent a test specification for the functional units in the system. As functional units, components can be analyzed to produce a test frame based both on analysis of the component's interface and on its metadata.

```
public class BankingAccount {
  //@ invariant ( ((balance  > 0) || (status == OVERDRAWN)) && \
  //@                 ((timeout < LIMIT) || (logged == false))  );

  public void open() throws CantOpenException,
                            InvalidPINException {
    //@ pre (true);
    //@ post (logged == true);
    //@ aspects (Collaborative Wok);
  }
  public float withdraw(float amount) {
    //@ pre    (logged == true) && \
    //@         (amount < balance) ) ;
    //@ post ( (return == balance' ) && \\
    //@          (balance' == balance – amount) ) ;
    //@ aspects (Collaborative Work, Persistency, User Interface);
  }
  public float deposit(float amount) {
    //@ pre   (logged == true) ;
    //@ post ( (return == balance' ) && \\
    //@          (balance' == balance + amount) ) ;
    //@ aspects (Collaborative Work, Persistency, User Interface);
  }
}
```

Fig. 5. BankingAccount fragment of the component metadata.

Figure 6 illustrates, for the methods *withdraw* and *deposit*, a possible set of categories, choices, and constraints on the choices derived by applying the category-partition method to the component *BankingAccount*.

We can now select test cases by applying the meta-procedures *M1* and *M2*. First of all, we consider compatibility of pre- and post-condition(s) grouped into different aspect sets. When analyzing the withdraw method, Collaborative Work, Persistency, and User Interface are influencing aspects. For example, from the point of view of Collaborative Work, there is only one precondition to consider, which is logged == true, and two possible values – available and unavailable – defined in the frame. In the same way, there is only one pre-condition from the Persistency point of view, that is, amount < balance, only one post-condition, that is balance' = balance - amount, and several possible combinations of values – amount greater than balance, balance greater than amount, etc.

Next, we combine pre- and post-condition(s) from different points of view to get a suitable set of conditions for test cases which relate to different aspects. Iteratively, we should construct a combined expression for all influencing aspects on the component interface, and define its associated test cases. After that, we proceed building an evaluation driver and performing interface probing.

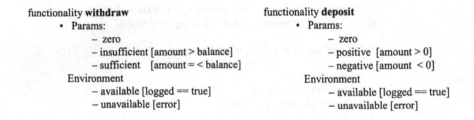

Fig. 6. A possible set of categories, choices, and constraints for withdraw and deposit.

3 An Aspect-Based Environment for Component Testing

One of the ways in which COTS-based systems result in higher quality compositions is by having an automated environment in which properties of integrations are dynamically tested [62]. An environment should support and exploit component self-description or meta-information that is stored directly inside the component; the environment should support a development process comprising component development and application composition; and so on. For example, the WREN [249] approach for visual composition requires components to have a specific format to provide minimum self-description. A component is a Java file that can contain Java classes, interfaces, and resources. It must contain a self-description class, which provides information about the component. Components can also contain a diagrammatic representation of themselves, so that they can be represented in component diagrams that are created in the environment.

Interfaces are central to this approach. A component is characterized by the interfaces of the data types it provides or requires. WREN interfaces are self-description wrappers around Java interfaces that can provide additional natural language documentation and additional information about individual operations in the interface. Each operation can have an additional self-description wrapper to provide information about itself. In particular, this wrapper can define post-condition(s) to assert constraints on the execution of the operation at runtime.

As another example, the work in [68] presents an overall architecture of an Aspect-Oriented Enterprise JavaBeans (EJB) Server. This architecture is based on the notion of *metaobject* (an object that contains information about a base object and/or controls the execution of the base object) and *baseobject* (a base-level object that is managed by a meta object). A metaobject corresponds to a container in EJB, but is more generalized. A metaobject is created for a baseobject and has sufficient information about the baseobject. That information, called metadata, is gathered from a deployment descriptor of the baseobject. Also, additional information, such as current status of baseobject, is updated during run-time. A metaobject has the full control of a baseobject: creating and destroying the baseobject, hooking incoming method calls of the baseobject, and then delegating them to aspects according to the metadata.

Following the latter approach, we have developed a tool to to include an EJB component's metadata for testing. Using two predefined interfaces (*EntityBean* and *SessionBean*), developers can build three types of EJBs:

- Stateless beans receive requests from client applications, process them, and send them a response. They do not maintain information about the connection with the client.
- Stateful beans maintain information about the connection and can then receive multiple related requests at different moments and provide a set of "also-related" responses.
- Entity beans maintain information about the connection and, moreover, their instances represent persistent objects that are saved in some kind of secondary storage.

Stateless and stateful EJBs must implement the *SessionBean* interface, whereas entity EJBs must implement the *EntityBean* interface. EJBs are managed by a component container that receives client requests through the *Remote* interface of the component. Previously, the client must have located the desired component via its *Home* interface. So the *Remote* interface includes the declaration of the business methods, which are those used by the clients to make use of the component functionalities. The *Home* interface also includes the headers of some methods to find instances and to provide persistence to instances (in Entity EJBs). In practice, the component must implement the methods defined in both the *Remote* and the *Home* interfaces, although this point is later checked at runtime by the component container, since there is no direct implementation relationship from the component to its interfaces, that is, the compiler does not detect whether a method in either the *Remote* or the *Home* interface is not implemented by the component (even the names of the methods in the *Home* interface are not the same as in the component).

This fact is illustrated in Fig. 7, which shows on the right hand side the indirect nature of the implementation relationship among the *AccountEJB* component and its two interfaces (really, the only direct implementation relationship is from the component to the interface representing its type of EJB, *EntityBean* in this example). Both interfaces are actually exposed by the container as a means for the component to communicate with clients: in fact, the client application uses the component functionality by using the *Account* interface (the *Remote* interface). The container is in charge of linking the interface with the component.

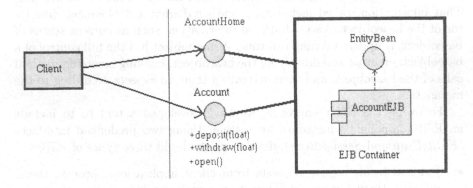

Fig. 7. Client and server sides in a generic EJB application.

From components like the *AccountEJB* and its two interfaces, what we want is to apply the method described in the previous section to generate aspect-depending test cases. To do so, we build a special type of EJB that has enough internal structure and behavior to manage testing. Therefore, our components do not directly implement the afore- mentioned predefined Java interfaces (*EntityBean* or *SessionBean*), but are subclasses of *EntityTesting* or *SessionTesting*, two special types of components we have developed.

Both *EntityTesting* and *SessionTesting* include in their definitions an instance of the *Metadata* class that has the relevant information for testing, as in the diagram in Fig. 8.

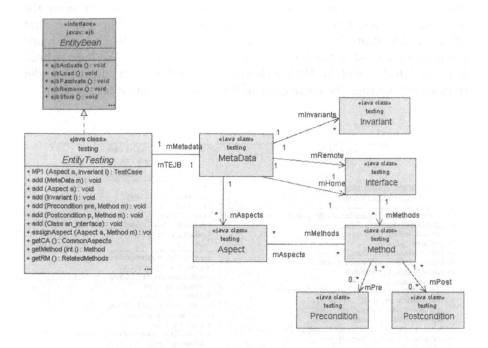

Fig. 8. Structure of the *EntityTesting* component.

As it is seen, the *EntityTesting* class knows one instance of *MetaData*, a representation of the actual information required for testing. *EntityTesting* (*SessionTesting* is exactly the same, excepting the interface it implements) has the set of methods needed to add all types of testing metadata to the component; so, the component's user can add pre- or post-condition(s) to a method, invariants, or aspects. Especially interesting is the second operation listed in *EntityTesting*, *add(Class an_interface)*, that builds and adds to the component the information about its *Remote* and *Home* interfaces by means of the Reflection API provided by Java. With Reflection, one object can know at runtime many details about its implementation, such as its set of methods, parameters of each method, superclasses, and interfaces implemented. In this way, one instance of *EntityTesting* can ask for the interfaces it implements by executing the operation *this.getClass().getInterfaces()*, which returns an array of objects whose class is *Class* (Fig. 9 reproduces a fragment of some classes used in the Reflection API). However, if we execute this call on our *EntityTesting* component, we would obtain the *EntityBean* interface, which is the only interface really and directly implemented by the component (recall from Fig. 7 that the implementation relationships between the component and its *Remote* and *Home* interfaces are not resolved at compilation time, but at runtime by the container), and not the *Remote* or the *Home* interface, in which we are interested. Therefore, we must pass in two turns the *Remote*

and the *Home* interfaces to the component as a *Class* parameter using the
add(Class) method that launches the execution of a set of operations that
fill in the MetaData instance with two instances of *Interface* and as many
instances of *Method* as there are methods in the interfaces. We have defined
both the *Interface* and the *Method* classes, shown in Fig. 8, on purpose in order
to efficiently manage the complexity of the Test case generation problem.

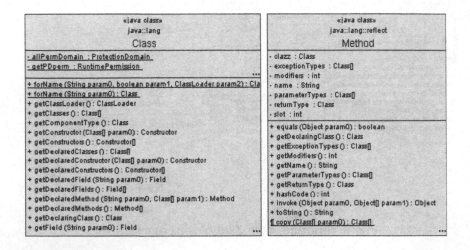

Fig. 9. Two useful Java classes for Reflection and some of their operations.

From the structure shown in Fig. 8, the *AccountEJB* component of
Fig. 7 can be converted into a component suitable for doing testing if we
make it a specialization of *EntityTesting*. Note that *EntityTesting* (as well
as *SessionTesting*) is an abstract class because it does not implement the
operations in the standard Java interface *EntityBean* (or *SessionBean*). So,
with the following lines of code, we could add invariants, pre-conditions, and
post-condition(s) to the component:

public class AccountEJB extends EntityTesting   //EntityTesting is already an
EntityBean (Fig. 8)

```
          ...
          public void build() throws Exception {
          Method deposit=getMethod(0);
          Precondition pre=new Precondition("logged()==true");
          add(pre, deposit);
          Post-condition post=new Postcondition("return==balance && " +
               "balance=balancepre+amount");
          add(post, deposit);
          Aspect cw=new Aspect("Collaborative work");
          Aspect pers=new Aspect("Persistence");
```

```
Aspect ui=new Aspect("User interface");
add(cw); add(pers); add(ui);
assignAspect(cw, deposit);
assignAspect(pers, deposit);
assignAspect(ui, deposit);
    ...

    ...
}
```

Obviously, it is much more comfortable to use a graphic tool to add data to the component instead of writing this manually. We have connected a single screen to manage our class structure (Fig. 10). The tool shows the relevant information about the *Remote* and *Home* interfaces in the EJB, as well as the addition of pre- and post-condition(s) to their methods, invariants, and aspects. It is also possible to assign methods to every aspect created. As the *MetaData* class is serializable, all the data introduced are saved in a file when the user closes the window, and they can be later recovered to be edited or modified.

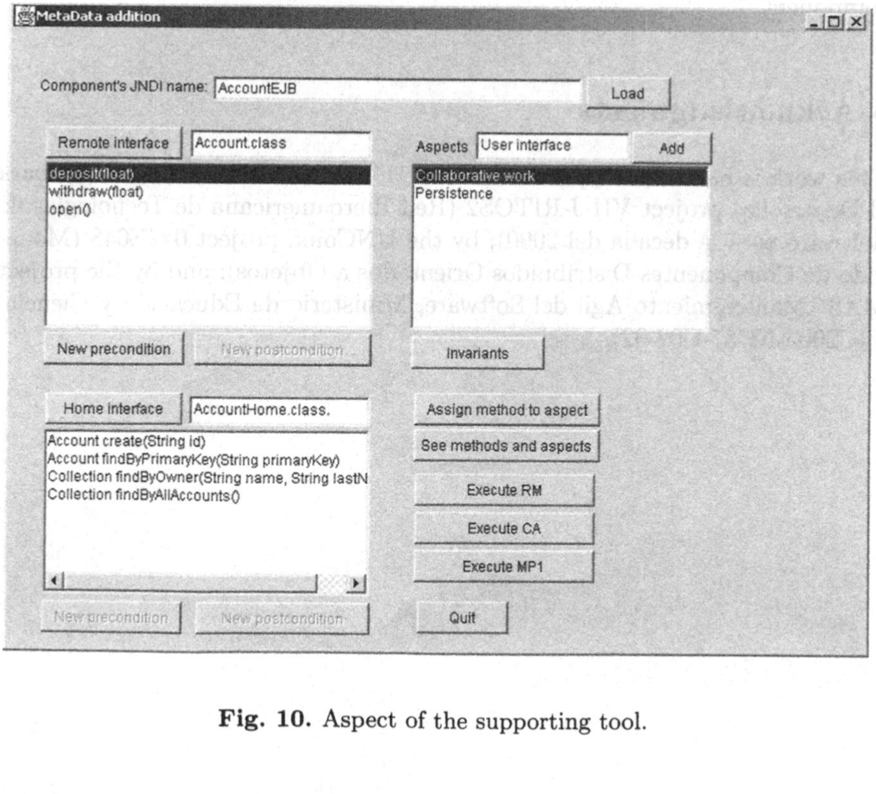

Fig. 10. Aspect of the supporting tool.

4 Conclusion and Future Work

Our approach is based on packaging additional information together with a component, so documentation for testing is included into the component as metadata. In particular, aspects allow us to classify metadata information to improve the test selection activity by reducing complexity of analysis. Splitting metadata according to aspects brings the possibility of applying separation of concerns, as a principle, on component testing selection.

There are many open issues to work on in the future, of course: different scenarios should be empirically analyzed to investigate positive and negative effects of our approach. Also, in this chapter we have not considered the use of metadata and aspects by looking at the problem from the angle of identifying and addressing proper component requirements and specification prior to development, perhaps constrained by specific contexts or domain applications. The attention was drawn on (i) constructing metadata for testing based on a set of relevant aspects, (ii) offering a way of organizing information prior to development, and (iii) supplying a class structure, which provides a complete support for the method proposed, and it is easily expandable to include more relevant metadata, as information for regression testing (as proposed by [186]), or other types of desirable data, such as metrics about the component.

5 Acknowledgments

This work is partially supported by the CYTED (Ciencia y Tecnología para el Desarrollo) project VII-J-RITOS2 (Red Iberoamericana de Tecnologías de Software para la década del 2000); by the UNComa project 04/E048 (Modelado de Componentes Distribuidos Orientados a Objetos); and by the project MAS (Mantenimiento Agil del Software, Ministerio de Educación y Ciencia, TIC2003-02737-C02-02).

Automatic Testing of Exception Handling Code

Christof Fetzer[1], Karin Högstedt[2], and Pascal Felber[3]

[1] Dresden University of Technology
  Dresden, Germany
  christof.fetzer@inf.tu-dresden.de
[2] AT&T Labs—Research
  Florham Park, NJ, USA
  karin@research.att.com
[3] Institut EURECOM
  Sophia Antipolis, France
  felber@eurecom.fr

Summary. Robust applications have to gracefully handle runtime errors that occur during program execution. Recent studies have shown, however, that code related to error handling is the most likely to contain software bugs: first, because it is almost never exercised under normal operation; and second, because errors modify the control flow of the program and render error handling code inherently complex. It is thus of utmost importance for software robustness to carefully and systematically test error handling code.

In this chapter, we describe automated tools to exercise and validate error handling code in modern programming languages that support exceptions, such as C++ and Java. We first introduce the notion of "failure atomicity," which informally states that a software component must remain in a consistent state after an exception has been thrown for the error to be recoverable. This property is essential, because it constitutes a prerequisite for using the component in a robust application. We then propose automated mechanisms based on code instrumentation for injecting exceptions in a program and verify consistent operation of the error handling code. Experiments illustrate the usefulness of our techniques with real-world applications.

1 Introduction

Robust applications have to gracefully handle errors that occur during program execution. They have to deal with many different types of errors, like resource depletion, memory corruption, unexpected user input, and software bugs. Hence, the error handling functionality of robust applications usually constitutes a large portion of the program's code. Studies have shown that code related to error handling is the most likely to contain software bugs ([75, 259]): first, because it is almost never exercised under normal operation;

and second, because errors modify the control flow of the program and render error handling code inherently complex. It is thus of utmost importance to carefully and systematically test error handling code to achieve software robustness. This is a challenging task, however, because one needs to accurately anticipate possible errors, simulate them, and detect incorrect program recovery behavior.

Modern languages like Java and C++ simplify error handling by providing language-level exception handling mechanisms. When a semantic constraint is violated or when some exceptional error condition occurs, an exception is *thrown*. This causes a non-local transfer of control ¿from the point where the exception occurred to a point, specified by the programmer, where the exception is *caught*. An exception that is not caught in a method is implicitly propagated to the calling method. The use of exceptions is a powerful mechanism that separates functional code from the error handling code and allows a clean path for error propagation. It facilitates the development of applications that are robust and dependable by design.

Exception handling code must however be programmed carefully to ensure that the application is in a consistent state after catching an exception. Recovery is often based on retrying failed methods. Before retrying, the program might first try to correct the runtime error condition to increase the probability of success. However, for a retry to succeed, a failed method also has to leave changed objects in a consistent state. Consistency is ensured if any modification performed by the method prior to the exception's occurrence is reverted before the exception is propagated to the calling method. This behavior is hard to implement because, when catching exceptions, a programmer has to consider all possible places where an exception might be thrown, and has to make sure that none of these exceptions can cause a state inconsistency.

In this chapter, we describe a tool to exercise and validate exception handling code. While this tool can be used by a component developer, its main user base is developers of large component-based systems. Indeed, the complexity of exception handling code validation is further increased when an exception causes a non-local transfer of control between two components. For example, a developer might not know the complete set of components that another component will depend upon at runtime (directly or indirectly), nor the exhaustive set of methods and statements that might throw exceptions. Our tool helps component-based system developers by systematically injecting exceptions into components and verifying consistent operation of the exception handling code.

We address this problem by introducing the notion of "failure atomicity." Informally, the definition of failure atomicity states that a software component must remain in a consistent state after an exception is thrown. This property is essential, because it constitutes a prerequisite for using the component in a robust applications. Experiments illustrate the usefulness of our techniques with real-world applications.

The organization of this chapter is as follows. In Sect. 2, we first discuss related work. Section 3 introduces failure atomicity, and Sect. 4 presents our approach for detecting failure non-atomic methods. In Sect. 5 we discuss the implementation details of our system, and Sect. 6 elaborates on the performance of our C++ and Java infrastructures. Section 7 concludes the chapter.

2 Related Work

Exception handling has been investigated for several decades. Goodenough [146] proposed to add explicit programming language constructs for exception handling in 1975, and Melliar-Smith and Randell [268] introduced the combination of recovery blocks [341] and exceptions to improve the error handling of programs in 1977.

Exception handling is still actively investigated. For example, a complete issue of ACM SIGAda Ada Letters [5] was recently dedicated to exception handling, and a 2001 Springer LNCS book addresses advances in exception handling [348]. One of the major issues addressed by researchers is a better separation of functional code and exception handling code. Recent studies have proposed to combine exception handling and reflection to increase this division [286], or to use aspect-oriented programming for reducing the amount of code related to exception handling [246].

Although the goal of exception handling code is to increase the robustness of programs, it has been noted by Cristian in [75] that exception handling code is more likely to contain software bugs (called *exception errors* [259]) than any other part of an application. This can be explained intuitively by a couple of factors. First, exceptions introduce significant complexity in the application's control flow, depending on their type and the point where they are thrown. Second, exception handling code is difficult to test because it is executed only rarely and it may be triggered by a wide range of different error conditions. Furthermore, 50% of security vulnerabilities are attributed to exception handling failures [259]. Therefore, eliminating exception failures would not only lead to more robust programs, but also to more secure programs.

Several approaches have been proposed to address the issue of exception errors [259]: code reviews, dependability cases, group collaboration, design diversity, and testing. Testing typically results in less coverage for the exception handling code than for the functional code [75]. The effectiveness of dependability cases, design diversity, and collaboration for reducing exception handling errors has been studied in [259]. In this chapter we introduce a novel approach based on exception injection to address certain kinds of exception errors. We do not consider our approach as a replacement of other approaches; rather, we believe that it complements techniques like dependability cases and collaboration. The advantages of our approach lie essentially in its highly automated operation and fast detection of functions that contain certain exception errors.

The robustness of programs can be evaluated using fault injection techniques [12]. There exist software-implemented, hardware-implemented, and simulation-based fault injectors. Our tool performs software-implemented fault injections. Software-implemented fault injectors have been investigated for various types of failures, such as memory corruption [7, 363], invalid arguments [237], or both [119]. There are also various techniques for injecting faults. Some tools like FERRARI [219] and Xception [59] inject faults without modifying the applications. Tools like DOCTOR [164] modify the application at compile time, and others modify it during runtime. Our tool injects faults in the form of exceptions by modifying the application either at compile time or at load time. Unlike FIG [46], which tests the error handling of applications by returning error codes to system calls, our tool injects only application-level exceptions.

3 Problem Description and Motivation

Robust software has to be able to detect and recover from failures that might occur at runtime. One way of performing failure recovery is to take advantage of the language-level exception handling mechanism. Using this mechanism, a method can signal to its caller that it has encountered a failure, be it memory depletion or the unexpected result of a calculation, by throwing an exception. The exception can then be caught by the caller, providing the programmer an opportunity to recover from the failure and, consequently, to increase the robustness of the application.

Failure recovery, however, is likely to fail, unless extreme care is taken during the programming of the exception handling code. Due to the incomplete execution of the method that threw the exception, a component might be in an inconsistent state. Unless consistency is restored, the application might crash or terminate with an incorrect result.

The tool presented in this chapter helps programmers detect which methods might leave an object in an inconsistent state when an exception is thrown (automatic techniques for *masking* such errors are presented in [124]). To do so, we introduce the notions of *object graphs* and *failure atomicity*.

Definition 1. *An object graph is a graph whose nodes are objects or instances of primitive data types, and whose edges are part-of and refers-to relationships, with a single distinguished root object. The object graph of an object o is the graph rooted at o.*

This definition corresponds to the notion of object graphs traditionally used in object-oriented languages to delimit the scope of deep copying. It follows that the object graph of an object o holds the state of o (i.e., the values of its fields), as well as the state of all objects referenced directly or transitively by o.

Definition 2. *Let C be a class. A method m of class C is* failure non-atomic *if there exist an object o of class C and an execution E in which m is invoked on o with arguments* $\alpha_1, \cdots, \alpha_m$, *such that the object graphs of o and* $\alpha_1, \cdots, \alpha_m$ *are not equal before m is invoked and right after m has returned with an exception. A method is* failure atomic *if it is not failure non-atomic.*

```
1   class HashMultiMap {
2     int count;
3     Bucket[] b;
4     // ...
5     void add(Object k, Object v) {
6       count++;
7       b[k.hashCode()%b.length].append(new Pair(k, v));
8     }
9     int nb_elements() { return count; }
10    static public void main(String[] args) {
11      HashMultiMap map = new HashMultiMap();
12      try {
13        String k = f.readLine();
14        String v = f.readLine();
15        map.add(k, v);
16      } catch(Exception e) {
17        // Handle error
18      }
19    }
20  }
```

Fig. 1. Sample class with a failure non-atomic method *add*.

To better understand these definitions, consider the code shown in Fig. 1. Method *add*, which associates a value with a given key in a hash map, may exhibit failure non-atomic behavior if an exception is thrown on line 7, e.g., if the key is `null`. In that case, the method leaves the hash map in an inconsistent state: the element count was incremented but the value was not inserted. More formally, the value of *count* in the object graph after the invocation of the method is different from its value before the invocation, as can be observed in Fig. 2. If the exception is caught and execution of the program continues, this inconsistency is likely to cause fatal errors at a later point in time, rendering such bugs very hard to isolate. In this example, swapping lines 6 and 7 would be sufficient to render the *add* method failure atomic.

4 Detecting Failure Non-Atomic Methods

Our goal is to isolate failure non-atomic methods so that they can be fixed by the developer, or automatically masked as proposed in [124]. Unfortunately, it can be shown that the problem of determining whether a method is failure atomic is not computable. To address this issue, we relax the accuracy requirement: our system classifies a method as non-atomic only if it has found an

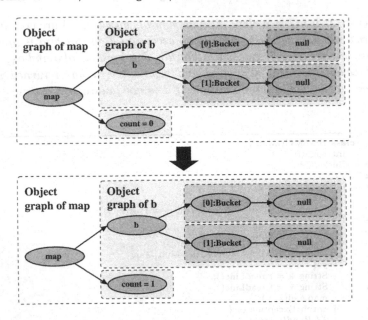

Fig. 2. Sample object graph of an object of type *HashMultiMap* before and after invocation of the *add* method with $k = null$.

execution for which the method does not behave atomically, i.e., if the method is provably failure non-atomic. Other methods are conservatively classified as atomic.

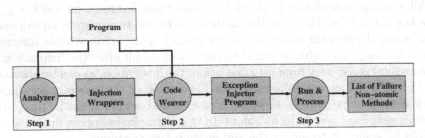

Fig. 3. We automatically transform applications to inject exceptions during their execution. The output of these test runs are automatically processed to determine non-atomic methods.

We test the exception handling code of software components by performing automated experiments on test programs (ideally test scripts, written by the component developer, that instantiate and call the code with various inputs) and/or end user applications that use these components. To that end, we *automatically* transform the application code to inject exceptions at specific points of the execution. The transformed "exception injector" programs are then run repeatedly to generate a list of all the failure non-atomic methods that have been discovered. This process consists of three steps, as depicted in Fig. 3.

Step 1: To create an exception injector program P_I ¿from a program P, we first determine which methods are (potentially) called by P, and, for each of them, the exceptions that may be thrown (this includes all the exceptions *declared* as part of the method's signature, as well as generic runtime exceptions that can be thrown by any method).

The *Analyzer* tool then creates an *injection wrapper* for these methods as follows. Assume that method m declares exceptions of types $E_1, \cdots, E_k$ and may also throw runtime exceptions $E_{k+1}, \cdots, E_n$. The *Analyzer* creates an injection wrapper *inj_wrapper_m* (shown in Fig. 4), which either throws one of these exceptions or calls method m. In the injection wrapper of m, there are n potential injection points (lines 2 to 5). We decide whether to throw an exception at any of these injection points based on the value of a global counter (*Point*). The counter is incremented every time the control flow reaches one of the potential injection point. An exception is injected when the counter reaches a preset threshold value (*InjectionPoint*).

```
1   return_type inj_wrapper_m(α₁, ··· , αₘ) throw (E₁, ··· , Eₖ) {
2     if (++Point == InjectionPoint) throw E₁();
3     if (++Point == InjectionPoint) throw E₂();
4       ...
5     if (++Point == InjectionPoint) throw Eₙ();
6     pre_invocation_graph = create_object_graph(this, α₁, ··· , αₘ);
7     try {
8       return m(...);
9     } catch (...) {
10        if (pre_invocation_graph.equal(this, α₁, ··· , αₘ))
11          mark("m", "atomic", InjectionPoint);  // Atomic in this call
12        else
13          mark("m", "non−atomic", InjectionPoint);
14        throw;
15    }
16  }
```

Fig. 4. Pseudo-code for the injection wrapper of method m.

Step 2: After the *Analyzer* has created the injection wrappers for all the methods called by P, the *Code Weaver* tool makes sure that these wrappers, instead of the original methods, are called. Modifications can be performed on the program's source files (source code transformation), or by directly instrumenting the application's code or bytecode (low-level transformation); both approaches are discussed in more detail in Sect. 5. The result of this transformation is an exception injector program P_I.

Step 3: Once the exception injector program P_I has been created, we execute it repeatedly. We increment the threshold value *InjectionPoint* before each execution to inject an exception at a different point in each run (as we shall discuss shortly, injections can also be performed in a more efficient manner). Each wrapper intercepts all exceptions and checks if the wrapped method is failure non-atomic before propagating the exception to the caller.

To determine whether a method m is failure non-atomic, the injection wrapper (Fig. 4) makes a copy of the state of the invoked object, as well as of all arguments passed in as non-constant references (line 6), before calling method m (line 8). This copy represents a snapshot of the object graphs of the invoked object and its arguments. If m returns with an exception, the wrapper catches the exception and compares the saved snapshot with the current value of the object graphs. If they are equal, we mark the method as failure atomic; otherwise, we mark it as failure non-atomic. Since different injections may result in different classifications for a method, we classify a method m as failure atomic if and only if it is never marked as failure non-atomic, i.e., if and only if for each injection the "before" and "after" object graphs are equal. The output of this step is a list of all the failure non-atomic methods detected in the original program.

4.1 Speedup of Exception Injections

In a program P with N method calls and K exception classes, our system injects $N * K$ exceptions. The approach sketched above performs this task by executing the program $N * K$ times. The time complexity of Step 3 (in terms of number of methods called) is hence $O(N^2 K)$. For large values of N, this process can be time consuming in comparison to the normal running time of $O(N)$. Therefore, we implemented an optimized variant with a lower complexity of $O(NK)$.

To reduce the execution time of Step 3, we checkpoint the application state before injecting an exception by forking a child process. The child process injects the exception while the parent process waits for the child process to terminate. The child process needs to check the atomicity of all methods that are in execution at the time the exception is injected, i.e., of all methods for which there exist a return address on the stack at the time of the exception injection.

If an application can tolerate the injected exception, i.e., the injected exception does not terminate the application, the child process will run to completion. Hence, for such applications the time complexity is still quadratic, even if the system is using application state checkpointing. To reduce the time complexity, the system terminates a child process as soon as the exception stops propagating. Note that the failure atomicity property is restricted to methods returning with an exception, i.e., the system stops learning about method failure atomicity after an injected exception has finished propagating.

A child process can thus terminate in two distinct manners after an exception has been injected. First, if the exception propagates to the topmost wrapper on the call stack of the child process, the wrapper terminates the child immediately after determining the failure atomicity classification of the wrapped method. Second, any wrapper that detects that an injected exception has stopped propagating terminates the child process. When using early process termination, Step 3 now has a time complexity in $O(NK)$. The performance gain resulting from this optimization is discussed in Sect. 6.

4.2 Pure and Dependent Failure Non-Atomicity

Some methods might exhibit failure non-atomic behavior only because they call methods that are failure non-atomic. In other words, if all the methods called by such a method were modified to be failure atomic, then the method would automatically become failure atomic (with no modification required). We call this property *dependent failure non-atomicity*:

Definition 3. *A dependent failure non-atomic method is a failure non-atomic method that would be failure atomic if all the methods that it calls (directly or indirectly) were failure atomic. All other failure non-atomic methods are pure failure non-atomic.*

A dependent failure non-atomic method m will exhibit failure atomic behavior if one corrects all the non-atomic methods that it calls. Thus, by definition, method m is no longer failure non-atomic and it is not necessary to correct it. Therefore, distinguishing between pure and dependent failure non-atomic methods can help programmers focus on the methods that really need to be fixed.

To distinguish dependent from pure failure non-atomic methods, we examine the order in which failure non-atomic methods are reported during exception propagation for each run of the exception injector program (Step 3 in Fig. 3). If there exists a run in which method m is the first method to be reported as failure non-atomic, then m is pure failure non-atomic. Indeed, any failure non-atomic method called by m would be detected and reported before m because of the way exceptions propagate from callee to caller (see Fig. 4). If there exists no such run, then m is dependent failure non-atomic.

4.3 Limitations

The approach that we use to detect non-atomic methods has some limitations. First, it does not address external side effects of methods: we do not attempt to detect inconsistent external state changes caused by an exception, nor do we try to mask such external state inconsistencies. The proper handling of external state changes in the face of exceptions remains the task of the code that catches such exceptions.

Second, as our system executes the instrumented program repeatedly to inject exceptions at each possible injection point of an execution, we can guarantee only that all possible injection points of an execution are covered if the program is deterministic. The fork-based injector does not suffer from this limitation. One should note that our system tests only the methods that are called by the original program, and the completeness of the results depends on how extensively the program exercises its own objects and methods.

5 Implementations

We have investigated two approaches for implementing our system: source code and compiled code program transformation techniques. The first approach requires access to the source code of a program, while the second does not. However, transforming compiled code might not be possible with all programming languages, and the resulting instrumented programs generally suffer from higher performance overhead than the ones with source code transformation.

Both kinds of transformations can be aided by the use of aspect-oriented programming [226], which allow programmers to easily capture and integrate crosscutting concerns in their applications. We have used AspectC++ [372] for our source code transformations.

5.1 Source Code Transformation

We have implemented a first prototype of our system that performs source code transformations to inject and mask non-atomic exception handling in C++ applications. We use the C/C++ interpreter CINT [149] to parse the source code of a given program and gather the type information necessary to generate the checkpointing code and wrappers for each method during the detection phase. The wrappers are implemented as *aspects* for the AspectC++ [372] aspect-oriented language extension for C++, which are then woven with the source code of the program in such a way that each call to a method m calls, instead, the wrapper of m. We also generate, for each class, a function *create_object_graph* to checkpoint the state of an instance of that class. The exception injector program is executed repeatedly to inject exceptions at all possible injection points (for the given program input), and the results of online atomicity checks are written out to log files by the injection wrappers. These log files are then processed offline to classify each method.

Due to restrictions of C++ and the tools we are using, our implementation has a few limitations. First, CINT does not support templates and ignores exception specifications. Using a better C++ parsing tool would solve this limitation. Second, checkpointing C++ objects is not trivial. In particular, C++ allows pointer manipulations that make it hard, in some situations, to discover the complete object graph of an object at runtime. While there exist techniques to address this problem (e.g., copying the whole process state), these techniques can be prohibitively expensive. Third, unlike Java, C++ does not enforce thrown exceptions to be declared as part of the method's signature. Hence, the C++ exception injector might have to inject a wide range of different exception types in applications that do not declare exceptions. This problem can be solved using source code analysis or through automated fault injection experiments.

5.2 Bytecode Transformation

With languages that offer adequate reflection mechanisms, it is possible to add functionality to an application without having access to its source code by applying transformations on the compiled bytecode. We have followed this second approach in the Java version of our infrastructure for detecting and masking non-atomic exception handling.

To inject and mask failures in Java classes, we have developed a tool, called the Java Wrapper Generator (JWG) [120], which uses load-time reflection to transparently insert pre- and post-filters to any method of a Java class. These generic filters allow developers to add crosscutting functionality (as with aspect-oriented programming) to *compiled* Java code in a transparent manner. Filters are attached to specific methods at the time the class is loaded by the Java virtual machine by using bytecode instrumentation techniques based on the BCEL bytecode engineering library [391]. Filters can be installed at the level of the application, individual classes, instances, or methods. They can modify the behavior of a method by catching and throwing exceptions, bypassing execution of the active method, or modifying incoming and outgoing parameters.

The Java implementation of our framework works along the same lines as its C++ counterpart, with just a few notable differences. Wrappers are attached to the application at load-time, by instrumenting the classes' bytecode. These wrappers have been programmed to be generic, i.e., they work with any class; they obtain type information about classes, methods, parameters, and exceptions at runtime using Java's built-in reflection mechanisms. The methods that checkpoint the state of an object are also generic; they essentially perform a deep copy of the object's state using Java's reflection and serialization mechanisms.

A major limitation with Java bytecode transformation is that a small set of core Java classes (e.g., strings, integers) cannot be instrumented dynamically. This limitation applies to all systems that perform Java bytecode transformations, and is not specific to our implementation. It can be overcome by instrumenting the bytecode of core classes offline and replacing their default implementations by the instrumented versions.

6 Experimental Results

Table 1. C++ and Java application statistics.

	Application	#Classes	#Methods	Total # Injections
C++ Applications	adaptorChain	16	44	10122
	stdQ	19	74	9585
	xml2Ctcp	5	19	6513
	xml2Cviasc1	23	102	12135
	xml2Cviasc2	23	89	13959
	xml2xml1	18	70	8068
Java Applications	CircularList	8	58	5912
	Dynarray	7	50	2528
	HashedMap	10	40	3271
	HashedSet	8	32	1149
	LLMap	10	41	7543
	LinkedBuffer	8	38	2737
	LinkedList	9	62	7500
	RBMap	11	55	7133
	RBTree	9	51	8056
	regexp	4	32	1015

To validate our exception injection tool, we first developed a set of synthetic "benchmark" applications in C++ and Java. These benchmarks are functionally identical in both languages, and contain the various combinations of (pure/dependent) failure (non-)atomic methods that may be encountered in real applications. We used these benchmarks to make sure that our system correctly detects failure non-atomic methods. These applications were used for the code coverage experiments and to obtain some of the performance figures presented in the section.

We then tested the robustness of some legacy applications. For that purpose, we tested two widely-used Java libraries implementing regular expressions [392] and collections [241]. Such libraries are basic building blocks of numerous other applications and are thus expected to be robust. We also tested Self* [123], a component-based framework in C++ that we are currently developing. We ran experiments with several applications that use Self* to help us detect failure non-atomic methods and improve the robustness of the framework.

Table 1 lists the number of classes and methods used in the applications we used for our experimental evaluation, together with the total number of exceptions injected (note that this value corresponds to the number of method and constructor calls during the execution of the test programs). We ran separate experiments for each individual application; however, because of the inheritance relationships between classes and the reuse of methods, some classes have been tested in several of the experiments.

Experiments were conducted following the methodology described in Sect. 4: we generated an exception injector program for each application, and ran it once for each method and constructor call in the original program, injecting one exception per run. The C++ experiments were run on a 866 MHz Pentium 3 Linux machine (kernel 2.4.18) with 512 MB of memory, and the Java tests were run using Java 1.4.1 on a 2 GHz Pentium 4 Linux machine (kernel 2.4.18) with 512 MB of memory.

6.1 Fault Injection Results

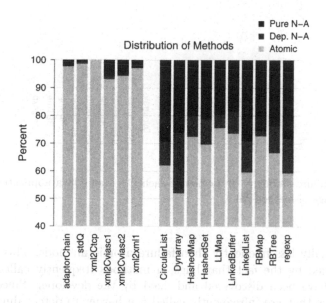

Fig. 5. Failure-atomicity properties of each C++ and Java application, in terms of percentage of methods.

We first computed the proportion of the methods defined and used in our test applications that are failure atomic, dependent failure non-atomic, and pure failure non-atomic. The results, presented in Fig. 5, show that the proportion of "problematic" methods, i.e., those that are pure failure non-atomic, remains pretty small for C++. This may indicate that the tested Self★ applications have been programmed carefully, with failure atomicity in mind. In contrast, the Java results exhibit a different trend. The proportion of pure failure non-atomic is pretty high, as it averages 20% to 25% in the considered applications. The proportion of dependent failure non-atomic methods is smaller, but still significant. These relatively high numbers tell us that our system is indeed useful, and that the programmer could eliminate many potential problems by making these methods failure atomic.

Figure 6 represents the same data, weighted by the number of invocations to each method. Results show that failure non-atomic methods are called

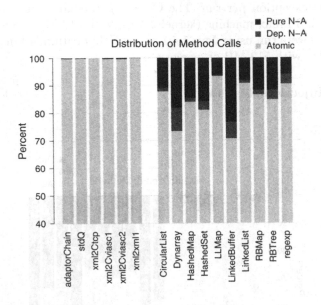

Fig. 6. Failure-atomicity properties of each C++ and Java application, in terms of percentage of method calls.

proportionally less frequently than failure atomic methods. This trend may be explained by the fact that bugs in methods frequently called are more likely to have been discovered and fixed by the developer. Since problems in methods that are infrequently called are harder to detect during normal operation, our tool is valuable in helping a programmer find the remaining bugs in a program. For example, the pure failure non-atomic methods of the "xml2Cviasc" applications are called very rarely, and would probably not have been discovered without the automated exception injections of our system.

As another illustration of the usefulness of our system, the output of the fault injector allowed us to discover some severe bugs in rarely executed error handling code of the *LinkedList* Java application. In particular, when adding a set of elements to a list, if any of the new elements but the first is invalid (e.g., it has a `null` value), an "illegal element" exception is correctly thrown and the elements are not inserted; however, the variable storing the size of the list is incremented, which leaves the list in an inconsistent state that soon triggers a fatal error. This kind of bug is hard to detect without automated exception injections. Using trivial code modifications, and by identifying methods that never throw exceptions, we managed to reduce the number of pure failure non-atomic methods in that application ¿from 18 (representing 7.8% of the calls) to 3 (less than 0.2% of the calls). This further demonstrates the importance of carefully testing error handling code.

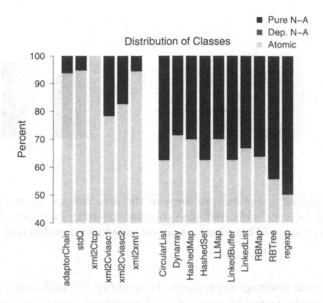

Fig. 7. Failure-atomicity properties of each C++ and Java application, in terms of percentage of classes.

Figure 7 shows the proportion of the classes in our test applications that are failure atomic (i.e., only contain failure-atomic methods), pure failure non-atomic (i.e., contain at least one pure failure non-atomic method), and dependent failure non-atomic (i.e., all other classes). The results clearly demonstrate that failure non-atomic methods are not confined to just a few classes, but spread across a significant proportion of the classes (up to 25% for C++ tests, and from 30% to 50% for Java tests).

6.2 Code Coverage

As previously mentioned, our system helps detect problems in code and methods that are only rarely executed. In particular, exception injections allow us to systematically test exception handling code and to increase the line and branch coverage by executing the statements in *catch* blocks. Moreover, even for programs without *catch* blocks, branch coverage can be increased with exception injections because of the "hidden" branches that are exercised only during the propagation of exceptions. These branches are taken, for example, during the unwinding of the stack to call the destructors of the objects that were allocated on the stack, and they are important because the programmer has to make sure that the program maintains failure atomicity for each branch.

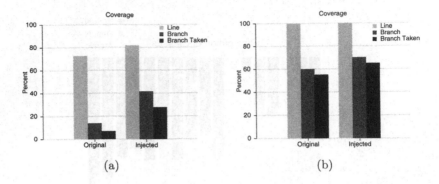

Fig. 8. Injecting exceptions can increase the line coverage by exercising *catch* blocks. Even for code with 100% line coverage, injecting exceptions can help to improve the coverage of branches that are evaluated and branches that are taken.

We ran test coverage experiments to quantify the additional portions of code that can be tested by our system. Experiments were conducted on two benchmark programs: the first one had a *catch* block, while the second did not. To ensure a fair comparison of the coverage, these two programs were not transformed; instead, exceptions were injected by external methods. The first application shows an increase in line and branch coverage (Fig. 8(a)). The second application already has 100% line coverage and, hence, shows no increase in line coverage (Fig. 8(b)). The branch coverage, however, is more than 10% higher with exception injections. Code coverage can thus strongly benefit from automated exception injections: not only does the line coverage increase for code with *catch* blocks, but increases the branch coverage for code without catch blocks also.

6.3 Speedup of Fork-Based Injection

To evaluate the performance gain resulting from the fork-based optimization described in Sect. 4.1, we measured the time needed to inject exceptions in an application, both with and without forking child processes. Figure 9 clearly shows the linear increase in injection time when forking a child process, versus the quadratic increase without a fork. This optimization is thus very useful for applications with large numbers of injections points.

7 Conclusion

In this chapter we defined the failure atomicity problem and described a system designed to detect failure non-atomic methods. This system operates by injecting exceptions at runtime into each method executed by an application,

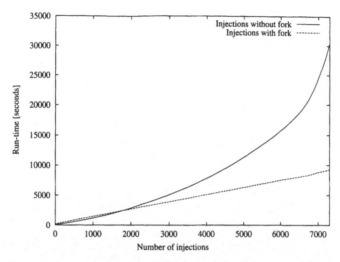

Fig. 9. Time needed to inject x exceptions at the first x injection points of an application (*xml2Cviasc*).

and by comparing the states of the objects before the method is called and after it terminates with an exception. Methods that cause an object to enter an inconsistent state are classified as failure non-atomic.

Our exception injection system alerts the programmer on finding failure non-atomic methods. In many situations, the programmer can correct the problem by applying simple modifications to his code (such as reordering a couple of statements). In other cases, more elaborate modifications are required to implement failure atomicity.

Ideally, our tool will be used by a developer to make sure that his or her components are failure atomic. Exception injections are performed by instrumenting and repeatedly executing a test harness for the code, if it exists, or any application that uses the component (our empirical study has shown that failure non-atomic behavior can indeed be detected for most methods with only a few test case).

Our tool can also be used for integration testing. Connecting different components might create new "exception paths" in the program that none of the component developers was aware of during the design. Our tool can be of valuable help in checking for failure non-atomicity in such cases.

We have implemented our infrastructure for detecting non-atomic exception handling in both Java and C++. Experimental results have shown that our system is effective and can be of great help to the developer of robust applications.

Part II

Testing Components in the Context of a
System

A Process and Role-Based Taxonomy of Techniques to Make Testable COTS Components

Atif M. Memon

Department of Computer Science and Institute for Advanced Computer Studies
University of Maryland
College Park, MD 20742, USA
atif@cs.umd.edu

Summary. An important activity in component-based software development is the testing of each component in its context of use. Since a component developer cannot anticipate all possible applications of the component, this task is usually left to the component user. What makes testing of component-based software especially challenging for the user is the lack of source code and partial knowledge of the working of the component. To ensure high quality of the overall software, the component user must perform testing tasks, i.e., generate test cases, create test oracles, evaluate coverage, and perform regression testing, all without access to the component's source code or complete semantic knowledge. The developer of the component can facilitate the execution of these testing tasks by augmenting the component appropriately with information that improves its testability. This chapter describes techniques that can be employed by developers to build testable COTS components. A taxonomy of these techniques based on the phases of software testing and the role of the component developer/user is presented, followed by a description of an important subset of the following techniques: (1) State Machine Models, (2) Built-In Tests, (3) Built-In Contract Testing, (4) Interface Probing, (5) Traceable Components, (6) Metacontent, (7) Binary Reverse Engineering, (8) Fault Injection Support, (9) Testable Beans, (10) Retro Components, (11) Component Test Bench, and (12) Self-Testing Components. Finally, a discussion summing up all the techniques is presented.

1 Introduction

Development of component-based software presents two significant challenges for quality assurance [169, 371], both stemming from the fact that the component is created by one party (usually referred to as the *developer* of the component) and used by another party (referred to as the *user* of the component) [395]. First, although the developer can employ commonly available techniques to test the component both in isolation and in a few application-specific contexts/environments, the developer cannot anticipate all possible contexts of use, and hence cannot test the component completely in all possible environments [292, 403]. Second, the burden of testing the component is shifted to the user, since the user has full knowledge of the application context. However, the unavailability of source code and partial knowledge of the working of the component hinders the testing process for the user. For example, the user cannot use conventional white-box (code-based) testing techniques [162]. Details of a user-oriented framework for component deployment testing is presented in the chapter 'A User Oriented Framework for Component Deployment Testing'.

With limited knowledge of the functionality of the component, the user may generate a few black-box (specification-based) test cases to perform limited testing. For example, a specification-based approach to facilitate component testing is presented in the chapter 'Using a Specification Approach to Facilitate Component Testing'. This testing is inadequate because (1) black-box testing can be used to detect only certain classes of defects and (2) test case generation is only one aspect of testing. The user needs to perform other steps to complete the testing process.

The testing steps for conventional software tailored for components follow:

- *Determine what to test*
  During this first step of testing, *coverage criteria*, which are sets of rules used to determine what to test in a software, are employed. In components, a coverage criterion may require that each input parameter value be used to determine whether it executes correctly.
- *Generate test input*
  The test input is an important part of the test case and is constructed from the software's specifications and/or from the structure of the software. For components, the test input may consist of method calls, parameter values, etc. Test cases for components may be either provided by the developer or generated by the user from information provided by the developer.
- *Generate expected output*
  Test oracles generate the expected output, which is used to determine whether or not the software executed correctly during testing. A *test oracle* is a mechanism that determines whether or not the output from the software is equivalent to the expected output. In components, the expected output may include expected values of output parameters. Users of COTS components face the problem of determining the exact functionality of the components to create the test oracle. They have to identify properties of COTS components to properly test them [145]. The functionality of the component may specify some of its expected properties. For additional properties, the user may interface with the component through its application program interface (API). The user may also employ new methods for understanding the component that do not require source code, re-

ferred to as black-box understanding methods. There are several methods of black-box understanding, e.g., binary (object code) reverse engineering and interface probing. The actual observed behavior may be used to create a model of the expected behavior.

- *Execute test cases and verify output*
  Test cases are executed on the software and its output is compared with the expected output. Execution of the component's test case may be done by setting up the environment, plugging in all the inputs specified in the test case, and comparing the actual output to the expected output as given by the test oracles.
- *Determine if the component was adequately tested*
  Once all the test cases have been executed on the implemented software, the software is analyzed to check which of its parts were actually tested. Note that this step is important because it may not always be possible to test in a component implementation what is required by the coverage criteria.

New versions of the component may become available as vendors add more functionality. Modifications lead to regression testing [165, 318], i.e., retesting of the changed software.

- *Perform regression testing*
  Regression testing is used to help ensure the correctness of the modified parts of the software as well as to establish confidence that changes have not adversely affected previously tested parts. A regression test suite is developed, consisting of (1) a subset of the original test cases to retest parts of the original software that may have been affected by modifications, and (2) new test cases to test affected parts of the software, not tested by the selected test cases.

Any testing method for components must perform all of the above steps. Unfortunately, the component user cannot do all the above steps in their entirety because of lack of information (e.g., source code).

To facilitate the testing process, the component developer must provide additional information/tools with the component. This chapter describes some techniques that the developer can employ to aid the user testing. Briefly, these techniques are as follows:

- *State Machine Models:* The developer creates and associates state machine models with the component that allow the component user to generate specific types of test cases.
- *Built-In Tests:* The developer packages the component with test cases. These test cases may be executed on the component by using a test executor also supplied with the component or by using a user-developed test executor. Detailed discussion of this approach is provided in the chapter 'COTS Component Testing through Built-In Test'.

- *Built-In Contract Testing:* The set of rules governing the interaction of a pair of components is defined as a *contract*. The component developer creates contract test cases that determine whether the servers to which they are plugged at deployment time will fulfill their contract. Approaches for modeling and implementation of built-in contract tests are also provided in the chapter 'Modeling and Implementation of Built-in Contract Tests'.
- *Interface Probing:* Interface probing is a technique that the component user may employ to understand the component's functionality. This functionality may then be used as the basis for creating test oracles [95, 96, 345]. The component developer may reduce the effort required to determine component properties by automating certain aspects of interface probing.
- *Traceable Components:* The developer may create traceable components. Traceability is a facility that a component provides to track its internal and external behavior. Traceability may be used to create test oracles.
- *Metacontent:* The developer may associate metacontent with the component. Metacontent is a collection of information and methods associated with a component that allows testing tasks to be performed on the component without compromising IP rights. An approach for COTS component testing through aspect-based metadata is described in the chapter 'COTS Component Testing through Aspect-Based Metadata'.
- *Binary Reverse Engineering:* The developer may compile/build the component in such a way as to enable binary reverse engineering. Binary reverse engineering is used to automatically derive a design structure of a component from its binary code, e.g., a call graph, a control flow graph.
- *Fault Injection Support:* Fault injection is a process to examine the behavior of a software component under controlled anomalous circumstances. A component user may examine the behavior of the overall software if invalid outputs are produced from a component. The developer may provide mechanisms to guarantee that such outputs are never produced. The chapter 'Automatic Testing for Robustness Violations' discusses automatic testing techniques for robustness violations.
- *Testable Beans:* The developer may package the component as a testable bean. A component augmented with capabilities to support test execution and test observation is called a testable bean. A testable bean is deployable, traceable, implements the test interface, and includes the necessary provisions to interact with external testing tools.
- *Retro Components:* The developer may package the component as a retro component. A component enhanced with information concerning tests conducted by the component provider and indications for tests to be conducted by the component user, and with capabilities (e.g., queries) to gather information during tests of the component user, is called a retro component.
- *Component Test Bench:* The developer may package the component as a component test bench, augmenting a component with test specifications that describe implementations of a component, the interfaces provided by

each implementation, and the concrete sets of test cases appropriate to an interface.

- *Self-Testing Components:* The developer may create a self-testing component. The underlying idea of this strategy is to augment a component with the functionality of analysis and testing tools. A component augmented accordingly is capable of conducting some or all activities of the component user's testing processes.

Table 1 shows a taxonomy of the techniques presented in this chapter. Note that the taxonomy is based on the different phases of testing. The columns show the different phases of testing. An × is used to indicate that a technique may be applicable during a specific phase. Subsequent sections provide details of these techniques. This chapter concludes with a summary outlining the application contexts in which the techniques may be used.

Table 1. A Taxonomy of Techniques Based on Phases of Testing.

Technique	Test Adequacy & Coverage	Test Case Generation	Test Oracle Creation	Test Case Execution	Regression Testing
State Machine Models		×			
Built-In Tests		×			
Built-In Contract Testing		×			
Interface Probing			×		
Traceable Components			×		
Metacontent					×
Binary Reverse Engineering			×		
Fault Injection Support		×			
Testable Beans		×		×	
Retro Components			×		
Component Test Bench		×		×	
Self-Testing Components	×	×	×	×	

2 State Machine Models

2.1 General Idea

The developer creates and associates state machine models with the component that allow the component user to generate specific types of test cases. A mapping between the abstract states of the model and the concrete states of the implementation is also needed to create test cases.

This section describes the specific approach presented by Beydeda and Gruhn [35]. Each component is represented by a *component state machine* (CSM), which is a special type of finite state machine. The mapping between the states of the model and the concrete states is provided by using Java code annotations. The component state machine is constructed as follows:

1. The abstract states of a component are identified, and form the nodes of the CSM. The CSM also includes two special states, called the *initial* and *final* states, i.e., the states of the component before it is created and after it is destroyed, respectively. Note that CSMs are similar to *class state machines* defined by Hong et al. [183]. As in class state machines, CSMs also have an error state that represents the state of a class (or, in this case, a component) after an error has occurred. Components enter the error state after the occurrence of an event that is either not specified for a particular state or does not fulfill one of the guards (described next).

2. Each transition between states is represented by a directed edge. More specifically, each transition is formally represented as a 5-tuple (source, target, event, guard, action). The source and target are states, guard is a predicate that has to be TRUE before the transition can occur, and action defines operations on component variables during the transition. Note that guard and action are defined in terms of a Java statement.

The key idea for developing a CSM is that each transition be annotated with Java code to allow automatic generation of test cases by the component user.

2.2 Role of the Developer

The developer defines a component state machine for each component. Consider the example of an *account component* that simulates a bank customers' account. It encapsulates ID and account balance and provides suitable methods to check and alter it. After an account component is initialized, it enters a state in which it is ready to receive deposit and withdrawal requests. After each deposit request, the account component remains in the ready state. Withdrawal requests can imply a change to the error state, which is entered when clients of the account component try to overdraw the account. The account component also provides an observer method, called balance(), for checking the account balance. A change to the final state is triggered by invoking the remove() method.

2.3 Role of the User

The component user generates test cases by combining all the CSMs to create a **component-based software flow graph** (CBSFG), which is similar to a class control/data flow graph [34]. The graph represents information from both the specification and source code of a component. Hence both white- and black-box test cases can be generated from a CBSFG. The CBSFG contains a main component for the software.

The steps required for building a CBSFG are:

1. Transform each transition $t = (source, target, event, guard, action)$ to a nested if-then-else construct, as shown below,

```
if (predicate(source)) { // state
  if (guard) { // guard
    action; // action
  }
  else throw new ErrorStateException();
}
else throw new ErrorStateException();
```

where `predicate(source)` refers to the predicate of the source state, i.e., the predicate of component variables defining the occurrence of the state labeled `source`.

2. After transforming each transition to the corresponding `if-then-else` construct, those having the same event type are combined together as a prototype.

3. The next step consists of constructing control flow graphs for the generated prototypes and combining them with those based on component source code. Due to the predefined structure of automatically generated prototypes, they permit identification of data flow defined in the specification of the corresponding component.

Since a CBSFG is a directed graph visualizing both control and data flow within component-based software, each method of the main component is represented by two *subgraphs*: (1) a control flow graph of the prototype generated on the basis of the specification and (2) a control flow graph determined using the source code of the method. In contrast to a method within the main application, a method in another component is represented only by a flow graph visualizing its prototype, because a control flow graph of a method can be built only if its source code is available, which is not the case.

Each subgraph is interlinked with others using three types of control and data flow edges:

a) *Intra-method control and data flow edges:* Intra-method control and data flow edges represent control and data dependencies within a single subgraph. An intra-method data flow edge connects a node representing a definition of a variable with another node representing a use in the same method.

b) *Inter-method control and data flow edges:* These edges represent control and data flow between subgraphs of the same type. An invocation of a method within another method is modeled by an inter-method control flow edge leading from the node representing the invoking statement in the calling method to the node representing the entry statement of the called method. Similarly, an inter-method control flow edge also models the triggering of an event in a CSM within the action part of a transition of another CSM. Inter-method control flow edges connect with each other both method control flow graphs and prototype control flow graphs.

c) *Specification-implementation edges:* This type of edge represents the connection between specification and source code by connecting the two subgraphs of main component methods. Thus, a specification-implementation edge leads from the node representing the action within a prototype to the node representing the entry node of the method.

Once the CBSFG is constructed, the remaining task is to generate test cases. As a first step for test case generation, definitions and uses of variables have to be identified. Definitions and uses of local variables within methods can be identified by considering their source code. In contrast to associating local definitions and uses, associating definitions and uses of component variables has to take into account the possible method sequences defined by the appropriate CSM. A definition and a use can only be associated to each other if the method that contains the use can be invoked after an invocation of the method that contains the definition. It is important to ensure that the component variable is not redefined. Definitions and uses within control flow graphs of prototypes are associated with each other according to the *all-definitions* criterion. Test cases are generated covering those def-use pairs.

3 Built-In Tests

3.1 General Idea

The developer packages the component with test cases. These test cases may be executed on the component by using a test executor also supplied with the component or by using a user-developed test executor.

A component may contain test cases that may be accessed by the component user. Thus, the component user does not need to generate test cases. Built-in tests can be integrated with component-based development [213]. The underlying philosophy behind built-in testing is that an upfront investment on verification infrastructure pays off during reuse [425]. This adds considerable value to the reuse paradigm of component-based software development, because a component can complain if it is given something unsuitable to interact with, or if it is mounted into an unsuitable environment. The benefit of built-in verification follows the principles common for all reuse methodologies. The additional effort of building the test software directly into the functional software results in an increased return on investment depending on how often such a component is reused. Hence, built-in tests offer a feasible and practical approach for validating the semantics of components.

Each component's method possesses a *testing* method that invokes it with predefined arguments. An oracle [344] is implemented by means of component invariants and method pre- and post-conditions. Invariants and pre- and post-conditions are determined based on the specification of the component, and are embedded by the component provider in the source code of the component. The functionality necessary to validate them and other functionality, such as that necessary for tracing and reporting purposes, is implemented by a framework, which technically requires that the component, or the main class of the component, implements a certain interface. As in the above approach, the built-in testing capability can be passed to subclasses by inheritance. The component user typically has to assume that the built-in tests are sufficient.

Another built-in test approach, the component+ approach, can be found in http://www.component-plus.org/. A shortcoming of the conventional built-in testing approach is that test cases (or a description of their generation) need to be stored within the component. This can increase the resource consumption of the component, which, taking into account that the built-in testing capability of a component is often required only once for deployment, can be an obstacle to its use. To avoid this shortcoming, an architecture consisting of three types of components, namely BIT components, testers, and handlers, can be defined. The BIT components are the built-in testing enabled components. These components implement certain mandatory interfaces. Testers are components which access the built-in testing capabilities of BIT components through the corresponding interfaces and which contain the test cases in a certain form. In the above approach, a built-in testing-enabled component also encompasses the functionality of the testers. Here, however, they are separated, with the benefits that they can be developed and maintained independently and that they do not increase resource requirements of BIT components in the operational environment. Finally, handlers are components in this architecture that do not contribute to testing, but can be required, for instance, to ensure recovery mechanisms in the case of failures.

3.2 Role of the Developer

A component developer can create test cases. For example, if the component is implemented as a class, we suggest implementing built-in testing by additional methods which either contain the test cases to be used in hardwired form or are capable of generating them. The integral benefit of such an implementation is that the methods for built-in testing can be passed to subclasses by inheritance.

Besides various modes of operation, a component may be implemented using object-oriented languages, Java in particular. Built-in testing is implemented by additional methods. Each component method that is testable by built-in testing capabilities possesses a testing method

3.3 Role of the User

The component user thus does not need to generate test cases. Difficulties that the component user would otherwise face, thus, can in principle not complicate the component user's test.

A component user can operate each component in two modes, namely a normal mode and, a maintenance mode. In the normal mode, the built-in test capabilities are transparent to the component user and the component does not differ from other, non-built-in testing-enabled components. In the maintenance mode, however, the component user can test the component with the help of its built-in testing features. The component user can invoke the respective methods of the component, which execute the test, evaluate autonomously its results, and output a test summary.

Although built-in tests can simplify a component user's test insofar that the component user might not need to generate test cases, they might in some cases be not appropriate. The reasons include:

- Firstly, the built-in testing approaches explained are static in that the component user cannot influence the test cases employed in testing. A component that is "built-in testing-enabled" according to one of the approaches explained contains either a predetermined set of test cases or the generation, even if conducted on demand during runtime, depends solely on parameters which the component user cannot influence. Specifically, the component user cannot specify the adequacy criterion to be used for test case generation. However, the component user might wish to test all components to be assembled with respect to a unique adequacy criterion. Built-in testing approaches do not allow this.
- Secondly, built-in testing approaches using a predefined test case set generally require considerable storage. Specifically, large components with high inherent complexity might require a large set of test cases for their testing. A large set of test cases obviously requires a substantial amount of storage that, however, can be difficult to provide taking into account the storage required, in addition, for execution of large components. This is also the case if test cases are stored separately from the component, as proposed by component+ approach.

4 Built-In Contract Testing

4.1 General Idea

The set of rules governing the interaction of a pair of components is defined as a contract. The component developer creates contract test cases that determine whether the servers to which they are plugged at deployment time will fulfill their contract.

The correct functioning of a system of components at run-time is contingent on the correct interaction of individual pairs of components. Component-based development can be viewed as an extension of the object paradigm in which the set of rules governing the interaction of a pair of components is typically referred to as a contract that views the relationship between a component and its clients as a formal agreement, expressing each party's rights and obligations [33]. The relationship between a component and its clients may be described as a formal agreement or contract, expressing each party's rights and obligations in the relationship. This means that individual components define their side of the contract as either offering a service (this is the server in a client/server relationship) or requiring a service (this is the client in a client/server relationship).

Testing the individual client/server interactions against the specified contract goes a long way toward verifying that a system of components as a whole will behave correctly. Contract-based testing is based on the notion of building contract tests into components so that they can ensure that the servers into which they are plugged at deployment time will fulfill their contracts. The objective of built-in contract testing is to ensure that the environment of a component does not deviate from what it was developed for.

4.2 Role of the Developer

Consideration of built-in tests needs to begin early in the design phase, as soon as the overall architecture of a system is developed and/or the interfaces of components are specified. Built-in contract testing therefore needs to be integrated within the overall software development methodology. In order to check contractual properties dynamically when a system is configured or deployed, test cases can be built into the components alongside the normal functionality. The developer may choose among several implementation models.

First, the developer may develop *tester components*. Rather than associate a test with a single method, it is more in the spirit of component technology to encapsulate it as a full tester component in its own right. The tester component contains tests that check the semantic compliance of the server that the client acquires. The tests inside the client's tester component represent the behavior that the client expects from its acquired server. A client also has built-in test software since it is able to test its associated servers. Tester components that are embedded in testing components provide the optimal level of flexibility with respect to test weight at both runtime and development time. In general, the testing component (client) will contain one or more built-in contract testers for checking its servers. These testers are separate components that include the test cases for implicitly or explicitly acquired components. Obviously, if the runtime system is invariant, a component will not include any server testers for the underlying platform. A client that acquires a server will typically exhibit a configuration interface through which a particular server component may be set. This can be a method, such as **setServer (Component Server)**, that assigns a particular component to a component reference in the client. The **setServer()** method is typically invoked when the system is configured and deployed. However, before the assignment is established, the client will execute its built-in tester components to perform a full semantic check on this new server. The tester executes a simulation on the services of the newly acquired component and may raise an exception if the test fails. The tests may be derived through any arbitrary test case generation technique such as requirements-based, equivalence partitioning, boundary value analysis, or structural testing criteria [296]. According to the applied testing criteria, it may represent an adequate test suite for the individual unit. The size of the built-in tester is also subject to efficiency considerations.

Second, the developer may create *testable components*. Component-based development is founded on the abstract data type paradigm with the combination and encapsulation of data and functionality. State transition testing is therefore an essential part of component testing. This means that in order to check whether an operation of a component is working correctly, the component must be brought into an initial state before the test case is executed, and the final state of the component as well as the returned values of the operation must be checked after the test case has been applied (pre- and post-conditions). A test case for an abstract data type therefore always consists of three parts: ensure precondition, execute event, compare post-condition with expected post-condition. This presents a fundamental dilemma. The basic principles of encapsulation and information hiding dictate that external clients of a component should not see implementation and state variables. The test software outside the encapsulation boundary cannot therefore set or get internal state information. Only a distinct history of operation invocations on the functional interface, results in a distinct initial state required for executing a test case. Since the tests are performed in order to verify the correctness of the functional interface it is unwise to use this interface for supporting the testing (i.e., setting and getting state information). A testable component under the built-in contract testing paradigm is a component that can be tested, which means it provides some built-in support for the execution of a test by an external client. The required support is provided in the form of a contract testing interface.

Third, the developer of a testable component can also provide an introspection interface which provides access to and information about the supported testing interfaces. This may be implemented in form of a Java interface that realizes a BIT testability contract. A testable component contains a built-in contract testing interface which extends the component's normal functional interface with operations to support contract testing. The most basic contract testing interface consists of state assertions realized as operations that are invoked by a tester to see whether the component is residing in a defined logical state. This is the most fundamental and well known state checking mechanism. This technique is based on additional operations of abstract data types that implement the assertion checking code. If the assertion fails, the whole test fails; otherwise, the test event is invoked and the final state assessed through the assertion operation. The disadvantage of having only a state checking mechanism is that for some tests a long history of operation invocations may be necessary in order to satisfy the preconditions. This can be circumvented through additional state "setup" operations that can directly manipulate the state variables according to the logical states. This may be simple and straightforward for many simple components, but for some components substantial reimplementation of the component's functionality may be required. However, specific BIT libraries may alleviate this effort. State checking and setting operations of the testing interface enable access to the internal state variables of a component for contract testing by breaking the encapsulation boundary in a well-defined manner while leaving the actual tests outside the encapsulation boundary. The clients of the component use the contract testing interface in order to verify whether the component abides by its contract (contract test). In this way, each individual client can apply its own test suite according to the client's intended use or the usage profile of the component.

4.3 Role of the User

When "individually correct" components are assembled and deployed to form a new system or to reconfigure an existing system, there are two things that can go wrong. First, explicitly acquired servers or implicitly acquired servers within a component's deployment environment may behave differently from those in its original development environment. Since such servers are either acquired explicitly from external sources or implicitly provided by the runtime system, they may not abide by their contracts (semantically) even if they conform syntactically to their expected interfaces. Second, clients of the component may expect a semantically different service than that provided, although they may be satisfied with the syntactic form of the client.

There are consequently two things that should ideally be tested to ensure that a component will behave correctly within its deployed environment. First, the deployed component must verify that it receives the required support from its servers. This includes explicitly acquired servers and implicitly presumed servers (i.e., the runtime system). Second, clients of the deployed component must verify that the component correctly implements the services that it is contracted to provide. In other words, clients of the deployed component must ensure that it is meeting its contract.

5 Interface Probing

5.1 General Idea

Interface probing is a technique that the component user may employ to understand the component's functionality. This functionality may then be used as the basis for creating test oracles [95, 96, 345]. The component developer may reduce the effort required to determine component properties by automating certain aspects of interface probing.

A component user can gain understanding of a component by executing test cases. After an initial set of test cases is used, the user may design additional test cases to gain better understanding of the component and to clarify its functionality and limitations. This approach may be an effective way of understanding of overall component functionality. However, one of the major disadvantages of this approach is that frequently a large number of test cases have to be created and analyzed. Some component properties can be easily determined by simple interface probing, but identification of other properties may require significant interface probing and may be very labor-intensive, tedious, and expensive [232]. In addition, users may frequently miss major component limitations and incorrectly assume certain component functionality that does not represent the actual component functionality. This may lead to incorrect use of the component when it is integrated with a software system under development.

5.2 Role of the Developer

The developer can reduce the effort required to determine component properties by automating the interface probing search process. The search may identify component inputs on which a property of interest is revealed. In order to specify the search, the developer has to provide the description of the property and the scope of the search. Assertions may be used to describe component properties, and the existing automated test generation methods for black-box testing and white-box testing may be used to generate inputs to the component to determine whether it has the property of interest. One of the major advantages of this approach is that after the search specification is provided by the developer, the approach is fully automated. In addition, by using this approach, as opposed to manual interface probing, chances of missing some component properties are minimized.

5.3 Role of the User

Types of component properties that the user may be interested in depend on the degree of detail provided in a component description. On one extreme, no description of a component may be provided. As a result, the user has to identify all properties of the component. This may be a significant discovery process, requiring a large amount of effort when manual interface probing is used. The major task for the user is to identify (guess) the functionality of the component based on a set of test cases. On the other extreme, a very detailed component description is provided, i.e., its functionality, limitations, constraints, etc. Even if a detailed description of the component is provided, the user may want some confidence that the component exhibits properties in its description. As a result, the user may want to go through some validation process. If this process is successful, the user may have more confidence that described properties represent actual component properties.

In most cases, the user is dealing with a partial component description. As a result, in black-box understanding of COTS components, the user is dealing typically with two types of processes: a discovery process and a validation process. In the discovery process the user does not know, or is not sure, whether the component has a certain property and, therefore, is interested in revealing this property. In a validation process the user knows, from the component description, that the component has (or should have) a certain property. However, the user wants to have some confidence that the component actually has this property. As a result, the user is interested in the validation of the property of interest. In a typical process of black-box understanding, a user designs a set of test cases (some test cases may be provided with a component). Based on the given set of test cases the user is able to identify some properties of the component, but there may be other properties that these test cases may not reveal or may only partially reveal.

The goal is to specify a search that may reveal a property of the component and use automated search methods that identify component inputs on which the property is revealed. In order to specify the search the user has to provide a description of the property and a search scope. In this approach assertions are used to describe properties of a component. After the assertions describing properties of the component are provided, the user specifies the search, e.g., ranges of values for input parameters used. Next, the search engine (an automated test case generator) performs the search to identify component inputs that exhibit the specified property. If such inputs are found, the component has the specified property. On the other hand, when the search fails to find such inputs, the component most likely does not have the specified property.

Assertions can be used to describe properties of components. Assertions are recognized as a powerful tool for automatic runtime detection of software errors during debugging and testing. An assertion specifies a constraint that applies to some state of a computation. When the assertion evaluates to false, there exists an incorrect state in the program. The first systems supporting simple assertions were reported in 1970s. It has been shown that assertions may be very effective in detecting runtime errors. Programmers create assertions to detect erroneous program behavior and to expedite debugging during software development. The effort in constructing assertions pays off in quick and automatic detection of faults. Assertions are supported by some programming languages, e.g., Eiffel and Turing. For languages that do not support assertions, specialized tools have been developed, e.g., APP tool supports assertions for C programs. These tools recognize assertions that appear as annotations of the programming language. There are many different ways in which assertions can be written. In general, an assertion can be written as a Boolean formula, a predicate calculus formula, or as executable code. An assertion as a Boolean formula is a logical expression that can evaluate to true or false value. Assertions can also be written as predicate calculus formulas. A special language is used to describe assertions in this format. Assertions as Boolean formulas or predicate calculus formulas are recognized by a special preprocessor that substitutes assertions with corresponding source code in some programming language, e.g., in C.

Although many assertions may be described in a format of Boolean formulas or predicate calculus formulas, a large number of assertions cannot be described in this way. Therefore, assertions can also be written as executable code (e.g., as a program function) that returns true or false values. The major advantage of assertions in this format is that programmers can write very complex assertions.

All three formats of writing assertions can be used to describe properties of COTS components. Since source code of COTS components is not available, assertions used to describe properties of components describe only relations between output parameters or between input and output parameters of components.

After properties of a component are described, the user may provide a search scope. Typically, in the search scope, input parameters and their ranges (possible values) that are to be used in the search are identified. In addition, the user may be interested in finding only certain values of an input parameter because many values of that particular input parameter may satisfy the property of interest; or the user may be interested in finding, for example, the maximum (or minimum) parameter value that satisfies the property. The user may also indicate interest in finding one component input, a fixed number of inputs, or as many component inputs as possible that satisfy the property of interest. If no search scope is identified, the search engine uses values allowed by data types of input parameters.

6 Traceable Components

6.1 General Idea

The developer may create traceable components. Traceability is a facility that a component provides to track its internal and external behavior. Traceability may be used to create test oracles.

Another technique that the component user can employ to develop test oracles is component traceability. The developer can facilitate this task by developing traceable components.

6.2 Role of the Developer

The component developer can provide the following traceability features:

1. *Behavior traceability:* It is the degree to which a component facilitates the tracking of its internal and external behaviors. There are two ways to track component behaviors. One is to track internal behaviors of components. This is useful for white-box testing and debugging. Its goal is to track

the internal functions, internal object states, data conditions, events, and performance in components. The other one is to track external behaviors of components. It has been used for black-box testing, integration, and system maintenance. The major purpose is to track component public visible data or object states, visible events, external accessible functions, and the interactions with other components.

2. *Trace controllability:* It refers to the extent of the control capability in a component to facilitate the customization of its tracking functions. With trace controllability, users can control and set up various tracking functions such as turn-on and turn-off of any tracking functions, and selections of trace formats and trace repositories.

To enable successful traceability, the developer should adhere to the following basic requirements for component tracking:

- The developer should use a standardized trace format and understandable trace messages. This is essential to generate trace messages that are easy to understand. The trace message format should be defined to include proper information for users in problem isolation, program understanding, and behavior checking. For example, each trace message must contain proper identification information, such as component identifier, thread identifier, object id, and class function name. All error messages and exception handling must be classified and defined with a fixed format.
- The developer should provide mechanisms to minimize the users' efforts to add or remove tracking code in the component. Users may hesitate to use a provided tracking mechanism unless it is easy to use and effective for debugging and performance testing.
- The developer should provide flexibility on selecting different trace types. Since each trace type has its special use in testing and maintenance of a component based program, it is important to provide diversified trace types and facilities for users to use according to their needs.
- The developer should add the tracking capability in components with a minimum system overhead. There are two types of tracking overheads: (a) system CPU time and (b) extra system resources such as system space for tracking code and storage space for trace messages.
- The developer should provide mechanisms to manage and store trace messages. Component users will need this function for debugging, component testing, and maintenance to help them manage and monitor the trace messages.

The tracking capability of a component may be described at the following levels:

1. Software components are constructed with ad hoc tracking mechanisms, trace formats, and functions. For components at this level, developers need to spend more time in understanding, debugging, and testing during system testing and software maintenance.

2. Software components are built according to a predefined standard tracking mechanism, trace format, and a set of predefined functions. Using standardized tracking in component construction enhances the understanding of component behaviors in distributed software and reduces costs of debugging and system testing. However, there is a programming overhead cost involved in adding built-in tracking code to components.

3. At this level, software components are designed with a systematic tracking mechanism and capability; therefore, developers can monitor and check their behaviors, and manage and store their traces in an automatic manner. Since a consistent tracking mechanism is used for building traceable components, developers' programming efforts involved in tracking are reduced.

4. Software components are designed to facilitate the support of component tracking functions and their customization. Achieving customizable tracking in component construction provides the flexibility to define, select, and configure the tracking functions and trace formats. Moreover, it helps developers to set up a systematic tracking and monitoring method and environment for supporting component-based software.

The component developer can use the following systematic tracking mechanisms. Each mechanism has its own pros and cons. In practice, a combination is needed to support different types of tracking for a program and its components.

- *Framework-based tracking:* In this approach, a well-defined tracking framework (such as a class library) is provided for component developers to add program tracking code. It usually is implemented based on a trace program library. Component developers can use this library to add tracking code into components. This approach is simple and flexible to use. It can be used to support all trace types, especially for error trace and GUI trace. However, it has a high programming overhead.

- *Automatic code insertion:* This approach is an extension of the previous one. Besides a tracking framework, it has an automatic tool, which adds the tracking code into the component source code. A parser-based tracking insertion tool is a typical example. To add operational tracking code, it inserts it into each class function, at the beginning and the end of its functional body, to track the values of its input data and output parameters. Similarly, it can insert the operation tracking code before and/or after each function call. Performance tracking code can be added into a component in the same way to track the performance of each function. Although this approach reduces a lot of programming overhead, it has its own limitations. First, due to its automatic nature, it is not flexible enough to insert diverse tracking code at any place in components. Second, it requires a very complex parser tool. Since a component-based program may consist of components written in different languages, this leads to high complexity and cost of building parser tools.

- *Automatic component wrapping:* This approach is another extension of the first one. Unlike the second method, where tracking code is inserted by parsing component source code, this approach adds tracking code to monitor the external interface and behaviors of components by wrapping them as black-boxes. The basic idea is to wrap every reusable component with tracking code to form an observable component in the black-box view. With the tracking code, users can monitor the interactions between a third-party component and its application components. This approach is very useful for constructing component-based software based on third-party software components, for example, Enterprise JavaBeans. Compared with the other two methods, it has several advantages. One of the advantages is its low programming overhead. In addition, it separates the added tracking code from component source code. Since no source code is required here, this method can be used for both in-house reusable components and COTS components. However, it is not suitable to support error tracking and state tracking because they are highly dependent on the detailed semantic logic and application domain business rules.

The above points presented a few examples of the approaches that developers may use. To design and construct traceable components, developers need more guidelines on component architecture, tracking interface, and supporting facilities.

6.3 Role of the User

The component user can make use of the facilities to collect the following types of traces and use them for test oracles [270]:

1. *Operational trace* that records the interactions of component operations, such as function invocations. It can be further classified into two groups: (a) internal operation trace that tracks the internal function calls in a component and (b) external operation trace which records the interactions between components. External operation trace records the activities of a component on its interface, including incoming function calls and outgoing function calls.
2. *Performance trace* that records the performance data and benchmarks each function of a component in a given platform and environment. Performance trace is very useful for testers in identifying the performance bottlenecks and issues in performance tuning and testing. According to performance traces, the component user can generate a performance metric for each function in a component, including its average, maximum, and minimum speeds.
3. *State trace* that tracks the object states or data states in a component. In component black-box testing, it is very useful for testers to track the public visible objects (or data) of components.

4. *Event trace* that records the events and sequences occurring in a component. The event trace provides a systematic way for GUI components to track GUI events and sequences. This is very useful for recording and replaying GUI operational scenarios.
5. *Error trace* that records the error messages generated by a component. The error trace supports all error messages, exceptions, and related processing information generated by a component.

7 Metacontent

7.1 General Idea

The developer may associate metacontent with the component. Metacontent is a collection of information and methods associated with a component that allows testing tasks to be performed on the component without compromising IP rights.

This section will present the use of component metacontent in the context of automated *regression testing* [321, 322]. Note that software components already provide some form of metacontent, although not specifically for regression testing. For example, DCOM, Enterprise JavaBeans, supply limited information, e.g., names of the functions and types of parameters that are used during compilation and execution.

What makes regression testing of components different from first-time testing is that the user may have a test suite available. The problem addressed in this section is the *regression test selection* problem, which focuses on selecting a subset from this test suite. More specifically,

1. given an application A that has been tested with test suite T and that uses a set of components C,
2. when new versions C' of the components are available,
3. the problem of regression test selection is to build a test suite T' ⊆ T that can reveal possible regression faults in A due to changes in C' and that does not include test cases not impacted by the changes.

7.2 Role of the Developer

To assist in regression testing, the component developer associates metacontent with the component. The metacontent should satisfy the following requirements.

1. It should be accessible by the component user.
2. It should provide information about several aspects of the component, e.g., dynamic and static.

3. It should have two parts – metadata and metamethods. Information about the component should be packaged as metadata; metamethods are used to retrieve and perform operations on the metadata.

In the context of this section, metacontent should help in the regression test selection process.

The developer may employ two approaches for providing component meta-content for regression test selection:

1. *Code-based*, using which the test selection is based on code elements. This approach is extended from conventional code-based regression testing. The developer may provide three types of metacontents as metamethods or metadata:

   - Metadata to associate each test case with edges in the program-flow graph. This information may be used to compute the edge coverage achieved by the test suite with respect to the component.
   - Metamethods to identify the component, i.e., query its version.
   - Metamethods to query/identify changes in the component between two versions.

   Note that the above metacontent has been described in terms of edges in the component's program-flow graph. This may be impractical for large programs. Hence, for large programs, the same type of metacontent may be described at different levels of granularity, e.g., at the method, class, or subsystem level.

2. *Specification-based* using which the test selection will be based on the functional description of the program. For the sake of clarity, consider a popular specification-based technique, say the category-partition method [323]), in which test frames that represent test specifications for the functional units in the system are created. Three types of metacontent may be provided by the component developer in the context of the category-partition method:

   - Metamethods that compute coverage [272] achieved by the test suite with respect to the test frames for the component.
   - Metamethods to query the component version.
   - Metamethods to retrieve the test frames affected by the changes in the component between two versions.

7.3 Role of the User

Depending on the metacontent made available by the developer of the component, the user can employ either code-based [6, 40] or specification-based regression testing techniques [106, 107, 271, 321]. Note that even though the term "code-based" is used, the source code of the component need not be available; the metacontent will help to perform the analysis.

Code-based: As in the above discussion, this idea will be presented in terms of program-flow graph edges. However, the technique is general and may be done for any program element. Also, the discussion will focus on *a safe regression test selection* approach [321]. The component user can employ the metacontent to perform safe regression test selection in the following steps:

1. Construct a program-flow graph for the original component and, for each test case, determine the edges covered by the test case. Note that metamethods are available to perform this step.
2. Assume that the new version of the component, with associated metacontent, is available.
3. Create the program-flow graph for the new component and determine which edges were modified in the revision. Metamethods are made available for this step.
4. Choose all test cases that cover at least one edge. Use the chosen test cases for regression testing.

Specification-based: Recall that this regression testing approach is based on the functional description of the program. In conventional specification-based regression testing, a software tester performs the following steps:

1. The tester chooses a technique (say, category-partition method [323]) in which test frames are created that represent test specifications for the functional units in the system.
2. The tester analyzes the specification to identify the individual functional units in the system.
3. For each unit, the tester identifies the parameters and environmental factors. The parameters are inputs to the unit whereas environmental conditions are elements outside the code that affects the behavior of the unit.
4. The tester partitions the parameters and environmental conditions into mutually exclusive choices.
5. The tester identifies constraints among choices based on their interactions.
6. The tester develops a set of test frames for each functional unit by computing the cross product of the choices. Note that the constraints (identified above) are used to eliminate certain combinations of choices, usually those that the tester considers meaningless and/or contradictory.
7. The tester records the coverage of the original test suite with respect to the entities in the functional representation. In this case, the test frames are the entities that are covered by the test cases. A test case in T covers a test frame if (a) the parameters of calls to single functionalities match the corresponding choice in the test frame and (b) the state of the component matches the environmental conditions in the test frame. This step may be performed by instrumenting the code

according to the test frames. That is, when a test case is executed, the output of the instrumenter will be a set of test frames that it covers. The coverage of a test case will be the set of test frames.

8. For regression testing, the tester identifies the test frames that are affected by the changes and runs only those test cases that cover affected test frames.

9. The only remaining issue is identifying the affected test frames. Intuitively, each test case identifies a family of paths within the component, i.e., the paths executed by the test case. A change affects a test frame if at least one of the paths associated with the test frame traverses a statement either changed or eliminated in the new version.

Note that the metacontent provided by the component developer is sufficient to perform the above steps.

8 Binary Reverse Engineering

The developer may compile/build the component in such a way as to enable binary reverse engineering. Binary reverse engineering is used to automatically derive a design structure of a component from its binary code, e.g., a call graph, a control flow graph.

Binary reverse engineering is used to automatically derive a design structure of a component from its binary code, e.g., a call graph, or a control-flow graph. Source code of the component can also be partially extracted. There are, however, several limitations of binary reverse engineering: it is not always possible to automatically extract the whole component design (some design extraction has to be done manually), names of procedures and variables are meaningless because binary reverse engineering tools assign names "blindly" without any consideration to their purpose, and no comments in the source course are generated by these tools. As a result, the process of component understanding may still be very time consuming and difficult. Binary reverse engineering is used mainly for understanding a component design. To a lesser extent, it is used to understand component functionality. Note, however, that when source code for the component (even with meaningless names of procedures and variables, and no comments) is provided, one may still determine, frequently with significant effort, the component functionality.

The component developer can make the task of binary reverse engineering easier for the component user by adding more information into the component. For example, the component may be compiled and linked with "symbols", similar to the approach used for debugging. Note that this technique does not require any extra effort on the part of the developer.

9 Fault Injection Support

9.1 General Idea

Fault injection is a process to examine the behavior of a software component under controlled anomalous circumstances. A component user may examine the behavior of the overall software if invalid outputs are produced from a component. The developer may provide mechanisms to guarantee that such outputs are never produced.

Consider a software system Y that contains a component X. Let X have three different output variables – A, B, and C. To determine which failure modes from X cannot be tolerated by the overall software system, fault injection [88, 189, 409] is used to forcibly corrupt (modify) the information stored in one of A, B, C, or some combination. Note that the fault is not produced naturally by X. The fault is artificially introduced using fault injection processes [410]. The goal is to study Y's reaction or response to the faulty output from X. Fault injection provides a nice basis from which to reason about how actual corrupt information will impact an overall software system that is composed of components.

The key idea is that the component user goes through several steps: (1) identifies the inputs and outputs of the component and (2) uses fault injection to identify those output values that cause problems. These outputs can be masked using wrappers, or the developer can do some analysis that guarantees that these error outputs will never be produced.

9.2 Role of the Developer

The approach involves performing fault injection first, and then performing the mitigation processes. For the developer of a suspicious component, static fault tree analysis, backward static slicing (with testing), and wrapping are three mitigation strategies that will enable a developer to show the integrity of the components.

Static fault tree analysis (SFTA) can prove (by contradiction) that certain failure classes are not possible from the software, even if we were to receive bad input data from the rest of the system. Static fault tree analysis assesses the causal relationship between events in a process. Software fault tree analysis is simply the application of static fault tree analysis to software. It was brought over to software engineering from systems safety engineering. Those outputs of the component that caused problems in the overall software will be the top events in the fault tree. These events will be ORed together. The underlying events represent failures of subcomponents or failures of external components upon which the software depends for input information. Fault trees allow a developer to prove that certain faulty values cannot be produced by a component. If during this analysis a branch exists that does not result in a logical contradiction, then the analysis has uncovered events that can lead to undesirable outputs from the component. This means that there are harmful outputs from the component that the system must be protected against.

Backward static slicing from the variables that were corrupted by fault injection can establish which slices need concentrated testing. This provides an argument that those failure modes are not possible. The component developer can also perform slicing and then perform slice testing. Slicing and slice testing, unlike fault tree analysis, does not prove that the output events are impossible. The results from slicing and slice testing are statistical. Even though these approaches to impact analysis are different, the results from these techniques demonstrate that certain output events are unlikely. And this is precisely what is needed to mitigate the potential of those outputs that fault injection has warned of. After the static slices are discovered, the slices must be thoroughly tested to determine whether those values were even output from the component. This is referred to as slice testing. Note that generating test cases to exercise a slice can be a difficult task, and like almost all problems that involve test case generation for code coverage, it can suffer from undecidability problems. In summary, if certain values do not occur during slice testing, confidence in the component is increased.

9.3 Role of the User

The component user can perform fault injection to determine the outputs of the component that cause problems for the overall software. Once identified, the user can give feedback to the developer for assurances that these outputs will not be produced. If the component developer does not provide convincing evidence that the component cannot produce these values using the previous two mitigation strategies, there is still another alternative that the component user can undertake – software wrappers. Software wrappers are a family of technologies that force components to behave in specified, desirable ways. A software wrapper is a software encasing that sits around the component and limits what the component can do with respect to its environment. (There is also another type of wrapper that limits what the environment can do to the component.) To accomplish this, two different wrapper approaches can be used. One approach ignores certain inputs to the component and thus does not allow the component to execute on those inputs. This clearly limits the component's output. The other approach captures the output before the component releases it, checking to ensure that certain constraints are satisfied, and then allowing only output that satisfies the constraints. Recall that fault injection pointed out which outputs from the component were undesirable (with respect to the system state of Y for corrupt outputs). Wrappers should be based on that information. One option for accomplishing this is to build tables that contain undesirable corrupt states (along with the system states for which they are undesirable). If these states are seen, the wrapper can halt their being output. Another option is to use artificial intelligence approaches to build heuristics that can classify the results of fault injection, and if outputs that satisfy the heuristics are observed, they too can be thwarted.

10 Testable Beans

10.1 General Idea

The developer may package the component as a testable bean. A component augmented with capabilities to support test execution and test observation is called a testable bean. A testable bean is deployable, traceable, implements the test interface, and includes the necessary provisions to interact with external testing tools.

10.2 Role of the Developer

Component testability depends, besides other factors, on the ability of a component to aid in the testing process. Testability can thus be increased by augmenting a component with capabilities in order to support testing tasks. The testable beans approach is a possible answer to this requirement.

A component needs to satisfy certain requirements and to possess certain features to become a testable bean. These requirements and features include:

1. A testable bean is deployable and executable. A testable bean can be used in exactly the same way as a regular component, and that does not require specific provisions for its operation.
2. A testable bean is traceable. A testable bean possesses certain capabilities that permit the component user to observe its behavior during a test, something that would have to be encapsulated without such capabilities.
3. A testable bean implements the test interface. A testable bean implements a consistent and well-defined interface that allows access to the capabilities supporting its testing.
4. A testable bean includes the necessary provisions to interact with external testing tools. The approach suggests functionally separate business logic implemented from the testing-specific logic at an architectural level.

10.3 Role of the User

From a component user's point of view, the test interface is the only difference between a testable bean and a regular component. The test interface provides mechanisms to initialize a test given the class and method to be tested and the test case; another method executes the test as it is initialized; the last method evaluates the test. The methods declared by the test interface and implemented by a testable bean can be used in two possible ways. These are as follows:

- Firstly, the test interface can be used by other tools. For instance, it can be used by tools in the environment in which the testable bean is embedded, for example, test agents and tracking agents. The first triggers the tests whereas the second has mainly the purpose of monitoring.
- Secondly, the test interface can also be used by the testable bean itself. A testable bean can contain built-in test scripts which access the methods declared in the test interface as necessary. These test scripts, possibly embracing test cases, can initialize tests, execute them, and evaluate the results autonomously.

11 Retro Components

11.1 General Idea

The developer may package the component as a retro component. A component enhanced with information concerning tests conducted by the component provider and indications for tests to be conducted by the component user, and with capabilities (e.g., queries) to gather information during tests of the component user, is called a retro component.

Retrospection as provided by a retro component is similar to introspection widely found in component models. Both retrospection and introspection are mechanisms for exchanging information between the component provider and component user. However, two significant differences can be identified. Firstly, introspection is static, whereas retrospection is dynamic. A retro component can autonomously gather information during the testing and operation of a component. Both the component provider and component user can benefit from this. The component provider can gain a better insight into the use of the component and the component user can carry out tasks that otherwise would require access to information not available. Secondly, introspection only facilitates unidirectional information flow, whereas retrospection bidirectional. A retro component possesses the capability of gathering information during its test and operation at the component user site that can be delivered to the component provider. Such a flow of information does not occur in introspection.

11.2 Role of the Developer

The developer needs to technically enhance a component so that the component user can collect relevant information during testing.

From a technical point of view, the component developer is in charge of enhancing a component with retrospection. For this task, the component developer can use predefined retrospection facilities that provide a default retrospection behavior. The component is assumed in this context to be implemented using an object-oriented language such as Java. The predefined facilities consist of a certain framework of classes that can be integrated with the component under consideration by inheritance and by implementing certain interfaces.

The component can provide two types of information. First, the information exchanged can be static. A retro component can offer information to the component user describing, for instance, the component developer's assumptions for tests conducted, adequacy criteria used, and test histories. Static information can also embrace indications for further tests in the form of recommendations for the component user. Second, the information can be dynamic. A retro component is capable, for instance of computing adequacy of a test case set and collecting information describing its use. Computation of adequacy can be specifically conducted according to a white-box criterion, which obviates source code access to the component user for such a task.

Information gathered during test and use of a component, which can be valuable for perpetual testing and further development, can be delivered back to the component provider. Thus, the retro component approach supports, to some extent, a bidirectional information flow.

11.3 Role of the User

The user can operate the default implementation in distinct modes, including the modes of test time and runtime. Retrospection can be used during testing, i.e., in test time mode, and during operation, i.e., in runtime mode, to access static information and to gather dynamic information. The information accessible can be processed by external tools, such as test case generators.

12 Component Test Bench

12.1 General Idea

The developer may package the component as a component test bench, augmenting a component with test specifications that describe implementations of a component, the interfaces provided by each implementation, and the concrete sets of test cases appropriate to an interface.

A component test bench contains information that can be used for analysis and testing. A difference between the other approaches and this approach is that information provided here is restricted to test specifications.

Note that a component might be implemented in different programming languages. Implementations in different programming languages might even coexist with each other, and a specific operation can have multiple implementations. Furthermore, test specifications also support components offering several interfaces. A component can offer several interfaces, for instance, in order to provide several views to its operations depending on the application environment or for compatibility with previous versions. A set of test cases is associated with each interface of a component. An element of such a set is called a test operation. A test operation defines the necessary steps for testing a specific method in one of the interfaces of a component.

12.2 Role of the Developer

The developer creates test specifications and represents them in a standard format such as XML. The benefits gained by using a standard notation (XML) is that such specifications can be automatically processed by third-party tools once the tags are known. Third-party tools can be applied to read, interpret, and modify test specifications.

12.3 Role of the User

The concrete test inputs and expected test output packaged in a test operation can be determined, as usual, by testing. Depending on the type of testing intended, test inputs can be determined using black- and white-box techniques.

A test operation does not only include the arguments of the corresponding method, it also encompasses other provisions necessary, for instance, to enter the component in a necessary state. The arguments and the provisions necessary for a test can be defined in various ways. A test specification can be defined by (1) using a regular text editor to assemble XML descriptors, (2) using an XML editor which can offer more support than a text editor, (3) using a graphical interface with input boxes for each element, (4) using a data flow visual editor as suggested by the authors, and (5) using a program fragment consisting of a subset of Java.

The approach also encompasses certain tools that can be used to automate the definition of test specifications and the execution of tests. These tools, however, are not described here, since the majority of them (except a test pattern verifier) are intended to be used by the component provider. The test pattern verifier is a stand-alone module that the component user can apply to test the component with the test cases specified.

13 Self-Testing Components

13.1 General Idea

The developer may create a self-testing component. The underlying idea of this strategy is to augment a component with the functionality of analysis and testing tools. A component augmented accordingly is capable of conducting some or all activities of the component user's testing processes.

A self-testing component contains all the mechanisms to test itself [236, 238, 435]. The component can operate in two modes – a normal mode and a maintenance mode. In the normal mode, the built-in test capabilities are transparent to the component user and the component does not differ from other components. In the maintenance mode, however, the component user can test the component with the help of its self-testing features. The component user can invoke the respective methods of the component, which execute test cases, evaluate results, and output a test summary.

For example, if the component is implemented as a class, self-testing can be implemented by additional methods that either contain the test cases to be used in hardwired form or are capable of generating them. The primary benefit of such an implementation is that the methods for built-in testing can be passed to subclasses by inheritance.

13.2 Role of the Developer

The self testing strategy meets the demands of both the component provider and component user.

The component provider does not need to disclose detailed information. This does not mean that such information is not processed during tests conducted by the component user. Such information is either available to the component in an encapsulated form or is generated on demand by it during testing. In both cases, the corresponding information is not accessible to the component user but is nevertheless processed by the component. As a consequence, the information processed can be very fine-grained. For instance, source code, which the component provider would not disclose to the component user, can be packaged in a certain form into the component and can be used for test case generation. Even if the generated test cases are returned to the component user, source code still remains hidden.

13.3 Role of the User

The component user can parameterize tests as required. A self-testing component possesses the functionality of an analysis and testing tool and provides the component user the full functionality of such tools. As an example, the component user does not need to test a component according to the adequacy criterion anticipated by the component provider. The component user can generate test cases exactly as in the case of having access to the source code of the component and using a separate analysis and testing tool for test case generation.

The self-testing technique impacts several activities of a component user's testing process [105]. In particular, the activities of a typical testing process are impacted as follows:

Test plan definition: Some of the decisions made during the definition of test plans are addressed by conventions of the self-testing strategy and its actual implementation [27]. Such decisions concern, for instance, the target component model and framework. The actual implementation might assume, for instance, the Enterprise JavaBeans component model and framework. Another decision can concern the technique used for analysis and testing, such as the test case generation technique. Related to test case generation, the actual implementation of the self-testing strategy might also prescribe a certain type of completion criterion used to measure testing progress.

Test case generation: Generation of test cases is the integral constituent of self-testability. Test case generation needs to be conducted entirely by the self-testing component due to the absence of its source code and necessary white-box information for the component user, who therefore cannot carry out this task. Various types of test case generation techniques can be embedded in the actual implementation of the self-testing strategy. Test cases as generated in this context do not necessarily include expected results, depending on whether or not the specification of the component is available in a form in which it can automatically processed.

Test driver and stub generation: The component user does not need to generate test drivers for component method testing. The actual implementation of the self-testing strategy usually includes the provisions necessary to execute the methods of the component considered. Stubs, however, might be necessary if the method to be tested needs to invoke those of absent components. A component can often be embedded in a wide variety of application contexts and the specific application context therefore often cannot be anticipated [287]. The component user needs either to provide the stubs or to embed the component in the target application context.

Test execution: The execution of the methods under consideration with generated test cases can also be conducted by the implementation of the self-testing strategy. As one possibility for test execution, a dynamic technique, which iteratively approaches appropriate test cases and successively executes the method to be tested, can be used for test case generation purposes. As another possibility for test execution, test cases generated can be stored and executed in a separate testing phase.

Test evaluation: The evaluation of tests needs to be addressed either by the component user or by the implementation of the self-testing strategy, depending on whether or not the specification or expected results are available to the implementation. In the case in which the specification or expected results are available, this task can be conducted by the implementation of the self-testing strategy. Otherwise, expected results have to be determined and compared to those observed during and after test execution by the tester, i.e., component user.

14 Conclusions

This chapter presented techniques that can be employed by developers to build better testable COTS components. The focus of this chapter was to present the techniques using a taxonomy based on the phases of software testing and the roles of the component developer/user. A description of an important subset of the techniques was presented: (1) State Machine Models, (2) Built-In Tests, (3) Built-In Contract Testing, (4) Interface Probing, (5) Traceable Components, (6) Metacontent, (7) Binary Reverse Engineering, (8) Fault Injection Support, (9) Testable Beans, (10) Retro Components, (11) Component Test Bench, and (12) Self-Testing Components.

Practical deployment of a particular technique depends on the context of use, the overhead that can be tolerated, and the effort that the component developer and user want to put into the testing process. For example, the state machine model-based approach requires that the developer put in the effort to develop the models, and the user to combine them. The representation and storage of the state machines themselves will add to the overall "weight" of the component in terms of extra storage space. Similar overhead issues are seen with metacontent and fault injection (wrappers). However, these techniques give the component user flexibility, allowing the definition of different types of test cases. On the other hand, built-in tests provide no flexibility in terms of choosing the test cases – the user (with no test case generation effort) has to execute what is given by the developer. The other techniques also offer a spectrum of tradeoffs between user flexibility and effort. For example, interface probing (and traceable components) restricts the user to only those properties that the developer wants to make available, perhaps limiting the user's testing options. The software development life cycle and its phases also play a role in choosing techniques. For example, in many applications, built-in contract tests need to be designed at software design time, since the contracts are defined at that time. The application context, such as the implementation platform, restricts the application of some techniques; for example, retro components are easier to implement if the underlying language has built-in support. Platforms create several limitations for binary reverse engineering. It is not always possible to automatically extract the whole component design (some design extraction has to be done manually); names of procedures and variables are meaningless because binary reverse engineering tools assign names "blindly" without any consideration to their purpose; and no comments in the source course are generated by these tools. As a result, the process of component understanding may still be very time consuming and difficult.

The intention of using such a practical taxonomy was to give the reader a perspective on the narrow scope offered by some techniques. For successful practical application, these techniques will need to broaden their scope to address all phases of testing. After all, the component user will need to perform all testing tasks.

Evaluating the Integrability of COTS Components – Software Product Family Viewpoint

Anne Immonen, Eila Niemelä, and Mari Matinlassi

VTT Technical Research Centre of Finland,
P.O. Box 1100, FIN-90571 Oulu, Finland
Anne.Immonen@vtt.fi, Eila.Niemela@vtt.fi, Mari.Matinlassi@vtt.fi

Summary. COTS (Commercial-Off-The-Shelf) components are increasingly used in product family-based software engineering. Within product families, components are assembled using a disciplined process and a common product family architecture. However, the black-box nature of COTS components and insufficient component documentation make the integration of components difficult. Successful component integration requires that the component match the functional, quality, and system requirements and interoperate with other components of the systems family. Ensuring component integrability is an important task, especially within product families, where the ineffective use of COTS components can cause extensive and long-term problems. This chapter discusses the characteristics of architecture, components, and product families that affect the integrability of COTS components, as well as the evaluation techniques that an integrator can use in the assessment of the integration capability of COTS components.

1 Introduction

Integrability is the ability to make separately developed components of the system work together correctly. Software systems are based on integrated components as the components are used as building blocks in product development. The use of COTS components promises a lot of benefits to system integrators, such as lower costs, products better tested, and possible maintenance support. However, the use of COTS components brings out several problems compared to the use of in-house components. The black-box nature of COTS components prevents component integrators from modifying the component to better meet requirements. In addition, COTS components are usually documented insufficiently, so the integrators do not receive the detailed behavioral specifications they need. Architectural mismatches may occur when the interaction and architectural assumptions of the components are not known. Furthermore, integrators have no control over the component, its evolution, or its maintenance, but are dependent on the component developer.

Ensuring the integrability of a component is a great challenge in software product family engineering. A software product family is a group of products that are developed from a common set of assets (i.e., reusable requirements, software architecture, and components) but which differ from each other by having distinct features that affect the buying behavior of different customer groups [10,43,212,305]. The use of COTS components is increasing in software product families, mainly because building systems as component-based product families promises large-scale productivity gains, decreased time to market, increased product quality, efficient use of human resources, and changeable and extensible systems. The quality of a COTS component is particularly important in product families because an unwanted property or a side effect of a component can cause higher additional expenses than in a single system.

The owner of the product family, i.e., the integrator, can affect integrability by modifying the architecture of the product family to better support the integration of COTS components. Several architecture-related properties affect the integrability of COTS components, e.g., dependencies, component models, and interfaces. The integrator can also affect integrability through COTS evaluation. The evaluation of COTS components is about assessing component properties against evaluation criteria. This assessment is done mainly in the selection phase of COTS components. Therefore, the evaluation is about testing components and software from the perspective of architecture. Architecture testing usually focuses on various quality attributes involved in software architecture; here, we concentrate only integrability.

Because component documentation is often the only source for the assessment of information, it has become important since the use of COTS components has increased [388]. In many cases, the evaluation of COTS components — and especially integrability evaluation — is difficult to perform when based on documentation alone, and, therefore, testing is required. However, integrators do not have much influence on component testing. They are dependent on testing support that the component developer provides (or the developer makes the component testable).

In this chapter, we discuss the factors affecting the integrability of COTS components. Architectural properties have a great influence on the interoperability of components. We discuss briefly the common architectural characteristics and use two approaches that assist in interoperability evaluation: the model-based approach and the component-based approach. In the model-based approach, we apply our Quality-driven Architecture Design and quality Analysis method (QADA^{SM})[1] to assist in mismatch detection from the architectural models. In the component-based approach, we discuss the integrator's demands and the means for component integration, and define the required architectural properties of components that ensure integrability. In both ap-

---

[1]SM = Service Mark of VTT Technical Research Centre of Finland.

proaches, we define issues specific to product families. This chapter also describes two integrability evaluation methods: assessment through documentation and assessment through testing. We emphasize the value of component documentation in the component evaluation phase and define the importance of documentation and its contents from the integrator's point of view. We then discuss COTS component testing and define the testing methods that are applicable to integrators. Finally, we conclude the chapter.

2 The Impact of Architectural Properties on Integrability

In spite of careful component selection, COTS components may not necessarily work with other components of a product family. "A component is 'integrable' if its interfaces are well defined and well documented so that it can potentially be wrapped for commonality with other components" [70]. The success of component integration is not simple, but it is a sum of several aspects. Integrability depends on the external complexity of the component, the interaction mechanism and protocols, and how well and completely the interfaces have been specified [22]. In addition, integrability depends on the functionality assigned to the component, and how that functionality is related to the functionality of the component's new environment.

The product family integrator may need to adapt the architecture to support COTS components. There are a number of properties that are desirable for an architecture that adapts COTS components. For example, the architecture must support the substitution of components so that a component can be replaced without influence on the system [399]. For the same reason, the architecture must allow component isolation. Dependencies between the components and the insufficient control of these dependencies usually restrict the component substitution. The use of totally replaceable components would be an ideal situation, but unfortunately no such component model yet exists [361]. Therefore, the integration architecture must provide a mechanism for hiding the unwanted functionality of a component, because functionality of COTS seldom totally corresponds to the functionality that the integrator wants. The mechanism usually takes the form of an "integration component" or an integration technique, such as glue or a wrapper. The architecture must also include the capacity of COTS debugging and testing. The testing of a COTS component requires special attention, and the observation of the component is often the only way to verify component behavior at runtime.

In addition to adapting the architecture to support COTS components, the COTS components may have to be adapted to the architecture. However, the adapting of COTS components can be done only within the limits of component interfaces. Therefore, the use of open interfaces and standard component architecture, i.e., a component model, improve the integrability of the component. Within integration, other issues might arise that have an impact on integration but that cannot be described within interfaces or observed externally. These are dependencies that can include, for example, other components, external resources, platforms, standards, and protocols.

The qualitative properties of the COTS component are often difficult to find, and the incompleteness of components may lead to additional cost to component integrators. A proposal has been made of the quality attributes that measure the characteristics of COTS components [26]. It uses the ISO 9126 quality model of software [199] as a basis but modifies it, claiming that not all the characteristics of a software product defined by it are applicable to COTS components. The quality attributes are divided into two main categories: attributes measurable at runtime and attributes observable during the product's life cycle. The first category includes accuracy, security, recoverability, time behavior, and resource behavior. The second category includes suitability, interoperability, compliance, maturity, learnability, understandability, operability, changeability, testability, and replaceability. The attributes of the second category are especially crucial to integrators for ensuring the suitability of a component for a product family. However, when considering these properties, interoperability is the one to be examined first because a component's suitability for a product family is heavily dependent on interoperability.

Software architecture presents a set of characteristics that pertain to the expected data and control exchange of components. When assessing the integrability of components, software architecture characteristics should be comparable. Architectural mismatches occur mostly when composing system components and when dealing with inconsistencies of different views. Two approaches have been suggested for use together to estimate and avoid integration mismatches these two cases: model-based integration and component-based integration [104]. The approaches are different, but their results are complementary. The purpose of both approaches is to identify clashes, which yield mismatches. Corresponding to the approaches, two types of clashes/mismatches can be detected:

- Model-based integration yields model constraint and rule clashes/mismatches
- Component-based integration yields component feature clashes/mismatches.

The model-based integration approach needs more information to start with than the component-based approach, and, therefore, it is more precise and can handle large amounts of redundant information. The approach tries to combine information from different views to allow precise reasoning. Integrating architectural views means that problems and faults are still relatively easy (and inexpensive) to fix, because architectural issues are considered early in the development life cycle.

The component-based integration approach is high-level and can be used early for risk assessment while little information is available. The approach uses a set of conceptual features for describing components and the connections between the components. When composing systems, many potential architectural mismatches can be detected by analyzing their various choices for conceptual features. Feature mismatches may occur when components have different or same (collision) characteristics for some particular feature, such as concurrency, distribution, dynamism, layering, encapsulation, supported data transfers, triggering, or capability. Component features can be derived through observation and assumptions of their external behavior (black-box analysis) without knowing their internal workings.

2.1 Model-Based Integration

Every component has been developed for a particular architecture, and, therefore, the components have assumptions about their interactions. An architectural mismatch occurs when the integrated component has wrong assumptions about the surrounding system. Four main categories of architectural mismatches in component integration have been identified [139]. These categories are based on assumptions the components make about the structure of the system and its environment. Assumptions about the nature of components and connectors include the substrate on which the component is built, the components (if any) that control these sequences of computation overall, the way in which the environment will manipulate data managed by a component, the pattern of interaction characterized by a connector, and the kind of data communicated. The assumptions about the global architectural structure include the topology of the system communications and the presence or absence of particular components and connectors. In addition, the components make assumptions about the construction process, i.e., the order in which pieces are instantiated and combined in an overall system.

Integrability is related to interoperability and interconnectivity. Interoperability is a subcharacteristic of integrability, and partially defined by interconnectivity, the ability of software components to communicate and exchange information. Thus, interconnectivity is a prerequisite for interoperability, the ability of software to use the exchanged information and provide something new originating from exchanged information. Interconnectivity and interoperability are execution qualities, whereas integrability has a larger scope, impacting the development and evolution of a system. Therefore, integrability is to be considered together with the features of a product family, domain requirements, high-level coarse-grained architectural elements, and the ways to develop and maintain a product family and derive a product from it. Interoperability is considered when components and their interactions are defined in detail and finally observed as executable models, simulations, and running systems.

We know from literature that there exists a multitude of architectural characteristics that play a part in component interoperability. By examining multiple aspects of characteristics, Davis et al. [86] have grouped, associated, and appended the characteristics in a structured manner, and thus developed a single definition of characteristics (Table 1). They form a set of 21 architectural characteristics from the initial set of more than 70, and organize them into the three categories according to [222]: system, data, and control. They use three levels of abstraction, orientation, latitude, and execution, that represent the point at which the value of an architectural characteristic can be assigned during the design effort. The system category is concerned with the system as a whole and with how the characteristics shape the component system on the orientation level. Data characteristics deal with how data resides and moves within software components. Data characteristics are defined on the latitude and execution levels. Similarly, control characteristics address control issues on the latitude and execution levels.

Table 1. Categorized architectural characteristics.

Category	Characteristics	Abstraction level
System	Identity of components	Orientation level
	Blocking	Orientation level
	Modules	Orientation level
	Connectors	Orientation level
Data	Data Topology	Orientation level
	Supported Data Transfer	Orientation level
	Data Storage Method	Orientation level
	Data Flow	Latitude level
	Data Scope	Latitude level
	Data Mode	Latitude level
	Method of Data Communication	Execution level
	Data Binding Time	Execution level
	Continuity	Execution level
Control	Control Topology	Orientation level
	Control Structure	Orientation level
	Control Flow	Latitude level
	Control Scope	Latitude level
	Method of Control Communication	Execution level
	Control Binding Time	Execution level
	Synchronicity	Execution level
	Concurrency	Execution level

The characteristics of the orientation level are related to the high-level architectural style of the component, and their values can be gleaned from the developer's documentation. The characteristics of the latitude level demarcate where and how communication moves through a system. The characteristics of the execution level are further refined to the extent of providing execution details. Furthermore, the semantic network is employed from these architectural characteristics and their abstraction levels. The semantic network defines the intra- and inter-level relationships of these characteristics [86]. The intra-level relationships provide insight into the dependencies of the characteristics at similar abstraction levels. The inter-level relationships connect characteristics across the previously defined levels to indicate a linkage between detail and generality.

In order to evaluate interoperability, the architectural characteristics should be detected directly from the architectural models. We found the QADA^{SM} method to be best suitable for assisting in interoperability analysis because the method determines software structures based on the quality requirements and uses different viewpoints to address certain quality attributes [257, 338]. The main difference between QADA^{SM} and other analysis methods is that QADA^{SM} is designed to be used especially within product families, including commonality and variability analyses [338]. It considers architecture on two abstraction levels: conceptual and concrete. For both levels, QADA^{SM} has four viewpoints: structural, behavior, deployment, and development. The structural viewpoint concerns the component composition, whereas the behavior viewpoint concerns the behavioral aspects of the architecture. The deployment viewpoint embeds and allocates the components to various computing environments, whereas the developmental viewpoint presents the components, their relationships to each other, and the actors responsible for their development. The mapping of the characteristics of orientation, latitude, and execution levels to the viewpoints of QADA^{SM} for interoperability evaluation is introduced next.

Orientation Level

In the conceptual structural viewpoint, the functional and quality responsibilities are decomposed and mapped to conceptual services and components. The characteristics of the orientation level can be detected partly from the decomposition model, which describes the components (system components, subsystem components, leaf components, classes) and relationships (passes-data-to, passes-control-to, uses, is-inherited-from, is-part-of). The decomposition model is used, for example, for selecting architectural styles that support quality attributes derived from quality requirements.

The components to be developed or acquired are presented in the conceptual developmental viewpoint. The conceptual development viewpoint of QADA^{SM} describes the technological choices made basing on standards, communication technologies, and enabling technologies. In this viewpoint, the COTS components to be acquired are mapped to the system architecture. The viewpoint uses the constraints model for mapping existing standards and technologies to the structural viewpoint of the conceptual architecture. The constraints model describes the standards and technologies the services and components have to conform with. Therefore, we map the rest of the characteristics of the orientation level to the developmental viewpoint.

The mappings of characteristics are compiled in Table 2. An example of the mapping is presented in Fig. 1.

Table 2. Mapping the orientation-level characteristics to the structural and developmental viewpoints.

Conceptual structural view	Orientation-level characteristics
Decomposition model	control topology, control structure, data topology, data storage method, identity of components, blocking

Conceptual developmental view	Orientation-level characteristics
Constraints model	supported data transfers, modules, connectors

Figure 1 shows an example of the decomposition model of the structural viewpoint that has been drawn using the diagramming and drawing tool Visio2000. The sample architecture (Fig. 1) supports a client/server architectural style, allowing the services to be centralized to a server and clients to be located across the network. Service components are independent units and aware of each other. Used protocols and other technical standards can be detected from the constraint model. For example, the model can describe that a particular service is based on message-based communication and the User Datagram Protocol (UDP), supporting both synchronous and asynchronous communication modes. Architectural relations of the decomposition model reveal the control topology, as well as the data topology on the orientation level.

Latitude Level

The characteristics of the latitude level can be detected using the concrete behavior viewpoint of QADA^{SM}. The concrete behavior viewpoint defines the behavior of individual components and interactions between component instances, i.e., how components exchange messages and invoke one another's interfaces and operations to achieve the overall system functionality. The concrete behavior viewpoint represents a state diagram that describes the components (capsules) and relationships (ports, in and out signals) and a message sequence diagram that describes the components as capsules and relationships as interactions between capsules. The state diagram is used for refining internal behavior of concrete components (i.e., intra-level relationships), whereas

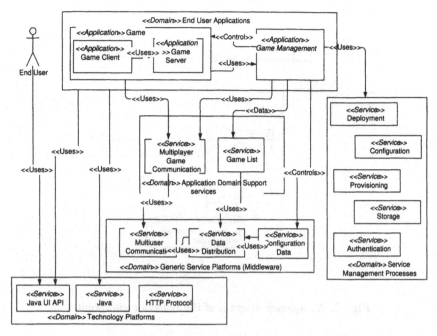

Fig. 1. An example of the decomposition model.

the sequence diagram is used for refining external behavior of concrete components (i.e., inter-level relationships) and analyzing interoperability from the concrete architecture. The characteristics of the latitude level are mapped to the state diagram and the sequence diagram of the behavior viewpoint (Table 3).

Table 3. Mapping the latitude-level characteristics to the concrete behavior viewpoint.

Concrete behavior view	Latitude-level characteristics
State diagram	control flow, control scope
Sequence diagram	data flow, data mode, data scope

Data mode, flow, and scope can be detected from the sequence diagram (Fig. 2). Additional information, when needed, can be attached to the diagram, for example, with a note shape, which is a diagram comment having no semantic influence on the model elements.

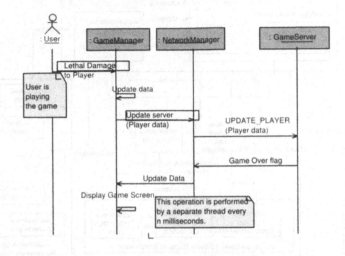

Fig. 2. A sequence diagram of the behavior viewpoint.

Execution Level

The characteristics of the execution level can be detected when examining interfaces. The concrete developmental viewpoint of QADA^{SM} shows the interfaces between developed concrete components. The developmental viewpoint also describes the development-time software structure and links to an asset repository with UML structural diagrams (packages and associations), that supports assessment of integrability. In addition, the development viewpoint describes the technology layers. The characteristics of the execution level are mapped to interface descriptions and the descriptions of technology layers (Table 4).

Table 4. Mapping the execution-level characteristics to the concrete developmental viewpoint.

Concrete development view	Execution-level characteristics
Interface description	Method of data communication, method of control communication, continuity, synchronicity
Technology layers	Data binding time, control binding time, concurrency

We describe component interfaces using a two-level interface description model. The first level illustrates the interfaces from the architectural point of view, describing the responsibilities of the interface. The second level is a detailed description of the transformation of the interfaces, i.e., how the interfaces are mapped to the implementation. Tables 5 and 6 present examples of interface descriptions.

Table 5. Architectural-level interface description.

Interface	Responsibility	Operation
srvMgm_ITF: asynchronous EJB (RMI/IIOP)	Allows the access to Service Management Services, such as the authentication and authorization of a user, user profile management and accounting.	authenticate/ authorize

Table 6. Transformation-level interface description.

srvMgm_ITF: EJB (RMI/IIOP)				
Method	Responsibility	Parameters	Return	Exceptions
authenticate: request-response	Wraps a call to the Authentication Service. The method returns true if the credentials provided are correct.	user: String, password: String	Boolean	authentication failed
authorize: request-response	Wraps a call to the Authorization Service.	user: String, service: String	Boolean	authorization failed

The technology layers describe technologies to be used and their relationships between each other. The descriptions can be informal, but to assist in the detection of the execution-level characteristics, the technology/protocol used should also have comprehensive specifications.

In summary, the architectural characteristics that affect interoperability can be mapped to the particular diagrams of the viewpoints defined in QADA[SM]. This provides the information needed for the evaluation of the interoperability (and interconnectivity) of components at the architectural level, and therefore assists in the evaluation of COTS components for product families.

The Impact of the Product Family Approach

The architectural characteristics cannot all be directly detected from the architectural models if the standard UML (Unified Modeling Language) is used. Therefore, the modeling notation had to be extended to support the development of product family architectures. This was made by a PFE (Product Family Extension) profile that describes the architectural elements and relationships required in the viewpoints of QADA^{SM} [98].

The PFE profile [98] is realized by the UML extension mechanisms: constraints, tags, and stereotypes. The main architectural elements defined as stereotypes are *system, subsystem, leaf component, service component, deployment node, and unit of deployment*. Thereafter, some special architectural elements were defined for service architectures: *domain* (i.e., the name of a set of related services) and *application* (a containment of services visible to end users). The set of proposed stereotypes for architectural relations such as *use, control, data,* and *sequence of actions* can be *mandatory, optional, alternative, or optional-alternative*. Furthermore, there are *is-allocate-to, require,* and *exclude* relationships.

The PFE profile was developed based on experiences of several architectural design case studies [240, 256, 394]. These case studies collected and defined information about how to describe architectures with UML, and how to extend UML to describe variability. The justification for two separate levels of abstraction and the need for multiple viewpoints in architectural representation is given in [306].

Architectural analysis requires special effort within software product families. Traditional software architectural analysis examines whether the architecture supports the requirements of the system. For example, the widely used Architecture Tradeoff Analysis Method (ATAM) enables the comparison of the results of the analyses to the requirements [69]. ATAM is also tailored to deal more specifically with the issues associated with COTS-based systems [401]. The main difference between ATAM and other analysis techniques is that ATAM helps to identify dependencies among quality attributes. However, the architectural analysis of the product family has to examine whether or not a proposed architecture supports both the shared requirements for all systems in the product family and the distinct requirements pertaining to individual systems in the product family. This means that the analysis method has to consider product family-specific techniques such as commonality analysis [97]. The emphasis of recent product family techniques has been on developing the product family architecture rather than on analyzing and evaluating the existing product family architectures [250]. Thus, a quality-driven method like QADA^{SM} is required for product family architecture analysis.

2.2 Component-Based Integration

Software architecture defines the relationships that a component has with other components. Each relationship defines an interface that defines a contract between a component that provides certain functionality and components that require that functionality [22]. Thus, interfaces determine how a component can be used and interconnected with other components. Interfaces hide the details of a component from its environment while enabling access to the component. Therefore, the interface description helps integrators decide what integration strategy to use. There are a few strategies by which the interfaces can be controlled:

- Using de facto and industry-defined standards (preferably open standards).
- Specifying as many assumptions about a component's interface as feasible.
- Wrapping the components with source code controlled by the user/integrator.

A number of the existing standards define how to access particular functional components. These standards take the form of an Application Programmer Interface (API) that defines how to link to a local procedure call, or they take the form of a protocol that defines how to access a service over a network. By using an accepted standard, component developers allow the integrators a much greater capability to mix and match components. However, accepted standards exist only in domains that are relatively mature, such as relational databases and directories. In many other application areas, no standards exist or, alternatively, many standards exist but the component providers have not yet accepted them [400].

Parameterized interface and negotiated interface are techniques for avoiding interface mismatch [22]. A parameterized interface is an interface whose assumptions about the environment can be changed by changing the value of a variable before the component service is invoked. A negotiated interface is a parameterized interface with self-repair logic. This kind of interface can parameterize by itself or by an external agent.

The integration of a COTS component depends mainly on the interfaces of the component. However, the integrators have several means for integrating the COTS component into a system. Wrapping, bridging, mediating, and tailoring are used to form an interface for a COTS component, which is then used by other software components to interact with the COTS. Wrappers, bridges, and mediators are defined in QADA^{SM} as part of the decomposition model or in a separate integration model of the structural view of the architecture. A wrapper is a piece of code that isolates the COTS component from other system components and filters unwanted inputs that could make the component behave improperly. Wrappers are also used to control the levels of component interaction and to limit undesirable dependencies [166]. A bridge translates data from one form to another without knowing its clients.

Mediators exhibit properties of both bridges and wrappers. Tailoring means adding some element to the component to provide it additional functionality, for example, with scripts or plug-ins. Tailoring does not involve, in this case, modifying the source code of the component.

Integrators may apply *integration elements*, such as design patterns and connector models, in component integration. The integration elements can be classified into the translator, controller, and extender [223]. The translator and controller are connector models of integration functionality defined as design patterns on the architectural level and based on solving incompatibility problems among components. The extender is a connector model whose functionality enhances the functionality provided by translators and controllers. The basic function of a translator (e.g., a bridge, adapter, filter, or converter) is to convert data and functions between component formats and to perform semantic conversions. It does not change the content of the information. A controller (e.g., a broker) coordinates and mediates the movement of information between components using predefined decision-making processes or strategies. The extender is a connector model whose functionality can vary extensively, (e.g., buffering, polling, and security checks) and is specifically used as part of an integration architecture in which the translator and controller cannot accommodate the full functional need. The proxies, wrappers, and decorators contain at least one translator and one extender integration element.

A number of promising component architectures are used in component development to eliminate possibilities of architectural mismatch [86]. However, the interoperability of component models still requires consideration. All component models define two elements: components and containers [294]. A component model provides the template from which practical components are created. The container part of the component model defines a method for combining components together into useful structures. Containers provide the context for the components to be arranged and to interact with one another. The main element of a component model is the interconnectivity standard (i.e., connection standard, wiring standard) that defines the communication and data exchange among components. In addition, a component model provides a set of standards for component implementation, naming, customization, composition, evolution, and deployment.

The Impact of the Product Family Approach

The basic elements of component models are far too general when examining component interoperability in the context of product families. Using our product family approach, we defined three viewpoints to examine component integrability: domain-based, standard-based and product family architecture (PFA)-based. In the domain-based view, our approach was a distributed service platform that provides a variety of services that are mobile and enable spontaneous networking. In the standard-based view, the importance of standards on interoperability was examined from both domain and PFA viewpoints. Finally, in the PFA-based view, the interoperability was examined in the context of product family architecture. Using these views, we found several required properties for component models (Table 7).

The interoperability requirements of components (Table 7), especially in distributed systems, are derived from industrial case studies in which a proprietary software bus with a specific component model [307] and CORBA-compliant middleware with a CORBA component model [304] were applied.

The product family approach also has great impact on the COTS selection. The selection of the component is usually based on vendor qualification and the COTS evaluation results [280]. Several selection methods have been proposed for the COTS selection for a single system, such as OTSO (Off-The-Shelf Option) [230] and PORE (Procurement-Oriented Requirements Engineering) [302]. However, in product families, the selection criteria have to be defined from the perspective of the product family, and not of a single system. Therefore, the COTS selection criteria must have several points of view. As far as we know, only one selection method is related to product families. The National Product Line Asset Center (NPLACE) has developed evaluation criteria that help select a COTS component for any product family [301]. A hierarchical certification model for certifying COTS components for product families has been developed from these criteria [428]. The certification model has four levels, each of which considers different aspects of a component when trying to determine if the component is suitable for a product family. Moreover, the certification model identifies categories that were not considered by NPLACE criteria, such as testability criteria, efficient implementation, generality, retrievability, and usefulness.

Hierarchical COTS certification levels are

- COTS-Worthiness: functionality and quality of component
- Domain Pervasiveness: usefulness of the component in the domain
- Architecture Conformance: usability of the COTS component in a given product family context
- Application Adequacy: adequacy of the component for one particular product of the product family

Every product of the product family shares a common architecture that is expected to persist over the life of the product family. Therefore, the impact of COTS has to be eliminated or scaled to as small as possible. The COTS components can be product-specific components only used in a single product, or they are included in the asset base of the product family in which case they can be used in multiple products. Because core assets need to be dependable over a long period of time, several stability factors need to be noted when considering COTS components to be used as core assets [70]. Ineffective COTS utilization can cause problems throughout the life cycle of a software product family. Therefore, a special risk analysis is required when using COTS

Table 7. Important properties of component models for product family architecture (PFA).

Examination view	Required property	Definition
Application domain view: embedded, networked system	Distributed computing support	A component model provides a remote method specification to allow communication of components over the network.
Standard based view	Standard protocol	A component model defines a standardized protocol that is used in communication between components.
Standard based view	Standard IDL, language-neutral IDL	The description of interfaces and their elements using an implementation-independent notation.
PFA view	Platform and programming language neutrality	If the component model allows the implementation of components in a different language, the component model can assure the interoperability of components by providing binary interface structure and standard calling conventions at the binary level.
PFA view	Customization	The ability to adapt the component for use (e.g., customization interfaces).
PFA view	Communication between different component models	A component model provides a specification about how to bridge communication among implementations of different component models.
PFA view	Packaging	A component model gives instructions on packing a component in a way that it can be deployed independently. The content of the package can be defined in a deployment model.

components in product family architecture. We divide risk factors into risks concerning a COTS product and risks concerning a COTS vendor, and define the risks from the product family architecture viewpoint (Table 8).

Table 8. Risk factors of COTS components.

Product related risks	Vendor related risks
Maturity and robustness of the products	Expected product update schedule
Interoperability with a wide variety of products	Stability of the vendor
Trojan horses: unexpected behavior of the component	Frozen functionality
Defective or unreliable COTS software	Incompatible upgrades
Complex or defective middleware which mediates information between COTS and custom software	

The risk factors of Table 8 are applied in [217], in which the risk factors of the use of commercial components are realized in three industrial cases.

3 Evaluation Methods of COTS Components for Integrability

The common obstacle in the adoption of COTS is not knowing the quality of components and not knowing how the systems will tolerate them. Component evaluation is performed by acquiring information about the component and assessing how well the component meets the evaluation criteria. Component documentation assists in assessing component properties. However, because of insufficient documentation of COTS components, testing is often the only way for evaluating the component.

3.1 Assessment through Documentation

Documentation is perhaps not considered an attractive subject but rather a forced phase of software engineering; however, most of the software community is aware of the importance of documentation. But the community suffers from a lack of standards and appropriate tool support. Therefore, the threshold for keeping documentation up-to-date is high. Product family architecture documentation is needed for sharing the vision of software systems and, therefore, supporting communication between different stakeholders and sharing architecture between developers and development organizations. Documentation also tracks design decisions, and is used for training and tutoring novices and storing knowledge of the architecture for others' use (i.e., reuse of software architecture).

Software component documentation is equally important because it shares knowledge of components inside and outside an organization. A self-contained documentation for software components is required, especially when reusing and selling components. Component documentation is the only way of assessing the applicability, credibility, and quality of a COTS component. It assists in the selection of components for a product or for product families, and in their integration into and adaptation to a system [387].

As with architectural documentation, the importance of component documentation is ignored. Traditionally, components have been documented as part of the software systems in which they are used. Furthermore, there are several standards for software documentation, such as for software design descriptions [196], software user documentation [195], software test documentation [197], and software quality assurance plans [198]. None of these considers the component as an independent product, but as part of a larger context. However, COTS components are intended to be used in different contexts and by several component integrators. The lack of a standard documentation model causes inconsistent and inadequate component documents [388].

A work is in progress for a standard proposal for a component documentation pattern [388]. The pattern is defined as a model that can be repeatedly reused and applied to different occasions, and is independent of the methods of implementation. The pattern guides how to describe the component's general properties and responsibilities from the architectural point of view, and how to provide a detailed description of the component's design and implementation. In addition, the pattern introduces information required for validating the quality of the component, as well as for the use and maintenance of the component. Therefore, the documentation that follows the defined pattern allows the integrators to evaluate the component for software product families. The developed documentation pattern also supports the hierarchical COTS certification model defined in [428].

In the component evaluation phase, the requirements for the component are converted into evaluation criteria sets. With the help of component documentation, the properties of components are compared with the criteria. As an example, we discuss the requirements classification and selection of a commercial database for the family of mission critical systems. The software requirements were collected by interviewing the representatives of an industrial company, the owner of the product family, and by reviewing the documents of the different types of products developed earlier. The requirements were then classified into five categories: Customization (C), User (U), Environment (E), Functions (F), and Production (P). The customization class defines the requirements common to the product variety, and application software used in different products has to fulfill these requirements. The user class defines mainly properties of user interfaces. The environment class defines the requirements on how the application software will be installed. The function class describes requirements of the primary services. The production class focuses on the ease of the production or the update of the application software. An example of each category is shown in Table 9.

Table 9. A fragment of the list of categorized requirements.

Category	Identifier	Requirement
Customization	C6	The same software architecture will be used in all products. So, scalability and adaptability will be supported, especially for user interfaces, communication interfaces, and the size of the database.
User	U2	Graphical images have to be reusable components. Graphical components must be able to be stored in the database.
Environment	E2	The integration of commercial and application software requires adaptive interfaces.
Functions	F2	Basic services are configured during the development.
Production	P6	Version control should be supported by the database.

Further, the requirements were mapped to the evaluation criteria (Table 10). The evaluation criteria of commercial databases were categorized into five classes: Software Development, Functionality, Safety, Fault Tolerance, and Performance. The importance of a criterion was ranked in one of four levels: no, low, medium, and high.

The evaluation was done for the three most advanced object-oriented databases. An example of the evaluation is shown in Table 11.

At the end of the evaluation, the conclusions were drawn. Based on the evaluation table above, the Objectivity/DB was chosen for the family of mission critical systems. While examining the documentation of COTS components, it was discovered that the technical details and general information about the components were documented well. Functional specification was defined in the form of component overview. Detailed functional specifications were not available. In addition, interface descriptions were unsatisfactory in most cases. Information on the design rationale, quality, and testing was not available. Therefore, the integrator can compare technical details, but cannot be sure of the quality of the components and how it is made. With this approach, the integrator cannot be sure if the component is suitable for his or her product family.

Table 10. A fragment of an evaluation table.

Evaluation criteria	Application requirements	Importance for the product family
1 Development requirements		
1.2 DB interfaces		
1.2.1 Interactive interface	C3, U3, U4, U5, U910, U11, U12, P6, P10	MEDIUM
1.2.2 Programming language	C3, C6, F3, F4, F6, P1, P4, P10, P12	HIGH
1.2.3 Portability (environments, standards)	C6, U8, U10, U11	HIGH
1.4 Data model complexity		
1.4.1 Complex relationships (many-to-many)	C1, C14, U12, U13, F1	HIGH
1.4.2 Composite objects (structural hierarchies of components)	C1, C2, C13, C14, C16, C17, U12, E1, E2	HIGH
1.4.3 Complex objects (variable length of data, pictures)	C13, C14, F1	HIGH

As a summary, the importance of component documentation cannot be ignored within commercial components. From the integrator's point of view, component documentation assists in the following [388]:

- selection of components,
- validation of the interoperability of components,
- analysis of combined quality attributes, and
- maintenance of components.

Consistent and extensive component documents are required for component comparison and evaluation. Therefore, a standard model for documentation is required to define the consistent content and structure for component documentation. As far as we know, no such model yet exists, but several proposals have been made. However, none of these proposals has been widespread or adapted by the software community.

Even with a standard model for component documentation, tool support is required. Today's design tools support documentation only partly. In the

Table 11. A fragment of the evaluation of object-oriented databases.

Evaluation criteria	Objectivity/DB release 4.0	Object store release 4.0	Versant release 5.0
1 Development requiremets			
1.2 DB interfaces			
1.2.1 Interactive interface	SQL++	SQL	SQL
1.2.2 Programming language	DDL-preprocessor, C++, Smalltalk	Smalltalk, C, C++, type-checking	C++, Smalltalk, Java: transparent integration of the languages, STL, Tools.h++
1.2.3 Portability (environments, standards)	SQL, ODBC, ODMG-93	ODBC, CORBA-interface for Orbix (single threaded version)	ODMG-93, CORBA object references; multithreaded database client and server; ODBC, JDBC
1.4 Data model complexity			
1.4.1 Complex relationships (many-to-many)	dynamic uni- and bidirectional associations, clustering	bidirectional association between two objects	many-to-many relationships
1.4.2 Composite objects (structural hierarchies of components)	propagation of delete and locking operations, object clustering	collections: performance-tuning, default behavior, multiple representations	arrays, strings, sets, lists
1.4.3 Complex objects (variable length of data, pictures)	dynamic sized, inheritance, large objects: memory management	inheritance, polymorphism, Image Object Manager (not only binary large objects)	graph-structure for complex objects

following points we sum up our experiences from the point of view of the documentation support:

- Rose-RT[2] includes a documentation window feature. The documentation window enables the user to add comments directly to individual modeling elements. It is possible to generate a Word document including component

---

[2]http://www.rational.com

names and attached comments as a documentation of the system. It is also possible to add attributes, operations, and their descriptions. However, this document includes only text comments, not diagrams; so diagrams have to be added manually.

- Visio2000[3] is a technical diagramming and drawing tool. Visio offers the ability to create custom master shapes in a stencil. Visio does not itself easily support attaching long descriptive information to shapes. Therefore, we used the VisiNotes tool that provides a simple user interface for attaching text to shapes. It is a user-friendly editor for adding up to three different notes. We applied the VisiNotes add-on tool to document service and component responsibilities directly to the architectural model. Component responsibilities were saved in text files, and they could therefore be inserted directly into architecture documents and updated with shortcut keys (a word processor feature). As with Rose-RT, this documentation feature supports only text, and diagrams, if wanted as a part of the architectural or component document, have to be added manually. '

- Rhapsody[4] is a UML-compliant visual design tool especially for developers of real-time embedded software. Rhapsody enables the user to add textual description directly to every individual modeling element, such as class, attribute, or operation. The entire software system can be documented by generating the descriptions into a document in a text or rich text file. Rhapsody's XMI (XML Metadata Interchange) interface enables the generation of an XML (Extensible Markup Language) format file from UML diagrams. Therefore, developers may export and import design data between Rhapsody and other tools supporting the XMI standard. The component developer and integrator are not forced to use the same UML tool.

- Together[5] is a tool for UML modeling. With this tool it is possible to manage and present the diagrams easily by generating an HTML (HyperText Markup Language) document. HTML documentation is generated using a template provided by Together. The document is structured with hyperlinks and can be used on the Web.

Visio provides manual support for component and architecture documentation. Rose-RT is considered a semiautomatic document generation tool, whereas Together and Rhapsody provide the best support for automatic documentation. However, the documentation support requires commitment of various tool suppliers. The tool suppliers have to see documentation as an important activity of architecture and component design. A documentation tool integrated into a software design tool would enable automatic generation of documentation.

---

[3]http://office.microsoft.com
[4]http://www.ilogix.com
[5]http://www.borland.com

3.2 Assessment through Testing

The testing is usually a part of the software verification and validation process. Within components, the purpose of the testing is to prove the quality of the component, i.e., the component satisfies its requirements, both functional and non-functional. When used in product families, the components have also to satisfy the functional and quality requirements of the product family architecture.

The initial and final states of a COTS component are usually hidden from external clients of a component, something which makes testing a COTS component more challenging than testing traditional in-house software or component. Component testing should assure the integrator that the functionality of the COTS component is consistent with the integrator's need, that the component is reliable, and that there is no mismatch between the component and the system.

In the software world, both software developers and integrators are frequently demanding that independent agencies certify that programs meet certain criteria. By paying Software Certification Laboratories (SCL) to grant software certificates, independent vendors partially shift responsibility to the SCL for whether or not the software is good. However, for small components, the use of software certification may not be productive. The use of SCL brings with itself several limitations, such as cost, liability problems, developer resources needed to access SCLs, and applicability to safety-critical systems [293]. Therefore, the SCL certification may be practical only for large software systems and applications, where the cost of software failure is high.

The goals of COTS testing are to ensure that the component is functionally correct, externally secure, internally secure, and robustly responds to anomalous inputs. Component testing techniques are traditionally divided into white-box and black-box testing. Black-box testing is an important but limited technique in assessing the quality of the component. Quality is not just a matter of component quality, but also a matter of integration compatibility. Black-box techniques test that the component's behavior is consistent with its specification. Therefore, the test criteria should already be defined during the component specification. White-box testing cannot usually be used with COTS components because they require access to source code and design documents.

The methodology defined by Voas [407] uses three quality assessment techniques to determine the suitability of a candidate OTS component: black-box testing, system-level fault injection, and operational system testing. Black-box testing is used to determine whether the component is of high enough quality. This requires that the integrators generate test inputs, build test drivers, and create a technique that determines if a failure has occurred. However, black-box testing may not catch serious problems, such as unknown functionality. The system-level fault injection technique called interface propagation analysis (IPA) is used to determine how well a system will tolerate a failing component. IPA stimulates failure in a predecessor component, determining whether the system can tolerate anomalies in a component. Operational system testing is used to determine how well the system will tolerate a properly functioning component. Operational system testing embeds the component and executes the full system.

Basically, traditional testing includes the building of a testing environment, the installation of software to this environment, and the execution of the test cases. As an example (Table 12), we present a performance test between two CORBA implementations. The environment for the evaluation was the same for both implementations. The implementations were isolated from the network with a bridge to minimize the influence of network load on the measurement. Due to good documentation and instructions, no problems occurred during the installation phase of the software.

Table 12. A fragment of the performance test results between two CORBA implementations.

Type of activity	Orbix QNX	CHORUS/COOL
Client initializations before being able to make invocations	0.20 – 0.30 s	0.16 – 0.21 s
Invocation with 4 bytes of data (two-way/one-way)	5 ms / 1 ms	13 ms / 4ms
Invocation with 1024 bytes of data	5 ms / 3 – 13 ms	14 ms / 8 ms
Invocation with 2048 bytes of data	6 ms / 20 – 30 ms	16 ms / 10 ms
Invocation with 4096 bytes of data	8 ms / 20 – 60 ms	19 ms / 14 ms
Invocation with 8192 bytes of data	70 ms / 30 ms	25 ms / 20 ms

As a result of the test it was discovered that the performance times were not dependent on data types (char, double, structures) used. The essential thing that seemed to have an effect on performance was the size of the message in bytes. Orbix had a remarkable variation in the execution of one-way messages, whereas Chorus did not have this property.

However, traditional testing is a time consuming task for component integrators, and often impossible because of the black-box nature of COTS components. According to our experiences, we state that integrators can ensure integrability through testing in the following two cases:

1. The integrator receives information on testing (i.e., test cases, test environments, test results) from the component developer.

2. The integrator builds the testing environment and uses the standard test interfaces and tester components. However, this requires that the COTS components support built-in testing.

The integrator's effort can be facilitated when a component developer provides a test program that corresponds to the testing executed by the developer or to the information on component testing. In this way, component integrators are able to verify how the component's functionality and quality have been validated and how exhaustive the tests have been. If developers are to supply test sets to purchasers, they will need a standard, a portable way of specifying tests, so that a component user can estimate how much testing the component has undergone. Potential customers can then make an informed judgment on the risk of the component failing in their application, keeping in mind the nature of the tests and the intended application.

A standard test specification has been suggested for software component certification [293]. With this approach, software developers supply test certificates in a standard portable form, so that purchasers can determine the quality and suitability of a component. XML was chosen for representing test specifications because it adheres to a standard developed by an independent organization responsible for several other widely accepted standards. In addition, XML has achieved broad acceptance across the industry, and it is designed as a language to provide structured documents. The advantages of this approach are:

- Reduced costs. The incremental cost to developers is small because they have produced extensive tests as part of their own verification procedures. Without such tests, they cannot make any claim for component reliability.
- Guaranteed trust. Purchasers receive the test data and the means to interpret it. Most XML editors can use the XML DTD to display the test specification's structure and content. Furthermore, purchasers receive a means for running the tests and verifying that the developer's claims for correctness are sustainable.
- Confirmed conformance. To confirm a developer's claims regarding a given product's testing level, purchasers can review the tests to judge how well they conform to their understanding of the specification.
- Augmented functional requirements. The test specifications augment the functional requirements, which are usually in plain language and therefore laden with potential ambiguities. The specifications and accompanying results provide a precise if voluminous specification of actual component behavior.
- Added value. The test specifications add considerable value to a software component. In many cases they already exist in collections of test programs, scripts, and test procedures, requiring only a standard format for packaging and supplying with a component to a purchaser.

The product family architecture itself may provide support for component testing, usually with test interfaces. The test interfaces allow self-test functionality to be invoked. The self-test functionality provides capability to determine whether the system is currently operational. Standard test interfaces allow an easy evaluation of COTS components that support built-in tests (BITs). BITs offer two major benefits: the component user can check the behavior of the component and the component can check if it is deployed in an inappropriate environment [103].

We map a BIT component in the context of product family architecture (Fig. 3). When deployed in new systems, built-in test (BIT) components can check the contract-compliance of their server components through the build-in test interface, and thus automatically verify their ability to fulfill their own obligations [13]. Therefore, the BIT interface gives access to the built-in tests and provides the system with the information needed in order to verify certain aspects of the component, without revealing information about the internal workings of the component. The standardization of test interfaces is required for the use of components developed by independent vendors. The tester components are separated from the BIT components and therefore can be changed at any time in order to best suit the context in which the component operates. The product family architecture may use its own testers, if they obey the standardized test interfaces, to directly test the COTS components. COTS components can also be published with accompanying testers.

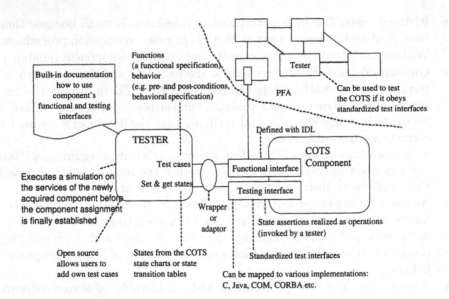

Fig. 3. The deployment of a COTS component in product family architecture.

4 Conclusions

In this chapter, we discussed the issues that affect component integrability, and how the integrability can be evaluated. The integrability of COTS components means that the component is able to communicate and exchange information with other components and use the exchanged information for providing some new functionality originating from exchanged information. Integrability also means easy adaptation of a component to the context of a product family, considering requirements, architecture, and existing components, and the use of COTS in product derivation.

We discussed the integrability of COTS components when applying the product family approach. We approached the product family and architecture development by mapping architectural characteristics related to integrability to the quality-driven architecture design. We also discussed the kind of influence component architecture has on the component's integrability and defined the requirements for the architectural properties of components from the point of view of product family architecture. Finally, we defined COTS evaluation techniques that integrators can use. COTS integrability is ensured by evaluating it against a set of criteria. This can be achieved only by analyzing component documentation and by testing.

A User-Oriented Framework for Component Deployment Testing

Andrea Polini and Antonia Bertolino

Istituto di Scienza e Tecnologie dell'Informazione - "Alessandro Faedo,"
Area della Ricerca del CNR di Pisa, Via Moruzzi 1
I-56124 Pisa, Italy {andrea.polini, antonia.bertolino}@isti.cnr.it

Summary. The capability to test an externally acquired software component deployed within the target application environment can help establish the compliance of a candidate component to the customer's expectations, and helps "increase trust." To this end, in this chapter we introduce the CDT framework that is conceived to ease the planning and the execution of test suites by the component user. We discuss the main challenges raised by the new component-based software production methodology and how the proposed framework can facilitate the evaluation of candidate components. Notably, CDT permits codifying a component deployment test suite in the early stages of development without reference to any (yet unknown) real implementation, and, later, during the integration stage, adapting and executing the test suite on a found candidate component.

1 Introduction

The last several years have been characterized by increasing pervasiveness of information processing systems. Many new application fields have been explored and many new software systems have been developed. On the one hand, this testifies that trust in software has generally grown, to the effect that it is used more and more in risky activities, of which the online banks are perhaps one of the most evident examples. On the other hand, this also makes it necessary to enhance the Quality of Service of the software produced, while assuring a high dependability, or the consequences can be otherwise catastrophic. This trend has not given any sign of finishing, and, as a result, the complexity of software systems is continuously increasing. At the same time, to stay competitive, software developers need to cope with the constant shrinking of time to market.

The answer to these challenges is being sought with the potential of obtaining complex systems by composing prefabricated and adequate pieces of software called "components". Following examples provided by other engineering disciplines, the simple underlying idea is that building complex systems by assembling already produced subsystems (components) should be faster and easier than building them from scratch. At the same time, it is assumed that the reuse of subsystems, whose qualities have been verified earlier by operating them as part of "successful" systems, should grant a higher reliability. However, some laboratory experiments [139] and even catastrophic events [245] have early on warned that composing components is not an easy task and much research is necessary to realize this vision.

Different perspectives and aspects have been considered while trying to address the problem of "composition of components," which involves issues coming from three new fields:

- Software Architecture (SA): basically, the overall system structure is specified in terms of the descriptions of the constituent components and of their interactions (*connectors*). Several dedicated Architectural Description Languages (ADLs) (e.g., Darwin [254], C2 [265], Wright [9]) have been proposed for this purpose, as well as domain-specific architecture styles [141], but the study on SA is still far from ending;
- Middleware: it is the layer between distributed system components and network operating system components that solves those issues related to heterogeneity and distribution and simplifies the communication among distributed software components [108];
- Component-Based Software Standards: they define a set of rules that the developer has to follow to guarantee the interoperability of a developed component with other components in the system and to use the services defined in the component standards (e.g., transaction, persistence, security) [282, 309, 380].

The interest from both academia and industry, and the importance of this new discipline, is evident through the spread of related events (e.g., [81]) and journal articles (e.g., [2, 80, 258]), and by the launch in the market of the first component-oriented technological products and platforms (e.g., CCM [309], EJB [380], COM+/.NET [282]).

However, although it is generally agreed that the implementation of a system from components needs specific approaches, clear guidelines and new processes have not yet been established. As for the other development phases, the testing stage also needs rethinking in order to address the peculiar characteristics of CB development [31]. One distinctive feature of CB production is the coexistence through the development process of several and new stakeholders. A CB process must in fact foresee and manage the spreading, in time and space, of different tasks among several uncoordinated subjects [31]. For testing purposes, in particular, we must distinguish at a very minimum between two subjects, the *component developer* and the *component user*. The first needs to test the software component in order to validate its implementation, but cannot make any assumption on the environment in which the component will be employed[1]. The second, instead, needs to (re)test the component as an interacting part of the larger CB system under development. In this respect, an important requirement is that the component user, on the basis of what he or she expects from a searched component, i.e., with reference to the system specification or architecture, be able develop a test suite and then routinely (re-)execute these tests – without too much effort – to evaluate any potential candidate components. The latter is precisely the issue that we address here.

A testing campaign by the component user, possibly in combination with usage of formal methods and Design by Contract (DBC) approaches [275], is also recognized as a suitable means to alleviate a new emerging problem in the area of CB production, generally referred to as the *Component Trust Problem* [279]. This problem points to the component user's exigency of instruments to gain confidence on what a component produced by someone else does and how it behaves. Obviously this issue is especially hard for components built by third parties and for COTS (Component-Off-The-Shelf), which are generally delivered without the source code. However, even in the case of components reused internally in an organization, the difficulties of communication between teams and the lack of clear documentation can to some extent produce similar effects. Moreover, even though a component has already undergone extensive testing by its developer, since complete testing is clearly impossible (since the developer cannot know in advance all the possible application domains or what other components will interact with the his component), some kind of testing against the component user's specifications is always necessary [420]. In this sense, it is also illusory to hope that reuse drastically diminishes the need for testing [39, 420].

On the foundational side, Rosenblum [350] outlines a new conceptual basis for CB software testing, formalizing the problem of test adequacy (with reference to a particular criterion) for a component released by a developer and deployed by one or more customers. He introduces the complementary notions of *C-adequate-for-P* and of *C-adequate-on-M* for adequate unit testing of a component and adequate integration testing of a CB system, respectively (where C is a criterion, P is a program, and M is a component). The cited paper constitutes a starting point for a revision of the theoretical concepts related to testing components, but a lot of work remains to be done.

Instead, with regard to the practical aspects of testing from the component user point of view, we cannot talk about *one* generic testing approach. For testing purposes, components can, in fact, be classified depending on the information that is carried with the component. In this sense, we could figure out a continuous spectrum of component types, at one extreme of which there are fully documented components whose source code is accessible (for

---

[1]An overview of component developer's techniques is provided in the chapter 'A Process and Role-Based Taxonomy of Techniques to Make Testable COTS Components'

instance, in the case of in-house reuse of components or open source components), and at the other extreme of which there are components for which the only available information consists of the signatures of the provided services, typical of COTS (commercial off-the-shelf) components. Clearly, the testing techniques that can be applied by the component user will be quite different depending on the type of component. For instance, in the case of COTS, the unavailability of code hinders the possibility of using any of the traditional code-based testing techniques.

In view of all the needs depicted above, and considering a scenario in which no information is made available by the component developer in addition to the component interface signatures (the extreme COTS example), we have developed the Component Deployment Testing (CDT) framework presented here. CDT supports the functional testing of a to-be-assembled component with respect to the customer's specifications, which we refer to as *deployment testing*. CDT is both a reference framework for test development and codification, and an environment for executing the tests over a selected candidate component. In addition, CDT can also provide a simple means to enclose, with a component, the developer's test suite, which can then be easily re-executed by the customer.

The key idea at the basis of the framework is the *complete decoupling* between what concerns deriving and documenting the test specifications and what concerns execution of the tests over the implementation of the component. Technically, to achieve such a separation, the framework requires the capability of retrieving, at runtime, information about the component relative to the methods signature. For this purpose, the component to be tested must enable runtime introspection mechanisms [225].

Before going ahead with the description of CDT, it is necessary to clarify what we mean by the "component" from a more technical point of view. In fact, the term has an ambiguous interpretation in the literature. A succinct and often quoted definition is due to Szyperski [385]:

A software component is a unit of composition with contractually specified interfaces and explicit context dependencies only. A software component can be deployed independently and is subject to composition by third parties.

For the sake of generality, we have adopted in our experiments a simplified view, identifying a component with a system or subsystem developed by one organization, deployed by one or more different organizations, and provided without the source code. According to this definition, we will consider a class or a set of classes as an extreme example of a component.

In the next section we expand our deliberations on the needs for a revised process for CB development. In Sect. 3 we present some of the approaches of the literature, somehow related to the approach that we propose, to increase trust in an externally acquired component. Section 4 gives an overview of the motivation for and features of the CDT framework. Section 5 presents a case study that will be used in Sect. 6 to discuss how an hypothetical component assembler can use the framework. In Sect. 7 some technical details on the actual implementation of the framework will be provided. Finally, we conclude the chapter outlining some conclusions and possible work directions.

2 CB Development Process and Testing Phase

In this section we discuss some issues related to the definition of a CB development process. It is not our intent (nor could it be done in only one section) to completely unravel this topic. The interested reader can refer to [64, 79], while an overview of CB life cycle processes embedding quality assurance models can be found in the chapter 'A Generic Environment for COTS Testing and Quality Prediction'. Our goal is to relate the framework that we have developed to the relevant phases of the development process and to provide information useful to better understand how the framework can be used.

The idea of producing software systems out of components is older than thirty years [261], but it is only in recent years that strong efforts have been made toward the wide adoption of this new methodology. Today, many component models exist, and from a pure technological point of view it is "quite easy" to build systems by composing components. Technology advances have in fact delivered component models and middleware addressing the questions of composition, interaction, and reuse of components. However, a comparable progress has not been made in the definition of a process apt to develop component-based systems. Thus, designing a system that will be implemented by "composing components" still remains a challenging activity, and further study on the subject is needed.

Some general considerations concerning such a process and the various activities that compose it can be discussed. The *implementation phase* deals mainly with the development of what is generally referred to as the "glue" code. This code is the instrument necessary to facilitate the correct interactions among the different components. The components are not generally implemented, but are looked for in the in-house repositories or on the market, in what is generally referred to as the *provisioning phase*. After one or more candidate components have been identified, it is necessary to evaluate their behavior when integrated with the other already chosen components. This phase can be referred to as the *selection and validation phase*. Obviously, in this phase, testing can play an important role. In fact, on the basis of the specifications for the searched component, testers can develop useful (functional and architectural) tests to be executed to evaluate each candidate component.

If the above requirements for the implementation phase can seem obvious, less clear but perhaps most important considerations can be discussed for what concerns the *specification phase*. In the new process, the emphasis of this phase must be on the reusability and interoperability of the elements that will be part of the system. As stated in the introduction, an important instrument toward this target has been identified in the *software architecture* [9]. In fact, using the specification mechanisms developed for the software architecture, the structure of a system is explicitly described in terms of components and connectors. In a CB development environment it is important to establish a direct correspondence between the architectural components and the runtime components. In other words, the components forming the software architecture and the interconnections among them must remain clearly identifiable, even dynamically, during execution. This feature, in fact, affects the quality of the system in terms of *reuse* and *replaceability*, and makes the management of system *evolution* easier. All of these features are clearly major targets in a CB development process.

Finally, we discuss some considerations about the *testing phase*. For this activity, what we need to figure out is a testing methodology that can allow for the effective testing of a component by someone who has not developed it, and within an application context that was completely unknown when the component was developed.

Traditionally, the development of complex systems involves three main testing phases. The basic phase is *unit testing*, and concerns a relatively small executable program; for instance, in object-oriented systems a unit can consist of a class or a group of logically related classes. A second phase is generally referred to as *integration testing*. In this phase a system or subsystem obtained from the integration of several (already tested) units is tested with the purpose of evaluating their mutual interfaces and cooperation. Finally, the phase of *system testing* focuses on the various quality attributes and on the functionalities that characterize the entire system [39]. These three phases are performed along a defined process, keeping the step with the process of system construction.

In CB development, the three traditional testing phases have to be reconsidered and extended (see Fig. 1). The component here naturally becomes the smallest test unit. *Component testing* is performed by the component developer and is aimed at establishing the proper functioning of the component and at detecting early any possible failures. The tests established by the developer can rely not only on complete documentation and knowledge of the component, but also on the availability of the source code, and can thus in general pursue some kind of coverage. However, such testing cannot address the functional correspondence of the component behavior to the specifications of the system in which it will be later assembled. In fact it is not possible for the developer to consider all the environments in which the component could be subsequently inserted.

The phase of integration testing corresponds to the stage we denote by *deployment testing*, however different conceptually the two tasks may be. Performed by the component customer, the purpose of deployment testing is the validation of the implementation of the components that will constitute the final system. In our study we divide this phase in two successive subphases. In the first subphase, the component will be tested as integrated in an environ-

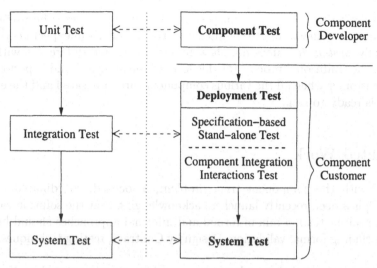

Fig. 1. Adapting the test process to CB development.

ment constituted of stubs that roughly implement the components as foreseen by the specifications. This way, we check if the component correctly interacts with the "ideal" environment foreseen. In order to do this we need a driver that executes the test cases by directly invoking the services provided by the component. In the second subphase, we verify the integration between several chosen components. In order to do this we need means to monitor the interactions among the actual implementations of the architectural components during the execution of some test cases. In this manner we can check whether some wrong interactions among the components occur. Particularly useful to this purpose can be the definition of a "contract" [275] between the provider and the client of a service, as we will better explain shortly. It is worth noting that potential mismatches discovered by the customer during deployment testing are not in general "bugs" in the implementation. Rather, they highlight the non-conformance of the expected component with the tested one (and hence the need to look for other components).

Also, for deployment testing (as for integration testing), we can consider adopting an incremental strategy, allowing for the progressive integration of components into larger subsystems. In the presentation of CDT, we speak for clarity in terms of a single component; however, the framework could be identically applied to the deployment testing of a subsystem, with the introduction of specific mechanisms allowing for the monitoring of the interactions among its components (we return to this in Sect. 6).

A particular case of deployment testing is when a real component comes equipped with the developer's test suite, and the customer re-executes those tests in his or her environment. These tests guarantee that the "intentions" of the developer are met in the final environment and their execution generally leads to a more comprehensive evaluation. They can include test cases not relevant to the customer's purposes, but that can however be useful for evaluating the behavior of the component with customer's unexpected entries.

Finally, *system test* does not show major conceptual differences with respect to the traditional process (at this level of the analysis) and is performed by the customer when all the various components are integrated and the entire system is ready to run.

3 Related Work

To deal with the component trust problem, a focused, coordinated initiative [279] has been recently launched, acknowledging that the solution cannot be universal; instead, a mix of formal and informal approaches should be applied, including formal validation, Design by Contract, testing techniques, and others.

In this section we give a glance to several proposed approaches, in some manner related to testing from the component user's view. The approaches cannot be considered alternatives; rather, the combined use of more than one of them can certainly give better results than selecting only one. Obviously, the list is not exhaustive, but reflects our comprehension and our best knowledge of the literature.

Built-in testing approach

The idea behind the "Built-in testing" (BIT) approach is that the component developer can increase the trust of the component user by augmenting the provided component with executable test cases. Running the provided test cases, the component user can validate, in the final environment, the hypotheses made by the component developer. To provide test cases with the component, the basic technique [416] is to distinguish between two different "modes" of component execution: the *normal mode* and the *maintenance mode*. In the maintenance mode the component user can invoke particular methods, enclosed with each class constituting the component, that have been added to codify dedicated test cases. Being part of the class, these methods can access every private variable and invoke every method. So the mechanism provides the component user with a powerful means of evaluation, without requiring the component customer to use any specific framework or tool for testing purposes.

The proposed approach suffers of some drawbacks though. The first, and technical, is that the memory required at runtime to instantiate the objects from a class can become huge and dominated mainly by the need for space to allocate the testing methods; these, obviously, are completely useless in normal mode. The second, and more conceptual, concerns the meaningfulness to the component user of the developer's defined test cases. As advocated by different authors [420], it is in fact important that the customer develop his or her own test suites so to ascertain that a candidate component be "compliant" with the requirements for the searched component.

Further details on the BIT approach can be found in the chapters 'COTS Component Testing through Built-In Test' and 'Modeling and Implementation of Built-In Contract Tests'.

Testable architecture approach

This approach can be seen as a special case of the approach previously described, and in fact shares the same aims. However, being different from built-in testing, this approach prevents the problem concerning the huge amount of memory required at runtime. The idea is to develop a specific testable architecture that allows the component user to re-execute the test cases provided by the developer, without the need for enclosing them in the component itself.

In [136], Gao et al. require that each component implement a particular interface for testing purposes. This interface has the goal of augmenting the testability of the component. In this manner the developer can then provide the component user with test cases coded for clients that use the testing interface. By foreseeing the presence in the test-oriented interface of methods that use the introspection mechanisms, which are generally provided by component standard models, the power of the built-in testing approach can be obtained in terms of access to methods and variables not otherwise visible to clients.

Another interesting approach, also relying on the definition of a particular framework for component testing, has been proposed by Atkinson and Groß [13]. Being different from the previous approach, it does not use the introspection mechanisms provided by the various component models. As a consequence, the framework cannot attain the same power of the built-in testing approach. However, this approach is not intended for the execution of generic test cases, but focuses on providing the customer with specific test cases derived from contract specifications. To check the validity of a contract, the authors suppose that a component developer implements specific methods for state introspection. In particular, these states are defined at a logical level using a component model based on KobrA [56], a modeling tool developed in the area of Product Line Design.

Certification strategy approach

The approaches belonging to this class are based on the general observation that the customer of a component is generally suspicious about the information and proof of quality provided by the component developer. Hence, to increase the trust of a customer on a component, some authors have proposed different forms of "component certification." A first approach proposes the constitution of independent agencies (or Software Certification Laboratories [405]) for software component evaluation. The main duty of such an agency should be the derivation and verification of the qualities of a component. To this end the agency should extensively test (from both functional and performance points of view) the components and then publish the results of the executed tests and the environments used. However, the inherent difficulties in establishing these agencies suggested that, as an alternative, warranties be derived as the result of extensive operational usage, following some notable open source examples (e.g., Linux). By coordinating the users of a particular software, a "user-based software certification" could be established [408].

A different approach to certification has been proposed by Morris et al. [54] [293], starting from the remark that using the services of a certification agency could be particularly expensive for a small software company. To overcome this problem, a developer's software certification approach is proposed. This approach relies on the specification and release, to the component customer, of test cases written in an XML format. This format should guarantee a better understanding, on the component customer's side, of the test cases that have been executed by the developer on the component. According to the authors, on the one hand this should increase the trust of the customer on the component behavior; on the other hand, by using suitable tools, it should be possible for the customer to (re-)execute the XML test cases in the target environment. In view of this feature, the approach can also be seen as another variant of built-in testing.

Metadata approach

As observed, the scarcity of component documentation is the main source of customer suspicion. The proposal behind the metadata approach [320] is to augment the component with additional information in order to increase the component customer's analysis capability. Obviously, it is important at the same time to develop suitable tools for easing the management and using the metadata provided. Different kinds of information can be provided by the developer, such as a Finite State Machine (FSM) model of the component, pre- and post-conditions for the provided services, regression test suites [321], and so on. Also, the proposal of Stafford and Wolf [375], who foresee the provisioning of pathways expressing the potential of an input to affect a particular output, can be redirected to this approach. Whaley et al. [424] propose to supply models that express acceptable method call sequences. In this manner the customers can evaluate their use of the component and check that illegal calls are not permitted. Finally, an aspect-based approach to classify metadata information, so as to better support test selection, is suggested in chapter 'COTS Component Testing through Aspect-Based Metadata'.

Customer's specification-based testing approach

To different extents, all of the above approaches rest on some cooperation and goodwill from the component developer's side: that some specified procedure is followed in producing the component, or that some required information or property about the component behavior and/or structure is provided. However, we cannot assume that this is generally the case, and often components are delivered supplemented with little information. At this point, the only means in the hands of the customer to increase his or her trust on the component behavior is the execution of test cases that he or she has defined on the basis of the specifications for the component. This is the approach we follow here. The use of test cases developed on the basis of the component user's specification and in the target environment is useful in any case, but especially when only black-box test techniques can be used. The application of this kind of approach requires, however, the development of suitable tools and methodologies for test case reuse and derivation. It is also of primary importance to develop new means for the derivation of relevant test cases from the specifications.

In our work, we consciously make the least restricting assumptions on how the component is developed or packaged, taking a hint from the observation that in practice COTS components may be delivered with scarce, if any, useful information for testing purposes. Starting from this assumption, we developed our framework for facilitating the execution of test cases derived from the customer architectural specifications.

4 Overview of the CDT Framework

The CDT framework [33] has been designed to suit the needs of component deployment testing, as discussed in Sect. 2. In particular, we have focused on developing suitable means for facilitating **customer's specification-based testing**, as outlined above. Our objective is to develop an integrated framework within which the component user can evaluate a component by testing it against its expected behavior within the assembled system. The main features of such a framework should include:

- the possibility of the **early definition of the test cases** by the component user, based on the expected component behavior within the target system;
- an **easy reuse of the defined test cases**, in order to evaluate a set of candidate components;
- the **easy configuration/reconfiguration of the assembled system**, in order to execute the test cases;
- the **easy extensibility of the testing framework**, in order to add new features and functionality for testing control purposes;
- the **reduction of the number of test cases** to be re-executed when a component is substituted.

In our approach we distinguish among "virtual," "concrete," and "real" components. The first represents an ideal component conforming to the architectural definition. A concrete component is instead a candidate implementation of this virtual component, which has to be validated through testing. Finally, a real component is a component as it can be obtained from the market or retrieved from the in-house repositories. While concrete and real components may coincide, we are more likely to implement a concrete component by combining more than one real components.

We assume that the component user has identified some requirements for a component derived, for instance, from the system architectural specifications. On the basis of such requirements, he or she designs a reference component model that we call the "virtual component." The framework allows for the codification of the virtual component interface in a particular class that will be used as the target of testing (we will expand on this in Sect. 6).

The framework subsumes a component user's development process, according to the considerations expressed in Sect. 2. We intervene at the stage in which the component user is searching for a candidate concrete component matching the virtual component's requirements. The process can be roughly summarized in the following steps:

1. definition of the system architecture, with identification of the components and of the associated provided and required interfaces;
2. coding of the interfaces, as identified in the previous step, into precise interface specifications implemented by the virtual component (these specifications will be successively used as a sort of wrapper for the candidate concrete component);
3. definition of the test cases, starting from the architectural description, to test the defined virtual component;
4. identification of one or more candidate concrete components that could match the virtual component;
5. evaluation of each candidate component on the defined test cases, possibly using stubs if not all services required by them are already implemented.

A main feature of the CDT framework is the decoupling of the specification of the test cases and the actual implementation details of a component candidate for assembly. In other words, our framework allows a component user to start designing the executable test cases before any specific component implementation is available.

We illustrate this feature in Fig. 2. As shown on the left hand side, following a conventional test strategy, the design of a test case can start only after a concrete component has been identified. Moreover, different test designs may be necessary for each concrete component. Using CDT instead, the process is simplified, as shown on the right hand side. In fact, CDT makes it possible to perform test design in advance, based on the virtual component specification. Later on, when one or more candidate (concrete) components are identified, they can be tested by using the framework, without need to revise the test

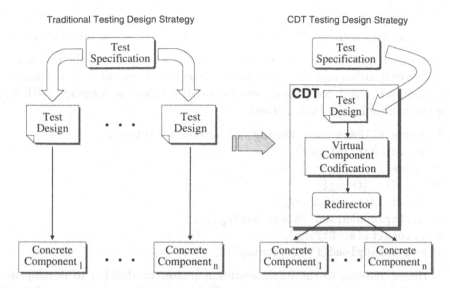

Fig. 2. CDT usage scheme.

design. It is the framework that, when switching from a concrete component to another, performs the redirection of the invocations (that a test case always makes to the virtual component) toward different candidate components. In this manner, a clear saving of coding effort can be obtained.

5 A Case Study

In this section we present a case study that will be used subsequently to illustrate the features of the CDT and how it can be employed during development. It is a proof-of-concept system that has been developed to validate our ideas and to conduct a first experimentation.

Our idea was to develop a CB FTP service system allowing for multiple session clients, i.e., clients that can maintain several FTP sessions open at the same time and transfer files to and from the various servers with which a connection is established. A simple client/server system for FTP service was already available in our laboratory, previously developed as the result of an undergraduate exam project. However, we were completely unaware of the structure of this piece of code. We decided to make an attempt to reuse the real components from this existing system, and to employ the CDT for evaluation.

We started from the specification phase, inspired at large by the process followed in [64]; we identified in the system to develop two main components:

1. a **session manager component**, i.e., a component capable of maintaining a reference to all open connections,

2. an **FTP client component**, i.e., a component capable of establishing a connection with an FTP server and transferring files via this connection.

For both components, we then defined an interface according to their architectural specifications and the interactions foreseen between them. In particular, for the FTP client component, we defined the following interface, with an intuitive meaning for each method:

1. `connect(IPAddress: String, clientPort: Integer, serverPort:Integer)`,
2. `close()`,
3. `list(): String[]`,
4. `download(file:String)`,
5. `multipleDownload(files: String[])`,
6. `upload(file: String)`,
7. `multipleUpload(files:String[])`

Hence, passing to the implementation phase, we decided to develop in-house the session manager component. This was, in fact, a rather specialized component. Instead, we decided to reuse the FTP client already available to realize the virtual FTP client component. Therefore, we started to analyze the services provided by the real component (the one already existing). To adhere to our hypothetical process allowing for the reuse of black-box components, even though we could have had access to the source code, we tried to understand the services that were effectively provided by analyzing only the associated documentation in Javadoc format. The real FTP component implemented the following interface:

1. `open(IP: String, portaC:int, portaS: int)`,
2. `exit()`,
3. `list(): String[]`,
4. `put(file:String)`,
5. `get(file:String):String`

Several differences between the interfaces of the actual and the virtual component can be noticed. From the syntactic point of view, no two methods (except for `list()`) in the two interfaces had the same signature, and the differences were at various levels. On a first examination there were some methods that presumably were performing the same service and differed only in the method's name. A little more difficult were those cases in which the difference concerned the parameter types. Finally, the biggest problem was the absence of methods in the real FTP component allowing for the multiple download/upload services foreseen in the definition of the virtual component. In the following section, we illustrate how using the CDT framework we were able to overcome these differences and how we defined and used some test cases to validate the implementation.

We notice that CDT is meant for use during development in order to evaluate selected candidate components for reuse within a specified architecture.

Once, and if, the CDT testing is successful, adequate coding (e.g., wrapping) might be necessary to allow for the effective deployment of the tested component within the system assembly.

6 Using CDT

In this section we illustrate how a system developer, who intends to build a complex system by assembling externally produced components, can use the CDT framework for evaluating any retrieved component. To use the framework, the component user must essentially develop for each component three main artifacts, as introduced by the following list:

1. The **Spy classes**, which constitute the fully conforming codification, in some programming language, of the services provided by the "virtual component."
2. The **test cases**, which must be developed to validate a possible implementation of a virtual component. They refer to the virtual component interface referred to in the previous point.
3. The **XMLAdapter**, a file in which the user must establish some rules expressing how a virtual service is provided at runtime by a concrete component.

In the rest of this section we provide more details of how and when these artifacts can be built, with reference to the case study presented.

As already noted, such artifacts are not conceived to be used during normal operational usage due to the high performance overhead caused by reliance on introspection mechanisms. However, they can be usefully employed for the development of application prototypes as cooperative glue code.

"Virtual Components" and Spy classes

The Spy classes play a key role in facilitating the decoupling between the virtual components and the real components. In short, we foresee that once an architectural component is specified, sufficient information is available to codify a plausible interface (as that illustrated, for instance, in the case study section). Using this interface as a reference, the component user can thus implement a "virtual component" that has the same interface and can be invoked by the test cases. This "virtual component" is implemented in a Spy class. The implementation of the methods of Spy has not to be very elaborate; in fact, the methods act only as a form of delegation toward the CDT "Driver" component instance (this component will be presented in Sect. 7). Considering the case study of the previous section, we can codify the required component interface as shown in Fig. 3.

Therefore, the Spy represents an interface of the services necessary to launch the test cases. But, as presently illustrated, the association between

```
1 InformationSwap {
2
3   public void connect(String IPAddr, Integer cPort, Integer sPort) {
4     Object[] parameters = new Object[] {IPAddr,cPort,sPort};
5     Object ris = driver.executeMethod("connect", parameters);
6   }
7
8   /* All the other methods foreseen in this inteface are not shown
9    * since they share a similar structure with the connect method
10   */
11
12 }
```

Figure 3. Extract of the virtual component codification for the *FTP client compo-nent.*

the services provided by the Spy and a real implementation will be established only at runtime.

We also introduced, at this level, mechanisms for the specification, and for the runtime checking, of contracts. The approach to the specification of pro-vided services using contracts has emerged first in the area of object-oriented programming [275]. However, with the advent of the CB paradigm the em-phasis on this approach has grown: in fact, contracts have been recognized as a valuable means to transfer information concerning the service behavior between the component developer and component user.

Considering the potential of this approach, we decided that the system architect could specify contracts for the services of the virtual components as an additional means of validating the choice of a concrete component. To do this, the component user should annotate the Spy with the definition of the expected behavior of the component in the form of a contract. The syntax to specify the contract depends from the specific components (as explained in the next section). Basically, contracts can be enclosed in the codification of the Spy, and they will be checked at run time for each invocation of the Spy methods.

Developing the test cases

After the Spy has been implemented, the testing teams can develop the de-ployment test cases taking as a reference the "virtual component" codification. Each test case is coded as a method that belongs to a class, which in turn is part of a suite, according to the JUnit [1] conventions. The latter is a well known open source test tool developed and used inside the eXtreme Program-ming (XP) community. The goal of JUnit is to provide the developers with a means for the easy codification and execution of the test cases concurrently with development, following the motto "*code a little, test a little, code a little, test a little. . . .*" JUnit sets some conventions for the naming and organization of the test cases. Two main reasons convinced us to follow the same syntac-tic conventions (with some minor exceptions) established by JUnit. The first

```
1 public void testNoOverwrite() {
2   java.io.File file = new java.io.File(serverDirectory + forDownload);
3   ((SpyFTPClient)spy).download(serverDirectory + forDownload);
4   long lastModified_1 = file.lastModified();
5
6   ((SpyFTPClient)spy).download(serverDirectory + forDownload);
7   long lastModified_2 = file.lastModified();
8
9   assertTrue(lastModified_1 == last_Modified_2);
10 }
```

Figure 4. A possible test-case codification.

reason is the reduction in by learning effort required to the testers (already knowledgeable with JUnit) using the CDT framework. The second reason, is related to the reduction in the effort of developing our framework, as we can directly integrate part of JUnit in it. Moreover, by reusing JUnit we have provided CDT with the capability of organizing the test cases in "*target equivalence classes.*" Thanks to this feature, when we need to modify a virtual component by substituting some internal parts, we can reduce the number of test cases that on average must be re-executed. Obviously, it is necessary to apply regression test selection mechanisms to identify the test cases necessary to re-execute.

Thanks to the reuse of JUnit, it is easy to add a new test case to a test suite. This is obviously an important factor since new test cases can always be derived as development proceeds. At the end of the test cases elicitation stage, the test cases are packed in a JAR file containing the corresponding Spy. Then, to add a new test class, it is sufficient to identify the JAR file containing the specific suite.

With reference to the FTP case study, we report in Fig. 4 an example of a test case that checks the behavior of the component for the overriding of a file (i.e., a file with the same name as that just downloaded is found in the directory).

We are also introducing mechanisms for tracing the execution of the test cases [32]. We foresee the use wrappers for the real components to intercept all the invocations. For each invocation, the wrapper records all parameters and return values, to reuse them when the component will be modified and/or substituted.

Drawing up the XMLAdapter

As stated, a Spy is not a real component and its purpose is only to codify the desired functionality for a component so as to permit the early establishment of test cases. In parallel, on the basis of the same specifications, a searching team can start searching the internal repository or the market for components that match the virtual components. We think it reasonable to focus at this stage only on the behavioral aspects of the specification. In other words, we search for components that (seem to) provide the desired functionality, neglecting in this search possible syntactic differences. As a result, several differences at various levels can exist between the virtual component (codified in a Spy) and the candidate instances of it found.

Now we clarify which the second artifact is that the system developer needs to build for using CDT: the XMLAdapter serves the purpose of specifying the correspondence among real and virtual components to overcome the possible differences among them, so as to permit the execution of the specified test cases. To establish this correspondence, a customer can rely on his or her intuition of what the methods of the candidate components likely do. This intuition can be based on the signatures of the methods, and on any additional documentation accompanying the components, such as the Javadoc description of each method. Obviously, this process (which is always the most delicate part of a CB development) is subject to misinterpretation (especially if the components are not adequately documented), and a candidate component could actually behave differently from what is expected. However, deployment test execution should highlight such misunderstandings.

An ad hoc XMLAdapter must be drawn up every time a possible implementation for the virtual component has been identified. We defined a Document Type Definition (DTD) scheme that specifies the legal building box of the XMLAdapter. The information that must be specified in this file can be classified into two categories that are reflected also in the structure of the file. In the first part, the component user must specify which are the candidate real components that we intend to test. In the current implementation it is possible to specify the real components using the name of a package that contains the component. Alternatively, it is also possible to specify a name registered in a naming service registry. In the same part, the user must also specify which are the test cases to be executed on the candidate implementation. They are identified simply by specifying the name of the package and of the class containing them. The necessary test cases will be retrieved from one of the JAR files created by the testing teams by packaging the test cases and the corresponding Spy. The second part of the XMLAdapter contains information that specifies, for each method in the virtual component codification, how it can be implemented by the methods in the real candidate components. In other words, this part allows for the adaptation of the virtual interface to the real service provided. In particular, we have analyzed the following levels of possible differences between these two types of components:

1. differences in the method names and signatures:
   a. the methods have different names;
   b. the methods have the same number and types of parameters, but they are declared in different order;
   c. the parameters have different types, but can be made compatible through suitable transformations. It may be also necessary to set some default parameters;

```
 1<?xml version="1.0" ?>
 2<!DOCTYPE Matahari>
 3<matahari>
 4  <test_package name="it.cnr.isti.test.components" />
 5  <test_class name="ClientFTPTest" />
 6  <real_package name="it.cnr.isti.component.clientFTP" />
 7  <create_object class="REAL_PACKAGE.Client" object_name="client" />
 8  <virtual_method name="connect" parameters="serverName_portaClient_portaServer">
 9    <exec_method object="portaClient" name="intValue" put_result_in="clientP" />
10    <exec_method object="portaServer" name="intValue" put_result_in="serverP" />
11    <exec_method object="client" name="open">
12      <parameter value="serverName" />
13      <parameter type="int" value="clientP" />
14      <parameter type="int" value="serverP" />
15    </exec_method>
16  </virtual_method>
17  <virtual_method name="close">
18    <exec_method object="client" name="exit" />
19  </virtual_method>
20  <virtual_method name="download" parameters="file">
21    <exec_method object="client" name="get">
22      <parameter value="file" />
23    </exec_method>
24  </virtual_method>
25  <virtual_method name="upload" parameters="file">
26    <exec_method object="client" name="put">
27      <parameter value="file" />
28    </exec_method>
29  </virtual_method>
30  <virtual_method name="multipleDownload" parameters="files">
31    <recover_field object="files" field="length" put_value_in="length" />
32    <for counter="i" from="0" to="length-1">
33      <exec_method object="client" name="get">
34        <parameter value="files[i]" />
35      </exec_method>
36    </for>
37  </virtual_method>
38  <virtual_method name="multipleUpload" parameters="files">
39    <recover_field object="files" field="length" put_value_in="length" />
40    <for counter="i" from="0" to="length-1">
41      <exec_method object="client" name="put">
42        <parameter value="files[i]" />
43      </exec_method>
44    </for>
45  </virtual_method>
46  <virtual_method name="list">
47    <exec_method object="client" name="list" put_result_in="output" />
48  </virtual_method>
49</matahari>
```

Figure 5. Example of XMLAdapter related to the case study.

2. one method in the Spy class corresponds to the execution of more than one method in the real implementation of the component.

Obviously the instances listed above are not mutually exclusive; for instance, it is possible to have different method names with different signatures. It may be worth noting that the case symmetric to type 2 (more methods in the Spy correspond to one method in the real implementation) is not generally relevant. In fact, the Spy is kept simple and typically contains a minimal number of necessary methods. If, say, two methods in the Spy correspond to one method in the real implementation, then either the real implementation is not compatible, or we do not need to invoke the two methods alone, but always together and in the same sequence. If so, then it would be more intuitive to indicate only one method in the specification of the Spy. We imagine that the differences between a virtual component and a candidate implementation are generally not so big. We think, in fact, that large differences in the interfaces can hardly lead to the eventual adoption of the candidate component. Nevertheless, even though it is in principle possible to have a one-to-many correspondence in the implementation of a virtual component, we think that, in a well established development process, an architecture developed by experts should generally lead to a one-to-one correspondence between virtual and real candidate components.

As a final consideration, the drawing up of the XMLAdapter is certainly not an easy task. However, this task can be partially automated and alleviated with the implementation of suitable tools and graphic interfaces.

In Fig. 5 we report an excerpt of the XMLAdapter for the case study illustrated in the previous section. In this file we record all the information that permits an instance of the "Driver" component (see next section) to create the environment for the test phase. In particular, we solve all the differences between the two interfaces in this file.

An interesting result we discovered, executing the test case in Fig. 4, was that the component overwrote any file with the same name as the file that was currently downloaded. Since we required a more careful behavior, we needed to implement a "patch" to this component.

The graphical user interface

To make easier the use of the framework, we are planning the development of a graphical user-friendly interface for the CDT framework. Currently, the interface developed can interact with the user only to start the test phase. We are studying possible extensions for the semiautomatic drawing up of the XMLAdapter when the candidate implementation of a component has been identified. We briefly describe the features of the current implementation of the CDT interface as shown in Fig. 6.

Since the interface provides, at this time, functionalities only for the test execution phase, it assumes that the previous steps, such as the Spy codification, test case specification, and XMLAdapter drawing up, have already been performed. Then, as first step, the user must choose an XMLAdapter relative to the virtual component that the user intends to test, and the test cases to execute. The user can then choose the run test option (the two check boxes in the upper part of the interface in Fig. 6 provide this choice). A first possible use case is to run the application only in order to instrument a Spy definition with contract specifications. In such a case the framework will retrieve the JAR file containing the test cases and the virtual component codification and

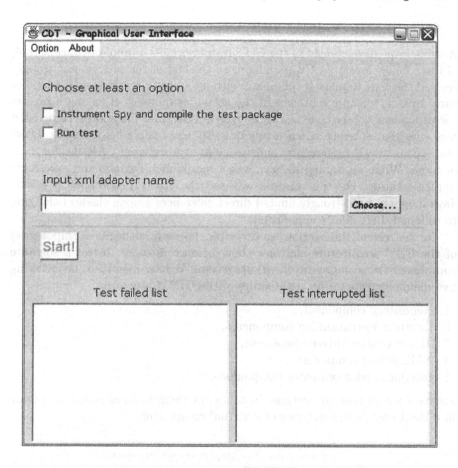

Fig. 6. The CDT framework interface.

create another JAR file that contains the same test cases and an instrumented version of the Spy. A second possible use case is to execute a testing session. In this case, the application will "create" the system architecture instantiating the real components specified in the XMLAdapter, and then the test cases specified will be retrieved and executed. It is also possible to execute the two tasks in a sequence.

In the lower part of the interface, the user, when the test phase execution mode has been chosen, can identify the test cases that, for some reason, did not finish correctly. In particular, we distinguish between the two different cases of "failed test" (the result obtained does not match with the expected one) and "interrupted test" (as a consequence of the raising of an exception). The test cases interrupted because of the violation of a contract belong to the second set.

7 Framework Architecture

Although the development of the CDT framework, as a proof-of-concept tool, did not follow a priori a CB paradigm, at the end of the process we strongly revised the code to make it compliant with an a posteriori developed architecture. In fact, we were conscious of the actual advantages of having a precise correspondence of the code to a high-level architecture. Therefore, the revision was aimed at isolating as much functionality as possible belonging to different architectural components, and we created a different JAR file for each of them. What we wanted to have was a modifiable, flexible, and extensible implementation. For this purpose we used the `interface` construct of the Java language and strongly limited direct references among classes belonging to different JAR files (components).

In the rest of this section we describe the main elements (components) of the CDT architecture and how they interact in order to test a software component, or a component-based subsystem. We have identified the following five main elements in the architecture of the CDT framework:

1. Repository component,
2. Contract instrumenting components,
3. Test execution driver component,
4. XML parser component,
5. Interface and coordinator components.

Figure 7 shows how, at runtime, instances of these main elements cooperate in order to test a real instance of a virtual component.

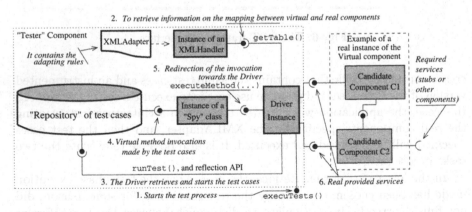

Fig. 7. The Structure of the CDT framework.

Repository component

We have seen in the previous section how a generic user must codify, following the JUnit test "template," the test cases that will be successively used to test a real implementation of a virtual component. Correspondingly, we need to foresee in the system architecture a repository component that should provide suitable services for the storage of a specified test suite, and suitable services for the retrieving of one of them when its name is specified. In our implementation we have chosen to pack a test suite and its corresponding Spy class in a JAR file. At this point we can identify the test suite by the name of this file. Therefore, in the current implementation, the component providing the repository service is abstracted by the Java API for file management, and it is actually implemented by the file system running on the machine. The services provided by the file system are used by two other components:

1. the component that can be used to instrument the Spy class with contract definition,
2. the component that needs to retrieve a test suite to start a test phase

Contract instrumenting component

As seen, we allow testers to insert contract specifications in the definition of the methods of a Spy. Obviously, in the case of the virtual component definition, the specification of a contract can only contain references to the methods foreseen in the definition of the Spy. No access to a feature of a real implementation of the component, such as a field, can be had. We chose to integrate an externally developed component for the management of contracts, and all technical details concerning contract definition (e.g., source instrumentation using a special tag in Javadoc comments) reflect the requirements of the integrated component. There are several options introducing contract checking in the Java language, and we chose to integrate **iContract** [235], a free (not open source) component that can be downloaded from the Internet.

iContract works as a preprocessor and generates, from an instrumented Java source file, a source and a class file in which each method starts and finishes with contract checking invocations. The tags that must be used to define a contract are "@invariant," "@post," and "@pre," be followed by strings conforming to the format

<ContractExpression>[#ExceptionClassName]

in which <ContractExpression> is a boolean expression that represents the contract, and [#ExceptionClassName] is the name of an exception that must be raised if the boolean expression is evaluated to *false* (if no exception is declared, a RuntimeException is launched). A contract can be defined using any legal boolean expression following the Java syntax. Moreover iContract provides the following operators that can be used to define more complex contract expressions:

1. **forall**: this operator permits us to specify a rule that must be true for all the elements in a set,
2. **exists**: this operator is evaluated to true if the expression following it is true on at least one element in a set,

3. **implies**: an expression of the form "I implies C" means "if I then check C;" then, if the expression I is true, C must also be evaluated.

The *contract instrumenting component* interacts with the *Repository component* in order to retrieve Spy classes that must be instrumented, and to store the instrumented version of the retrieved virtual component definition.

Test execution driver component

This constitutes the core of the approach. The main duties of this component are the correct setting of the test environment and the redirection of the invocations made on the virtual component to a real implementation of it. To set up the test environment, the component asks the *XML parser component* for information concerning the correspondence among the virtual component and the real components. The real components can be provided as packages and classes that must then be instantiated by a specified constructor, or simply by names registered in the registry used by a naming service.

Two different services are provided on an instance of this component:

1. `execuTests()`: the invocation of this method starts the deployment test. Hence, as the first thing, the Driver retrieves the information reported in the "XMLAdapter" via an instance of the XML parser component, and acts as described above. At this point it needs to retrieve the test cases to be executed. Hence, the Driver, using the service provided by the repository component, retrieves the JAR file containing the test cases corresponding to the virtual component under test. The tests to execute can also be a subset of the tests contained in the package, and the choice is made following the JUnit rules. After having identified the tests and the Spy, the Driver instance sets itself as the target for the invocations of the retrieved Spy class. At this point the test phase can be started with the execution of the first test case.
2. `executeMethod (String name Object[] par)`: this service is invoked by the instance of the Spy class that has been created by the invocation to the method described above. The aim of this invocation is "to inform" the Driver instance of the method invoked by the test case. On the basis of this information, and of the data retrieved from the "XMLAdapter," the Driver can determine the corresponding method (or methods) to invoke in the real implementation of the component.

From the description it is clear that this component is at the center of the system architecture, from where it interacts with the *repository component* to retrieve the test cases and with the *XML parser component* to retrieve information concerning the set up of the system under test. At the same time, the Driver is started by an instance of the *interface and coordinator component*.

XML parser component

This component provides a parser to handle the XML file that we defined to define the information concerning the "test plan." Its services are accessed by the *Driver component* in order to retrieve information for setting up the test environment.

Interface and coordinator components

This component implements the functionality for interaction with the user. We have already described the elements of the interface that can be used by the user to instrument a Spy class or to execute a test session. After that information has been inserted in the graphical interface, this component creates an instance of the Driver component and starts the execution of the test phase.

8 Conclusions and Future Work

In this chapter we presented a framework for the easy and efficient execution of test cases in a component-based environment. The framework is meant to give a partial answer to the need for new techniques for test derivation and execution, since the traditional ones have been recognized as being inadequate. In particular, the main objective of the framework is to provide a simple mechanism for the execution of test cases derived by the component user on the basis of the system architecture specification and to validate the choice of possible candidate components. We verified our ideas on a simple case study that has been used in this chapter to present how a generic component user can take advantage of the framework. In the future we will further investigate the advantages that the use of the framework can bring, and develop add-on tools to aid the user of the framework. In summary, the main advantages that we have seen in using the framework include:

- Decoupling of test specification and test design from the component implementations;
- No ad hoc requirements imposed on the candidate components for testing purposes;
- Easy reuse of test cases;
- Test suite flexibility (it is easier to add new test cases);
- Simple mechanisms to group test cases for regression testing purposes.

Currently we are also focusing on the definition of new methodologies for the derivation of test cases. In particular, we conducted a first investigation on the use of test cases, derived from a system architectural description, for functional component validation [29]. We are also planning an integration of the framework with new methodologies for non-functional analysis, in particular with reference to performance analysis [30].

Acknowledgments

Andrea Polini's PhD grant is supported by Ericsson Lab Italy in the framework of the Pisatel initiative.

We thank Matteo Barontini for his contribution to the implementation of the CDT framework, and Daniele Polini for having provided the case study.

Modeling and Implementation of Built-In Contract Tests

Hans-Gerhard Gross[1], Ina Schieferdecker[2], and George Din[2]

[1] Fraunhofer IESE
   Kaiserslautern, Germany
   grossh@iese.fhg.de
[2] Fraunhofer FOKUS
   Berlin, Germany
   {schieferdecker|din}@fokus.fhg.de

Summary. Built-in contract testing is based on the idea of building tests directly into components, so that each component can assess whether it will be integrated into a suitable environment, and the environment can assess whether a newly integrated component will be acceptable.

Component technologies such as CCM, .NET, or EJB are more and more being supported by model-based approaches like the OMG's Model Driven Architecture (MDA). The idea is to gain considerable momentum in the development of component-based architectures through high-level modeling and automatic code generation. However, the emphasis with these approaches is currently more on system design and development and not as much on system validation and testing, so the expected reductions in component-based development in terms of time and effort can only be realized in component and application construction and not during test development. Lengthy and costly in-situ verification and acceptance testing, that is mainly still performed manually, undermines the benefits of these modern development approaches.

This chapter demonstrates how built-in contract testing can be integrated with and made to supplement automatic approaches to derive application testing from system models, represent them on the model level, and generate executable tests from these models. This model-based testing approach increases the degree of automation in generating and realizing built-in contract tests; therefore, it also increases the quality of the built-in tests and reduces the resources required for developing them.

1 Introduction

The vision of modern recursive model-driven development approaches is for applications to be specified and designed at high levels of abstraction through graphical representations, for available components to be identified and assembled on this abstract level, and for the missing links or the adaptors between the components to be easily derived from the models, to a large extent through automatic code generation [57]. This allows software vendors to avoid the overheads of traditional development methods by assembling new applications from high quality, prefabricated, reusable parts that are specified and realized with models and to integrate them easily, almost in a plug-and-play fashion. Although there has been considerable recent effort to put this vision into reality, it has been almost exclusively dedicated to the model-based design and implementation of the functional software rather than the testing. If test software development and testing will not be supported in the same way as is the case with functional software, we will in fact create a gap in the overall development life cycle, since functional development will be readily supported largely by sophisticated automatic tools but testing will not be. In other words, applications that are becoming increasingly more complex will be developed with increasing speed, but their assessment and validation will continue to be performed traditionally, and will actually slow down the momentum gained in the first stage. This will drastically increase the validation effort of a typical project instead of decreasing it, or developers will simply reduce the overall testing activity. In our opinion, both scenarios are unacceptable.

Built-in contract testing [155–157] is a step in the right direction to integrate the efforts for functional and test development. The philosophy of the technology is parallel modeling and implementation of the functional software together with the test software, and the derivation of the test models from the functional models. Since the test software is built directly into the functional software, it merely represents an additional development effort that is performed almost in exactly the same way as any other software development for a system's original functionality (rather than its testing).

With the principles of built-in contract testing, we already have a powerful means for modeling and implementing test software in tandem with the functional software. However, testing is based on a number of very specific concepts that are not typically needed for a system's normal functionality. For model-based test development, we can now apply the recently released UML testing profile [315] that is put forward by the Object Management Group (OMG) and represents a very distinct extension to the core UML. Additionally, for implementation and execution of the test software, we can resort to the Testing and Test Control Notation (TTCN-3) [114–116] that is traditionally used in the telecommunication domain, although it is also suitable for any software domain. This realizes a generic way of specifying the test software and transforming it into a concrete implementation automatically.

This chapter presents an introduction to each of the technologies, and illustrates how they can supplement each other and be integrated into an overall model-based test development process for component-oriented applications. We believe the integration of these technologies represents a simple yet powerful way of realizing test design and development in the spirit of the MDA. In addition to the introduction of the technologies, we show how such a model-driven test development process may be applied to a subcomponent of a large communication platform.

2 Built-In Contract Testing

The correct functioning of a system of components at runtime is contingent on the correct interaction of individual pairs of components according to the client/server model. Component-based development can be viewed as an extension of the object paradigm, in which the set of rules governing the interaction of a pair of objects (and, thus, components) is typically referred to as a contract [277]. This characterizes the relationship between a component and its clients as a contract, a formal agreement, expressing each party's rights and obligations in the relationship. This means that individual components define their side of the contract as either offering a service (the server in a client/server relationship), or requiring a service (the client in a client/server relationship). Testing the correct functioning of individual client/server interactions against their specified contracts therefore represents a validation that a system of components as a whole will behave correctly.

The ideas and the technology behind built-in contract testing [155–157] have been mainly developed within the European Union funded project Component+ [71], and the technology focuses on verifying these pairwise client/server interactions between two components when an application is assembled and integrated. It is based on the notion of building contract tests into components so that they can validate that the servers into which they are "plugged dynamically", at deployment time, will fulfill their contracts. Consideration of built-in test artifacts begins early in the design phase, as soon as the overall architecture of a system is developed and/or the interfaces of components are modeled. Built-in test artifacts can, and should, be derived from the system model, and they should be developed in an integrated process, together and in parallel with the system design, the system model, and the system implementation.

2.1 Built-In Tester Components and Testing Interfaces

The configuration of a system involves the creation of individual pairwise client/server relations between the components in that system. This is usually done by an outside "third party," which we refer to as the context of the components. It creates the instances of the client and the server, and passes the reference of the server to the client (thereby establishing the client connection between them). In order to fulfill its obligations toward its own clients, a component that acquires a new server must verify the server's semantic compliance to its client contract. This means that the client must check that the server provides the service that the client has been developed to expect. The client is therefore augmented with built-in test software in the form of a tester component. This is called a server tester component, and is executed when the client is configured to use the server. In order to achieve this, the client will pass the server's reference to its own server tester component. If the test fails, the tester component may raise a contract testing exception and point the application programmer to the location of the failure. The client's tester component will be realized according to the specification of the client's required interface.

The object-oriented and, as a consequence, the component-based development paradigms build on the principles of abstract data types, which advocate the combination of data and functionality in a single entity. The compliance of the component's externally visible states and transitions to the expected states and transitions of the specification state model must therefore be checked. These externally visible or logical states are part of a component's contract that a user of the component must know in order to use it properly. However, because these externally visible states of a component are embodied in its internal state attributes, there is a fundamental dilemma. The external test software of a component cannot therefore get or set any internal state information. This means that expected state transitions, as defined in the specification state model, cannot normally be tested properly. The contract testing paradigm is therefore based on the principle that components should expose their logical or externally visible (as opposed to internal) states by extending the normal functional interface of a component through a so-called testing interface. A testing interface provides additional operations that read from and write to internal state attributes that collectively determine the logical states.

2.2 Basic Model of Built-In Contract Testing

The distinction between clients and servers in the previous section is intended only to refer to the roles that can be played in a pairwise interaction between two components. When viewed from a global perspective, individual components can, and usually do, play the role of both client and server. Any of the client/server relationships of components may be subject to contract tests. In the server role, a component provides a testing interface that supports the tests performed by its client's tester components, and in the client role, the component owns tester components that use the testing interfaces of its associated servers. A component that plays both roles (i.e., provides a testing interface to its clients and contains its own tester components to test its servers) is called Built-in Test (or BIT) component [71].

Figure 1 displays the organization of the contract testing architecture (in the shaded box). Each tested component, or each server role, provides a testing interface that extends the original component, and provides testing operations that associated client tester components may use for the testing. The testing interfaces enhance a server's testability. The testing interface comprises typical operations for state information, or assertion checking. The chapter 'COTS

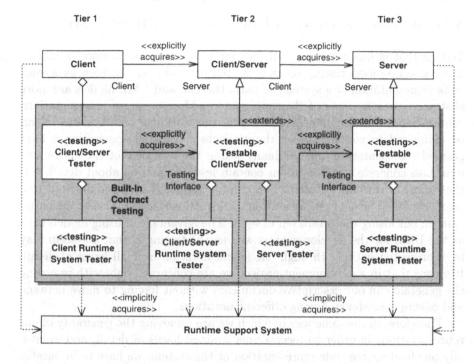

Fig. 1. Basic model of built-in contract testing in a typical 3-tier architecture.

Component Testing through Built-In Test' provides more detailed information on how testing interfaces may be designed and implemented; in this chapter, we focus more on the implementation and automatic generation of a testing architecture that is based on built-in contract testing, and on the design and generic realization of tester components.

Each testing component, or each client role, owns a server tester component that contains test cases. The test cases check the server's semantic compliance to its contract with the client. The tests in the client's tester component are defined according to the specification of the client, and not of the server. They represent the client's expectations of the tested server, and can be derived according to any existing test case generation technique, e.g., traditional coverage criteria and functional testing techniques, or, more specifically, according to model coverage criteria as proposed in [154].

In addition to testing the explicit components in a component framework, built-in contract testing addresses also the testing of the implicit server components that are provided by the underlying component platform, by the runtime system, or by the operating system. These components are implicitly acquired servers because they are available to be used by the explicit component framework of the developed application. Implicit and explicit servers represent the entire import interface of a component.

3 Generation of Built-In Contract Tests from UML

Testing that is based on the UML has many concepts in common with traditional code-based testing techniques. Source code can be seen as a concrete representation of a system, or parts thereof, and UML models are more abstract representations of the same system. More concrete representations contain more detailed information about the workings of a system. It can be compared to zooming in on the artifacts considered, generating a finer grained representation, but gradually losing the overview of the entire system. Less concrete representations contain less information about details but show more of the entire system. This can be compared with zooming out to a coarser grained level of representation, making it easier to overview the entire system, but losing the details out of sight. The advantage of using models such as the UML for the development as well as the testing is that a system may be represented entirely through one single notation over all levels of detail. It means that in a development project we are concerned only with removing the generality in our descriptive documents without having to move between and ensure consistency among different notations.

Therefore, in the same way in which we are removing the generality of our representations in order to receive finer grained levels of detail, and eventually our final source code representation of the system, we have to in parallel remove the generality of the testing artifacts for that system and move progressively towards finer grained levels of testing detail. So, the system models in UML have to be accompanied by test models in UML, and the UML Testing Profile [314, 315] has been defined in order to support the development of the testing models in UML explicitly.

3.1 Black- and White-Box Coverage Criteria and the UML

Coverage is an old and fundamental concept in software testing. Coverage criteria in testing are based on the assumption that only the execution of a faulty piece of code or a faulty specification may exhibit the fault in terms of a malfunction or a deviation from what is expected. If the faulty section is never executed in a test, it is unlikely to be identified through testing, so path coverage testing techniques, for example, are among the oldest software testing and test case generation concepts [418] in software development projects. The idea of coverage has led to quite a number of functional and structural testing techniques over the years that are primarily based upon flow graphs and specification pieces (e.g., function points) [24]. These traditional testing criteria all have in common that they are often based on documents (i.e., flow graphs, source code) very close to the implementation level. Traditionally, these coverage criteria are applied only at the unit level which sees the tested module as a white box for which its implementation is known and available to the tester. On a higher level, in an integration test, the individual modules are only treated as black-boxes for which no internal knowledge is assumed.

An integration test is traditionally performed on the outermost subsystem that incorporates all the individually tested units, so that we assume white-box knowledge of that outermost subcomponent, but not of the integrated individual units. Traditional development separates only between these two levels: white-box test in unit testing, and black-box test in integration testing. Additionally, there may be an acceptance test of the entire system driven by the highest-level requirements.

More modern recursive and component-based development approaches do not advocate this strict separation, since individual units may be regarded as subsystems in their own right, i.e., components for which no internal knowledge is available, or integrating subsystems, i.e., components for which internal knowledge may be readily available. Particularly, in component-based development where we cannot strictly separate units from subsystems, both approaches may be readily applied in parallel, according to whether only black-box information, e.g., external visible functionality and behavior, or, additionally, white-box information, e.g., internal functionality and behavior, are available. Here, we can also apply all the traditional testing criteria, although on different levels of abstraction. The difference is that, at the beginning of a development project, models will provide only part of the information that is required for testing; but, since we are progressively moving our project toward more concrete representations, we will eventually be able to also extract more concrete information for the testing.

3.2 Test Specification with the UML Testing Profile

Since the majority of tests are developed manually as automated test derivation techniques, they still bear several limitations (or they are extended and enhanced manually), their separate specification and realization is advantageous. From this motivation, the Object Management Group has initiated the development of a UML testing profile that is specifically addressing typical testing concepts in model-based development [315]. The UML testing profile is an extension of the UML 2.0 that is also based on the UML meta-model [314]. It defines a modeling language for visualizing, specifying, analyzing, constructing, and documenting the artifacts of a test system that can be developed in parallel with the original functional system. The testing profile particularly supports the specification and modeling of software testing infrastructures. It follows the same fundamental principles of the UML in that it provides concepts for the structural aspects of testing such as the definition of test components, test contexts, and test system interfaces, and the behavioral aspects of testing such as the definition of test procedures, test setup, execution, and evaluation. The core UML may be used to model and describe testing functionality, since test software development can be seen as any other development for functional software properties. However, as software testing is based on a number of special test-related concepts, these concepts are provided by the testing profile as extensions to the UML. The concepts are grouped mainly into test architecture, test behavior, and test data. A test architecture specifies the structural aspects of a test system and includes:

- The System Under Test (SUT), where one or more objects within a test specification can be identified as the SUT.
- Test components, defined as objects within the test system that can communicate with the SUT or other components to realize the test behavior.
- A means for evaluating test results derived by different objects within the test system in order to determine an overall verdict for a test case or a test suite. This evaluation process is called arbitration. Users can either use the default arbitration scheme of the profile (i.e., the classical functional arbitration, where negative results have priority over positive results), or define their own arbitration scheme using an arbitration test component.

Test behaviors specify the actions and evaluations that are necessary to check the test objective, which describes what should be tested. For example, UML interaction, state, and activity diagrams can be used to define test stimuli, observations from the SUT, test control invocations, coordination, and actions.

However, when such behaviors are specified as tests, the primary focus is given to the definition of normal or expected behaviors. The handling of unexpected messages is achieved through the specification of defaults providing the means to define more complete yet abstract test models. This simplifies validation and improves the readability of test models. The separate behavior of defaults is triggered if an event is observed that is not explicitly handled by the main test case behavior. The partitioning between the main test behavior and the default behavior is the designer's responsibility. Within the testing profile, default behaviors are applied to static behavioral structures. For example, defaults can be applied to combined fragments (within interactions), state machines, states, and regions. The testing profile also introduces concepts that are necessary for test behavior specification, such as:

- A test case, which is an operation of a test suite specifying how a set of cooperating test components interact with the SUT to realize a test objective.
- A verdict, which is a predefined enumeration specifying possible test results, e.g., pass, inconclusive, fail, and error.
- A validation action, which can be performed by the local test component to denote that the arbiter is informed of a local test result.
- A log action, which is used to log entries during the execution for further analysis.
- A finish action, which is used to denote the completion of the test case behavior of a component, without terminating the component.

Another important aspect of test specification is the use of wildcards in test data. For example, pattern matching and regular expressions are very useful when specifying behavior for handling unexpected events, or events that contain many different values. The UML testing profile introduces wildcards for dealing with that, and permits the specification of "any value," denoting any value out of a set of possible values, and "any or omitted values," denoting any value or the lack of a value (in the case where multiplicities range from 0 upward). All these concepts provide the capabilities that are required to construct precise test specifications and to develop systems and tests in an integrated way in parallel by using the UML. This also applies to built-in tests, as they require the same concepts, as well as to traditional black-box tests.

4 Implementation and Execution of Built-in Tests

If the built-in tests have been defined in terms of what the UML testing profile is suggesting, their executable versions can be generated with mappings according to existing test execution environments, e.g.,

- JUnit is an open source unit testing framework, which is widely used by developers who implement unit tests in Java. The mapping focuses primarily on the JUnit framework. For instance, when no trivial mapping exists to the JUnit framework, existing JUnit extensions, such as for repeated test case runs or for active test cases, can be used. It is important to note that built-in contract tests are not unit tests of the same tenor. A unit test is defined according to the specification of the tested unit, whereas a contract test is defined according to the specification of the client's usage profile of the tested unit. In other words, a unit test is performed according to the component developer's mind, whereas a contract test is performed according to the component customer's mind.
- TTCN-3 (Testing and Test Control Notation [114]) is a widely accepted standard for test system development in the telecommunication and data communication domains. TTCN-3 is a test specification and implementation language that can be used to define test procedures for black-box testing of distributed systems. Although TTCN-3 was a basis for the development of the testing profile, they differ in some respects; but the UML testing profile specifications can be represented by TTCN-3 modules and executed on TTCN-3 test platforms. TTCN-3 is the chosen platform throughout the rest of this chapter.

Although the testing profile and TTCN-3 are used on different levels of abstraction, with TTCN-3 on a more detailed and concrete test case specification level and the testing profile on a more abstract level, TTCN-3 can also be used on more abstract levels by defining just the principal constituents of a test objective, or of a test case, for example, without giving all the details needed to execute the tests. While this is of great advantage in the test design process, since it hides too much detail we have to add that missing information later on in order to generate executable tests. For example, the expressiveness of UML 2.0 sequence diagrams allows us to describe a whole set of test cases with just one diagram, so test generation methods have to be applied in order to derive these tests from the diagrams. TTCN-3 represents a powerful way to manage and execute built-in contract tests, and it comes with its own tool suite [390]. It is built from a set of basic testing concepts that make it quite universal, and independent of any particular application or domain. A TTCN-3 test specification consists of different parts including type definitions for test data structures, template definitions for concrete test data, function and test case definitions for test behavior, and control definitions for the execution of test cases. The semantics of these concepts is well-defined and the main principles of test execution are defined in the form of TTCN-3's test execution interfaces [115, 116]. All the required parts of a TTCN-3 test specification are derived from the built-in test models in the testing profile, including, e.g., test type and data definitions and the definition of test behavior functions and test cases. A built-in tester component is then implemented through component-specific executable versions of the automatically generated TTCN-3 tests, together with access to a TTCN-3 runtime environment for test execution. This sounds bulky, but it represents a very elegant way of managing the built-in contract tests in an abstract form and instantiating them automatically for any required component platform.

5 A Working Example

This section shows, by means of an example system, how the individual parts in the previously described testing process are put together, and it elaborates the steps that we have to take in order derive executable tests from abstract models that have been developed according to the philosophy of built-in contract testing. The example is a Resource Information Network (RIN) from Fraunhofer IGD in Darmstadt, Germany [193, 357], one part of a larger communication system that supports working floor maintenance staff in their everyday working tasks. The large communication system hosts multiple communication devices that are interconnected through a radio network and controlled and supported by a number of desktop workplaces. The desktop workplaces help the maintenance staff accomplish their tasks, and provide additional information. They can guide a worker through complex tasks by looking at the video signals from the worker's video facility, giving advice to the worker through the audio device, and providing additional information, for example, online user manuals or video repair guides. Each of the communication devices has defined capabilities that are made public to all the other devices through the RIN. Every device that is part of the network will have a RIN client, a RIN server, and a number of RIN plug-ins installed. The server controls the resource plug-ins and communicates with the clients of connected devices. The client gets the information from the associated device's RIN server. All the devices within the range of the communication system can, before they communicate, retrieve information from their associated nodes through the RIN about what things they are capable of doing at a given time. This way, the individual nodes are never overloaded with data that they cannot process as expected. For example, the video application of a desktop station may determine the current memory state of a handheld device, and decide based on that information whether it can send colored frames or only black-and-white frames; it may also reduce the frame rate, or ask the handheld device to momentarily remove some of its unused applications from its memory. These decisions depend on the profile of the user and the priority of the applications that use the RIN. As shown in Fig. 2 the RIN system represents a 3-tier architecture with: RINClient, RINServer, and RINSystemPlugin.

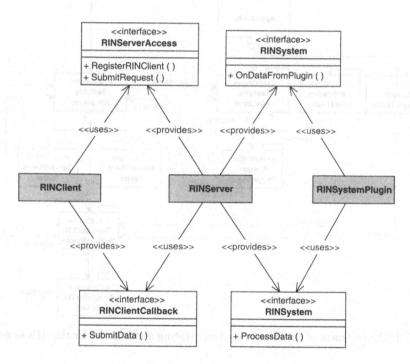

Fig. 2. UML-style structural organization of the Resource Information Network.

- RINClient requires system information, such as "system memory state" or "system power state," from an associated host. It connects to the host's RINServer for such requests. For this, RINClient uses the RINServer's provided interface, RINServerAccess. The RINClient provides also an interface RINClientCallBack. This interface is used by RINServer in order to re-transmit required information to RINClient.
- RINServer resides on each host, receives the client's requests (via RINServerAccess), and transmits it to the appropriate RINSystemPlugin. This provides the interface RINSystem for receiving client requests and returning responses to the server through RINServerCallBack.

- **RINSystemPlugin** resides in each **RINserver**, and provides different system information. After **RINSystemPlugin** has collected all required information, it returns all data via the server's **RINServerCallBack** interface.

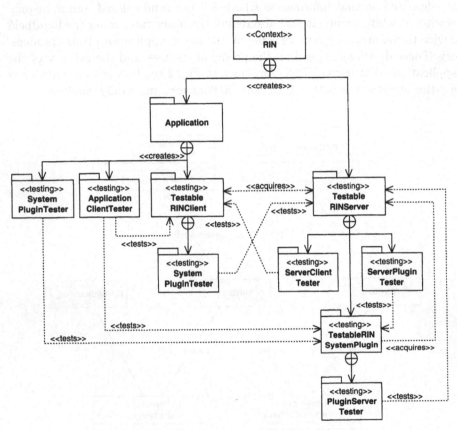

Fig. 3. Containment of the built-in contract testing architecture for the RIN system.

Since the integrating communication application is supposed to execute on quite a different number of hosts, the RIN system must be tested on each of these different platforms and configurations. This can be seen as a deployment or platform test that checks the correct connection to the underlying middleware platform. An additional feature is the provision of different system plug-ins, based on how a device that is equipped with hardware must be checked. For testing this means, that different types of plug-in components may be added to the servers on different platforms, and they must all abide by the contract that the server is implementing for communicating with the plug-ins. The previously described tests are all carried out on a lower level of abstraction, the network or communication level. An additional application-

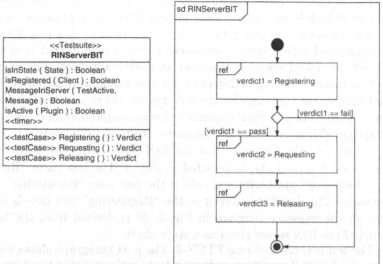

Fig. 4. Specification of the BIT server component with its testing behavior.

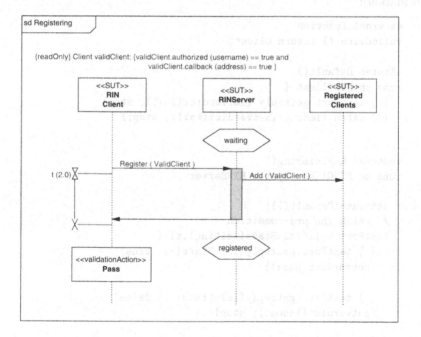

Fig. 5. Sequence diagram for the test case "Registering".

level test assures that the application (the large communication system) retrieves the right information from the respective plug-ins. This means that a number of high-level requests must be sent from the application to the plug-in (via the server) in order to assess its correctness. Each application will be augmented with a tester component for each plug-in that it is accessing. All tests are based solely on the contract testing approach. The model of the built-in contract testing architecture for this example is displayed in Fig. 3. For example, the test cases for the server cover the registration of clients (test case "Registering"), normal requests or bypass requests from clients (test case "Requesting"), or releasing the resources (test case "Releasing"). The set of test cases, i.e., the test suite, for the RIN server, together with the execution order of these tests, is depicted in Fig. 4. The test cases "Requesting" and "Releasing" are performed only if the test case "Registering" has been successful. The detailed behavior of the "Registering" test case is illustrated through the sequence diagram in Fig. 5. It is derived from the behavioral model of the RIN server given as a state chart.

The test is translated into TTCN-3. The next paragraph shows a simplified form of a TTCN-3 specification for this test (without giving test type and data information):

```
external function
validClient() return Client;

altstep Default()
runs on RINClient {
  [ ] testPort.getreply {setverdict(fail); stop}
  [ ] catch.timeout {setverdict(fail); stop;}
}

testcase Registering()
runs on RINClient system RINServer
{
  activate(Default());
  // check the pre-condition
  testPort.call(IsInState(waiting),t) {
    [ ] testPort.getreply(IsInState(-): true)
    {setverdict(pass)}

    [ ] testPort.getreply(IsInState(-): false)
    {setverdict(inconc); stop}

    [ ] catch.timeout {setverdict(inconc); stop;}
  }

  // main test body
  testPort.call(Register(validClient),t) {
    [ ] testPort.getreply(Register(validClient))
    {setverdict(pass)}
```

```
    }
    // check the result
    testPort.call(IsRegistered(validClient),t) {
      [ ] testPort.getreply(IsRegistered(-): true)
      {setverdict(pass)}
    }
    // check the post-condition
    testPort.call(IsInState(registered),t) {
      [ ] testPort.getreply(IsInState(-): true)
      {setverdict(pass)}
    }
  }
```

The external function `validClient()` is used to retrieve the information about a valid client from the environment. The test case "Registering" can be executed by the client's built-in test component and test RINServer component. It initially activates a default test to handle all unexpected responses from the server. The test validates the pre-condition for the tests, and then proceeds with the main body by trying to register the valid client. Afterward, the result is checked: is the client really registered; and is the RINServer in the state **registered**? All valid executions of the tests will result in the verdict "pass." Invalid executions lead to "fail." If the pre-condition for the test is not fulfilled, "inconclusive" will be returned. The tests in TTCN-3 are detailed enough to generate executable code. For the example, we generate Java code. The compiled Java bytecode is deployed and executed in a TTCN-3 execution environment.

The test execution architecture of the TTCN-3 suite is displayed in Fig. 6. In order to connect the test components with the target components, a test adapter according to the TTCN-3 execution interfaces TRI [116] and TCI [115] is required. The test adapter uses so-called connectors to mediate between different communication middleware (e.g., CORBA, CCM, RMI, Siena, UDP, etc.), which make the adapter generic and reusable for built-in test components in various execution contexts. The adapter implements the abstract operations of the test system (e.g., **connect**, **send**, **receive**, **call**, **getreply**, etc.). For the RIN system, the CORBA connector is used to invoke the RIN server methods.

6 Summary and Conclusion

This chapter has presented and introduced an integrated model-driven development and test process based on novel and existing technologies: Built-In Contract Testing, the UML Testing Profile, and the Testing and Test Control Notation, in its third incarnation, TTCN-3. Built-in contract testing represents the overall framework for testing component-based applications. It provides guidelines on how to augment functional components with the capability

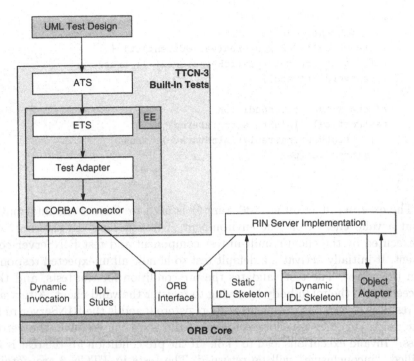

Fig. 6. Architecture of the TTCN-3 suite.

to test other associated server components and to be tested by other client components. For modeling the high-level built-in contract testing architecture, the core UML provides sufficient support. Because the testing architecture is not really focusing on concrete test concepts, such as test behavior, or test data. But if the specification of the testing artifacts becomes more concrete further down the design of a project, the UML testing profile provides all necessary concepts for the specification of the nitty-gritty testing details. In the next step, we have to implement the testing infrastructure, and this is the case mainly for test components and their incorporated test suites. Integration of the components is carried out according to the integration rules of the underlying component platform, e.g., through IDL-type interface mappings, or through component adapters that realize functional, behavioral and semantic mappings between two components. Since all the testing artifacts are readily built in, they are also part of these mappings, and they are treated as normal functionality. The TTCN-3 permits a generic implementation of the test components and their respective test cases out of the UML testing models, independently of any concrete underlying component platform or programming language. The "embodiment" into concrete source code is performed automatically. TTCN-3 supports a number of implementation technologies, such as Java, C++, and some newer component models.

Currently, the test generation from system models in UML and the mapping from the UML testing profile specifications into TTCN-3 are still performed manually because of a lack of appropriate tools. From TTCN-3 onward, everything is automatic. Future work must attempt to increase the automation throughout the entire process, especially in the early modeling phases and for the extraction of tests from models. The development and provision of suitable tools for the test generation and translation is therefore one of the most important future activities. Another important route is the assessment and improvement of the UML testing profile, through more case studies, in order to validate its expressiveness and improve its application for built-in contract testing. Overall, we believe that the topics described in this chapter, and, of course, their integration, can make a significant contribution to component-based system development.

Acknowledgment

This work has been partially funded by the German National Department of Education and Research (BMBF) under the MDTS project acronym. The project deals with model-driven development and testing methods for telecommunication systems.

Using a Specification Approach to Facilitate Component Testing

Duane Hybertson

The MITRE Corporation
dhyberts@mitre.org

Summary. This chapter does not describe a component test method directly, but rather it describes an approach to specification of components and system architectures that is intended to facilitate component user testing. The approach is a synthesis of specification ideas that are known individually–such as Design by Contract, explicit dependencies, quality of service, cost of service–but are not being followed collectively in practice. The argument is that clearer specification content and structure by system architects and COTS component vendors enables more efficient and effective component search, selection, and testing in component-based systems. Further, the approach here includes component specification variations that facilitate both consideration of the maximum number of candidate components for a given system and the maximum market for a given component. These are achieved through generalizing specifications while retaining precision. A test structure is given that shows how the approach can be used for component testing and integration, and a simple example illustrates the approach.

1 Context and Orientation

The context for the approach in this chapter, and for Part 3 of this book in general, is a situation in which a component user–system engineer, system architect, or system integrator–is building a system out of components, and for each component that is needed, must find, test, and integrate an available component that meets the need of the system.

The basic test and integration problem of a component user is: How do I test whether a component meets my system needs given that (1) I have no knowledge of the source code and therefore cannot do white-box testing[1] and (2) the component was not built specifically for my system context? Also, how do I reassess the fit of a new version of the component, or the fit of an existing component if my system context changes?

---

[1] In some situations, such as certifying safety critical code, component object code is reverse engineered, and then white-box testing is done on the source code produced. But this chapter does not assume such an approach.

My answer to this question is to define proper specification information both for the component and the system context. Proper specification information is not the *full* solution to component testing; other chapters in this part of the book describe additional elements of a larger solution. But my claim is that proper specification is an *essential* part of the solution; without it, no amount of testing improvement will suffice to solve the problem.

In summary, the thesis of the approach here is that more precise and complete specifications will enable component testing and simplify it. In fact, better specifications will be a primary enabler of COTS-based and component-based software engineering. This chapter describes a specification approach as such an enabler. The approach places requirements on both developer and user, but the focus and orientation of this chapter is the user.

The specification approach presented here is general, i.e., it is not tied to any specific component model, such as Java-based J2EE from Sun Microsystems, or the CORBA Component Model (CCM) from the Object Management Group (OMG), or .NET from Microsoft Corporation. Although the approach lends itself to formalization, it is not presented formally. The focus is more on precision than formalization. The approach represents a synthesis of ideas from the literature in software architecture, component specification, Design by Contract, specification matching, and the concept of a modeling space. Appropriate citations to this literature are given with each associated topic discussed in the chapter. In one sense, the approach defined in this chapter presents nothing new, in that none of the elements of the synthesis are new. In another sense, the approach defined in this chapter is beyond the state of current best practice, because no specifications being produced today address all the types of specification information designated here, and most languages do not yet provide adequate support for the approach. Therefore, the approach defined here may be thought of as a delineation of known specification elements whose sum total serves as a goal to achieve in the future.

The next section summarizes the general approach to specification. Section 3 describes how the general specification approach is applied to COTS component specification and user testing.

2 Specification Approach

This section provides a summary of a specification approach to systems and components based on both component and software architecture research. The emphasis is on precise specifications built on the basic principles of modularity, encapsulation, clear communication, and scalability. The scope of specifications in this section covers all of software systems engineering, but the emphasis is on specifying, testing, and integrating components.

2.1 Interaction Model

A general interaction model provides the context and structure for the approach to specifications in component-based systems. The model comes from the software architecture community [9, 364, 366], and consists of two general entity types: *components*, which serve as a locus of computation and decision making, and *connectors*, which serve as a locus of interaction between components. A connector provides not just an exchange medium, but also specification of roles and protocols involved in an interaction. Components and connectors have interface points called ports and roles, as shown in Fig. 1. The left side of the figure shows a basic interaction of components A and B via a connector. The center is a visualization of the component-port-role-connector model. The right side shows specification elements in this structure, which are further delineated in Sect. 2.2.

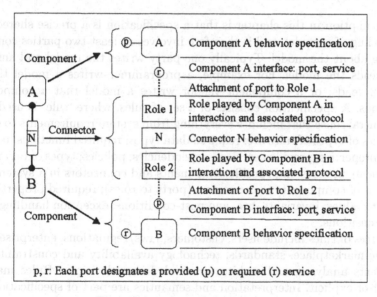

Fig. 1. Anatomy of an interaction.

A subtle but important aspect of this model is that attachment of components to connectors is not part of the specification of either component or connector. This separation preserves modularity. Components and connectors are attached only in the composition of specific interactions or systems. This approach differs, for example, from the nodes-edges example in chapter 'Testing Polymorphic Behavior of Framework Components' by Typer et al., in which nodes are analogous to components and edges are analogous to connectors, but attachment of edge to node is part of the edge specification.

The interaction model supports component-based software and COTS component testing in that the explicit treatment of interaction, connectors, and coordination provides a basis for integrating components into systems by clearly defining the integration context.

2.2 System and Component Specifications

As used in this chapter, the concept of specification is based on the concept of model. A model of a system is treated here as any explicit representation or abstraction of part or all of the system, where a part might be any subset of components, connectors, ports, etc. Traditional examples include a requirements document, data definition or model, architecture description, design description, source code, and executable code. Any UML diagram is considered a model.

What is a Specification?

The assumption in this chapter is that a specification is a precise shared understanding of a model, and it therefore involves at least two parties communicating about the model. Typically one party writes the model and another party reads the model. For example, a programmer writes a model that a compiler reads; or a component vendor writes a model that a component user reads. A specification consists of a set of rules, where 'rule' is used in a very general sense that includes everything from system requirements to code. Examples of types of rules are: required data types; required functions; performance properties; provided services; dependencies; policies; types of permitted components in a system; specific components and connectors in a system; attachment of components to connectors (ports to roles); required properties or attribute values; invariants, pre- and post-conditions; exception handling; and state transitions.

Sources of rules include users, customers, laws/regulations, enterprise policies, the marketplace, standards, technology availability and constraints, requirements analyses, and architecture and design decisions. Rules may be implicit or explicit. Interpretation and semantics are part of specifications.

A general source for the specification approach described here is [385]. An important element of achieving precision in specification is a clear understanding of dependencies. Traditional programming language-based specifications define what services are provided but not what services are required. Luckham et al. [248] describe an "object connection architecture" as an architecture of a system in which component interfaces define services provided but not services used or required. They suggest, instead, "interface connection architectures" that specify both services provided and services required. An approach that supports this concept is Design by Contract (DBC), defined by [276]. DBC originally emphasized contract provisions in the code itself, and the focus was primarily on behavioral or functional–as opposed to non-functional or performance–issues.

The component community has embraced the DBC concept and extended it for component use. First, the concept of trusted components has come into play. [278] defines a trusted component as a reusable software element possessing specified and guaranteed property qualities. In the same paper, Meyer defines a high road and a low road toward establishing high quality components. The low road is to start with today's COTS or open source components and move to certification based on contracts. The high road is to produce new components with correctness proofs by defining correctness properties based on contracts.

Second, DBC has been extended to include non-functional information (performance, quality of service or QoS) as well as cost. [3] describes an approach to QoS modeling that features the notion of QoS profile. A profile defines a QoS region in which a component operates. Multiple different QoS profiles may be defined for a given component–for example, one profile defined for a PDA platform and another for a desktop platform. [89] adopts a similar idea in defining a QoS model using UML extensions, and applies it to component frameworks. [397] also uses contracts to model non-functional constraints for embedded software.

The cost might be the initial purchase of the component; the purchase of ongoing maintenance updates; or the cost of "renting" the component on a per use basis. Cost may also be specified at a more granular level for each service.

Gross et al. describe in chapter 'Modeling and Implementation of Built-In Contract Tests' how built-in contract tests can help automate component testing. [82] discusses a tool to automate contract verification. [50] and [324] discuss different approaches to increasing formal support for contracts in UML and OCL. The specification approach described here incorporates these extended contract concepts. It does not require formal specification or automation, but it is fully consistent with these ideas.

Intertwining External and Internal Specifications

Specification types are derived from the interaction model and from the notion of composition–specifically, the intertwining of internal and external views. An *internal specification* of a system is a set of rules about the data, components, and connectors that are within the system, and about their structure and interaction. An *external specification* of a system or component is a set of rules about the external or 'black-box' view of that system or component. This includes observable data, behavior, ports, and services, as well as their observable properties or qualities. As shown in Fig. 2, the relation between the two specification types is that an internal specification of a system includes the external specifications of its components and connectors. The external view corresponds to what we traditionally call requirements or specification, and the internal view corresponds to what we traditionally call architecture, design, or implementation.

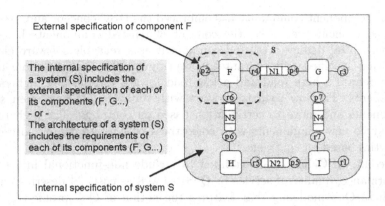

Fig. 2. Relation between internal and external specifications.

Service Structure

An external specification of an entity, such as a system or component, has two contract types. The first specifies what the component provides to users (services offered). The second specifies what the component requires of providers (dependencies). These two contract types effectively partition the environment of a component into two parts: a service environment to which the component provides services, and a dependency environment from which the component requires services. Both the service environment and dependency environment can generate a chain of indefinite length. Suppose we have a system E with components F, G, H, and I, as shown in Fig. 3. F requires a service (r6) that is provided by component H (p6), which in turn requires a service (r5), which is provided by component I (p5), which in turn requires a service (r1). But service r1 is not provided within system E. Therefore, E must propagate the dependency as a required service of system E. Likewise, any service offered by a component (e.g., p2 from F or p6 from H) is a candidate for a service to be propagated and offered by the encompassing system (E).

This propagation continues up the composition hierarchy. Provided services are a matter of choice; they may be exposed as provided services at any higher level system. Required services are a matter of necessity; they must be met, i.e., provided by another component or system at some level up the hierarchy, or the component that requires the service cannot fulfill its end of the contract.

Specification Contents

The three tables below show the types of information in an internal system specification. They reflect the relation shown in Fig. 2 above, namely, that an internal specification includes the external specifications of its components and connectors. Table 1 presents system-wide rules that specify internal system

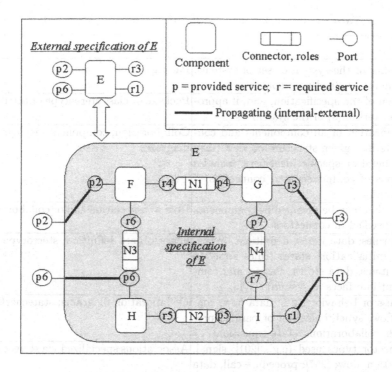

Fig. 3. Propagating services and dependencies.

structure and interaction. Table 2 shows the external specification information for each component in the system, and Table 3 shows the external specification information for each connector. All three tables also associate each set of rules with corresponding UML or OCL representations. A given specification has a defined scope and purpose, so in many cases only a select subset of the information called for in these tables will be in the specification.

Most of the details of simple well understood connector specifications, such as function calls or message passing, are usually implicit, because such types are mature and we have a shared understanding of them. However, more details of complex or higher-level connector specifications need to be explicit in order for us to avoid component mismatch. The approach described here does not require all the information in Tables 1-3 within the scope of a given specification to be explicit in that specification, but it does require all of it to be mutually understood by the interested parties. Over time, the part of specifications written down (i.e., the models) can become shorter because the proportion of the information that is mutually understood becomes larger.

2.3 Composition Levels

Software systems and components typically exhibit a whole-part hierarchy. The top and bottom levels of this hierarchy are respectively the largest com-

Table 1. Internal system specification content: system wide.

Rules	UML/OCL
Identifier of the system or set of systems: unique in a defined namespace	Package or class name
Version of the specification, and, if appropriate, version(s) of the system	Package or class stereotype or attribute
Identification of all components and connectors in a given structure or view (may be general or specific identifiers; includes versions of component and connectors, if appropriate)	Collaboration, component, deployment diagrams
Roles that may be assumed by components and specified in connectors	Role in association end or collaboration
Data rules: data items, definitions, invariants, initialization, states (rules apply to data items, data stores, classes, and component interfaces in system)	Class/object definition; stereotype
Process or behavior rules: data flow, control flow, synchronization of parallel processes, collaborations, state transitions...	Collaboration diagrams; statecharts
Connector types used (e.g., [201]: signal, operation, flow; [267]: procedure call, data access, linkage, stream, event, arbitrator, adaptor, distributor)	Associations specialized via stereotypes
Attachment of connector roles to component ports	Collaboration, component, deployment diagrams
System-wide constraints on supporting environment (e.g., must use Enterprise JavaBeans, or Windows, or Windows XP, or RDBMS, or Oracle 10g, or HTTP)	Annotations, stereotypes, OCL
Implementation rules (e.g., "write code in Java")	Annotations, stereotypes, OCL
Rules that constrain the processor(s) that execute(s) the system	Annotations, stereotypes, OCL
Creation, use, and deletion of resources in system	Annotations, stereotypes
Mapping between views	Annotations
Other constraints the system places on each component, or on each connector (e.g., security constraints)	Annotations, stereotypes, OCL

Table 2. Internal system specification content: external component.

Rules	UML/OCL
Component identifier (or anonymous)	Interface or class or object name
Version of the component specification	Interface or class stereotype or attribute
List of provided interfaces (ports) or services used by other components	Interface operations
List of required interfaces (ports) or services provided by other components	Interface stereotype or annotation
Component invariant over all provided services and all required services	Interface invariant in OCL or annotation
Component-wide properties	Interface attributes in OCL or annotation
Service interactions (sequence constraints, how one affects others, ...)	Interface invariant in OCL or annotation
For each port: data and control flow through port; data types	Class (associated with interface operation)
Cost of component (purchase, maintenance upgrades, rent)	Interface annotation or stereotype
For each *provided* service used in this context:	
-Access syntax (e.g., signature)	Interface operation
-Semantics:	Interface operation in OCL or stereotype or annotation
–What it requires of its users: precondition	
–What it provides its users	
–Part of invariant associated with service	
–Provided post-condition	
–Provided properties, QoS (performance, precision, reliability, ...)	
-Cost of service (CoS) constraints	Interface operation in OCL or stereotype or annotation
-Exceptions	Interface operation in OCL or stereotype or annotation
For each *required* service:	
–What it offers its providers: precondition	interface operation in OCL or stereotype or annotation
–What it requires of its providers: usage dependencies	interface operation in OCL or stereotype or annotation
–Part of invariant associated with service	
–Required post-condition	
–Required properties, QoS (performance, precision, reliability, ...)	
-Cost of service (CoS) constraints	Interface operation in OCL or stereotype or annotation
Rules that constrain the processor that executes the component	Interface operation in OCL or stereotype or annotation

Table 3. Internal system specification content: external connector.

Rules	UML/OCL
Connector identifier (or anonymous)	Association or link name
Version of the connector specification	Association or link annotation
Connector type	Association stereotype or annotation
List of roles of components attached to connector in this environment	Association ends
Specification of each role	Association end specification
Connector constraints on supporting environment	Association OCL or stereotype or annotation
Protocol specification: format, sequence, error checking, properties, QoS (e.g., throughput, capacity), services, semantics	Association OCL or stereotype or annotation

ponent or system of systems and the smallest indivisible component or unit. System and component can be used as relative terms. A system at one level may be a component of another system at the next higher level, and the same relations repeat at each level. The hierarchy is generated by the relation between external and internal specifications that was shown earlier in Fig. 2. Figure 4 illustrates how multiple levels can be generated. I is a component of system E, and in turn E is a component of system A. This relationship can be repeated at as many levels as necessary.

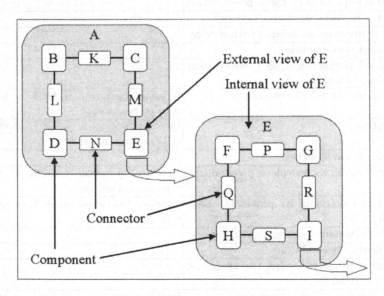

Fig. 4. Composition levels.

2.4 Variability and Generalization

In problem solving, problems are often similar, and solutions are often similar. There is a spectrum of similarity. At one end is complete equivalence–a set of problems or a set of solutions that have everything in common. At the other end is complete disjointness–problems or solutions that have nothing in common. The general issue is: how do we simultaneously exploit commonality among problems or solutions, and satisfy the uniqueness of each?

In the context of component-based systems, this issue has two complementary perspectives. First, how does a component vendor specify a component that fits into a large number of systems? Second, how does a system architect or integrator specify a required component that fits a large number of candidate components?

The general object-oriented approach to variability is to define a class hierarchy, in which higher level classes capture what is common across a broad set, and lower level classes capture what is unique among a small set. Several approaches have been defined to address the variability needs of component-based systems. Component frameworks have been defined to provide defined contexts for components, including specified platform dependencies. J2EE [383], OMG's CORBA Component Model (CCM) [311], and Microsoft Corporation's .NET [281] are well known frameworks. Ishikawa [210] investigates requirements for a component framework for ubiquitous computing, with a focus on identifying inter-component dependencies. In chapter 'Testing Polymorphic Behavior of Framework Components', Tyler et al. describe how variability is supported in frameworks through the use of template methods that are specialized by calling hook methods. Doucet [99] describes how variability is addressed in component frameworks through type abstractions in languages such as architecture description languages (ADLs) and module interconnection languages (MILs). The Aagedal [3] concept of QoS profile cited above in Sect. 2.2 can also be viewed as an approach to handling QoS variability.

The specification approach to variability in this chapter does not rely on a given class hierarchy or component model or a given framework. It is closer to an ADL approach, and relies on Design by Contract interfaces, explicit identification of dependencies, and generalization without a decrease in precision. The first two of these concepts have been described earlier in Sect. 2.2. The third, generalization and precision, will be described here.

A key potential benefit of the component paradigm is reuse–a component is intended to be usable in multiple systems or environments. The idea of general models and specifications supports this goal. Generalization is a form of abstraction in which information is removed to make a more general component or model that is useful in multiple environments or that allows multiple implementations. An example cited above is class hierarchy, where each class is a generalization of its subclasses. Another generalization mechanism is a design pattern, which specifies a general solution to a class of problems.

The specification approach defined here supports different levels of generality. In geometric terms, a specification typically defines a space rather than a point. For example, a component external specification defines a space that includes all components whose implementation satisfies the specification. The more general the specification, the larger the space.

An important goal is that general specifications should be no less precise than specific specifications. Generalization has to do with reducing the number of constraints, not increasing the fuzziness of the constraints, and, correspondingly, with increasing the size of the solution space, not increasing the fuzziness of the boundary around that space. From the perspective of an internal system specification, i.e., a component user, generalization allows consideration of the maximum number of potential components that meet a system requirement. From the perspective of a component vendor, generalization allows the maximum market or maximum number of contexts for a given component. The goal in both cases is to specify all necessary constraints, but no unnecessary constraints.

System and component specifications today typically violate this goal in both directions. Some necessary constraints are left unspecified, which results in mismatches and integration problems. At the same time, some unnecessary constraints are specified. A system architect who specifies unnecessary constraints precludes consideration of components that could in fact meet his system needs. A component developer who specifies unnecessary constraints precludes consideration of systems or environments in which his component could in fact be used.

Techniques exist for generalizing a specification without losing precision. Many of these involve relaxing or removing constraints. For example, consider these rules on managing data in a system: use Oracle version 10g; use Oracle; use a relational DBMS; use a DBMS; N (no constraint on data management). Each of these rules is successively less constraining than its predecessor, and is more general and defines a larger solution space. But all these rules are equally precise. Note that leaving a specification variable unconstrained (N in the list above) is a deliberate decision and can be part of the specification. The application of generalization and specialization of specifications to component testing is discussed in Sect. 3.

2.5 Specification Language and Universe of Discourse

I will use a statement from Barbier (chapter 'COTS Component Testing through Built-In Test') to raise the issue of specification language: "... CBD is increasingly organized around UML in which dedicated modeling constructs exist. ... In relation with this point, we also discuss the crucial need for the availability of *intuitive* component specifications for end users."

I interpret *intuitive* to mean representing an external specification in end user language, i.e., the language and universe of discourse of the problem domain in which a component is used. This leads to another interesting issue: a component might be used in multiple contexts. These contexts might reasonably be expected to fall in the same problem domain. But what if different problem domains can use the same generic component? Then perhaps a component provider needs to provide a component external specification in more than one language or universe of discourse, i.e., to interpret his abstract external specification in different ways, with different semantics. Perhaps this difference shows up in component catalogs of external specifications. A full exploration of this language topic is beyond the scope of this chapter, but it is important to point out the issue.

2.6 Integrating Specification Concepts for Future Investigation

The ideas concerning specification, composition, variability and generalization, and language have been brought together into a unified modeling space that has been described elsewhere [190, 191]. A full discussion of the modeling space is beyond the scope of this chapter, but a brief summary of elements is given here for two reasons. First, it indicates how the ideas presented in Sect. 2 tie together. Second, it provides a basis for further research on component specifications and their role in the varieties of testing needed for component-based systems.

The modeling space is an organizing structure for software engineering artifacts, including COTS and component-based software. Artifacts that are traditionally called requirements, architecture, design, source code, and executable code, are all characterized as models. The modeling space has five primary elements. The first three elements are dimensions that separate component-based software concerns. The elements are:

- A *composition* spectrum that represents a whole-part hierarchy ranging from the largest system to the smallest unit. It exhibits a repeating self-similar pattern in that a given whole is part of a larger whole.
- A *conceptualization* spectrum that ranges from problem domain languages to computer processor languages. This highlights the complicating fact that the modeling space is fundamentally multilingual.
- A *commonization* spectrum that represents "kind-of" and "is-a" hierarchies ranging from universal models to instance models. It exhibits a repeating self-similar pattern in that a model that is a generalization can in turn be further generalized.
- A *specification* approach that emphasizes contracts, precision, and semantics, and has two specification types for each component and connector: external and internal. The same kinds of specification information apply throughout the modeling space.
- A general *interaction structure* that relates components via connectors. This structure supports component interaction, coordination, and integration in a uniform way throughout the modeling space.

A specification occupies a point or range in each spectrum. That is, a specification is at some composition level, is represented in a language that falls somewhere between problem domain language and computer processor language, and is at some level of generalization. A reasonable interpretation of this is that composition, conceptualization, and commonization can vary independently, and thus collectively they structure the modeling space into three dimensions, as shown in Fig. 5.

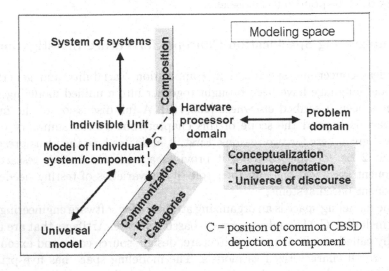

Fig. 5. Modeling space dimensions.

This structure can facilitate or at least provide an organizing context for further research and investigation in certain areas. For example:

- *Composition*: How can component-based systems, and associated testing, scale up to address "components of components" at multiple levels?
- *Commonization*: What additional techniques can be developed for handling variability, and for generalizing without losing precision?
- *Conceptualization*: How can language and representation facilitate component specification and testing, and how can a component vendor provide an intuitive specification of the same component for different contexts?

3 Application to COTS Component Testing

The approach to specification of systems and components in Sect. 2 above is specialized for COTS component specification and testing in this section. Variations of component specification are discussed in Sect. 3.1, and tests that are based on these specification variations are discussed in Sect. 3.2. Section

3.3 defines the criteria for determining whether one specification satisfies another, and gives a small example using the specification information. Section 3.4 summarizes the benefits of the approach described in this chapter.

3.1 Component Specification Variations

External component specifications are a key element of user testing of COTS components in a component-based system. Simplistically, one could assert that there is one external component specification of interest to a component user, namely, the one defined in the system architecture. The architect/user simply finds a component whose external specification matches the architecture component specification, i.e., selects an available component if and only if specification of available component = specification of desired component. But several factors motivate a more realistic criterion. First, two specifications are rarely, if ever, equal. We need to think of "satisfies" rather than "equals," and we need to define what it means for one specification to satisfy another specification. [434] and [178] discuss issues in specification matching from a formal perspective. Second, components evolve over time as COTS vendors produce new versions. We need to support a component user in determining whether a new component version still meets the system requirements. Third, systems also evolve, and the system requirements for a component may change. Does the existing component meet the revised system requirements?

These and related considerations motivate four external specification variations of a component in a component-based system. The distinctions are important for modularity and for the use of commercial (COTS) components and component-based architectures. Table 4 summarizes the four variations and shows how they are related.

A system architect and a component developer have two different perspectives on a component, and both of these perspectives have, or can have, two levels of generality. The relation between a required component (specification S1 in the table) and an available component (C2) is particularly crucial. With S1, a system architect has the perspective that the context of a component is specific and known and the component is general and unknown. With C2, a component developer has the perspective that the context is general and unknown and the component is specific and known.

S1 defines system requirements for the component, and is used to govern evolution and replacement of the component. That is, it defines a space of acceptability or satisfiability for the component, and new versions or potential replacements of the implemented component can be tested to determine if they still reside in this space, or, equivalently, if they still satisfy system requirements. S2 defines as-built or specific properties of the selected component version in the system. It is part of the answer to the question, "What is the specific architecture of the current implemented system?"

A general specification of a component developer may be used to define a component space that defines a component family–for example, a product

Table 4. External component specification variation.

Generality	Component User Perspective	Component Vendor Perspective
Generalized	S1–needed component	C1 (example: product family)
–Provided services	Services and QoS needed from component by system context. **p4**	Services and QoS provided by all components in family
–Required services–implementation independent	Services and QoS provided to component by system context. **r7**	Services and QoS required by all components in family
–Required services–implementation dependent	None	None
–Processor requirements	None; or estimated properties of needed processor(s) (language, speed, memory ...)	None; or constraints common to all components in family
Specialized	S2–selected component	C2–available component
–Provided services	Services defined in S1 (subset of those in C2); QoS defined in C2. **p4**	Full set of services, QoS provided by component to generalized environment [Goal: maximize] **p1, p4, p6**
–Required services–implementation independent	Services defined in both S1 and C2; QoS defined in C2. **r7**	Full set of implementation independent required services [Goal: minimize] **r7**
–Required services–implementation dependent	Services defined in C2 but not S1, or a subset of C2 services; QoS defined in C2. **r3**	Full set of implementation dependent required services [Goal: minimize] **r3**
–Processor requirements	Constraints defined in C2, or reduced constraints. **Pr**	Processor constraints to support provided contracts (language, speed, memory ...) [Goal: minimize] **Pr**

family defined by a common service but where each component in the family is targeted to a different processor or platform. Specification C1 would define the component space and C2 would define a component for a particular processor. We do not elaborate on C1 in this chapter because it is not used in user component testing. But the other three variations are heavily involved in user component testing and will be described here. The discussion explains the specification variations in Table 4 and the example specifications in Fig. 6. The table also refers to example services and dependencies (such as p4 and r7 in bold font) in the figure to help explain the table-figure connection.

Figure 6 shows a generic example of S1, C2, and S2. For purposes of the figure and the discussion that follows, we can stipulate with no loss of

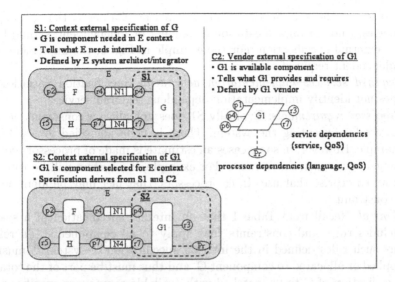

Fig. 6. Example of external component specification variations.

generality the following: The component user is a system architect/integrator who defines an internal specification or architecture of system E, in which a component G is required, with external specification S1. A component vendor has a component G1 with external specification C2 that the architect will find and test to see if it meets the requirements of system E for component G. If it does, the component is integrated and its external specification in the context of E is S2.

Discussion of S1

- *Provided services*: Specification S1 defines the information System E needs component G to provide. For the example in Fig. 6, the provided service is p4. As per Table 4, the information includes semantics and QoS specifications. Service cost is not necessarily provided in this variation, although it could be specified in terms of a maximum if the cost is likely to be based on per service use.
- *Required services–implementation independent*: There is probably no theoretical or formal basis for distinguishing between required services that are dependent on implementation of a component and those that are implementation independent. However, in many cases the distinction is obvious. For example, in a pipe-and-filter architecture style, a required service of a filter is an input data stream of some sort, regardless of how the filter is implemented. [412] discusses the distinction, and suggests specifying the required services that apply to all component implementations in the Component Interface (external) specification, and the implementation dependent required services into a different form, such as Annotations. The

position of the specification approach in this chapter is that all dependencies, whether implementation dependent or independent, should be in the external specification. For the example in Fig. 6, the implementation independent required service is r7.

- *Required services–implementation dependent*: Specification variation S1 does not identify implementation dependent required services.
- *Processor requirements*: Typically S1 does not place a constraint on processors for executing the system. There is none identified in the Fig. 6 example. However, in some cases an estimate is made of processor requirements, or a constraint is made. For example, if a system will be run only in an enterprise that uses Intel processors, that fact may be identified as a constraint.
- *General*: Recall from Table 1 that an internal specification of a system includes rules and constraints that apply to all components. Therefore, any such rules defined in the internal specification of system E must be applied or allocated to component G, and thus must be part of the total S1 specification of G to be matched with available component specifications, such as C2. One of the constraints might be the maximum cost allowable for any component, or for component G.

Discussion of C2

- *Provided services*: Specification C2 specifies all services that component G1 provides. For the example in Fig. 6, the provided services are p1, p4, and p6. Service cost is part of this specification if the cost is to be based on per service use. Otherwise, cost is associated with the component as a whole (see General below).
- *Required services–implementation independent*: Specification C2 specifies all required services, including implementation independent and implementation dependent. C2 may or may not distinguish between these two categories, i.e., C2 may specify all required services together, or may separate them into implementation dependent and implementation independent. For the example in Fig. 6, the required services are r3 and r7.
- *Required services–implementation dependent*: C2 specifies these services (see previous discussion).
- *Processor requirements*: C2 specifies constraints on processors for executing the component. For the example in Fig. 6, the processor constraints are designated Pr.
- *General*: If the cost is for the component as a whole instead of per service use, then that component cost is indicated as part of C2. For a COTS component, specification information, in addition to that in Table 4, is also recommended:
  - Provide component vendor information.

– If this is an update, provide a change specification, i.e., identify all changes from the previous version of the component specification, and if the implementation has changed, specify the new version number.

Discussion of S2

- *Provided services:* Specification S2 specifies the services provided by the selected component G1 and used in the system context. For the example in Fig. 6, the provided service is p4. The specification information comes from two sources. The actual provided services of this component used in the system are those specified in S1. The actual QoS of those services are specified in C2. Therefore, the S2 specification of provided services uses the S1 set of services and the C2 QoS, and, if applicable, service cost. For the Fig. 6 example, even though component G1 offers additional services beyond p4, in the system E context only p4 is used, so p4 is the only G1 provided service specified in the E context (S2). However, since G1 was accepted as satisfying S1, we can assume that the QoS specified in C2 met or in general exceeded the QoS specified in S1. For example, the reliability needed in S1 for p4 may be specified as at least .999, but the reliability offered of p4 in C2 may be specified as .9999. The actual reliability of the selected G1 is therefore the C2 QoS .9999, and that is what is specified in S2.
- *Required services–implementation independent:* A practical heuristic for distinguishing between implementation independent and implementation dependent required services can be defined even if the C2 specification does not distinguish between the two. This heuristic is that whatever required services are common to both S1 and C2 are assumed to be implementation independent, and the required services that are only in C2 and not in S1 are assumed to be implementation dependent. Using that heuristic, the implementation independent required service in Fig. 6 is r7. The QoS needed of r7 in S2 is taken from C2 because it defines the QoS needed of the actual component.
- *Required services–implementation dependent:* S2 identifies implementation dependent required services using the heuristic defined above. In the Fig. 6 example, this required service is r3. Obviously, the QoS for these services are also taken from C2. Note, however, that this type of service raises another issue that is seen in Fig. 6. This issue is that implementation dependent required services are not typically satisfied by the system into which the component is being integrated. In Fig. 6, there is no component in the E system context that provides the implementation dependent service required by r3. If component G1 is to operate in E, then either a component will have to be added to system E to provide the required service, or the required service will need to propagated up to E and become a required service of system E. The latter choice would show up in the external specification of E.

- *Processor requirements*: One might assume that the S2 processor requirements, i.e., requirements of G1 in E, are identical to the processor requirements in C2. This is reflected in Fig. 6. However, if only a subset of services of G1 is used in E, then the processor requirements of G1 in E may be less demanding than the C2 processor requirements. For example, assume in Fig. 6 that C2 provided process p1 is the driving force for the C2 Pr requirement, i.e., p1 requires a significantly more powerful processor than p4. Then the Pr requirement of G2 in E, i.e., Pr in S2, may be less than the Pr specified in C2, because only p4 is used in the E context.

The situation discussed thus far assumes that a candidate component consists of one COTS product. The specification approach described in Sect. 2, however, is fully scalable, and addresses other situations as well. In particular, the approach can be readily applied to the case of a component consisting of multiple COTS products. Using Fig. 6, suppose E is a component that includes COTS products F, H, and G. The component vendor acts first in the role of system architect or integrator, and applies the testing approach described above to select and integrate each of the COTS products as components of E. Next, E becomes a candidate component for some larger system (not identified in the figure). The test and integration of E into the larger system would follow the same pattern. That is, the E vendor would provide a C2 external specification of E. The architect of the larger system would define an S1 external specification of the needed E component, and if the vendor's E were selected for the system, the system architect would integrate it and define an S2 external specification for the integrated E component. The scenario as described here is not meant to imply that E must be integrated and available as a component before a system architect specifies the requirement for a component E. Consistent with the component approach in general, this approach allows either the system or the component to be defined first, or for both to be defined in parallel.

3.2 General Component Specification and Test Structure

Under the proposed approach, a component developer or vendor prepares three items: a catalog entry, a full component (external) specification, and a deployable implementation. The catalog entry is a subset of the full specification, because a full specification would make the catalog too large and would make the discovery process too slow. The component user (system architect) prepares an internal system specification, which includes the external specification of the desired component. The catalog entry has sufficient information to find a candidate component, but the full component specification is needed to test whether the component specification satisfies the requirement. The implementation is used in acceptance and integration tests, as described below.

Table 5 defines the names that will be used in the discussion of tests in this section.

Table 5. Test definitions.

Name	Definition
E	Implemented system in which a component is integrated
S1	User external specification of desired component in E context
EE	External specification of system E
EI	Internal specification of system E
C2	Developer/vendor external specification of offered component
G1	Developer/vendor component implementation (e.g., COTS executable)
S2	External specification of selected component in E context; becomes part of as-built EI specification
C2'	Modification of C2 (for example, new version)
S1'	Modification of S1
G1'	Modification of G1
EI'	Modification of EI
C2/C2'	Change specification of C2', i.e., specification of changes from C2 to C2'
S1/S1'	Change specification of S1', i.e., specification of changes from S1 to S1'
EI/EI'	Change specification of EI', i.e., specification of changes from EI to EI'

Table 6 shows the component user tests and test activities supported by the specifications. For test T3, if the test is for acceptance into system E, then the implemented component G1 is tested against S1. On the other hand, if an enterprise is testing component G1 as a potential enterprise resource for multiple systems, then it may wish to perform T3 as a test of G1 against C2 on enterprise processors.

Test T6 assumes that the component implementation changes from G1 to G1', but the external specification C2 does not change. This can occur, for example, with a fix or patch of an error. Test T7 assumes that the component implementation changes, and the external specification changes from C2 to C2'. This can occur, for example, with an upgrade. Test T8 assumes that the component context changes from S1 to S1', and the system internal specification changes from EI to EI', but the component G1 and its external specification C2 do not change.

3.3 Specification Testing and an Example

Testing an external specification to see if it satisfies another external specification is an important part of this approach. This section defines more specifically what specification testing means, and gives an example. Using the terms defined earlier in Sect. 3, we will delineate the conditions under which C2, the external specification of an available component, satisfies S1, the ex-

Table 6. COTS Component Test Activities.

Test	Name	Activity
T1	Component discovery	Search catalog for components whose catalog entry satisfies S1
T2	Component external specification test	Test C2 against S1
T3	Component acceptance test	Test G1 against S1 (or C2)
T4	System integration test	Test G1 and the other component and connector implementations against EI (which includes S2)
T5	System acceptance test	Test E (which includes G1) against EE
T6	Component change (G1′) regression test	Most conservative (and expensive) approach: Run tests T3-T4-T5 using G1′. Less conservative: any subset of T3-T4-T5 using G1′.
T7	Component change (C2′) regression test	Most conservative (and expensive) approach: Run test T2 using C2′ and tests T3-T4-T5 using G1′. Less conservative: Target specific subsets of tests T2-T3-T4-T5 based on change specification C2/C2′.
T8	Context change (S1′) regression test	Most conservative (and expensive) approach: Run tests T2-T3-T4-T5 using S1′ and EI′. Less conservative: Target specific subsets of tests T2-T3-T4-T5 based on change specifications S1/S1′ and EI/EI′.

ternal specification of a desired component in a defined system context. From a contract perspective, we can say that C2 satisfies S1 if and only if these two conditions hold. The services that C2 provides match or exceed in all respects the services that S1 provides, and the services that C2 requires are available from the environment of S1 (i.e., the other components in the system and the processor constraints of S1).

More specifically, an available component specified by C2 satisfies a system requirement specified by S1 if all of the following hold:

- C2 provides *at least* all the services that S1 provides ($C2(p) \supseteq S1(p)$)
- S1's environment provides *at least* all the services that C2 requires ($C2(r) \subseteq Env(S1(r))$)
- C2 invariants match S1 invariants
- Cost of C2 does not exceed the cost limit of S1 (or, if cost is specified per service use, the cost of each service does not exceed the cost limit of that service)
- For each service *provided* by C2 that is also provided by S1:
  - C2 preconditions do not exceed the preconditions specified for S1

- C2 post-conditions match or exceed the post-conditions specified for S1
- Data that passes through the C2 port is compatible with S1 data types
- Service protocol constraints of C2 are compatible with service protocol constraints of S1
- Each quality of service of C2 meets or exceeds the specified QoS for S1
- For each service *required* by C2:
  - C2 preconditions match or exceed the preconditions of S1's context
  - C2 post-conditions do not exceed the post-conditions of S1's context
  - Data that passes through the C2 port is compatible with S1 data types
  - Service protocol constraints of C2 are compatible with service protocol constraints of S1
  - Each quality of service of C2 does not exceed the QoS provided by S1's context

Example:

S1 has the following *provides* contract end:

- Specified data flow context: x (of specified type T) flows to S1; y (of type T) flows from S1
- Specified control flow context: control flows to S1 along with x; control flows from S1 along with y
- Provided square root service: precondition: $0 \leq x \leq 1000000000.0$; post-condition: $y \mid y * y \doteq x$.
- Provided QoS–Precision: $\mid y * y - x \mid \leq 0.000001$
- Provided QoS–Timing: $t2 - t1 \leq 0.01$ second, where t1 = time at which S1 receives x and acquires control, and t2 = time at which S1 returns y and releases control.

S1 has the following *requires* contract end:

- Required service: none
- Required processor: processor with available memory $\geq$ 100K and processing speed = 100 MIPS (this is specified because the system is intended to run on this processor)

C2 is an available component with the following *provides* contract end:

- Assumed data flow context: x (of type T) flows to C2; y (of type T) flows from C2
- Assumed control flow context: control flows to C2 along with x; control flows from C2 along with y
- Provided square root service: precondition: $0 \leq x \leq N$, where $N =$ largest number of type T representable on the processor; post-condition: y, where $y * y \doteq x$.
- Provided QoS–Precision: $\mid y * y - x \mid \leq 0.0000005$

- Provided QoS–Timing: $t2 - t1 \leq 0.5$ second/M, where $t1$ = time at which C2 receives x and acquires control, and $t2$ = time at which C2 returns y and releases control, and M = processor speed in MIPS.

C2 has the following *requires* contract end:

- Required service: none
- Required processor: processor with available memory $\geq$ 10K

So, does the available C2 specification satisfy the needed S1 specification? Yes, if $N \geq 1000000000.0$ and if cost of the component $\leq$ cost limit specified for S1. Why?

- Data and control requirements match
- Service (pre- and post-condition) matches
- QoS precision of C2 exceeds the requirement
- QoS timing (speed) of C2 exceeds the requirement on the provided processor
- Processor satisfies the C2 processor requirement
- C2 has no required service

This is a trivial example and smaller than a typical component, but it illustrates the kinds of specification information that we believe are needed for both user context and available component to support COTS component testing.

3.4 Benefits and Prospects

Benefits

The specification approach described here enables and strengthens black-box component testing by:

- Normalizing and reconciling developer specifications with user needs; this facilitates more comparable matching of available COTS products to system architecture needs
- Providing a general approach that can be instantiated in specific component-based environments/specifications; this explains what information is needed and provides a structure for organizing the information
- Providing an extensible approach–more black-box specification information related to testing can be added

The point is not that this approach offers a new way to test, but rather that this information offers a more precise and complete basis for testing than do traditional black-box specifications, especially informal ones. This approach has the virtue of achieving higher levels of precision without requiring high levels of formalization.

This approach can also incorporate other black-box approaches to component testing. For example, test frames could be added to component specifications to support regression testing, as described in the specification-based component testing in [321].

Testing candidate component specifications is now a more precise activity. The test of an available component external specification against a desired component external specification involves specification matching based on extended Design by Contract. Some of the difficulties Garlan observed [140] concerning architectural mismatch would be caught if this information were specified, i.e., if the approach in this chapter were followed. Thus, the result of analyzing a component specification now provides the component user much more information than under a traditional specification. Integration effort should be significantly reduced, because the difficulties and mismatches that now frequently occur are detected in specification matching. The approach helps identify changes more precisely, and thus should facilitate regression testing.

Finally, the approach frees system architects from having to pick a single component model, such as J2EE, because the specification information here applies to all models and vendors. In other words, the approach facilitates the testing and integration of heterogeneous systems. The approach also sets the foundation for moving into more dynamic component environments, such as service-oriented architectures and Web services.

Prospects

Some of the information called for in this approach is not typically provided by COTS vendors or in system architectures. The intent is to set a goal toward which the software industry–and in particular COTS vendors, component developers, and system architects–can begin to move to provide increasing support for testing of COTS components. Steps can be taken now to begin organizing and structuring specification information as described here, to see where the holes are, and to begin adding more semantic information both to architecture specifications and to COTS product specifications. The fact that the approach applies more broadly to software engineering in general should provide additional impetus for moving in this direction.

A Methodology of Component Integration Testing

Hong Zhu[1] and Xudong He[2]

[1] Department of Computing
Oxford Brookes University
Wheatley campus
Oxford OX33 1HX, UK
hzhu@brookes.ac.uk

[2] School of Computer Science
Florida International University
University Park
Miami, FL 33199, USA
hex@cs.fiu.edu

Summary. Integration testing plays a crucial role in component-based software development. It is also very difficult due to the common problem of lack of information about the design of the components and the unavailability of source code of commercial off-the-shelf (COTS) components. Addressing this problem, we investigate how to observe system's dynamic behavior in component integration testing. Based on a theory of behavioral observation developed in our previous work, this chapter proposes a formal model of component integration testing methods and a hierarchy of behavioral observation schemes suitable for component integration testing. Their properties and interrelations are studied. Incremental integration testing strategies are also investigated. The requirements for proper uses of test drivers and component stubs in incremental integration are analyzed.

1 Introduction

In recent years, software component technology has emerged as a key element of modularity in the development of large and complicated systems [100, 185, 385]. Ensuring the correct integration of software components is a critical problem in component-based software development(CBSD). Industrial practices in CBSD have shown a clear shift of development focus from design and coding to requirements analysis, testing, and integration, especially from unit testing to integration testing [77, 289, 371]. However, traditional testing methods have to be adapted to meet the new requirements of CBSD.

Generally speaking, software integration testing can be based on the requirements specification, the design or the code of the system under test, or, ideally, a combination of these. Most existing methods are based on the functional requirement specifications, e.g., [66, 438]. Their major weakness is that program structure and design information are not utilized in the testing. Design-based methods have been proposed to utilize the information contained in design documents, such as in UML models [4, 19], software architecture descriptions [27, 343], and structural design diagrams [446, 447]. However, in the context of CBSD, the design information of the components is usually not available in testing when components are commercial off-the-shelf (COTS) packages. Among code-based methods are inter-procedural data flow testing methods [130, 172, 325, 396], their extensions to coupling-based methods [214], and, more recently, interface mutation testing methods [91]. A weakness of code-based methods is that they rely on the availability of the source code of the components. This weakness becomes a serious problem when the component is a COTS package because source code is not usually available for component users. Moreover, these methods do not support incremental integration strategies. Consequently, even if the source code is available, analyzing the complete set of code becomes impractical when the software system is large. Therefore, their applicability to CBSD is also limited.

It is widely recognized that the lack of information flows between component developers and component users is one of the main causes of the difficulties of software testing in CBSD [37]. In particular, as discussed above, component users have limited access to information about component design and implementation details in the integration of components into their systems. This implies that testers as component users have very limited ability to observe the internal behavior of the components. On the other hand, component developers, in the design and implementation as well as in the testing of components, have very limited knowledge about their uses. Hence, they have limited knowledge about what should be provided to the component's users to observe the behaviors of the components. Therefore, how to observe the behaviors of components becomes a crucial problem of testing in CBSD.

This chapter addresses this problem based on a general theory of behavioral observation in software testing that we proposed in [441–443, 445]. We study the aspect of software testing in which a system's dynamic behaviors are observed and recorded so that the system's properties can be inferred. The focus of behavioral observation is one of the most important characteristics that distinguishes software testing activities at different development stages. For example, integration testing focuses its observation on the interactions between the components of the system, while unit testing focuses on the internal behaviors of the components. The former represents component users' view toward testing software components and the latter represents component developers' view. This chapter will take the component users' view toward testing in the integration of components into a system. However, the theory can be applied equally to the testing of components from the developers' view if the components are compositions of other components. It also sheds new light on what component developers should provide to component users in order to help integration testing of components. Based on our formal theory of behavioral observation, especially the 'design patterns' of software testing methods obtained in the study of existing testing methods [445], we can derive a number of testing methods suitable for component integration testing. Moreover, a collection of guidelines for the proper uses of incremental integration testing strategies can also be developed from the theory.

The remainder of the chapter is organized as follows. Section 2 briefly reviews our theory of behavioral observation and presents a set of design patterns of software testing methods. Section 3 applies the theory to component integration testing. We propose a formal model of white-box integration testing in which components can be treated as black boxes while the code that glues components together are treated as a white box. We then apply design patterns to derive a collection of testing methods that are suitable for white-box component integration testing. The effective uses of test drivers and component stubs in incremental integration testing will also be investigated. Section 4 concludes the chapter with a summary of the work reported in this chapter and a brief discussion of the directions for further work.

2 Overview of the Observation Theory

In software testing practices, observations on a system's dynamic behavior can be made on a number of different aspects of the execution of the system. For example, in addition to the correctness of the output, one can also observe the following:

(1) The set of executed statements, as in statement testing method;
(2) The set of exercised branches, as in branch testing method;
(3) The set of executed paths, as in path testing methods;
(6) The set of dead mutants, as in mutation testing;
(4) The sequences of communications between processes, as in the testing of communication protocols;
(5) The sequences of synchronization events, as in testing concurrent systems [389].

To render observed and recorded information meaningful, we require that observations be systematic and consistent. For example, it is not acceptable if sometimes we record executed statements, sometimes don't. We use the term 'observation schemes' to denote a systematic and consistent way of observing and recording a system's dynamic behavior in software testing. Here, a distinction must be made between an observed phenomenon and the dynamic behavior itself. A phenomenon is the result of an observation on a certain aspect of the dynamic behavior during a specific test execution of a software system. Employing different observation methods may result in observing different phenomena of the same behavior. Therefore, each observation method determines a universe of phenomena of the system's dynamic behavior observable from testing.

In this section, we review the theory that we developed in [441–443, 445] about the mathematical structure of the universe of observable phenomena, the mathematical properties of observation schemes, and the common structures of existing observation schemes in various software testing methods.

2.1 The Structure of Observable Phenomena

As argued in [441], the observable phenomena in testing a particular software system p using a well-defined testing method constitute an algebraic structure called Complete Partially Ordered set (CPO set). Formally, CPO sets are defined as follows.

Definition 1. *(CPO sets)*
A CPO set $\langle D, \leq \rangle$ consists of a nonempty set D and a binary relation $\leq$ on D, such that $\leq$ is a partial ordering and satisfies the following conditions:

(1) D has a least element, written $\perp$, i.e., for all $x \in D$, $\perp \leq x$;
(2) For all directed subsets $S \subseteq D$, S has a least upper bound, written as $\bigsqcup S$, i.e., for all upper bound u of S, $\bigsqcup S \leq u$;

where a subset $S \subseteq D$ is directed if for all $s_1, s_2 \in S$ there is $s \in S$ such that $s_1 \leq s$ and $s_2 \leq s$; an element $u \in D$ is called an upper bound of S if $s \leq u$ for all $s \in S$.   □

The partial ordering $\leq$ on observable phenomena represents the fact that different observed phenomena contain different information of the dynamic behavior of the system. The relation $\alpha \leq_p \beta$ means that phenomenon α contains less information than phenomenon β in testing system p.

Example 1. (The universe of observable phenomena in statement testing)
For example, in statement testing, the set of statements in the program executed during testing is observed in addition to the correctness of the output. A phenomenon of the dynamic behavior of a system is the set of statements executed during testing. All such sets constitute a universe of phenomena and the partial ordering relation on the universe is the set inclusion relation $\subseteq$. The more a program is tested, the larger the set of statements executed.   □

Within a CPO set, for all directed subsets S of elements, there is the least upper bound $\bigsqcup S$. In the context of software testing, the least upper bound of a set of observed phenomena serves as an operation that summarizes the observations and draws a general conclusion about the testing. The result is a phenomenon that puts information from all the independent observations together. It contains all the information in the individual observations and nothing more. For example, in statement testing, the union of the sets of executed statements is the summation operation on observable phenomena.

The set union operation is the least upper bound of two sets with respect to the set inclusion relation. This is consistent with the intuition that if two sets of statements are executed in two independent tests, the union of the sets of statements contains exactly all the tested statements.

The least element $\perp_p$ in the universe of observable phenomena in testing program p represents the phenomenon that can be observed if the system is not executed at all. Therefore, it usually is the phenomenon that contains no information about the dynamic behavior of a system. For example, in statement testing, the least element is the empty set, which means no statement is executed. Of course, any set of statements observed in a testing includes the empty set.

CPO sets have been well studied in denotational semantics of programming languages, and constitute domain theory. Readers are referred to [161] for a concise treatment of domain theory and its uses in the studies of the semantics of programming languages.

Note that, in many software testing methods, there is also a greatest element of observable phenomena in testing a software system p, written as $\top_p$. That is, for all phenomena α, we have that $\alpha \leq_p \top_p$. For example, the set of all feasible statements in a program is the greatest element in the observable phenomena in statement testing. In many cases, the greatest element can be observed only by testing on an infinite number of test cases. For example, the set of all feasible paths in a program is the greatest observable phenomenon in path testing. Usually, it can be covered only by infinite tests if the program contains loops. While such a greatest element might be useful, it does not necessarily exist in all testing methods. For the sake of generality, our theory does not assume its existence. The results obtained subsequently can also be applied to all phenomenon spaces, including those having the greatest elements.

2.2 The Notion of Observation Schemes

The notion of observation schemes is formally defined as a mathematical structure to represent systematic behavioral observation methods of software testing.

Definition 2. *(Observation scheme)*
A scheme $\mathcal{B}$ of behavioral observation and recording, or simply an observation scheme, is a mapping from software systems p to ordered pairs $\langle \mathbf{B}_p, \mu_p \rangle$, where $\mathbf{B}_p = \langle B_p, \leq_p \rangle$ is a CPO set that represents the universe of observable phenomena of p. Function μ_p is called the recording function, which is a mapping from test sets T to nonempty subsets of B_p. □

Informally, $\mu_p(T)$ is the set of all possible phenomena observable by testing p on test set T. In other words, $\sigma \in \mu_p(T)$ means that σ is a phenomenon that is observable by an execution of p on test set T. Note that, in testing a concurrent system, two executions of the same system p on the same test set

T may demonstrate two different behaviors due to nondeterminism. Consequently, one can observe more than one phenomenon in two executions of p on the same test set, say, σ and σ'. Both σ and σ' belong to the set of such observable phenomena for testing p on test set T, which is denoted by $\mu_p(T)$.

Note also that, to test concurrent systems, a test set T can be a multiple set (or bag) so that multiple executions of the system on the same test case can be described. In this chapter, the set of all multiple sets on a set X is denoted by $\mathbf{bag}(X)$. We write $\widehat{Y}$ to denote the set obtained by removing duplicated elements in a multiple set Y. The traditional set operators are used to denote their multiple set variants as well. Moreover, in the test of interactive or process control systems, a test case can be a sequence of input data without an upper limit on the lengths. In such cases, a partial ordering on the test cases of the system can be defined and the input space of the system forms a CPO set. Therefore, test sets can be elements of a power domain of the input CPO set. For the sake of generality, we assume that there is only a partial ordering on test sets and the collection of all test sets of a program forms a complete partially ordered set. The least element of the test sets means that the software is not dynamically tested. The greatest test set is the exhaust test, if it exists. For the sake of readability, we use the set inclusion symbol $\subseteq$ as the partial ordering relation between test sets, the empty set $\emptyset$ as the least element of the test sets, and the set union $\cup$ and intersection $\cap$ symbols as the least upper bound and the greatest lower bound of test sets, respectively. We also use the set membership symbol $\in$ to denote that a test case is contained in a test set. We will use P to denote the set of all software systems. The input domain of a software system p is denoted by D_p.

The following examples illustrate the notion of observation schemes.

Example 2. (Input/output observation scheme)
Let $IO_p = \{\langle x, y \rangle | x \in D_p \wedge y \in p(x)\}$, where $y \in p(x)$ means that y is a possible output of p when executed on input data x. The universe of observable phenomena is defined to be the power set of IO_p, and the partial ordering is set inclusion. The recording function $\mu_p(T)$ is defined to be the collection of sets of input/output pairs observable from testing p on T.

For instance, assume that $D_p = \{0, 1\}$, $p(1) = \{1\}$, and $p(0) = \{0, 1\}$ due to non-determinism. Let test data $t = 0$ and test set $T_1 = \{t\}$; then, $\mu_p(T_1) = \{\{\langle 0, 0 \rangle\}, \{\langle 0, 1 \rangle\}\}$, i.e., one may observe either $\{\langle 0, 0 \rangle\}$ or $\{\langle 0, 1 \rangle\}$ by executing p on input 0 once. Let test set $T_2 = \{2t\}$; then, $\mu_p(T_2) = \{\{\langle 0, 0 \rangle\}, \{\langle 0, 1 \rangle\}, \{\langle 0, 0 \rangle, \langle 0, 1 \rangle\}\}$, i.e., one of the following three different phenomena can be observed by executing p twice on the same input 0:

$\{\langle 0, 0 \rangle\}$ / p outputs 0 in two executions on input 0;
$\{\langle 0, 1 \rangle\}$ / p outputs 1 in two executions on input 0;
$\{\langle 0, 0 \rangle, \langle 0, 1 \rangle\}$ / p outputs 0 in one execution and outputs 1 in another execution on the same input 0. $\square$

Example 3. (Dead mutant observation scheme)
Consider the observation scheme for mutation testing [53,147,422]. Let Φ be a set of mutation operators. The application of Φ to a program p produces a set of mutants of p. Let $\Phi(p)$ be the set of such mutants that are not equivalent to p. Define the universe of phenomena to be the power set of $\Phi(p)$. The partial ordering is defined to be the set inclusion relation. For all test sets T, the recording function $\mu_p(T)$ is defined to be the collection of sets of mutants. Each element in $\mu_p(T)$ is a set of mutants that can be killed by one test of p on T.   □

Example 4. (Output diversity observation scheme)
The observation scheme in this example records the number of different outputs on each input data. A phenomenon observable from testing a concurrent system on a set of test cases consists of a set of records. Each record has two parts, $\langle t, n \rangle$, where t is a valid input, and n is the number of different outputs on the input data observed from the testing. Formally, an element of the universe of phenomena is a set in the form of $\{\langle t_i, n_i \rangle | t_i \in D_p, n_i > 0, i \in I\}$. The partial ordering relation on phenomena is defined as follows:

$$\sigma \leq \sigma' \Leftrightarrow \forall \langle t, n \rangle \in \sigma. \exists \langle t', n' \rangle \in \sigma'.(t = t' \wedge n \leq n').$$

The least upper bound of σ_1 and σ_2 is a set, written as $\sigma_1 + \sigma_2$, which contains elements in the form of $\langle t, n \rangle$ and satisfies the following conditions.

(a) $\langle t, max(n_1, n_2) \rangle \in \sigma_1 + \sigma_2$, if $\exists n_1, n_2 > 0.(\langle t, n_1 \rangle \in \sigma_1 \wedge \langle t, n_2 \rangle \in \sigma_2)$;
(b) $\langle t, n_1 \rangle \in \sigma_1 + \sigma_2$, if $\exists n_1 > 0.(\langle t, n_1 \rangle \in \sigma_1) \wedge \neg \exists n_2 > 0.(\langle t, n_2 \rangle \in \sigma_2)$;
(c) $\langle t, n_2 \rangle \in \sigma_1 + \sigma_2$, if $\exists n_2 > 0.(\langle t, n_2 \rangle \in \sigma_2) \wedge \neg \exists n_1 > 0.(\langle t, n_1 \rangle \in \sigma_1)$.
                                                                                      □

2.3 Test Adequacy Criteria

One of the most important elements of all software testing methods is the concept of test adequacy criteria. Since the introduction of the concept in 1970s [147], a large amount of research on test adequacy criteria has been reported in the literature; see, e.g., [437] for a survey.

Software test adequacy criteria can play at least two significant roles in software testing [437]. First, a test adequacy criterion provides an objective guideline to select test cases so that adequate testing can be performed. Many software test criteria have been proposed as such guidelines or test case generation and selection methods. A test set generated according to such a guideline or by using such a method is therefore adequate according to the criterion. In the research on the theories of software testing, test adequacy criteria are, therefore, usually formally defined as predicates on the space $\mathbf{T}$ of test sets and software systems P, i.e., as mappings $C : \mathbf{T} \times P \rightarrow Bool$, (cf [53, 67, 87, 132, 326, 327, 419, 422]). Second, a test adequacy criterion also provides a stop rule to determine whether a testing is adequate and can stop.

Such a stop rule is often used together with a metric to determine how much has been achieved by the testing so far. For example, the percentage of statements covered by testing is a metric for statement coverage criterion. Theoretically speaking, such a metric is a function that gives a mapping from test sets and software systems to a numerical scale such as the unit interval, i.e., $C : \mathbf{T} \times P \to [0, 1]$ (see, e.g., [439]).

A common feature of existing theories of test adequacy criteria is that they consider test adequacy as a property of test sets. However, as discussed in the previous sections, in the testing of concurrent and non-deterministic systems, the behavior of the system under test is not uniquely determined by the input test cases. Test adequacy is a property of the dynamic behavior demonstrated in the testing process. Therefore, we redefine the notion of test adequacy criteria as predicates of observed phenomena or as measurements on observed phenomena. Formally, let $\mathcal{B} : p \to \langle \mathbf{B}_p, \mu_p \rangle$ be an observation scheme. An adequacy criterion C as a stop rule is a mapping from software system p to a predicate C_p defined on B_p, such that, for any phenomenon, $\sigma \in \mu_p$, $C_p(\sigma) = true$ means that the testing is adequate if phenomenon σ is observed. An adequacy criterion C as a measurement is a mapping from software system p to a function M_p from B_p to the unit interval $[0, 1]$ of real numbers. For any phenomenon, $\sigma \in \mu_p$, $M_p(\sigma) = \rho \in [0, 1]$ means that the adequacy measurement of the testing is ρ if the phenomenon observed is σ.

In this framework, a software test method can be defined as an ordered pair $\langle \mathcal{B}, C \rangle$ of a behavioral observation scheme $\mathcal{B}$ and a test adequacy criterion C. In this chapter, we will focus on the observation schema because it is a difficult issue of testing in CBSD.

2.4 Properties and Axioms of Behavioral Observations

Having recognized that observation schemes are an essential part of all testing methods, we now discuss what a good observation scheme is. In [441], we proposed a set of desirable properties of observation schemes and studied the interrelationships between the properties. We now list the axioms. Their rationales can be found in [441].

Axiom 1. *(Empty set property)*
Nothing can be observed from the empty testing. Formally,

$$\forall p \in P, (\mu_p(\emptyset) = \{\perp_p\}). \tag{1}$$

□

Axiom 2. *(Observability)*
If a software system is tested on at least one valid input, some nontrivial phenomenon of the system's behavior can always be observed. Formally,

$$\forall p \in P, (T \cap D_p \neq \emptyset \Rightarrow \perp_p \notin \mu_p(T)). \tag{2}$$

□

A testing process is often incremental in the sense that more and more test cases are executed and observations are made cumulatively. Suppose that a system p is tested on test set T, and a phenomenon σ_1 is observed. Later on, some additional test cases are executed and a new observation σ_2 is made as the result of testing on T', where $T \subseteq T'$. The following axioms state the required properties for an observation scheme to be used in incremental testing:

Axiom 3. *(Extensibility)*
Every phenomenon observable from testing a system on a test set is part of a phenomenon observable from testing on any of its supersets. Formally,

$$\forall p \in P, (\sigma \in \mu_p(T) \wedge T \subseteq T' \Rightarrow \exists \sigma' \in \mu_p(T'), (\sigma \leq_p \sigma')). \tag{3}$$

□

Axiom 4. *(Tractability)*
Every phenomenon observable from testing a system on a test set T contains a phenomenon observable from testing on any subset T'. Formally,

$$\forall p \in P, (\sigma \in \mu_p(T) \wedge T \supseteq T' \Rightarrow \exists \sigma' \in \mu_p(T'), (\sigma \geq_p \sigma')). \tag{4}$$

□

A special case of incremental testing is to repeatedly execute a system on the same test cases. For testing concurrent systems, such repetition often reveals new behavior. However, the same phenomenon should be observable when repeating a test. Hence, we have the following axiom:

Axiom 5. *(Repeatability)*
Every phenomenon observable from testing a system p on a test set T can be observed from repeating the test of p on the same test set T. Formally,

$$\forall p \in P, (\sigma \in \mu_p(T) \Rightarrow \sigma \in \mu_p(T \cup T)). \tag{5}$$

□

Note that, in the above axiom, when the test set T is a multiple set of test cases, $T \cup T$ represents that all test cases in T are executed twice; hence, we may have that $T \cup T \neq T$.

Axiom 6. *(Consistency)*
For any given system p, any two phenomena observed from two tests of the system must be consistent. Formally,

$$\forall p \in P, (\mu_p(T) \uparrow \mu_p(T')), \tag{6}$$

where $\sigma_1 \uparrow \sigma_2$ means that the phenomena σ_1 and σ_2 are consistent, i.e., they have a common upper bound; $\Gamma_1 \uparrow \Gamma_2$ means that the sets Γ_1 and Γ_2 are consistent, i.e., for all $\sigma_1 \in \Gamma_1$ and $\sigma_2 \in \Gamma_2$, $\sigma_1 \uparrow \sigma_2$. □

In software testing practices, a testing task is often divided into several subtasks and performed separately. Such a testing strategy can be considered as testing on several subsets of test cases, and observations are made independently by executing on the subsets. These observations are then put together as the result of the whole testing effort. The following axioms are concerned with such testing processes:

Axiom 7. *(Completeness)*
Every phenomenon observable from testing a system on a subset is contained in a phenomenon observable from testing on the superset. Formally,

$$\forall p \in P, \left(\underset{i\in I}{\forall} \ \sigma_i \in \mu_p(T_i), (\exists \sigma \in \mu_p(T), (\sigma \geq_p \sigma_i)) \right), \tag{7}$$

where $T = \bigcup_{i\in I} T_i.$ □

Axiom 8. *(Composability)*
The phenomena observable by testing a system p on a number of test sets can be put together to form a phenomenon that is observable by executing p on the union of the test sets. Formally,

$$\forall p \in P, \left(\underset{i\in I}{\forall} \ \sigma_i \in \mu_p(T_i), \left(\bigsqcup_{i\in I} \sigma_i \in \mu_p(\bigcup_{i\in I} T_i) \right) \right). \tag{8}$$

□

Axiom 9. *(Decomposability)*
For all test sets T and its partitions into subsets, every phenomenon observable from testing a system p on the test set T can be decomposed into the summation of the phenomena observable from testing on the subsets of the partition. Formally, let $T = \bigcup_{i\in I} T_i;$ *we have,*

$$\forall p \in P, \left(\sigma \in \mu_p(T) \Rightarrow \underset{i\in I}{\exists} \ \sigma_i \in \mu_p(T_i), (\sigma \bigsqcup_{i\in I} \sigma_i) \right). \tag{9}$$

□

Figure 1 below summarizes the relationships between the axioms, where arrows are logic implications. Proofs of these relationships can be found in [441].

2.5 Extraction Relation Between Schemes

From a phenomenon observed under a given scheme, one can often derive what is observable under another scheme. For example, we can derive the set of executed statements from the set of executed paths. The following extraction relation formally defines such relationships between observation schemes:
Let $\mathcal{A} : p \rightarrow \langle \mathbf{A}_p, \mu_p^A \rangle$ and $\mathcal{B} : p \rightarrow \langle \mathbf{B}_p, \mu_p^B \rangle$ be two schemes.

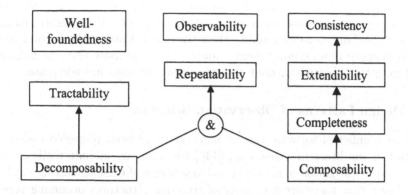

Fig. 1. Relationships between the axioms.

Definition 3. *(Extraction relation between schemes)*
Scheme A is an extraction of scheme B, written $A \triangleleft B$, if for all $p \in P$, there is a homomorphism φ_p from $\langle B_p, \leq_{B,p} \rangle$ to $\langle A_p, \leq_{A,p} \rangle$, such that

(1) $\varphi_p(\sigma) = \perp_p$ if and only if $\sigma = \perp_{B,p}$, and
(2) for all test sets T, $\mu_p^A(T) = \varphi_p(\mu_p^B(T))$.

$\square$

The extraction relation is a partial ordering on observation schemes.

Informally, scheme A being an extraction of scheme B means that scheme B observes and records more detailed information about dynamic behaviors than scheme A. The phenomena that scheme A observes can be extracted from the phenomena that scheme B observes. Consequently, if a fault in the system under test can be detected according to an observed phenomenon using A, the same fault can also be detected by using observation scheme B. In other words, A being an extraction of B implies that B has better fault detection ability than A.

Note that, first, extraction relations between observation schemas are similar to the subsumption relations on test adequacy criteria. A test adequacy criterion C_1 subsumes criterion C_2 if for all tests T, T is adequate according to C_1 implies that T is also adequate according to C_2 (cf [132,437,440]). However, the schema of testing method M_1 is an extraction of the schema of method M_2 does not imply that there is a subsumption relation between their adequacy criteria, or vice versa. Counterexamples can be found in [443]. In fact, a number of different test adequacy criteria can be defined on one observation schema. Second, subsumption relations between test adequacy criteria have been intensively investigated to compare testing methods, and are considered an indication of better fault detection ability. In posterior uses of test adequacy criteria, it does guarantee better fault detection ability [437]. However, it was proven that a subsumption relation cannot alone always guarantee better fault detection ability if the observation method used during testing is not taken into consideration [132]. In contrast, as discussed above, an extraction relation between two observation schemas can guarantee that one test method has a better fault detection ability than the other. Finally, the extraction relation between observation schemas allows us to compare the test methods' fault detection abilities without assuming that the tests are adequate.

2.6 Design Patterns of Observation Schemes

A great number of software testing methods have been proposed and investigated in the literature (see, e.g., [440] for a survey of unit testing methods). Our investigation of the observation schemes of existing testing methods has shown that there are a number of common structures occurring repeatedly [445]. These common structures can be considered as design patterns of observation schemes. They enable us to understand the strengths and weaknesses of testing methods from a very high level of abstraction, and to develop testing methods according to the desired features. They, therefore, provide guidelines for the design of testing methods. This section summarizes the common constructions of observation schemes and their properties. Readers are referred to [445] for details.

A. Set Construction

In statement testing, software testers observe and record the subset of statements in the software source code that are executed (see, e.g., [24, 299]). In this observation scheme, the execution of a statement is an atomic event to be observed. An observable phenomenon is a set that consists of such events that happened during testing. The partial ordering on observable phenomena is set inclusion. Such construction of a scheme is common to many testing methods. The following is a formal definition of this construction:

Definition 4. *(Regular set scheme)*
An observation scheme $\mathcal{B} : p \to \langle \mathbf{B}_p, \mu_p \rangle$ is said to be a regular set scheme (or simply a set scheme) with base $U_{p \in P}$ if, for all software systems $p \in P$, the elements in the CPO set $\langle B_p, \leq_p \rangle$ are subsets of U_p and the partial ordering $\leq_p$ is the set inclusion relation $\subseteq$. Moreover, the following conditions hold for the mapping μ_p:

(1) $U_p = \bigcup_{t \in D_p} (\bigcup \mu_p(\{t\}))$,
(2) $\mu_p(\emptyset) = \{\emptyset\}$,
(3) $T \cap D_p \neq \emptyset \Rightarrow \emptyset \notin \mu_p(T)$,
(4) $\mu_p(T) = \mu_p(T \cap D_p)$,
(5) $\mu_p(\bigcup_{i \in I} T_i) = \{\bigcup_{i \in I} \sigma_i | \sigma_i \in \mu_p(T_i), i \in I\}$.

□

The following theorem about the extraction relations between regular set observation schemes will be used later in the study of integration testing:

Theorem 1. *(Extraction theorem for regular set schemes)*
Let $\mathcal{B} : p \rightarrow \langle \mathbf{B}_p, \mu_p^B \rangle$ be a regular scheme. Let $\mathcal{A} : p \rightarrow \langle \mathbf{A}_p, \mu_p^A \rangle$. Assume that, for all software systems $p \in P$, there is a set U_p^A such that $\langle A_p, \leq_p \rangle$ is a CPO set of subsets of U_p^A with set inclusion relation $\subseteq$. If, for all $p \in P$, there is a surjection f_p from U_p^B to U_p^A such that $\sigma_A \in A_p \Leftrightarrow \exists \sigma_B \in B_p, (\sigma_A = \{f_p(x) | x \in \sigma_B\})$, and, for all test sets T, $\mu_p^A(T) = \{f_p(\sigma) | \sigma \in \mu_p^B(T)\}$, then we have that

(1) $\mathcal{A}$ is a regular scheme with base U_p^A, and
(2) $\mathcal{A}$ is an extraction of $\mathcal{B}$.

We say that $\mathcal{A}$ is the regular scheme extracted from $\mathcal{B}$ by the extraction mapping f_p. $\qquad\qquad\square$

In particular, observation scheme $\mathcal{A}$ is an extraction of scheme $\mathcal{B}$ if, for all programs p, $U_p^A \subseteq U_p^B$.

B. Partially Ordered Set Construction

In the set construction, there is no ordering relationship between the basic events to be observed. However, in some testing methods such as path testing, the basic events are ordered by a partial ordering.

Let X be a nonempty set and $\ll$ be a partial ordering on X. A subset $S \subseteq X$ is said to be downward closed if, for all $x \in S$, $y \ll x \Rightarrow y \in S$. Let $p \in P$. Given a partially ordered set (also called poset) $\langle A_p, \ll_p \rangle$, we define the universe B_p of phenomena to be the set of downward closed subsets of A_p. The binary relation $\leq_{B,p}$ on phenomena is defined as follows:

$$\sigma_1 \leq_{B,p} \sigma_2 \Leftrightarrow \forall x \in \sigma_1, \exists y \in \sigma_2, (x \ll_p y) \qquad (10)$$

It is easy to prove that $\leq_{B,p}$ is a partial ordering. Moreover, if the poset $\langle A_p, \ll_p \rangle$ has a least element $\perp_p$, the poset $\langle B_p, \leq_{B,p} \rangle$ is a CPO set with the least element $\{\perp_p\}$. The least upper bound of σ_1 and σ_2 is $\sigma_1 \cup \sigma_2$.

Definition 5. *(Partially ordered set scheme)*
An observation scheme $B : p \rightarrow \langle B_p, \leq_p^B \rangle$ is said to be a partially ordered set scheme (or poset scheme) with base $\langle A_p, \ll_p \rangle$ if its universe of phenomena is defined as above and the recording function has the following properties:

(1) $\mu_p(\emptyset) = \{\{\perp_p\}\}$,
(2) $T \cap D_p \neq \emptyset \Rightarrow \{\perp_p\} \notin \mu_p(T)$,
(3) $\mu_p(T) = \mu_p(T \cap D_p)$,
(4) $\mu_p(\bigcup_{i \in I} T_i) = \{\bigcup_{i \in I} \sigma_i | \sigma_i \in \mu_p(T_i), i \in I\}$. $\qquad\square$

Example 5. (Observation scheme for path testing [53, 188, 422])
Let p be any given program. A path in p is a sequence of statements in p executed in the order. Let A_p be the set of paths in p, and the partial ordering

$\ll_p$ be the sub-path relation. Let s be a set of paths in p. The downward closure of s is the set of sub-paths covered by s, written as $\bar{s}$. Let T be a test set. We define

$$\mu_p(T) = \{\bar{s}_{T,p} | s_{T,p}\},$$

where $s_{T,p}$ is a set of execution paths in p that may be executed on T.

It is easy to see that the function defined above satisfies conditions (1) through (4) in the definition of the poset scheme.   □

As in Example 5, we can define observation schemes that observe the sequences of a type of events that happened during test executions of a system, such as the sequences of communication and synchronization events. Such schemes have the same property as the scheme for path testing.

C. Product Construction

Given two observation schemes $\mathcal{A}$ and $\mathcal{B}$, we can define a new scheme from them by including the information observed by both schemes. The following defines the product scheme of $\mathcal{A}$ and $\mathcal{B}$:

Definition 6. *(Product construction)*
Let $\mathcal{A} : p \to \langle \mathbf{A}_p, \mu_p^A \rangle$ and $\mathcal{B} : p \to \langle \mathbf{B}_p, \mu_p^B \rangle$. The scheme $\mathcal{C} : p \to \langle \mathbf{C}_p, \mu_p^C \rangle$ is said to be the product of $\mathcal{A}$ and $\mathcal{B}$, written $\mathcal{C} = \mathcal{A} \times \mathcal{B}$, if for all software systems $p \in P$,

(1) $\mathbf{C}_p = \langle C_p, \leq_{C,p} \rangle$, where

$$C_p = \{\langle \sigma_A, \sigma_B \rangle | \sigma_A \in \mathbf{A}_p, \sigma_B \in \mathbf{B}_p\},$$

$$(\langle \sigma_A, \sigma_B \rangle \leq_{C,p} \langle \sigma'_A, \sigma'_B \rangle) \Leftrightarrow (\sigma_A \leq_{A,p} \sigma'_A) \wedge (\sigma_B \leq_{B,p} \sigma'_B);$$

(2) for all test sets T, $\mu_p^C(T) = \mu_p^A(T) \times \mu_p^B(T)$.   □

Example 6. (Typed dead mutant observation scheme)
In Example 3, an observation scheme is defined for mutation testing. In software testing tools, mutation operators are often divided into a number of classes to generate different types of mutants (see, e.g., [227]). Dead mutants of different types are then recorded separately to provide more detailed information. To define the observation scheme for this, let Φ_1, $\Phi_2, \cdots, \Phi_n$ be sets of mutation operators. Each $\Phi_i, i = 1, 2, \cdots, n$, defines a dead mutant observation scheme $\mathcal{M}_i$, as in Example 3. We define the typed dead mutant observation scheme $\mathcal{M}_{Typed} = \mathcal{M}_1 \times \mathcal{M}_2 \times \cdots \mathcal{M}_n$.   □

D. Statistical Constructions

An observation scheme in the set construction or partially ordered set construction observes and records whether certain types of events happen during the testing process. Another type of observation often used in software testing is the statistics of the number or frequency of certain events that happened in testing. Let $\mathcal{B} : p \to \langle \mathbf{B}_p, \mu_p^B \rangle$ be an observation scheme and N be any given set of numbers. Then, $\langle N, \leq \rangle$ is a totally ordered set under the less than or equal to relation $\leq$ on numbers. We can define a scheme $\mathcal{A} : p \to \langle \mathbf{A}_p, \mu_p^A \rangle$ as follows.

Definition 7. *(Statistical construction)*
An observation scheme $\mathcal{A} : p \to \langle \mathbf{A}_p, \mu_p^A \rangle$ is said to be a statistical observation scheme based on $\mathcal{B} : p \to \langle \mathbf{B}_p, \mu_p^B \rangle$ if there exists a set N of numbers and a collection of mappings $s_{p \in P} : B_p \to N$ such that, for all software systems $p \in P$,

(1) $A_p = N$, and $\leq_{A,p}$ is the less than or equal to relation $\leq$ on N;
(2) The mapping s_p from B_p to the set N preserves the orders in B_p, i.e.,
$$\sigma \leq_{B,p} \sigma' \Rightarrow s_p(\sigma) \leq s_p(\sigma');$$
(3) For all test sets T, $\mu_p^A(T) = \{s_p(\sigma) | \sigma \in \mu_p^B(T)\}$.   □

Informally, the observable phenomena in a statistical construction are numerical values ordered as numbers. The mapping s_p can be considered as the measurement of the sizes of the phenomena observed by the base scheme. This size measurement must be consistent with the ordering on the phenomena in the base scheme. In other words, the more the information contained in a phenomenon observed by the base scheme, the larger the size of the phenomenon. For example, statement coverage is a statistical construction based on statement testing:

Example 7. (Statement coverage)
Let $\mathcal{B} : p \to \langle \mathbf{B}_p, \mu_p^B \rangle$ be the regular scheme for statement testing, where $\mathbf{B}_p$ is defined in Example 1. Define $s_p(\sigma) = \|\sigma\|/n_p$, where n_p is the number of statements in program p and $\|\sigma\|$ is the size of the set σ. We thus define a statistical observation scheme for statement coverage. The phenomena observed by the scheme are the percentages of statements executed during testing.   □

Example 8. (Mutation score)
In mutation testing, mutation score is defined by the following equation and used as an adequacy degree of a test set [52, 93]:

$$MutationScore = \frac{DM}{NEM} \tag{11}$$

where DM is the number of dead mutants and NEM is the total number of non-equivalent mutants.

The mutation score can be defined as a statistical observation scheme based on the dead mutant observation scheme, defined in Example 3 with the mapping $s_p(\sigma)\|\sigma\|/m_p$, where $\|\sigma\|$ is the size of the set σ and m_p is the number of non-equivalent mutants of p generated by mutation operators. □

Note that the statement coverage scheme defined above is not decomposable, although the observation scheme for statement testing is a regular set construction that has decomposability according to Theorem 1. Similarly, the mutation score scheme does not have decomposability, while the dead mutation scheme has decomposability.

In software testing, statistics can also be made on the phenomena observed from testing on each test case. The following defines the construction of such schemes:

Definition 8. *(Case-wise statistical construction)*
An observation scheme $A : p \to \langle \mathbf{A}_p, \mu_p^A \rangle$ is said to be a case-wise statistical observation scheme based on $B : p \to \langle \mathbf{B}_p, \mu_p^B \rangle$ if there exists a set N of numbers and a collection of mappings $s_{p \in P} : B_p \to N$ such that, for all systems $p \in P$,

(1) $A_p = D_p \to N$, where $D_p \to N$ is the set of partial functions from D_p to N, and $\leq_{A,p}$ is defined by the equation

$$\sigma_1 \leq_{A,p} \sigma_2 \Leftrightarrow \forall t \in D_p.(\sigma_1(t) = undefined \lor \sigma_1(t) \leq \sigma_2(t)),$$

where $\leq$ is the less than or equal to relation on N;
(2) the mapping s_p from B_p to the set N preserves the order in B_p, i.e.,
$$\sigma \leq_{B,p} \sigma' \Rightarrow s_p(\sigma) \leq s_p(\sigma');$$
(3) for all test sets $T = \{n_i t_i | t_i \in D_p, n_i > 0, i \in I, i \neq j \Rightarrow t_i \neq t_j\}$, we have that $\sigma_A \in \mu_p^A(T)$ iff
   (a) $\forall i \in I.\exists \sigma_i \in \mu_p^B(\{n_i t_i\}).(\sigma_A(t_i) = s_p(\sigma_i))$, and
   (b) $t \notin T \Rightarrow \sigma_A(t) = undefined$.   □

Informally, a phenomenon in the universe A_p consists of a sequence of records. Each record represents the size of the phenomenon observed using the base scheme from the execution(s) of the concurrent system p on one test case. As in the statistical construction, the size function s_p must be consistent with the partial ordering relation defined on the base scheme.

Example 9. (Output diversity scheme)
The output diversity observation scheme defined in Example 4 is the case-wise statistical observation scheme based on the input/output observation scheme with the mapping s_p being the set size function.   □

In [442], we studied the properties of the observation schemes defined above. Table 1 below gives the properties of the above constructions in terms of the axioms that they satisfy. It also gives a typical example of observation

Table 1. Properties of the constructions of observation schemes.

Construction	Typical Examples	Properties (Axioms) 1 2 3 4 5 6 7 8 9
Regular set	Statement and branch testing Strong/weak mutation testing Def/Use data flow testing Decision/condition testing Partition testing	√ √ √ √ √ √ √ √ √
Partially ordered set	Path testing Interaction chain of data flow Definition context of data flow Def/Use data flow path testing	√ √ √ √ √ √ √ √ √
Product	Typed mutation testing	√ √ √ √ √ √ √ √ √
Statistics	Mutation score Statement/branch coverage Path coverage	√ √ √ √ √ √ √ × ×
Case-wise statistics		√ √ √ √ √ √ √ × ×

schemes in existing testing methods. Proofs of these properties can be found in [442].

Table 1 presented the properties of product, and statistical and case-wise statistical constructions proved under the assumption that the base schemes satisfy the axioms.

3 Behavioral Observation in Component Integration Testing

In this section, we apply the theory to the integration testing in CBSD. We study the axioms of behavioral observation for component integration testing, propose a set of observation schemes inspired by the design patterns of observation schemes, and investigate how test drivers and component stubs should be used properly in incremental integrations.

3.1 White-Box Integration Testing

At a high level of abstraction, a component-based software system can be regarded as a number of software components plugged into an architecture. Such an architecture can be considered a program constructor. In practice, it appears in the form of program code called glueware, while components may be in a number of forms, such as a module, a class, or a library.

In this chapter, we are concerned with white-box integration testing (WIT) methods in which the code of glueware is available and used in testing. Using a WIT method, the tester observes the internal dynamic behavior of the system rather than just the input/output. Moreover, the tester should be able to identify which part of the observation is about the components, and to separate such information from the rest.

A. Formal Model of White-Box Integration Testing

White-box integration testing methods can be formally defined using the theory of observation schemes as follows:

Definition 9. *(White-box integration testing methods)*
A white-box integration testing method contains an observation scheme $\mathcal{B}$:
$p \to \langle \mathbf{B}_p, \mu_p \rangle$. *For each component c in the system p under test, there exists a mapping φ_c from observable phenomena of the system in B_p to a universe $B_{c,p}$ of observable phenomena of the component c in the context of p. The mapping φ_c is called the filter for component c.*   □

Note that the universe of observable phenomena of a component determined by a WIT method should also be a CPO set, which may have a different structure from the whole system. This is because in integration testing we usually focus on the interaction between the components and their environment instead of the details of the behavior of the component.

It is worth noting that in Def. 9 we have not assumed whether observations on the internal behavior of a component are available. As we will see later, the approach is applicable to situations both when the internal behavior is observable and when the inside information of the components is hidden.

By a well-defined WIT method, we not only require that the observation scheme B satisfy the axioms listed in the previous section, but also that the partial ordering $\leq_{c,p}$ on $B_{c,p}$ and the filter φ_c satisfy the following axioms:

Axiom 10. *(Filter's well-foundedness)*
If no observation on the whole system is made, nothing is known for the component. Formally,

$$\varphi_c(\perp_p) = \perp_{c,p}, \tag{12}$$

where $\perp_p$ and $\perp_{c,p}$ are the least elements of $\langle B_p, \leq_p \rangle$ and $\langle B_{c,p}, \leq_{c,p} \rangle$, respectively.   □

Axiom 11. *(Filter monotonicity)*
The more the behavior observed of the whole system, the more one knows about the component based on the observation. Formally,

$$\forall \sigma_1, \sigma_2 \in B_p, (\sigma_1 \leq_p \sigma_2 \Rightarrow \varphi(\sigma_1) \leq_{c,p} \varphi(\sigma_2)). \tag{13}$$

□

Axiom 12. *(Filter continuity)*
The information about a component contained in the sum of a number of global observations is equal to the sum of the information about the component contained in each individual global observation. Formally,

$$\forall \Theta \subseteq B_p, \left(\varphi_c \left(\bigsqcup_{\sigma \in \Theta} \sigma \right) \bigsqcup_{\sigma \in \Theta} \varphi_c(\sigma) \right). \tag{14}$$

□

In white-box integration testing, we usually integrate a number of components into the system at the same time. Therefore, we generalize the notion of filter to a set of components. Let C be a set of components. A filter φ_C for a set C of components is therefore a mapping from the universe of the observable phenomena of the whole system p to the universes of observable phenomena of the component set C. We require that φ_C also satisfy the extended version of the above axioms, which are obtained by replacing φ_c with φ_C. Moreover, we require that for each c in C, there be a function ϑ_c such that $\varphi_c = \vartheta_c \circ \varphi_C$, where φ_c is the filter for the component c.

B. Some Basic WIT Observation Schemes

The following defines a hierarchy of observation schemes for component integration testing. Note that, although components may have structures, we will treat components as black boxes at the moment. We will discuss how the structure of components can be utilized in integration testing in Sect. 3.2.

(a) Interaction Statement Testing

This method is based on the regular set construction of observation schemes. We define the atomic events to be observed as executions of the statements in the glueware. Therefore, the set of statements executed during integration testing is observed and recorded. These sets of statements include activities related to interactions with the components, such as

(a) Initiating the execution of a component as a process or thread,
(b) Establishing or destroying a communication channel with a component,
(c) Creating or destroying an instance of a class defined in a component,
(d) Registering or unregistering a component into a system,
(e) Subscribing the data produced by a component,
(f) Publishing data that is subscribed,
(g) Invoking a component, as a function or procedure defined in a component,
(h) Sending a message to a process or thread of a component,
(i) Receiving a message from a process or thread of a component.

As in statement testing in unit testing, the details of the executed statement and their sequences of executions are not recorded. The method does not require observing and recording the execution of the statements inside a component. Therefore, the components are treated as black boxes. Formally, the interaction statement testing method can be defined as follows:

Definition 10. *(Interaction statement testing)*
Let U_p be the set of statements in the glueware of a component-based software system p. For each component c in the system, $U_{c,p} \subseteq U_p$, where $U_{c,p}$ is the subset of statements in the glueware that are related to the component c. The observation scheme $\mathcal{IS}_p$ of interaction statement testing is the regular set construction based on U_p. The observation scheme $\mathcal{IS}_{c,p}$ for a component c in p is the regular set construction based on $U_{c,p}$. The filter function φ_c for component c removes the statements not related to the component. That is, for all $S \subseteq U_p$, $\varphi_c(S) = \{s | s \in S, s \in U_{c,p}\}$. An adequacy criterion $\mathcal{ISC}_c$ for statement coverage of interaction with component c can be defined as follows:

$$\mathcal{ISC}_c = \frac{\|\varphi_c(S)\|}{\|U_{c,p}\|}, \tag{15}$$

where S is the set of statements in p executed during testing, ISC_c is the interaction statement coverage with respect to c. $\square$

It is easy to see that this testing method satisfies all the axioms of behavioral observation, as well as the axioms of filters in integration testing.

(b) Parameter Testing

The parameter testing method improves the observation on the dynamic behavior of a system by recording the set of component-related events with more details about the interactions with a component. Atomic activities in the interactions with a component often have parameters. For example, a call of a function/procedure defined in a component usually has parameters such as the values passed to the component in value parameters and values received from the component in variable parameters. Similarly, for a message passing event, the message also has contents. The values and contents passed across the interface of a component are not observed and recorded in interaction statement testing, but rather in parameter testing. In particular, in addition to what is observed in statement integration testing, parameter testing also observes and records the following information, and associates the information with the statements:

(a) The parameters used for initiating the execution of a component as a process or thread, if any, such as the name of the process, the value used for initialization of the process, etc.
(b) The parameters used for establishing or destroying a communication channel with a component, if any, such as the name, the identity number

of the communication channel, and the parameters used to set up the communication channel.

(c) The parameters used for creating or destroying an instance of a class defined in a component, such as the initial values used as parameters for the constructor.

(d) The parameters used for registering or unregistering from a component to a system, such as the name, network address, and any parameters of the component.

(e) The parameters used to subscribing for the data produced by a component, such as the name and/or format of the data.

(f) The details of publishing data that is subscribed to such as the value of the data, and any meta data such as format.

(g) Parameters used for invoking a component, such as the values of parameters and the names of the variable parameters in the invocations of functions or procedures defined in a component.

(h) The contents of messages sent to or received from a process or thread of a component, as well as any meta data associated with the message.

As with to interaction statement testing, this method itself does not require that the events happening inside a component be observed. It also treats components as a black box.

This scheme also has a set construction, but the base set is slightly more complicated here than in interaction statement testing. An element in the base set can be in the form of $\langle statement\ label, parameters \rangle$, which indicates that a statement is executed with its parameters. The observation scheme can be formally defined as follows:

Definition 11. *(Parameter testing)*
Let V_p be the set of statement-parameter pairs in the glueware of a component-based software system p, and $V_{c,p} \subseteq V_p$ be the subset of statement-parameter pairs where the statements are related to component c. The observation scheme $\mathcal{PT}_p$ of parameter testing is the regular set construction based on the set V_p. For each component c in the system p, the observation scheme $\mathcal{PT}_{c,p}$ for c is the regular set construction based on $V_{c,p}$. The filter function φ_c for component c removes the statement-parameter pairs that are not related to component c. That is, for all $S \subseteq V_p$,

$$\varphi_c(S) = \{s | s \in S \wedge s \in V_{c,p}\}.$$

□

An adequacy criterion for parameter testing cannot be defined as easily as interaction statement coverage because the set of statement-parameter pairs can be infinite if the parameter is, for example, a real number. Various methods to simplify the adequacy measurement can be applied to define practically usable adequacy criteria. For example, the domain of a parameter can be divided into a finite number of sub-domains so that each sub-domain is covered by at least one test case.

Note that, first, the observation scheme of statement testing is an extraction of the parameter observation scheme. This directly follows from Theorem 1. Second, the observation scheme of parameter testing is also a set construction. Therefore, it satisfies all the axioms of observation schemes. Finally, it is easy to prove that the filter satisfies the axioms of filters.

(c) Interaction Sequence Testing

Now, let us apply the partially ordered set construction to define a testing method similar to path testing.

The interaction sequence testing method for component integration testing observes and records the execution sequences of the statements in the glueware. Note that a component is still regarded as a black box. The base set is the set of paths in the glueware. Each path is a sequence of statements in the base set of interaction statement testing. There is a partial ordering between execution paths, which is the sub-path/super-path relation.

It is worth noting that interaction sequence testing in component integration can be applied not only to observe the sequences of interactions between a component and its environment (i.e., the glueware), but also to observe the interactions among a set of components. Therefore, the following defines the method in its most general form for integrating a set of components.

Definition 12. *(Interaction sequence testing)*
Let C be a set of components integrated into a component-based software system p, U_p be the set of interaction statements in the glueware of the system as defined in Def. 10 of interaction statement testing, and $U_{C,p}$ be the subset of U_p that is related to components in C as also defined in Def. 10. The observation scheme $\mathcal{ISQ}_p$ of interaction sequence testing is the partially ordered set construction based on $\langle Seq(U_p), \sqsubseteq \rangle$, where $Seq(X)$ is the set of finite sequences of elements in set X, and $\sqsubseteq$ is the sub-sequence/super-sequence relation between the sequences. The observation scheme $\mathcal{ISQ}_{C,p}$ of the component set C in p is the partially ordered set construction based on $\langle Seq(U_{C,p}), \sqsubseteq \rangle$. The filter function φ_C for component set C removes the statements not related to the components in C from the sequences of statements. That is, for each sequence q in $Seq(U_p)$, φ_C produces a sequence q' in $Seq(U_{C,p})$ by removing all the statements not in the set $U_{C,p}$. □

With this observation scheme, a variety of adequacy criteria can be defined, such as the coverage of simple sequences, which have no elements that appear more than once, and various path coverage criteria for loops (see, e.g., [436]).

Note that a finite sequence in the set $Seq(U_p)$ is a sequence of statements in p that represents an execution of the system. A finite sequence in the set $Seq(U_{C,p})$ removes any statement that is not related to interaction with the components in C. Therefore, it focuses on the interaction process between the glueware and the components.

From the properties of partially ordered constructions of observation schemes, we can prove that the observation scheme of interaction sequence testing satisfies all the axioms discussed in Sect. 2. It is also easy to prove that the filter function φ_C satisfies all the axioms of filters.

(d) Information Flow Testing

Similar to the interaction sequence testing method, information flow testing method is a generalization of parameter testing by applying the partially ordered set construction. The basic elements of observable phenomena are sequences of statement-parameter pairs. Each sequence records the execution of the system with detailed information about what has been passed across the interface to and/or from the components.

Definition 13. *(Information flow testing)*
Let C be a set of components integrated into a component-based software system p, V_p be the set of statement-parameter pairs in the glueware of the system as defined in Def. 11 of parameter testing, and $V_{C,p}$ be the subset of V_p that are related to components in C as defined also in Def. 11. The observation scheme $\mathcal{IFL}_p$ of information flow testing is the partially ordered set construction based on $\langle Seq(V_p), \sqsubseteq \rangle$. The observation scheme $\mathcal{IFL}_{C,p}$ of the component set C in p is the partially ordered set construction based on $\langle Seq(V_{C,p}), \sqsubseteq \rangle$. The filter function φ_C for component set C removes the statements not related to the components in C from the sequences. That is, for each sequence q in $Seq(V_p)$, φ_C produces a sequence q' in $Seq(V_{C,p})$ by removing all the elements not in the set $V_{C,p}$. □

The following theorem states the extraction relationships between the observation schemes defined above. They are also show in Fig. 2.

Theorem 2. *(Extraction theorem of basic WIT methods)*
The following extraction relations hold between the observation schemes defined above.

(1) $\mathcal{IS} \lhd \mathcal{PT}$; (2) $\mathcal{IS} \lhd \mathcal{ISQ}$; (3) $\mathcal{ISQ} \lhd \mathcal{IFL}$; (4) $\mathcal{PT} \lhd \mathcal{ISQ}$. □

The proof of Theorem 2 is straightforward.

3.2 Hierarchical Integration Testing

In large-scale and complicated component-based software systems, a component may also be a composition of other components. We call the components that directly constitute a software system the 1st order components. We call the components in a 1st order component the 2nd order components. Similarly, we define 3rd order components as components of 2nd order components,

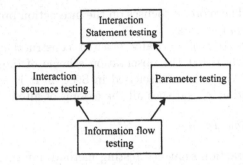

Fig. 2. The extraction relations between the testing methods.

and so on. We use high order components to denote all the components of any order. Therefore, each component can be modeled as a software constructor that consists of glueware and a number of higher order components. A component is called atomic if it does not contain any higher order components. In this case, the glueware is just the code of the component. Figure 3 below illustrates this view of a software system's structure. In the diagram, the overall system consists of three 1st order components B_1, B_2, and B_3. Each of these 1st order components is composed of some 2nd order components. For example, B_1 is composed of components $C_{1,1}$ and $C_{1,2}$. Component $C_{1,2}$ is composed of another smaller component, while $C_{1,1}$ is atomic.

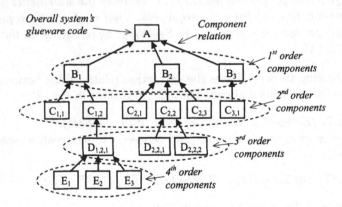

Fig. 3. Illustration of system structure from component view.

The integration testing methods studied in the previous section treat glueware as a white box and all components as black boxes. We call such a testing method a ground order white-box integration testing method. For each ground order method, we can generalize it to treat the 1st order components as white boxes and observe the same aspect of behavior inside the component. Meanwhile, the components of higher order than the 1st order are still treated as black boxes. We call such a generalized method a 1st order WIT method.

For example, the method obtained by generalizing the ground order interaction statement testing to the 1st order observes the statements at the architectural level glueware executed during testing, as well as the statements inside the 1st order components. All the statements of the glueware of the 1st order components are considered as related to the component. Therefore, the interaction statement coverage for integrating the component requires not only executing all the statements in the glueware of the whole system, but also all the statements of the glueware of the component.

For the interaction sequence testing of component integration, the generalization of the method from ground order to the 1st order requires testers to observe the execution paths that cross the interface of the 1st order components while treating higher order components as black boxes. Similarly, when the information flow testing method is generalized from ground order to the 1st order, testers are required to observe the execution paths that represent information flows between the glueware and the 1st order components. Such a path may start from the glueware and flow into the body of the 1st order components, then flow inside the body of the 1st order components, and finally come out the body, with the information being received and processed in the glueware. Before the execution path finishes in the glueware, it may well flow into other 1st order components.

A 1st order WIT method will not observe the same detail in the behavior of components of the 2nd and higher orders. It can be further generalized to kth order for any given natural number $k > 1$ by observing the same detail in the kth order components, while treating components of $(k+1)$th order as black boxes. The most powerful method is to treat all high order components equally, as white boxes. Such a method is called an infinite order WIT method. Figure 4 below illustrates the 2nd order WIT testing method, where all 2nd order components are treated as white boxes and higher order components as black boxes, shaded in the diagram.

Let $\mathcal{Z}$ be any given ground order WIT testing method. We write $\mathcal{Z}^{(k)}$ to denote the kth order generalization of $\mathcal{Z}$, and $\mathcal{Z}^{(\infty)}$ to denote the generalization of $\mathcal{Z}$ to an infinite order. It is easy to see that these observation schemes have the following extraction relationship. Its proof is omitted.

Theorem 3. *(Extraction relations on generalizations)*
For all WIT testing methods $\mathcal{Z}$, we have $\mathcal{Z} \lhd \mathcal{Z}^{(1)} \lhd \cdots \lhd \mathcal{Z}^{(K)} \lhd \mathcal{Z}^{(K+1)} \lhd \cdots \lhd \mathcal{Z}^{(\infty)}$,
for all $K > 0$. □

The generalization of ground order WIT testing methods also preserves the extraction relations. Formally, we have the following theorem [444].

Theorem 4. *(Preservation of extraction relations by generalizations)*
For all WIT testing methods $\mathcal{X}$ and $\mathcal{Y}$, we have that for all $n = 1, 2, \cdots, \infty$,
$\mathcal{X} \lhd \mathcal{Y} \Rightarrow \mathcal{X}^{(n)} \lhd \mathcal{Y}^{(n)}$. □

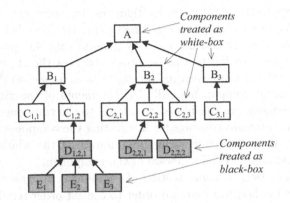

Fig. 4. Illustration of 2nd order WIT testing method.

A ground order WIT testing method can also be generalized heterogeneously so that some kth order components are treated as white boxes and some as black boxes. Figure 5 illustrates a situation in heterogeneous higher order WIT testing, where shaded components in the diagram are treated as black boxes and the others are treated as white boxes.

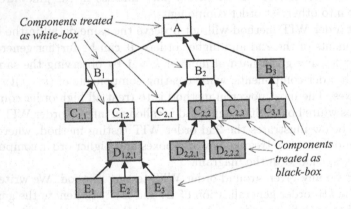

Fig. 5. Illustration of heterogeneous higher order WIT testing.

Let C be a subset of a system p's components that is to be treated as a white box in testing.

Definition 14. *(Consistent subset of components for WIT testing)*
A subset C of a system p's components is said to be consistent for WIT testing if a component of p being treated as a black box implies that all its subcomponents are also treated as black boxes. Formally, $\forall c \in C, (c \notin C \wedge (x$ is a subcomponent of $c) \Rightarrow (x \notin C))$. □

We write $\mathcal{Z}^{(C)}$ to denote the application of WIT testing method $\mathcal{Z}$ on software system p with a consistent collection C of components as white boxes and all other components as black boxes. Let C_1 and C_2 be two collections of components in a software system p. From Theorem 1, we can prove the following:

Theorem 5. *(Extraction relation on heterogeneous WIT testing)*
For all consistent collections C_1 and C_2 of components of any given software system p, $C_1 \subseteq C_2$ implies $\mathcal{Z}^{(C_1)} \lhd \mathcal{Z}^{(C_2)}$, i.e., $\mathcal{Z}^{(C_1)}$ is an extraction of $\mathcal{Z}^{(C_2)}$.
□

3.3 Incremental Integration Testing

In practice, integration testing is often carried out incrementally as components are gradually integrated into the system. Integration strategies such as top-down, bottom-up, and their combinations are employed. Applications of such strategies involve writing and using test drivers and component stubs. This section investigates the requirements on test drivers and component stubs in the light of behavioral observation theory.

For the sake of simplicity, we subsequently assume that program constructors are binary, i.e., they take two components as parameters. The result can be easily generalized to constructors of any number of components. Let $\otimes$ be a binary program constructor; $p = c_1 \otimes c_2$, where c_1 and c_2 are components. A component itself may be a composition of some other components, and formed by applying a program constructor, say, $c_1 = c_{1,1} \oplus c_{1,2}$.

A. Bottom-Up Integration Strategy

By applying the bottom-up strategy, we first put $c_{1,1}$ and $c_{1,2}$ together to form $c_1 = c_{1,1} \otimes c_{1,2}$ and test c_1 with a test driver to replace the constructor $\otimes$. After successfully testing c_1 and c_2 in this way, they are put together to form $p = c_1 \otimes c_2$ and tested. A test driver is in fact a program constructor, $\otimes'$, which, when applied to c_1, forms an executable program p'. During this testing process, we would like the test driver to act like the environment of c_1, as would be the case in the real program p. This means that if we can observe the behavior of component c_1 in the context of $\otimes$, we should be able to observe the same behavior in the context of the test driver $\otimes'$. Suppose that we use a WIT method with observation scheme $\mathcal{B} : p \to \langle \mathbf{B}_p, \mu_p \rangle$. Hence, there is a filter φ from p to c_1 and a filter φ' from p' to c_1. The requirements for a well developed test driver can be specified by the following axiom:

Axiom 13. *(Representativeness of test drivers)*
For all test suites T and all phenomena σ of the component that can be observed by executing the system p on T, there exist test suites T' for p' such that the same phenomena σ can be observed by executing p' on test suite T'. Formally, $\forall T \in \mathbf{T}_p,$

$$\forall \sigma \in \mu_p(T), \exists T' \in \mathbf{T}_{p'}, \exists \sigma' \in \mu_{p'}(T'), (\varphi(\sigma) \leq_{c_1} \varphi'(\sigma')), \qquad (16)$$

where $\leq_{c_1}$ is the partial ordering on B_{c_1}. $\qquad\qquad\qquad\qquad$ □

Note that Eq. 16 can be equivalently expressed as follows:

$$\forall T \in \mathbf{T}_{c_1 \otimes c_2}, \exists T' \in \mathbf{T}_{\otimes'(c_1)}, \left(\varphi(\mu_{c_1 \otimes c_2}(T)) \sqsubseteq_{c_1} \varphi'(\mu_{\otimes'(c_1)}(T'))\right),$$

where $\varphi(X) = \{\varphi(x) | x \in X\}$, and $X \sqsubseteq_{c_1} Y$ if and only if $\forall x \in X, \exists y \in Y, (x \leq_{c_1} y)$.

A test driver may simply pass input data to the component under test and then execute the component. Such test drivers serve as an interface between the tester and the component. For an observation scheme that observes only the functional aspect of behavior, such a test driver satisfies the representativeness axiom if it can pass all valid inputs to the component and pass out the result of the component's execution.

Sometimes, test drivers are written to combine other testing tasks, such as automatic generation of test cases, or select test cases from a repository of test data. Such a test driver usually does not have representativeness, because it generates only input data in a sub-domain. Therefore, it limits the space of observable phenomena. For all the test cases in the sub-domain, we require that the test driver be representative. Hence, we have the following weak form of Axiom 13.

Axiom 14. *(Representativeness on a sub-domain)*
For all test suites T in a sub-domain $S \subseteq D_p$ of the valid input of a system p, and all observable phenomena of the component from executing p on T, there is a test suite T' for the test driver for which the same phenomena can be observed in the context of the test driver. Formally, for all $T \in \mathbf{T}_S \subseteq \mathbf{T}_p$,

$$\forall \sigma \in \mu_p(T), \exists T' \in \mathbf{T}_{p'}, \exists \sigma' \in \mu_{p'}(T'), (\varphi(\sigma) \leq_{c_1} \varphi'(\sigma')) \qquad (17)$$

$\qquad\qquad\qquad\qquad\qquad\qquad\qquad\qquad\qquad\qquad\qquad\qquad\qquad$ □

B. Top-down Integration Strategy

A top-down strategy starts with testing the program constructor $\otimes$ by replacing components c_n with stubs c'_n, $n = 1, 2$. The difference between a real component c_n and a stub c'_n is that we would not be able to observe the internal behavior of c_n by executing c'_n. In fact, the internal behavior of c_n is not the focus of observation in integration testing. However, we would like that the interaction between the component c_n and its environment in p be faithfully represented by the stub c'_n. The requirements of the faithfulness of a component stub can be formally specified by the following axiom:

Axiom 15. *(Faithfulness of component stubs)*
For all test suites T and all phenomena σ observable by executing the system p

on T, the same observation can be obtained by executing the system p' obtained by replacing a component c with a stub c'. Formally,

$$\forall T \in \mathbf{T}_p, (\mu_p(T) = \mu_{p'}(T)). \tag{18}$$

□

An implication of the faithfulness axiom is that a stub can replace a component, if the observation scheme treats the component as a black box and if the observation scheme is concerned only with the functional aspect of a system. In that case, the stub is required to produce functionally correct outputs. Therefore, if a kth order WIT method is used, a component of $(k+1)$th or higher order can be replaced by a stub.

In software testing practices, stubs tend to provide only partial functionality of the component, and they faithfully represent the components' behavior only on a sub-domain of the component. This sub-domain is called the designated sub-domain of the stub. We require the stub to be faithful on the sub-domain. Hence, we have a weak form of Axiom 15. Assume that c is a component in system p, c' is a stub of c, and p' is obtained by replacing c in p with c'. We say that c' is faithful on a designated sub-domain S, if it satisfies the following axiom:

Axiom 16. *(Faithfulness of stubs on a designated sub-domain)*
For all phenomena σ observable by executing the system p on a test suite T, σ can also be observed by executing the system p' obtained by replacing the component c with a stub c' if, during the executions of p on T, the component is executed only on the stub's designated sub-domain. Formally,

$$\forall T \in \mathbf{T}_p \swarrow (c, S), (\mu_p(T) = \mu_{p'}(T)),$$

where $\mathbf{T}_p \swarrow (c, S)$ is the subset of $\mathbf{T}_p$ on which p calls the component only c on the designated sub-domain S.

□

The axioms of test stubs can also be extended for replacing a number of components by their corresponding stubs.

4 Conclusion

In this chapter, we reviewed the theory of behavioral observation in software testing and applied the theory to integration testing in component-based software development. We formalized the notion of white-box integration testing methods (WIT methods), in which the components can be treated as black boxes while the glueware of the system is treated as a white box. The basic properties of such testing methods are studied and a set of axioms is proposed to characterize well-defined observation schemes for such white-box integration testing. We also proposed four basic observation schemes for WIT, proved their satisfaction of the axioms, and investigated their interrelationships. These methods of component integration testing are

(a) interaction statement testing, which focuses on the statements in the glueware that interact with the components,

(b) interaction sequence testing, which observes the execution sequences of the statements in the glueware that interact with the components,

(c) parameter testing, which focuses on the interactions between the glueware and the components by observing the parameters of each interactive action,

(d) information flow testing, which focuses on the information flow in the glueware in the context of interaction with the components by observing the sequences of interactive actions and their parameters in each test execution of the system.

When details of components are available, our white-box integration testing methods also allow us to treat components as white boxes. In such cases, a component consists also of a glueware and a number of smaller components, which are called 2nd order or higher order components. In general, the components that directly comprise a software system are called 1st order components. The components that directly comprise a kth order component are called $(k + 1)$th order components. The basic WIT methods can be generalized to a kth order testing method, which treats components up to kth order as white box, while any higher order components are treated as black boxes. These testing methods and their generalizations fall into a nice hierarchical structure according to the extraction relation. Therefore, according to the availability of the code of components, appropriate testing methods can be used to achieve required test adequacy.

Integration testing of complicated large-scale software systems must use appropriate integration strategies. These involve writing and using test drivers and/or component stubs to enable the integration strategy to be applied. In this chapter, we also investigated and analyzed the requirements of test drivers and component stubs in bottom-up and top-down integration strategies.

There are several directions for future work. First, there are a number of testing methods proposed in the literature to support integration testing. We will examine whether these testing methods satisfy the axioms proposed in the chapter. Second, based on our understanding of the desirable properties of behavioral observation in integration, we will further investigate the algebraic structures of observable phenomena and their corresponding recording functions that satisfy these properties. The constructions of observation schemes that we proposed and investigated in [445] will also be further studied with regard to the axioms for integration testing. Finally, in [444] we have studied integration testing of software systems where components are integrated by applying parallel system constructors. We are further investigating some concrete system constructors that integrate components. In particular, we are applying the theory to specific component techniques.

5 Acknowledgments

This work was jointly funded by the NSF of USA under grant INT-0096143 and the NSF of China under grant 69811120643. X. He was also partially supported by the NSF of USA under grant HRD-0317692 and the NASA of USA under grant NAG2-1440. H. Zhu was also partially supported by China High-Technology Program under grant 2002AA116070.

Testing Component-Based Systems

Modeling and Validation of Publish/Subscribe Architectures

Luciano Baresi, Carlo Ghezzi, and Luca Zanolin

Politecnico di Milano – Dipartimento di Elettronica e Informazione
Piazza L. da Vinci, 32 – I20133
Milano (Italy)
baresi|ghezzi|zanolin@elet.polimi.it

Summary. The publish/subscribe component model is an emerging paradigm to support distributed systems composed of highly evolvable and dynamic federations of components. This paradigm eases the design of flexible architectures, but complicates their validation. It is easy to understand what each component does, but it is hard to foresee what the global federation achieves.

This chapter tackles the problem at the architectural level and describes an approach to ease the modeling and validation of such systems. The modeling phase specifies how components react to events. It distinguishes between the *dispatcher* and the other components. The former oversees the communication and is supplied as a predefined parametric component. The latter are specified as UML statechart diagrams. The validation uses model checking (SPIN) to prove properties of the federation defined as *live sequence charts* (LSCs). We do not start from LTL (*linear temporal logic*) formulae, the property language of SPIN, but we render properties as automata. This solution allows us to represent more complex properties and conduct more thorough validation of the modeled systems. The approach is exemplified on a simple application that controls an *eHouse*.

1 Introduction

The *publish/subscribe* [117] component model is an emerging paradigm to support software applications composed of highly evolvable and dynamic federations of components. According to this paradigm, components do not interact directly, but through a special-purpose element called *dispatcher*. The dispatcher receives events and forwards them to subscribers, that is, to all components registered to listen to them.

Publish/subscribe systems decouple the components participating in the communication: a sender does not know the receivers of its messages. Rather, receivers are identified by the dispatcher based on previous subscriptions. New components can dynamically join the federation, become immediately active, and cooperate with the other components without any kind of reconfiguration or refreshing of the modified application. They must simply notify the dispatcher that they exist by subscribing to particular events.

The gain in flexibility is counterbalanced by the difficulty to the designer in understanding the overall behavior of the application. Components are easy to reason about in isolation, but it is hard to get a picture of how they cooperate, and to understand their global behavior. Although components might work properly when examined in isolation, they can become faulty when put in a cooperative setting.

To solve these problems, we propose an approach, and a supporting environment, to model and validate publish/subscribe systems. We tackle the problem at the architectural level, where each component specifies how it produces and consumes events. The approach analyzes how the different elements cooperate to achieve a common goal, but does not address how they behave in isolation. Individual components are assumed to work as specified.

We point out explicitly that the goal of the chapter is to address validation of component-based software through formal analysis at the architectural level. In contrast with other contributions in this book, which focus on component testing, we address model-based validation. There is wide consensus that analysis and testing are complementary rather than competing techniques for validating software systems and improving their quality [330, 432]. This contribution stresses validation by proposing an innovative technique to analyze publish/subscribe systems that helps discover problems early during the design phase, but that does not replace component, integration, and system tests. Contributions to these subjects are presented in other chapters of this book.

Publish/subscribe systems are often implemented on top of a middleware platform that provides all event dispatching features. Implementors have only to configure it. The other components must be designed and coded explicitly. Our approach to modeling and validation exploits this peculiarity. Modeling the dispatcher is a complex task, but the effort is counterbalanced by the fact that the dispatcher is usually reused in different systems. The accurate representation of such a component would clearly impact the whole design phase, but its being application-independent eases the task. We do not ask designers to specify a new dispatcher (middleware platform) for each new application. By following a reuse approach at the modeling stage, we provide a parametric model of the dispatcher. Developers have only to configure it to render the communication paradigms they want to use. In contrast, application-specific components must be specified as UML statechart diagrams [354].

Once all components have been designed in isolation, modeled systems are validated through model checking. The global properties of the architectures, i.e., the federations of components, are rendered as *live sequence charts* (LSCs) [85]; both component models and properties are translated into Promela [181] and passed to the SPIN model checker [182]. We do not code properties as LTL (*linear temporal logic*) formulae, as is usual in the context of

SPIN, since they are not expressive enough. We render them as automata to represent more complex properties and to conduct more thorough validation.

The chapter is organized as follows. Section 2 introduces publish/subscribe systems through a simple example. Sections 3 and 4 describe how we model and validate their architectures. Section 5 presents the prototype toolset and Sect. 6 surveys the related work. Finally, Sect. 7 provides conclusions and outlines the possible directions of future work.

2 Our Approach

Our approach addresses publish/subscribe architectures [117,135]. These architectures are based on loosely coupled components that interact through events. The communication is based on a *dispatcher*. Components *publish* their events and *consume* those received from the dispatcher. They also *subscribe* (*unsubscribe*) to the dispatcher to define the events they want to receive. The dispatcher forwards (*notifies*) published events to all subscribers. This means that connections are not hardwired in the system, but are implicitly defined by means of published/subscribed events. New components can be added or new connections be established by simply subscribing/unsubscribing to events.

Figure 1 presents the architecture of such a system. It is an excerpt of a control system for an *eHouse*. Since we focus on a simple service that allows users to take baths, the architecture comprises the dispatcher and five application-specific components. When the user requires a bath, the service reacts by warming the bathroom and starting to fill the bathtub. When everything is ready, the user can take the bath.

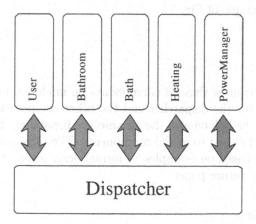

Fig. 1. Our example publish/subscribe architecture.

Notice that components do not communicate directly. More specifically, *User* publishes events to notify that he or she wants to take a bath. *Bathroom* is in charge of setting the bath and increasing the temperature in the bathroom. The bath and heating systems are described by *Bath* and *Heating*, respectively. When *Bath* receives the event from *Bathroom*, it starts operating and publishes another event when the bathtub is full. At the same time, *Heating* turns on the electric heating and increases the temperature of the bathroom.

PowerManager manages the provision of electricity. If there is a blackout, this component notifies this failure and switches from the primary to the secondary power supplier. The secondary power supplier is less powerful than the primary one, and some electric devices must be turned off for it. For instance, the electric heating turns itself off as soon as there is a blackout. Thus, the user cannot take a bath: the temperature in the bathroom cannot be increased since the electric heating does not work.

After sketching publish/subscribe systems and presenting a simple example, we can anticipate the main steps of our approach to modeling and validation:

1. The designer defines the specific dispatcher by instantiating a parametric component with suitable values for the parameters. Parameters tailor the main characteristics that differentiate the behaviors of the various dispatchers;
2. The designer specifies application-specific components by means of UML statechart diagrams;
3. The designer defines the properties against which the system should be validated through scenarios rendered as live sequence charts (LSCs);
4. Our tool validates the publish/subscribe architecture (against the properties defined above) using model checking techniques.

The following sections describe these three steps in detail and exemplify them on the example of Fig. 1.

3 Modeling

The approach requires that all components be modeled, but it suggests different methods for the dispatcher and the other components. In this section we first discuss the behavior of the parametric dispatcher. Then we show how statecharts can be used to model components. The presentation will be informal and mostly based on examples. A formal description of our approach will be provided in a future paper.

3.1 Dispatcher

The predefined dispatcher is instantiated by providing parameters that customize the dispatcher's behavior to reflect the different peculiarities of existing publish/subscribe middleware platforms. In fact, the market offers different alternatives, ranging from standards (e.g., Java Message Service (JMS) [379]) to research prototypes (e.g., Siena [60], Jedi [83]) to industrial products (e.g., TIBCO [393]). All these middleware platforms support the publish/subscribe paradigm, but their dispatchers offer slightly different characteristics. This means that the definition of the parameters that the dispatcher component should offer to the developer is a key issue. On the one hand, many parameters would allow us to specify the very details of the behavior, but, on the other hand, they would complicate the model unnecessarily. Moreover, we must consider that the target validation environment is based on model checking where state explosion hampers the actual analysis capabilities. Besides smart encoding techniques, the identification of the minimal set of parameters is essential: the simpler the model, the faster the verification.

Since the approach aims at verification at the architectural level, we assume that the model describes the interactions with components but does not address internal details. For example, the dispatcher could be implemented by middleware distributed on several hosts, but this is completely transparent to components and has no impact on functionality. The model describes how events are published and notified; it does not concentrate on how the dispatcher (middleware) works.

After several attempts, we have selected the following three characteristics as the key elements that define the "end-to-end" behavior of our dispatcher:

- **Delivery** Different middleware platforms may satisfy different requirements. For example, a middleware might be used to support cooperation among components in a mobile environment. In another case, it might be used for secure and reliable communication between components in a centralized system. These different cases require different guarantees to be met by the middleware in terms of event delivery. In the former case, we might tolerate the fact that some published events are not delivered to certain subscribers. In the latter, we might insist on the delivery of all published events. Thus, event delivery can be characterized by two alternatives: (a) all events are always delivered, or (b) some events can be lost.

- **Notification** The relationship between the order of event generation and event delivery can vary among different middleware implementations. Ideally, one might expect events to be notified in the same order in which they are published. This ideal behavior, however, can be easily enforced in a centralized setting, but is hard to achieve in a distributed environment. Thus, if we want to relate the order of publication to the order of notification, we can identify three alternatives: (a) they are the same, (b) the order of publication and notification are the same only when we refer to events published by the same component, or (c) there is no relationship, and events may be notified randomly. For example, if component A publishes the sequence of events x_1, x_2, and then component B publishes the sequence y_1, y_2, the dispatcher could notify these events to component C as follows:

  - case (a), $x_1 < x_2 < y_1 < y_2$

- case (b), $x_1 < x_2, y_1 < y_2$
- case (c), any permutation,

where $a < b$ means that event a is notified before event b.

- **Subscription** When a component declares the events it is interested in (i.e., *subscribes* to these events), it starts receiving them immediately. Similarly, unsubscribing is also instantaneous. However, the distributed nature of the system can make the dispatcher delay the response to new subscriptions/unsubscriptions. Thus, our parametric characterization identifies two alternatives: (a) the dispatcher immediately reacts to (un)subscriptions, or (b) these operations are not immediate and can be delayed.

The actual dispatcher comes from choosing one option out for these three main characteristics[1] (summarized in Table 1). These options of characterizations cover most of the guarantees that a dispatcher should satisfy. They are a reasonable compromise between balancing the need for light models of the dispatcher and capturing the many nuances of its possible behaviors. More sophisticated models – that is, more parameters to deal with problems like authentication and safety in message delivery – would have made validation heavier with no additional benefits (with respect to the problems we are interested in).

Notice that developers can always get rid of the predefined parametric dispatcher, implemented by a ready-to-use component, elaborate their particular model of the dispatcher as a UML statechart diagram (like any other component), and integrate it with the architecture. They would lose the advantages associated with reuse and well defined communication protocols, but can they could still follow our validation approach.

Table 1. Alternative guarantee policies associated with the *Dispatcher*.

Delivery	(a) All events are always delivered
	(b) Some events can be lost
Notification	(a) Orders of publication and notification are the same
	(b) Orders of publication and notification are the same only when we refer to the events published by the same component
	(c) No relationship and events may be notified randomly
Subscription	(a) The dispatcher immediately reacts to (un)subscriptions
	(b) Subscriptions are not immediate and can be delayed

Referring to the *eHouse* example, we assume that the architecture of Fig. 1 uses a dispatcher that (1) delivers all events, (2) keeps the same order of publication and notification, and (3) reacts immediately to all (un)subscriptions.

---

[1] The tool (Sect. 5) provides a set of check boxes to let the designer select the desired options.

3.2 Components

The designer provides for each component a UML statechart diagram whose transitions describe how the component reacts to incoming events. Events have a name and a (possibly empty) set of parameters. When components subscribe/unsubscribe to/from events, they can either refer to specific events or use wildcards to address classes of events. For example, *subscribe("bath", "ready")* means that the component wants only to know when the bath is ready, but *subscribe("bath",$)* means that it wants to subscribe to all *bath* events.

Transitions are labeled by a pair x/y, where x (i.e., the precondition) describes when the transition can fire, while y defines the actions associated with the firing of the transition. Either x or y can be missing. For instance, *consume("bath", "full")/publish("bath", "ready")* states that the transition can fire when the component is notified that the bathtub is full of water and publishes an event to say that the bath is ready.

The events notified to a component are stored in a *notification queue*. The component retrieves the first event from its notification queue, and if it does not trigger any transition exiting the current state, that is, no consume operation "uses" the event, the component discards the event and processes the following one. This mechanism allows components to evolve even if they receive events that cannot be processed in their current states.

Table 2. Glossary of events.

Event	Meaning
need,bath	The user needs a bath
bath,start	The bath starts running
bath,ready	The bath is full of water
bath,finished	The user finishes to take the bath
bath,notAvailable	The bath is not available
bath,full	The bath is full of water
bathroom,warm	The bathroom asks to increase the temperature
bathroom,freeze	The bathroom asks to decrease the temperature
bathroom, hot	The temperature in the bathroom is hot
bathroom, cold	The temperature in the bathroom is cold
heating, off	The heating is switched off
power, alarm	There is a blackout
power, ok	The electricity is on

Figure 2 describes component *Bathroom* of Fig. 1. To facilitate the intuitive understanding of these diagrams, Table 2 provides a glossary of events used. *Bathroom* starts in state *Idle*, waiting for events. At this stage, it is subscribed only to events that ask for a bath. When the user notifies that he or she needs a bath, *Bathroom* changes its state and notifies *Heating* that the

280   Luciano Baresi, Carlo Ghezzi, and Luca Zanolin

temperature should be increased and *Bath* should start to run. At the same time, the component updates its subscriptions by adding those relating to temperature, heating, and bath. This component exploits two variables that are used to store the status of the bath, *bathStatus*, and of the temperature, *temperatureStatus*. For example, the variable *bathStatus* set to *true* means that the bathtub is full of water.

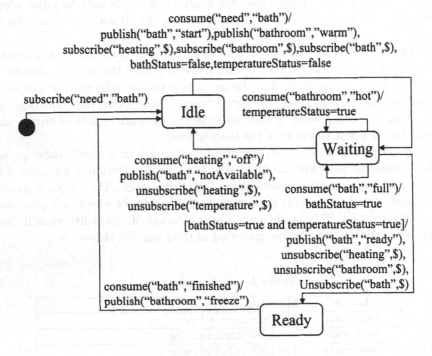

Fig. 2. Bathroom.

When the bathtub is full of water and the temperature is hot, the bath is *Ready*. In this state, the component is not interested anymore in events about bath and heating; thus, it unsubscribes from them. Finally, after the user takes the bath, *Bathroom* restores temperature to *cold*[2].

Figure 3 shows the statechart diagram of *Heating*. For simplicity, we suppose that, when this component starts, the power supplier is working correctly and temperature is *cold*. When *Heating* receives an event that asks for increasing the temperature, it moves to an intermediate state to say that the bathroom is warming. When the temperature in the bathroom becomes *hot*, *Heating* moves to the next state, i.e., *Hot*.

---

[2]For simplicity, we assume here that the temperature can assume only two values: cold and hot.

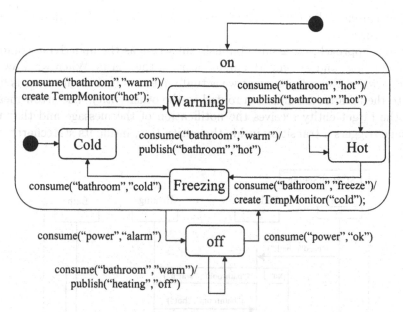

Fig. 3. Heating.

4 Validation

Validation comprises two main aspects: the definition of the properties that we want to prove on the federation of components and the transformation of both the model and properties into automata (i.e., Promela).

4.1 Properties

Our goal was to provide an easy-to-use graphical language to specify properties, which would allow designers to work at the same level of abstraction as statechart diagrams. For this reason, we did not use any temporal logic formalisms like *linear temporal logic* [331] (LTL), since they work at a different level of abstraction and, thus, developers would find them difficult to use. We chose *live sequence charts* (LSCs) [85] since they are a graphical formalism powerful enough to describe how entities exchange messages, which are a key aspect of the properties we wish to analyze.

Briefly, a basic LSC diagram describes a scenario of how the architecture behaves. LSCs allow us to render both existential and universal properties, that is, scenarios that must be verified in at least one or all the evolutions of the architecture.

Entities are drawn as white rectangles with names above them. The life cycle of an entity is rendered as a vertical line which ends in a black rectangle. The white and black rectangles denote the entity's birth and death, respectively. Messages exchanged between entities are drawn as arrows and are asynchronous by default. Each message has a label that describes the message contents.

In our approach, we assume publish/subscribe as the underlying communication policy, and we omit the middleware in the charts. When we draw an arrow between two entities, what we actually mean is that the message is first sent to the middleware and then routed to the other entity. The arrow means that the target entity receives the notification of the message and that the message triggers a transition inside the entity (i.e., inside its statechart).

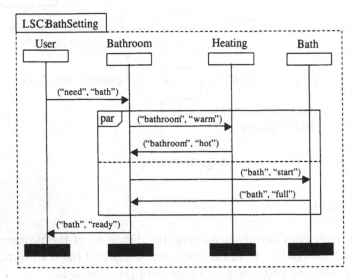

Fig. 4. A basic LSC: Bath setting.

Let us define some properties on our bath service. For example, we want to state that, when the user requires a bath, the temperature in the bathroom increases and the bathtub starts to fill. These two tasks are done in parallel and, after the termination of both, the user is notified that the bath is ready. These properties are described in Fig. 4, which shows a basic LSC scenario. *User* issues his/her request for a bath and *Bathroom* reacts by requesting that *Heating* must start to warm the bathroom and *Bath* to fill the bathtub. The two tasks are performed in parallel without any constraint on their order. This parallelism is described through the *par* operator, which states that its two scenarios (i.e., warming the bathroom and filling the bathtub) evolve in parallel without any particular order among the events they contain. When the bathtub is full and the bathroom is warm, *User* is notified that the bath is ready.

This chart describes only a possible evolution since we cannot be sure that *Bathroom* always notifies *User* that the bath is ready. In fact, if we had a blackout, *User* would receive a notification that the bath cannot be set. Thus, we do not require that the application always complies with this scenario.

Rather, we request that there be some possible evolutions that are compliant with it. In LSCs, these scenarios are called *provisional* or *cold* scenarios, and are depicted as dashed rectangles, as shown in Fig. 4.

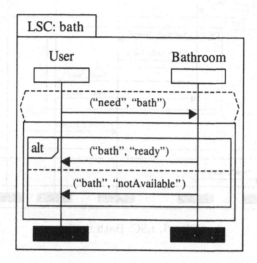

Fig. 5. LSC: Bath ready.

To fully specify the bath service, the designer also wants to describe the possible evolutions of the service, that is, when the user requires a bath, he or she always receives a positive or negative answer. This property is shown in Fig. 5. LSCs allow us to define such a property through a *mandatory* or *hot* scenario (depicted as a solid rectangle).

In general, it is difficult to identify global properties that must be satisfied in all evolutions. For this reason, LSCs support the definition of preconditions, that is, the property must hold in all the evolutions for which the precondition holds. Preconditions are drawn as dashed polygons, while the hot part of the scenario is depicted as a solid rectangle. For clarification, we can say that the precondition implies the hot scenario. The chart in Fig. 5 states that, for all the evolutions in which *User* requires a bath, *Bathroom* notifies two possible events, that is, either the bath is ready or it is not available. In this chart, we exploit *alt* (alternative), which is another operator supported by LSCs. This operator says that one of its two scenarios must hold. Thus, Fig. 5 describes that, after requesting a bath, an event will notify when the bath is ready, unless the bath notifies that it is unavailable.

Finally, we can redefine the previous property (Fig. 4) to state when the bath becomes ready: the bath must always become ready if no blackout occurs. This property is described in Fig. 6. If no blackout occurs while *Heating* warms the bathroom, the bath must always become available. In this chart, we introduce the *not* operator, which is not part of standard LSCs. This operator has two scenarios as parameters and states that while the first evolves, the

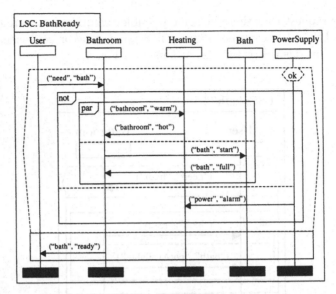

Fig. 6. LSC: Bath ready.

second cannot happen simultaneously: if no blackout occurs during the setup of the bath, *User* always receives a positive answer (i.e., the bath becomes ready).

4.2 Transformation

So far, we have shown how to model the architecture and define the properties. After these steps, we can start the analysis. We have decided to use the SPIN model checker [182] as verifier, but, as we already explained, we do not use LTL to describe the properties that we want to prove. Everything is transformed into automata and then translated into Promela [181].

After tailoring the dispatcher according to the parameters set by the developer, we can render it with Promela. Each alternative corresponds to a Promela package and the tool selects the right packages and assembles the model of the dispatcher directly. The translation of statechart diagrams into Promela is straightforward. We do not describe this translation since it has been done by others before (e.g., vUML [243] and veriUML [72]), and we have borrowed from these approaches a method to implement our translation.

Properties are translated in two different ways: cold scenarios are described through plain automata; hot scenarios need auxiliary LTL formulae also. This translation is rather complex since SPIN does not support natively the verification of existential properties. It can verify LTL formulae, which define universal properties but not existential ones.

To state an existential property through LTL, we could negate the LTL formula and verify that the system violates it: this means that there is at least one evolution in which the LTL formula is satisfied (i.e., its negation is violated). However, this approach would require that SPIN be run once for each property that we want to verify. We cannot compose the properties to eliminate executions: we would not find out if there are evolutions that satisfy our properties, but, rather if a single evolution satisfies all of them. Thus, instead of using LTL formulae or their translation into Büchi automata, we investigate a different solution that is based on representing properties (LTLs) as Promela processes. Reasoning on the state reachability feature provided by SPIN, we can compose properties, that is, we have some automata in parallel, and we verify if LSCs hold. However, automata are not enough to describe all LSC features, and, when required, we introduce local LTL formulae to overcome this problem. The transformation of an LSC into an automaton (and LTL) goes through the following four steps:

1. We simplify the property by downgrading all the hot scenarios to cold ones. This means that an automaton can describe the property.
2. We translate the simplified property into the automaton that recognizes the sequence of events described by the LSC. This task is quite easy since the structure of the automaton replicates the structure of the LSC.
3. We reintroduce the fact that the scenario is *hot* by identifying the states in the automaton in which the *hot* scenario starts and ends.
4. We describe the *hot* scenario through a constraint expressed as an LTL formula. The constraint states that if an automaton has reached the state that corresponds to the first message of the *hot* scenario, it must always reach the state that corresponds to the last message of the *hot* scenario. In other words, if the automaton recognizes the first message of the *hot* scenario, it must always recognize all the messages that belong to the same *hot* scenario.

The combination of the automaton and LTL formulae allows us to translate any LSC into Promela and verify it through SPIN.

For example, let us consider the LSC of Fig. 6 and the corresponding automaton of Fig. 7. This automaton has three types of arrows: solid, solid with a cross, and dashed. Solid arrows describe *standard* transitions and have labels that describe recognized events. For instance, if the automaton evolves from state b_1 to state b_2, this means that the event ("bathroom", "warm") has been published and consumed[3]. This type of arrow can end in a state or in a fork/join bar. Besides recognizing events, solid arrows with a cross disable the join bar in which they end. For instance, when the transition leaving d_1 fires, the join bar in the right hand side of the figure is disabled. Finally, dashed arrows do not define transitions between states, but constrain the evolution of the automaton. The constraint – described by an LTL formula – is always of the same kind: if the automaton reaches a state (i.e., the source state of

---

[3] For the sake of clarity, in Fig. 7 we do not describe who publishes or consumes events.

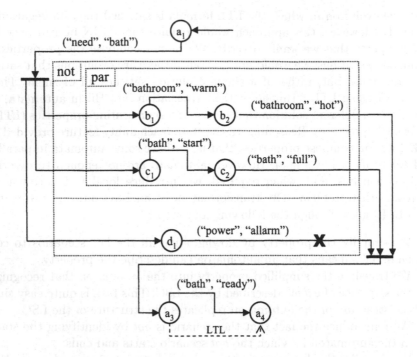

Fig. 7. The automaton that corresponds to the LSC of Figure 6.

the arrow), it must always reach the other state (i.e., the target state of the arrow).

The automaton of Fig. 7[4] has the same structure as the LSC of Fig. 6. This means that when the dispatcher notifies the first event, that is, *("need", "bath")*, the fork bar is enabled and the automaton splits its evolution into three different threads. Moving top-down, the first thread describes the warming of the bathroom, the second thread depicts the filling of the bathtub, and the last thread corresponds to the blackout. If the first two threads evolve completely while the third thread does not, the join bar is enabled and the automaton evolves to state a_3. This means that we do not have a blackout while the bathroom is warming and the bath tub is filling. Then, if the dispatcher notifies the last event (i.e., *("bath", "ready")*), the automaton reaches state a_4. Reasoning on state reachability, we can argue that if state a_4 is reachable, then there is at least one evolution that complies with the simplified property (i.e., the cold scenario). The property described by this automaton – with no LTL formulae – states that there exists an evolution in which no blackout occurs and, after set-up, the bath becomes available to the

---

[4]Readers can interpret this automaton as a statechart extended with inhibitor arcs (i.e., negative conditions). The diagram contains three parallel threads: The first two flows identify "positive" evolutions, while the third flow states a negative condition.

user. But this does not match the property of Fig. 6, which states that, if no blackout occurs, the bath must become available. This is why we must refine the automaton and add the dashed edge. Notice that, in this example, the hot scenario comprises only states a_3 and a_4. In fact, the scenario has only a single message (("bath", "ready")). All previous states define the precondition associated with the scenario, that is, the dashed polygon of Fig. 6. The hot constraint means that, if the precondition holds (i.e., all the previous events have already happened), then this event must always occur. This constraint is described by the following LTL formula:

$$\Box(In(a_3) \Rightarrow \Diamond In(a_4)),$$

where we require that when the automaton is in state a_3 (i.e., $In(a_3)$ holds), it must always reach state a_4.

We can verify this property by reasoning on the reachability of states. In particular, we require that the final state a_4 be reachable; thus, there is at least one evolution that complies with this property. If the model checker does not highlight any evolution in which the LTL formula is violated, we can say that when the precondition is verified, it is always the case that the post-condition is verified in the same evolution.

The validation of the bath services is performed by assuming that the available dispatcher provides the following guarantees: (1) events are always delivered, (2) the order of publication is preserved in the notification, and (3) the dispatcher immediately reacts to subscriptions and unsubscriptions. The validation process shows that the service is incorrectly designed since it violates the property shown in Fig. 5. This becomes clear if we consider the following scenario: *User* asks for a bath and *Bath* starts to fill the bathtub. At the same time *Heating* increases the temperature, but before its becoming *hot* we have a blackout that turns the heating off. At this point, *Bathroom* and *User* wait forever, since *Heating* notifies neither that it is switched off nor that the temperature is *hot*. This problem can be avoided by modifying the arrows between states *on* and *off* in *Heating* (Fig. 2) to introduce the publication of an event to notify that *Heating* fails.

5 Tool Support

Figure 8 shows the architecture of our prototype environment. Components, that is, UML statecharts, are translated directly into Promela. We do not need an intermediate step since Promela allows for easy coding of automata. Properties are translated as explained in the previous section. Both statecharts and LSCs are designed using UML-like CASE tools and supplied to the translator as XMI (XML Metadata Interchange [313]) files. In contrast, the dispatcher is specified by selecting the check boxes that correspond to the properties guaranteed by the middleware (as specified in Table 1). Each alternative is implemented as a package: the tool selects the appropriate parts and composes them in Promela directly.

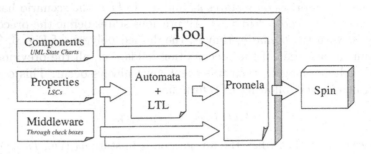

Fig. 8. The prototype toolset.

The whole translation – dispatcher, components, and properties – creates a specification that can be analyzed by SPIN. The initial version of the toolset does not support backward translation of analysis results. This feature, which will be part of the next version, visualizes results in different ways. It will represent a misbehavior either as a trace that highlights the error or as a warning that the scenario does not hold. This is the case, for example, of a violated *cold* scenario, that is, no evolution complies with the scenario. Execution traces would be meaningless; we can only say that the property is not satisfied.

6 Related Work

Finite state automata have been used for many years to model and validate complex software systems. In this chapter we investigated their use in the context of components and component composition. In this particular context, most previous work concentrated on validation via testing. These approaches identify the states through which a component can evolve, along with the meaningful transitions between them. They then identify test cases by applying suitable coverage criteria on the automata that mimic the behavior of the components [39, 134].

Our approach differs in the way we validate component-based software, which is based on model checking rather than testing. Several previous efforts applied this technique to the validation of software models, often specified as UML statechart diagrams, and the study of coordination among the components of distributed applications based on well defined communication paradigms.

vUML [243], veriUML [72], JACK [143], and HUGO [359] provide generic frameworks for model checking statecharts. All of these approaches support the validation of distributed systems, where each statechart describes a component, but do not support any complex communication paradigm. JACK and HUGO only support communication based on broadcasting, where the events produced by a component are notified to all the other components. vUML and veriUML support the concept of a channel, that is, each component writes and reads messages to or from a channel. These proposals aim at general purpose applications and can cover different domains, but are not always suitable when we need a specific communication paradigm. In fact, if we want to use them with the publish/subscribe paradigm, we must model the middleware as any other component. Moreover, the communication between components, and thus between the middleware and the other components, is fixed: it depends on how automata are rendered in the analysis language. For instance, vUML would not allow us to model middleware which guarantees that the order of publication be kept while notifying the events. These approaches also impose that channels between components be explicitly declared: vUML and veriUML do not allow software designers to specify architectures where components are created and destroyed at runtime and the topology of the communication is fixed.

The proposals presented so far do not support a friendly language to define properties. With vUML one can state only reachability properties, while with veriUML, JACK, and HUGO one can also define complex properties on how the application evolves; but, in all cases, the properties must be declared directly in the formalism supported by the model checker, that is, CTL, ACTL and LTL, respectively. All these formalisms are based on temporal logic and are difficult to use and understand by designers with no specific background in mathematical logic.

Two other projects try to overcome these limitations (i.e., the definition of properties and the communication paradigm). Inverardi et al. [209] apply model checking techniques to automata that communicate through channels. In this approach, properties are specified graphically through MSCs. They support two kinds of properties: (a) the application behaves at least once as the MSC, or (b) the application must always comply with the MSC. MSCs are directly translated into LTL, the property language supported by SPIN. Kaveh and Emmerich [221] exploit model checking techniques to verify distributed applications based on remote method invocation. Components are described through statechart diagrams where, if a transition fires, some remote methods are invoked. Only potential deadlocks can be discovered using this approach.

Garlan et al. [84] and the researchers involved in the Cadena project [173] apply model checking techniques to distributed publish/subscribe architectures. Neither of these approaches is not based on UML diagrams, but both define the behavior of components through their own specific language [84] or through an IDL-like specification language [173]. Garlan et al. provide different middleware specifications that can be integrated into the validation tool. The properties are specified in CTL, which is the formalism provided by the SMV [263] model checker. Although the ideas in this proposal and in our approach are similar, there are some differences: (a) we provide a complete graphical front-end for the designer who does not have to deal with any particular textual and logical formalism, (b) the set of guarantees supported by our middleware is richer (e.g., [84] does not deal with subscriptions), and (c) LSCs provide the operators for describing the communication among components in a graphical and natural way, whereas CTL is a general-purpose temporal logic.

Cadena is the other proposal that supports publish/subscribe architectures. It deals directly with the CORBA Component Model (CCM), and both, the description of component interfaces and the topologies of components, are given directly in CORBA. Cadena supports only the CORBA Component Model (CCM) as middleware, while we support a wider set of models: the CORBA dispatcher is one possible instantiation of our parametric component. In Cadena, the communication is established explicitly, that is, each component declares the components from which it desires to receive events. This particular implementation of the publish/subscribe paradigm does not allow the use of Cadena with other middleware platforms. Cadena supports the Bandera Specification Language [73] to specify properties against which the system must be validated.

The same research group which proposed Bandera and Cadena has also proposed Bogor [347], a special purpose modular model checker for analyzing software architectures. The main difference with respect to our approach is that they use their own modeling languages – instead of well known diagrammatic notations – to specify both components and properties. An interesting aspect of Bogoer is that it allows users to change its modules: the optimization phase is not in the encoding of models, but is shifted to within the model checker. The specification language is richer than those offered by the other model checkers, and the adoption of different modules allows users to investigate different alternatives during the checking phase. For example, in our approach we cannot change the algorithms embodied in SPIN. By using Bogor, we would instead be able to modify how the system works by both using its library of components and implementing our own strategies. This is an important aspect that changes the perspective in model checking software architectures and makes Bogor an interesting alternative as a support model checker for our approach.

7 Conclusions and Future Work

In this chapter we have presented an approach to model and validate distributed architectures based on the publish/subscribe paradigm. Application-specific components are modeled as UML statechart diagrams while the dispatcher is supplied as a configurable predefined component. Developers do not handle its internals directly, but only identify the desirable features by selecting some check boxes. We have validated this component by applying the same approach proposed here. We have built a federation of simple, dummy, components to stress all its possible configurations. The simplicity of components has allowed us to state that any misbehavior was due to the dispatcher itself.

Validation properties are described with *live sequence charts* (LSCs) and transformed to automata. Components, middleware, and properties are bundled together, translated into Promela, and then passed to SPIN to validate the architecture.

Our future work is heading in different directions. We would like to extend the approach to model time and probabilities associated with publication/notification of events. But we are also trying to understand how analysis can be performed in an incremental way. The concept is twofold and addresses both evolution of models and composition of properties. In the first case, we are interested in "adapting" properties to evolved systems. In the second case, we are trying to understand how to prove new properties incrementally by composing fragments of properties already verified.

We are also studying how to better support the designer while modeling applications. We are evaluating how the adoption of different model checkers may impact the quality of the results of analysis, and we are exploring the possibility of automatically generating code from these models.

Performance Testing of Distributed Component Architectures

Giovanni Denaro[1], Andrea Polini[2], and Wolfgang Emmerich[3]

[1] Università di Milano-Bicocca, Dipartimento di Informatica Sistemistica e
Comunicazione, via Bicocca degli Arcimboldi 8, I-20126 Milano, Italy.
Email: denaro@disco.unimib.it
[2] Istituto di Scienza e Tecnologie dell'Informazione "Alessandro Faedo," Area di
Ricerca del CNR di Pisa, via Moruzzi 1, I-56124 Pisa, Italy.
andrea.polini@isti.cnr.it
[3] University College London, Department of Computer Science, Gower Street,
WC1E 6BT London, UK.
w.emmerich@cs.ucl.ac.uk

Summary. Performance characteristics, such as response time, throughput, and scalability, are key quality attributes of distributed applications. Current practice, however, rarely applies systematic techniques to evaluate performance characteristics. We argue that evaluation of performance is particularly crucial in early development stages, when important architectural choices are made. At first glance, this contradicts the use of testing techniques, which are usually applied toward the end of a project. In this chapter, we assume that many distributed systems are built with middleware technologies, such as the Java 2 Enterprise Edition (J2EE) or the Common Object Request Broker Architecture (CORBA). These provide services and facilities whose implementations are available when architectures are defined. We also note that it is the middleware functionality, such as transaction and persistence services, remote communication primitives, and threading policy primitives, that dominates distributed system performance. Drawing on these observations, this chapter presents a novel approach to performance testing of distributed applications. We propose to derive application-specific test cases from architecture designs so that the performance of a distributed application can be tested based on the middleware software at early stages of a development process. We report empirical results that support the viability of the approach.

1 Introduction

Various commercial trends have led to an increasing demand for distributed applications. Firstly, the number of mergers between companies is increasing. The different divisions of a newly merged company have to deliver unified services to their customers, and this usually demands an integration of their IT systems. The time available for delivery of such an integration is often so short that building a new system is not an option, and therefore existing system components have to be integrated into a distributed system that appears as an integrating computing facility. Secondly, the time available for providing new services is decreasing. Often new services can only be effectively achieved if components are procured off-the-shelf and then integrated into a system rather than built from scratch. Components to be integrated may have incompatible requirements for their hardware and operating system platforms; they may have to be deployed on different hosts, forcing the resulting system to be distributed. Finally, the Internet provides new opportunities to offer products and services to a vast number of potential customers. The required scalability of e-commerce or e-government sites cannot usually be achieved by centralized or client/server architectures but demand the use of distributed software architectures.

In the context of this chapter, we take the perspective of the developer of a component-based system who is interested in devising systematic ways to ascertain that a given distributed software architecture meets the performance requirements of its target users. Performance can be characterized in several different ways. *Latency* typically describes the delay between request and completion of an operation. *Throughput* denotes the number of operations that can be completed in a given period of time. *Scalability* identifies the dependency between the number of distributed system resources that can be used by a distributed application (typically number of hosts or processors) and latency or throughput. Despite the practical significance of these various aspects, it is still not adequately understood how to test the performance of distributed applications.

Weyuker and Vokolos report on the weakness of the published scientific literature on *software performance testing* in [421]. To this date, no significant scientific advances have been made on performance testing. Furthermore, the set of tools available for software performance testing is fairly limited. The most widely used tools are workload generators and performance profilers that provide support for test execution and debugging, but they do not solve many unclear aspects of the process of performance testing. In particular, researchers and practitioners agree that the most critical performance problems depend on decisions made in the very early stages of the development life cycle, such as architectural choices. Even though iterative and incremental development has been widely promoted [42, 239, 285], the testing techniques developed so far are very much focused on the end of the development process.

As a consequence of the need for early evaluation of software performance and the weakness of testing, the majority of research effort has focused on performance analysis models [15, 25, 28, 111, 329, 333] rather than testing techniques. This research shares in general the approach of translating architecture designs, given mostly in the Unified Modeling Language (UML [41]), to models suitable for analyzing performance, such as Layered Queuing Networks (e.g., [329]), Stochastic Petri Nets (e.g., [25]) or stochastic process algebras (e.g., [333]). Estimates of performance are used to reveal flaws in the original architecture or to compare different architectures and architectural choices. Although models may give useful hints of the performance and help identify bottlenecks, they still tend to be rather inaccurate. Firstly, models generally ignore important details of the deployment environment. For example, performance differences may be significant when different databases or operating systems are used, but the complex characteristics of specific databases and operating systems are very seldom included in the models. Secondly, models often have to be tuned manually. For example, in the case of Layered Queued Networks, solving contention of CPU(s) requires, as input, the number of CPU cycles that each operation is expected to use. Tuning of this type of parameter is usually guessed through experience, and, as a result, it is not easy to obtain precise models.

With the recent advances in distributed component technologies, such as J2EE [365] and CORBA [273], distributed systems are no longer built from scratch [109]. Modern distributed applications often integrate both off-the-shelf and legacy components, use services provided by third parties, such as real time market data provided by Bloomberg or Reuters, and rely on commercial databases to manage persistent data. Moreover, they are built on top of middleware products (hereafter referred to as *middleware*), i.e., middle tier software that provides facilities and services to simplify distributed assembly of components, e.g., communication, synchronization, threading and load balancing facilities, and transaction and security management services [110]. As a result of this trend, we have a class of distributed applications for which a considerable part of their implementation is already available when the architecture is defined, for example, during the Elaboration Phase of the Unified Process. In this chapter, we argue that this enables performance testing to be successfully applied at an early stage.

The main contribution of this chapter is the description and evaluation of a method for testing performance of distributed software at an early stage of development. The method is based on the observation that the middleware used to build a distributed application often determines the overall performance of the application. For example, middleware and databases usually contain the software for transaction and persistence management, remote communication primitives, and threading policies, which have great impact on the different aspects of performance of distributed systems. However, we note that only the coupling between the middleware and the application architecture determines the actual performance. The same middleware may perform very differently in the context of different applications. Based on these observations, we propose using architecture designs to derive application-specific performance test cases that can be executed on the early available middleware platform a distributed application is built with. We argue that this allows empirical measurements of performance to be successfully done in the very early stages of the development process. Furthermore, we envision an interesting set of practical applications of this approach, that is, evaluation and selection of middleware for specific applications; evaluation and selection of off-the-shelf components;

empirical evaluation and comparison of possible architectural choices; early configuration of applications; evaluation of the impact of new components on the evolution of existing applications.

The chapter is further structured as follows. Section 2 discusses related work and highlights the original aspects of our research. Section 3 gives details of our approach to performance testing. Section 4 reports the results of an empirical evaluation of the main hypothesis of our research, i.e., that the performance of a distributed application can be successfully measured based on the early available components. Section 5 discusses the limitations of our approach and possible integration with performance modeling techniques. Finally, Section 6 summarizes the contributions of the chapter and outlines our future research agenda.

2 Related Work

In this section, we briefly review related work in the areas of performance testing of distributed applications and studies on the relationships between software architecture and middleware.

2.1 Performance Testing of Distributed Applications

Some authors have exploited empirical testing for studying the performance of middleware products. Gorton and Liu compare the performance of six different J2EE-based middleware implementations [148]. They use a benchmark application that stresses the middleware infrastructure, the transaction and directory services, and the load balancing mechanisms. The comparison is based on the empirical measurement of throughput for increasing numbers of clients. Similarly, Avritzer et al. compare the performance of different ORB (Object Request Broker) implementations that adhere to the CORBA Component Model [244]. Liu et al. investigate the suitability of micro-benchmarks, i.e., lightweight test cases focused on specific facilities of the middleware, such as directory service, transaction management, and persistence and security support [247]. This work suggests the suitability of empirical measurement for middleware selection, i.e, for making decisions on which middleware will best satisfy the performance requirements of a distributed application. However, as Liu et al. remark in the conclusions of their paper ([247]), "*incorporating application-specific behavior in to the equation in a simple and practical manner is still an open problem*" and "*it also remains to be seen how far the results from the empirical testing can be generalized across different hardware platforms, databases and operating systems.*" Our research tackles these problems. We study application-specific test cases for early performance evaluation (or also for comparing the performance) of distributed applications in specific deployment environments, which include middleware, databases, operating systems, and other off-the-shelf components.

Weyuker and Vokolos report on the industrial experience of testing the performance of a distributed telecommunication application at AT&T [421]. They stress that, given the lack of historical data on the usage of the target system, the architecture is key to identifying software processes and input parameters (and realistic representative values) that will most significantly influence the performance. Our work extends this consideration to a wider set of distributed applications, i.e., distributed component-based software in general. Moreover, we aim to provide a systematic approach to test definition, implementation, and deployment, which are not covered in the work of Weyuker and Vokolos.

2.2 Software Architecture and Middleware

Medvidovic et al. state the idea of coupling the modeling power of software architectures with the implementation support provided by middleware [264]. They notice that "architectures and middleware address similar problems - large-scale, component-based development - but at different stages of the development life cycle." They propose investigating the possibility of defining systematic mappings between architectures and middleware. To this end, they study the suitability of a particular element of software architecture, the *software connector*. Metha et al. propose an interesting classification framework of software connectors [267]. They distinguish among four types of services provided by connectors for enabling and facilitating component interactions: *communication*, i.e., support for transmission of data among components; *coordination*, i.e., support for transfer of control among components; *conversion*, i.e., support for interaction among heterogeneous components; *facilitation*, i.e., support for mediations of the interactions among components (e.g., participation in atomic transactions). A general set of software connector types is identified and classified in the framework, based on the combination of services that they provide. Although they draw on similar assumptions (i.e., the relationships between architecture and middleware), our research and that of Medvidovic et al. have different goals: we aim to measure performance attributes of an architecture based on the early available implementation support (of which the middleware is a significant part); Medvidovic et al. aim to build implementation topologies (e.g., bridging of middleware) that preserve the properties of the original architecture. However, the results of previous studies on software connectors and the possibility of mapping architectures on middleware may be important references for engineering our approach, as we further discuss in Sect. 3.2.

3 Approach

In this section, we introduce our approach to early performance testing of distributed component-based software architectures. We also focus on the aspects of the problem that need further investigation. Our long-term goal is to provide an automated software environment that supports the application of the approach we describe below.

Our performance testing process consists of the following phases:

1. Selection of the use case scenarios (hereafter referred to simply as *use cases*) relevant to performance, given a set of architecture designs.
2. Mapping of the selected use cases to the actual deployment technology and platform.
3. Generation of *stubs* of components that are not available in the early stages of the development life cycle, but are needed to implement the use cases.
4. Execution of the test, which, in turn, includes deployment of the Application Under Test (AUT), creation of workload generators, initialization of the persistent data, and reporting of performance measurements.

We now discuss the research problems and our approach to solving them for each of the above phases of the testing process.

3.1 Selecting Performance Use Cases

As it has been noticed by several researchers such as Weyuker [421], the design of test suites for performance testing is radically different from the case of functional testing. In performance testing, the functional details of the test cases, i.e., the actual values of the inputs, are generally of limited importance. Table 1 classifies the main parameters relevant to performance testing of distributed applications. First, important concerns are traditionally associated with workloads and physical resources, e.g., the number of users, the frequencies of inputs, the durations of tests, the characteristics of the disks, the network bandwidth, and the number and speed(s) of CPU(s). Next, it is important to consider the middleware configuration, for which the table reports parameters in the case of J2EE-based middleware. Here, we do not comment further on workload, physical resource, and middleware parameters, which are extensively discussed in the literature [247, 377, 421].

Other important parameters of performance testing in distributed settings are due to the interactions among distributed components and resources. Different ways of using facilities, services and resources of middleware, and deployment environments are likely to yield different performance results. Performance will differ if the database is accessed many times or rarely. A given middleware may perform adequately for applications that stress persistence and badly for transactions. In some cases, a middleware may perform well or badly for different usage patterns of the same service. The last row of Table 1 classifies some of the relevant interactions in distributed settings according to whether they take place between the middleware and the components, among

Table 1. Performance parameters.

Category	Parameter
Workload	Number of clients
	Client request frequency
	Client request arrival rate
	Duration of the test
Physical resources	Number and speed of CPU(s)
	Speed of disks
	Network bandwidth
Middleware configuration	Thread pool size
	Database connection pool size
	Application component cache size
	JVM heap size
	Message queue buffer size
	Message queue persistence
Application specific	Interactions with the middleware
	- use of transaction management
	- use of the security service
	- component replication
	- component migration
	Interactions among components
	- remote method calls
	- asynchronous message deliveries
	Interactions with persistent data
	- database accesses

the components themselves[4], or to access persistent data in a database. In general, the performance of a particular application will be largely dependent on how the middleware primitives are being used to implement the application's functionality.

We argue that application-specific test cases for performance should be given such that the most relevant interactions triggered specifically by the AUT are covered. According to this principle, the generation of a meaningful test suite for performance testing can be based on either of two possible sources: previously recorded usage profiles or functional cases specified in the early development phases.

The former alternative is viable in cases of system upgrade. In this situation, "histories" of the actual usage profiles of the AUT are likely to be available because of the possibility that they have been recorded in the field. The synthesis of application specific workloads based on recorded usage pro-

---

[4]Although interactions among distributed components map onto interactions that actually take place at the middleware level, they are elicited at a different abstraction level and thus considered a different category in our classification.

files is a widely studied and fairly well understood research subject in the area
of synthetic workload generation (e.g., [220, 373]).

In the case of the development of a completely new application, no recorded
usage profile may exist. However, modern software processes tend to define
the required functionality of an application under development in a set of
scenarios and use cases. To build a meaningful performance test suite, we
can associate a weight with each use case and generate a synthetic workload
accordingly. The weight should express the importance of each use case in the
specific test suite. Obviously, to have a reliable evaluation of the performance
characteristics of the application, we need to consider as many use cases as
possible. This should be a minor problem because it is often the case that
most of the use cases are available in early stages of a software process. For
instance, the iterative and incremental development approaches (such as the
Unified Software Development Process [42]) demand that the majority of use
cases be available at the end of the early process iterations. In such settings,
we can therefore assume that the software system developer can use these use
cases to derive test cases to evaluate the performance of the final application
before starting with the implementation phase. On the basis of the results
obtained, the developer can eventually revise the decisions taken in order to
obtain better "expected" performance. To this end, several possibilities are
available at this stage (less expensive with respect to late system refactoring,
which may be required due to poor performance), such as a revision of the
architecture or a recalibration of some choices concerning the middleware
configuration.

3.2 Mapping Use Cases to Middleware

At the initial stages of the software process, software architectures are generally defined at a very abstract level. The early use cases focus on describing
the business logic while they abstract the details of the deployment platform
and technology. One of the strengths of our approach is indeed the possibility of guiding software engineers through the intricate web of architectural
choices, off-the-shelf components, distributed component technologies, middleware, and deployment options, while keeping the focus on the performance
of the final product. The empirical measurements of performance may provide
the base for comparing possible alternatives. Consequently, to define a performance test case, the abstract use cases must be augmented with the following
information:

- The mapping between the early available components (if any) and the
  components represented in the abstract use cases;
- The distributed component technology and the actual middleware with
  respect to which the performance test is to be performed;
- The characteristics of the deployment of the abstract use cases on the
  actual middleware platform, i.e., the specification of how the described

component interactions take place through the selected component technology and middleware.

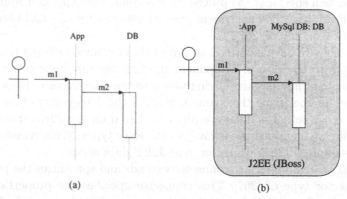

(b)

Fig. 1. A sample use case (a) and part of a corresponding performance test case (b).

The two former requirements can be trivially addressed. For example, Fig. 1 (a) illustrates a sample abstract use case in which an actor accesses the service m1 provided by the component App, which in turn uses the service m2 provided by the component DB. Correspondingly, Fig. 1 (b) illustrates a performance test case in which the component DB is referenced as the available MySQL database engine, while the component App is not early available; the whole application is deployed using the J2EE component technology and the JBoss application server as middleware. The rest of this section discusses the problem of specifying the deployment characteristics.

At the architectural level, the properties of the component interactions can be described in terms of *software connectors*[5]. Recent studies (e.g., [264]) have investigated the role that software connectors may play in software design, showing that they may relevantly contribute to bridging the gap between the high-level application view of a software architecture and the implementation support provided by distributed component technologies and middleware. [267] attempts to classify software connectors and identifies a general set of *connector types*, their characteristics (*dimensions*), and the possible practical alternatives for each characteristic (*values*). For instance, the procedure call is identified as a connector type that enables communication and coordination among components; synchronicity is one of the dimensions of a

---

[5]This is the spirit of the definition of software connectors given by Shaw and Garlan [366]: *connectors mediate interactions among components; that is, they establish the rules that govern component interaction and specify any auxiliary mechanisms required.*

procedure call connector; and **synchronous** and **asynchronous** are the possible values of such a dimension. When all dimensions of a connector type are assigned to specific values, the resulting instance of the connector type identifies a connector *species*, e.g., the **remote method invocation** can be considered as a species of the procedure call connector type. Our approach to the specification of the deployment characteristics leverages and extends the connector taxonomy of [267].

Up to now we have identified an initial set of connector types that specifically apply to the case of component interactions that take place through J2EE-compliant middleware. Giving values to the dimensions of these connectors allows for specifying the characteristics of the deployment of an abstract use case on an actual middleware platform based on the J2EE specification. Specifically, we identified the following connector types: J2EE remote service, J2EE distributor, J2EE arbitrator, and J2EE data access.

The *J2EE remote service* connector extends and specializes the procedure call connector type of [267]. This connector specifies the properties of the messages that flow among interacting components. We identified the following relevant dimensions for this connector:

- Synchronicity: A remote service can be either synchronous or asynchronous. Specifying a value for the synchronicity dimension allows to decide if the service is meant to be implemented as a synchronous method invocation or as an asynchronous event propagation.
- Parameters: This dimension specifies the number of parameters and their expected sizes in bytes. This allows for simulating the dependencies between performance and the transfer of given amounts of data between components. Moreover, if the component that provides the service is one of the early available components, types and values of the parameters must also be provided to perform the actual invocation during the test. In this case, if the service is expected to be invoked a number of times during the test, we can embed in the connector a strategy for choosing the values of the parameters:
  1. a single value may be given. This value will be used every time the service is invoked during the test;
  2. a list of values may be given. Each time the service is invoked, a value of the list is sequentially selected;
  3. a list of values and an associated probability distribution may be given. Each time the service is invoked, a value of the list is selected by sampling the distribution.

The *J2EE distributor* connector extends and specializes the distributor connector type of [267]. This connector allows us to specify the deployment topology. We identified the following relevant dimensions for this connector:

- Connections: This dimension specifies the properties of the connections among the interacting components, i.e., the physical hosts on which they are to be deployed in the testing environment and the symbolic names used to retrieve the component factories through the naming service.

- Types. This dimension specifies the (expected) implementation type of the interacting components. Possible values are client application, session bean, entity bean[6], and database table.
- Retrieving. This dimension specifies how to use the component factories (for components and interactions to which this is applicable) for retrieving references to components. In particular, either the default or finder method can be specified (non-standard retrieving methods of component factories are called *finders* in the J2EE terminology).

The *J2EE arbitrator* connector extends and specializes the arbitrator connector type of [267]. This connector specifies the participation in transactions and the security attributes of the component interactions. We identified the following relevant dimensions for this connector:

- Transactions: This dimension specifies the participation of a component interaction in transactions. Possible values are none, starts, and participates; *none* if the interaction does not participate in any transaction; *starts* if the interaction starts a new, possibly nested, transaction; *participates* if the interaction participates in the transaction of the caller.
- Security: This dimension specifies the security attributes of a component interaction. In particular, it specifies if services can be accessed by all users, specific users, or specific user groups, and which component is responsible for authentication in the two last cases.

The *J2EE data access* connector extends and specializes the data access connector type of [267]. This connector mediates the communication between J2EE components and a database, specifying the structure of the database and how the interactions are handled. In particular, we identified the following relevant dimensions for this connector:

- Tables: This dimension specifies characteristics of the tables and their respective fields in the database.
- Relationships: This dimension specifies the presence of relationships among the tables in the database.
- Management: In J2EE components, persistence can be handled either by implementing the access functions (e.g., queries) in the component code (this is called bean managed persistence, or BMP) or by using a standard mechanism embedded in the middleware (this is called container managed persistence, or CMP).

---

[6]Session beans are J2EE components that provide business services. Thus, session beans are often used as the interface between J2EE applications and client applications. Entity beans are J2EE components that represent persistent data within an application. Each database table is generally associated with an entity bean. The data in the entity bean are synchronized with the database. Thus, entity bean are often used as the interface between J2EE applications and databases.

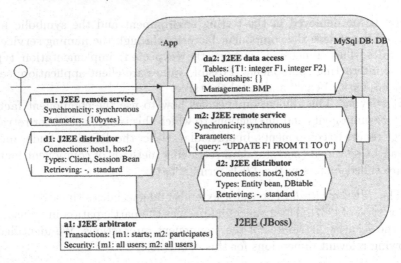

Fig. 2. A performance test case associated with the use case in Fig. 1.

Figure 2 illustrates the application of connectors to the sample use case of Fig. 1. As specified by the J2EE remote service connectors, the interactions m1 and m2 are both synchronous (i.e., they are assumed to be remote method invocations) and have just one input parameter. In the case of m1, only the parameter size is relevant since the server component App is not available early. Conversely, in the case of m2, the actual value of the parameter is needed, since the database is available. The parameter specified is the actual SQL code to be executed on the database, and the "single value" strategy is used. The database structure assumed is specified in the J2EE data access connector da2, and consists of a table (T1) with two integer fields (F1 and F2) and no relationship, while the interactions between the component App and the MySQL database are supposed to follow the bean managed persistence paradigm. The two J2EE distributor connectors, d1 and d2, specify that the component App and the database are deployed on the same host (host2), while the client is deployed on a different host (host1). The interface between the client and the component App is provided by a session bean EJB component, and the interface between App and the database is handled by an entity bean EJB component. The retrieving strategy, when applicable, uses the standard methods provided by the platform. Finally, the J2EE arbitrator connector specifies that m1 starts a transaction in which m2 participates, and no special security policy is considered. The information given in Fig. 2 identifies a specific performance test case associated with the use case in Fig. 1.

Notice that Fig. 2 is meant just for exemplification purposes, and not to suggest an approach in which use case diagrams must be annotated with connector information before testing. In a mature and engineered version of our approach, we envision the possibility that a tool analyzes the abstract use cases and extracts a simple list of alternatives for each interaction dimension. The performance engineer would then have the choice of selecting the best suited alternatives according to the performance requirements, or testing different alternatives to find out the one that works best (in a sort of what-if-analysis fashion). Software connectors provide the reasoning framework towards this goal. Furthermore, our current knowledge about all connector types needed and their dimensions is limited because it is based on a simple case in which we have experimented with the application of the approach (Sect. 4 gives the details of this). We believe that we are on the right path, even though we are aware that further work is still needed to understand the many dimensions and species of software connectors and their relationships with the deployment technologies and platforms possible.

3.3 Generating Stubs

So far, we have suggested that early test cases of performance can be derived from use cases and that software connectors can be exploited as a means to establish the correspondence between the abstract views provided by the use cases and their concrete instances. However, to actually implement the test cases, we must also solve the problem that not all the application components that participate in the use cases are available in the early stages of the development life cycle. For example, the components that implement the business logic are seldom available, although they participate in most of the use cases. Our approach uses *stubs* in place of the missing components.

Stubs are fake versions of components that can be used instead of the corresponding components for instantiating the abstract use cases. In our approach, stubs are adjusted specifically to use cases, i.e., different use cases will require different stubs of the same component. Stubs will ensure only that the distributed interactions happen as specified and that the other components are coherently exercised. Our idea of the engineered approach is that the required stubs are automatically generated based on the information contained in use case elaborations and software connectors. For example, referring once again to Fig. 2, if the component *App* is not available, its stub would be implemented such that it is able to receive the invocations of the service m1 and, consequently, invoke the service m2 through the actual middleware. The actual SQL code embedded in the remote service connector of m2 would be hardcoded in the stub. As for m1, it would contain empty code for the methods, but set the corresponding transaction behavior as specified. Of course, many functional details of *App* are generally not known and cannot be implemented in the stub. Normally, this will result in discrepancies between execution times of the stubs and the actual components that they simulate.

The main hypothesis of our work is that performance measurements in the presence of the stubs are good enough approximations of the actual performance of the final application. This derives from the observation that the available components, e.g., middleware and databases, embed software that mainly impacts performance. The coupling between such implementation support and the application-specific behavior can be extracted from the use cases, while the implementation details of the business components remain negligible. In other words, we expect thaialt the discrepancies of execution times within the stubs are of orders of magnitude less than the impact of the interactions facilitated by middleware and persistence technologies, such as databases. We report an initial empirical assessment of this hypothesis in Sect. 4 of this 'chapter, but are aware that further empirical studies are needed.

The generation of the fake version can be made easier if we can use UML to describe the software architecture. The use of UML in fact enables the use of all UML-based tools. An interesting investigation in this direction can be found in [266]. In this work the authors propose different techniques to introduce concepts as connectors and architectural styles as first order concepts inside an "extended" fully compliant UML.

3.4 Executing the Test

Building support to test execution shall mostly involve technical rather than scientific problems, at least once the research questions stated above have been answered. Part of the work consists of engineering the activities of mapping the use cases to deployment technologies and platforms, and generating stubs to replace missing components. Also, we must automate deployment and implementation of workload generators, initialization of persistent data, execution of measurements and reporting of results.

In particular, workload generators can be characterized in several different ways, and many different workloads can be found in the literature (e.g. [74, 367]). It is a developer's duty to choose the one that best represents the load that it expects for the application during normal use. Then, after the workload has been chosen, for instance, from a list of different possible choices, and the probability distributions have been associated with the relevant elements in that workload, it is possible to automatically generate the corresponding "application client" that generates invocations according to the chosen workload type and distributions.

4 Preliminary Assessment

This section empirically evaluates the core hypothesis of our research, i.e., that the performance of a distributed application can be successfully tested based on the middleware and/or off-the-shelf components that are available in early stages of the software process. To this end, we conducted an experiment in a controlled environment. First, we considered a sample distributed application for which we had the whole implementation available. Then, we selected an abstract use case of the application and implemented it as a test case based on the approach described in Sect. 3. Finally, we executed the performance test (with different numbers of application clients) on the early available components and compared the results with the performance measured on the actual application.

4.1 Experiment Setting

As for the target application, we considered the *Duke's Bank application* presented in the J2EE tutorial [355]. This application is distributed by Sun Microsystems under a public license; thus, we were able to obtain the full implementation easily. The Duke's bank application consists of 6,000 lines of Java code that are meant to exemplify all the main features of the J2EE platform, including the use of transactions and security. We consider the Duke's bank application to be adequately representative of medium sized component-based distributed applications. The Duke's bank application is referred to as DBApp in the rest of this chapter.

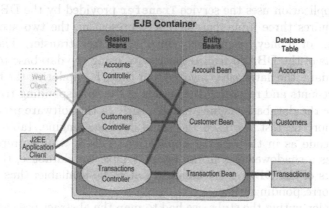

Fig. 3. The Duke's Bank application.

The organization of the DBApp is given in Fig. 3 (borrowed from [355]). The application can be accessed by both Web and application clients. It consists of six EJB (Enterprise JavaBean [365]) components that handle operations issued by the users of a hypothetical bank. The six components can be associated with classes of operations that are related to bank accounts, customers, and transactions. For each of these classes of operations, a pair of session bean and entity bean is provided. Session beans are responsible for the interface for users and entity beans handle the mapping of components to the underlying database table. The arrows represent possible interaction patterns among the components. The EJBs that constitute the business components are deployed in a single container within the application server (which is part of the middleware). For the experiment, we used the JBoss application server and the MySQL database engine, running on the same machine.

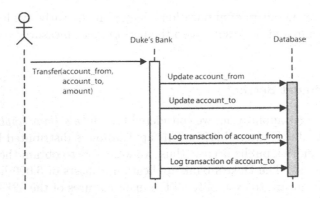

Fig. 4. A sample use case for the Duke's Bank.

Then, we selected a sample use case that describes the transfer of funds between two bank accounts. Figure 4 illustrates the selected use case in UML. A client application uses the service **Transfer** provided by the DBApp. This service requires three input parameters, representing the two accounts and the amount of money, respectively, involved in the transfer. The business components of the DBApp realize the service using the database to store the persistent data; the database is invoked four times for updating the balances of the two accounts and recording the details of the corresponding transactions. We assume the database engine available early in the software process.

Thus, for the test, we used the same database engine, table structure, and SQL code as in the original application. This is why we represent the database as a shadowed box in the figure. Unlike the database, the business components of the DBApp are assumed not to be available; thus we had to generate corresponding stubs.

For implementing the stubs, we had to map the abstract use case onto the selected deployment technology, i.e., J2EE. We already commented on the role that software connectors may play in the mapping. As for the interaction between the clients and the DBApp, we specified that the service **Transfer** is invoked as a synchronous call and starts a new transaction. As for the interaction between the DBApp and the database, we specified that the four invocations are synchronous calls that participate in the calling transaction and embed the actual SQL code. We set up the database factory such that the database connection is initialized for each call[7]. The DBApp uses entity beans and bean managed persistence to handle the interactions with the database tables. Based on this information, we implemented the stubs as needed to realize the interactions in the use case considered and we deployed the test version of the DBApp (referred to as DBTest) on the JBoss application server.

---

[7]Although this may sound like a bad implementation choice, we preferred to maintain the policy of the original application to avoid biases in the comparison.

Finally, we implemented a workload generator and initialized the persistent data in the database. The workload generator is able to activate a number of clients at the same time and takes care of measuring the average response time. For the persistent data, we instantiated the case in which each client withdraws money from its own account (i.e., there exists a bank account for each client) and deposits the corresponding amount to the account of a third party, which is supposed to be the same for all clients. This simulates the case in which a group of people is paying the same authority over the Internet. Incidentally, we notice that, in an automated test environment, initialization of persistent data would require to specify only the performance sensitive part of the information, with the actual values in the database tables being of little importance. For example, in our case, only the number of elements in each table and their relationships with the considered use case, i.e., whether each clients accesses the same or a different table row, are the real concerns.

With reference to the performance parameters of Table 1, we generated a workload to test both DBApp and DBTest with increasing numbers of clients, from one to one hundred. The two applications were deployed on a JBoss 3.0 application server running on a PC equipped with a 1 GHz Pentium III CPU, 512 MB of RAM, and the Linux operating system. To generate the workload, we run the clients on a Sun Fire 880 equipped with four 850 MHz Sparc CPUs and 8 GB of RAM. These two machines were connected via a private local area network with a bandwidth of 100 MBit/sec. For the stubs we used the same geographical distances as the components of the actual application. Moreover, in order to avoid influences among the experiments that could be caused by the concurrent existence of a lot of active session beans, we restarted the application server between two successive experiments. JBoss was run using the default configuration. Finally, the specific setting concerning the particular use case, as already discussed in the previous paragraphs, saw the use of remote method calls between the components and the use of the transaction management service to handle the data shared by the various beans consistently.

4.2 Empirical Results

We executed both DBApp and DBTest for increasing numbers of clients, and measured the latency time for the test case. We repeated each experiment 15 times and measured the average latency time. Figure 5 shows the results of the experiments. It plots the latency time of both DBApp and DBTest against the number of clients for all the repetitions of the experiment. We can see that the two curves are very near to each other. The average difference accounts for the 9.3% of the response time. The experiments also showed a low value for the standard deviation σ. The ratio between σ and the expectations are, in fact, definitively lower then 0.15, for both the DBApp and the DBTest.

The results of this experiment suggest the viability of our research because they prove that the performance of the DBApp in a specific use case is well

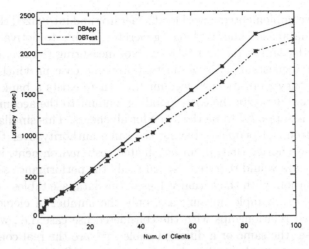

Fig. 5. Latency of DBApp and DBTest for increasing numbers of clients.

approximated by the DBTest, which is made of early available components. However, although the first results are encouraging, we are aware that a single experiment cannot be generalized. We are now working on other experiments to cover the large set of alternatives of component-based distributed applications. We plan to experiment with different use cases, sets of use cases for the same test case, different management schemas for transactions and performance, different communication mechanisms such as asynchronous calls, J2EE-based application servers other than JBoss, CORBA-based middleware, and other commercial databases and in the presence of other early available components.

5 Scope and Extensions

Our results support that using stubs for the application code, but the real middleware and database proposed for the application, can provide useful information on the performance of a distributed application. This is particularly true for enterprise information system applications that are based on distributed component technologies, such as J2EE and CORBA. We have already commented that for this class of distributed applications the middleware is generally responsible for most of the implementation support relevant to performance, e.g., mechanisms for handling distributed communication, synchronization, persistence of data, transactions, load balancing, and threading policies. Thus, in most cases critical contentions of resources and bottlenecks happen at the middleware level, while the execution time of the business components is negligible.

Our approach allows providers of this class of distributed applications to test whether, and to what extent, a given middleware may satisfy the performance requirements of an application that is under development. In this respect, our approach may perform better than pure benchmarking of middleware (e.g., [148, 244, 247]), because it enables application-specific evaluation, i.e., it generates test cases that take into account the specific needs of a particular business logic and application architectures. Moreover, the approach has a wider scope than solely testing the middleware. It can be generalized to test all components that are available at the beginning of the development process, for example, components acquired off-the-shelf from third parties. Based on the empirical measurements of performance, tuning of architectures and architectural choices may also be performed.

Despite these valuable benefits, however, we note that our approach cannot identify performance problems that are due to the specific implementation of late available components. For example, if the final application is going to have a bottleneck in a business component that is under development, our approach has no chance of discovering the bottleneck, since it would not be exhibited by a stub of the component. Performance analysis models remain the primary reference for evaluation of performance in such cases.

Currently, we are studying the possibility of combining empirical testing and performance modeling, aimed at increasing the relative strengths of each approach. In the rest of this section we sketch the basic idea of this integration.

One of the problems of applying performance analysis to middleware-based distributed systems is that middleware is in general very difficult to represent in the analysis models. For instance, let us consider the case in which one wants to provide a detailed performance analysis of the DBApp, i.e., the sample application used in Sect. 4. To this end, we ought to model the interactions among the business components of DBApp as well as the components and processes of the middleware that interact with DBApp. The latter include (and are not limited to) component proxies that marshal and unmarshal parameters of remote method invocations, the transaction manager that coordinates distributed transactions, the a database connectivity driver that facilitates interactions with the database, and the processes for automatic activation and deactivation of objects or components. Thus, although the application has a simple structure, the derivation of the corresponding analysis model becomes very costly.

We believe that this class of issues can be addressed by combining empirical testing and performance modeling according to the following procedure:

1. The analysis model is built and solved, abstracting from the middleware. The resulting model will generally have a simple structure.
2. Empirical testing is used to simulate the results of the model (e.g., frequency of operations) on the actual middleware, thus computing how the execution of the middleware and the contention of resources within the middleware affect the performance characteristics of the modeled interactions (e.g., the response time of a given operation may increase because it involves middleware execution).

3. Model parameters are tuned according to the testing results.
4. The process is repeated until the model stabilizes.

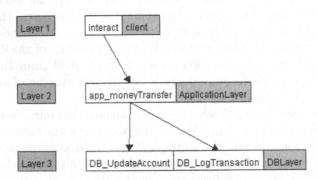

Fig. 6. A sample LQN model for DBApp.

For instance, Fig. 6 shows a Layered Queuing Network (LQN) corresponding to the use case of Fig. 4. A detailed description of LQN models is beyond the scope of this chapter, and we refer interested readers to [329]. The layers in Fig. 6 represent the main interacting components, i.e., the client, the application, and the database. Each component may be present in a number of copies (or threads). White boxes represent the services that each layer provides (limited to services of interest to the use cases considered). Connections between white boxes indicate client/server relationships between services, with arrows pointing to servers. In the specific case represented in the figure, clients interact with the application through the `moneyTransfer` service, which in turn uses services of the database layer to update accounts and log transaction details. Other important parameters of the model that are not indicated in the figure include the number of calls for each service (for example, both the database services are used twice in the considered case), the CPU and the CPU time used by each service and the service "thinking-times."

Although the middleware is not explicitly represented in the model, it is involved in the execution of each service and affects, for example, the ideal CPU time and thinking time. Once empirical measurements are available, the parameters of the LQN model can be tuned accordingly. On the other hand, by solving the model we can compute the frequency of invocations of each service for different numbers of clients. Thus, we can generate the test cases for the middleware accordingly.

The cost of the approach depends on the number of iterations of the process. We expect models to stabilize in a few iterations. However, experimental evidence of this is still missing, and further work is required to understand costs and benefits of the integrated approach.

6 Conclusions and Future Work

Distributed component technologies enforce the use of middleware, commercial databases and other off-the-shelf components and services. The software that implements these is available in the initial stages of a software process and, moreover, it generally embeds the software structures, mechanisms and services that mostly impact the performance in distributed settings. This chapter set out to exploit the early availability of such software to accomplish empirical measurement of performance of distributed applications at architecture definition time. To the best of our knowledge, the approach proposed in this chapter is novel in software performance engineering.

This chapter fulfilled several goals. It discussed the published scientific works related to ours, thus positioning our ideas in the current research landscape. It described a novel approach to performance testing that is based on selecting performance relevant use cases from the architecture designs, and instantiating and executing them as test cases on early available software. It indicated important research directions toward engineering such an approach, i.e., the classification of performance relevant distributed interactions as a base to select architecture use cases and the investigation of software connectors as a means to instantiate abstract use cases on actual deployment technologies and platforms. It reported experiments that showed that the actual performance of a sample distributed application is well approximated by measurements based only on its early available components, thus supporting the main hypothesis of our research. It finally identified the scope of our approach and proposed a possible integration with performance modeling techniques aimed at relaxing its limitations.

Software performance testing of distributed applications has not been thoroughly investigated so far. The reason for this, we believe, is that testing techniques have traditionally been applied at the end of the software process. Conversely, the most critical performance faults are often present very early because of wrong architectural choices. Our research tackles this problem, suggesting a method and a class of applications such that software performance can be tested in the very early stages of development. In the long term, and as far as the early evaluation of middleware is concerned, we believe that empirical testing may outperform performance estimation models, since the former is more precise and easier to use. Moreover, we envision the application of our ideas to a set of interesting practical cases:

- **Middleware selection:** The possibility of evaluating and selecting the best middleware for the performance of a specific application is reckoned important by many authors, as we already pointed out in Sect. 2 of this chapter. To this end, our approach provides a valuable support. Based on abstract architecture designs, it allows us to measure and compare the performance of a specific application with different middleware technologies.
- **COTS selection:** A central assumption of traditional testing techniques is that testers have complete knowledge of the software under test, as well

as of its requirements and execution environment. This is not the case for off-the-shelf components (COTS) that are produced independently and then deployed in environments not known in advance. Vendors may fail in identifying all possible usage profiles of a component, and therefore the testing of the component in isolation (performed by vendors) is not generally enough [349]. Limited to performance concerns, our approach allows us to test off-the-shelf components in the context of a specific application that is being developed. Thus, it can be used to complement the testing done by COTS providers and thus assist in selecting from several off-the-shelf components.

- **Iterative development:** Modern software processes prescribe iterative and incremental development in order to control risks linked to architectural choices (see, e.g., the Unified Process [42]). Applications are developed incrementally, through a number of iterations. During each iteration, a subset of the user requirements is fully implemented. This results in a working slice of the application that can be evaluated and, in the next iteration, extended to cover another part of the missing functionality. At the beginning of each iteration, new architectural decisions are made whose impact must generally be evaluated with respect to the current application slice. For performance concerns, our approach can be used when the life cycle architecture is established during the elaboration phase, because it allows us to test the expected performance of a new software architecture based on the software that is initially available.

We are now continuing experiments for augmenting the empirical evidence of the viability of our approach, and providing a wider coverage of the possible alternatives for component-based distributed applications. We are also working on engineering the approach, starting from the study of the research problems outlined in this chapter.

Acknowledgments

This work has been partially funded through the EU IST project SEGRAVIS.

A Generic Environment for COTS Testing and Quality Prediction

Xia Cai[1], Michael R. Lyu[1], and Kam-Fai Wong[2]

Dept. of Computer Science and Engineering, The Chinese University of Hong Kong, Hong Kong, China[1]
Dept. of System Engineering and Engineering Management, The Chinese University of Hong Kong, Hong Kong, China[2]

{xcai,lyu}@cse.cuhk.edu.hk,kfwong@se.cuhk.edu.hk

Summary. In this chapter, we first survey current component technologies and discuss the features they inherit. Quality assurance (QA) characteristics of component systems and the life cycle of component-based software development (CBSD) are also addressed. Based on the characteristics of the life cycle, we propose a QA model for CBSD. The model covers the eight main processes in component-based software systems (CBS) development. A Component-based Program Analysis and Reliability Evaluation (ComPARE) environment is established for evaluation and prediction of quality of components. ComPARE provides a systematic procedure for predicting the quality of software components and assessing the reliability of the final system developed using CBSD. Using different quality prediction techniques, ComPARE has been applied to a number of component-based programs. The prediction results and the effectiveness of the quality prediction models for CBSD were outlined in this chapter.

1 Introduction

Based on the component-based software development (CBSD) approach [403], software systems are developed using a well defined software architecture and off-the-shelf components as building blocks [335]. This is different from the traditional approach, in which software systems are implemented from scratch. Commercial off-the-shelf (COTS) components are developed by different developers using different languages and different platforms [342]. Typically, COTS components are available from a component repository; users select the appropriate ones and integrate them to establish the target software system (see Fig. 1).

In general, a component has three main features: 1) it is an independent and replaceable part of a system that fulfills a clear function; 2) it works

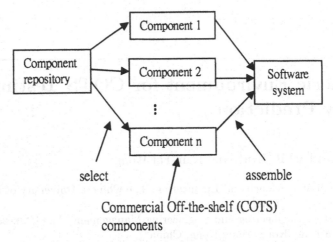

Fig. 1. Component-based software development.

in the context of a well defined architecture; and 3) it communicates with other components by its interfaces [47]. Current component technologies have been used to implement different software systems, such as object-oriented distributed component software [431] and Web-based enterprise applications [336].

The system architecture of a component-based software system is layered and modular [152, 176, 192]; see Fig. 2.

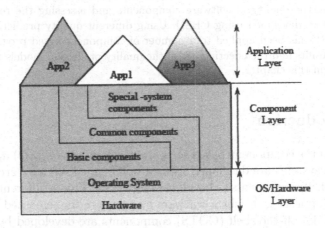

Fig. 2. System architecture of component-based software systems.

The top application layer entails information systems designed for various applications. The second layer consists of components for a specific system or application domains. Components in this layer are applicable to more than one single application. The third layer comprises cross-system middleware components and includes software and interfaces common to other established entities. The fourth layer of system software components includes basic components that interface with the underlying operating systems and hosting hardware. Finally, the lowest two layers involve the operating and hardware systems.

A CBSD-based software system is composed of one or more components that may be procured off-the-shelf, produced in-house, or developed through contracts. The overall quality of the final system depends heavily on the quality of the components involved. One needs to be able to assess the quality of a component to reduce the risk in development. Software metrics are designed to measure different attributes of a software system and the development process, and are used to evaluate the quality of the final product [360]. Process metrics (e.g., reliability estimates) [224], static code metrics (e.g., code complexity) [251], and dynamic metrics (e.g., test thoroughness) [411] are widely used to predict the quality of software components at different development phases [122, 360].

Several techniques are used to model the predictive relationship between different software metrics and for component classification, i.e., for classifying software components into fault-prone and non fault-prone categories [144]. These techniques include discriminant analysis [297], classification trees [334], pattern recognition [45], Bayesian network [121], case-based reasoning (CBR) [216], and regression tree models [144]. There are also prototypes and tools [224, 253] which use such techniques to automate software quality prediction. However, these tools employ only one type of metric, e.g., process metrics or static code metrics. Furthermore, they rely on only one prediction technique for overall software quality assessment.

The objective of this chapter is to evaluate quality of individual off-the-shelf components and the overall quality of software systems. We integrate different prediction techniques and different software metric categories to form a single environment, and investigate their effectiveness on quality prediction of components and CBS.

The rest of this chapter is organized as follows: we first give an overview of state-of-the-art CBSD techniques in Sect. 2, and highlight the quality assurance (QA) issues behind them in Sect. 3. Section 4 proposes a QA model which is designed for quality management in CBSD process. In Sect. 5, we propose ComPARE, a generic quality assessment environment for CBSD. It facilitates quality evaluation of individual components as well as the target systems. Different prediction models have been applied to real-world CORBA programs. In Sect. 6, the pros and cons of these prediction models are analyzed. Finally, Sect. 7 concludes this chapter.

2 A Development Framework for Component-Based Software Systems

A framework can be defined as a set of constraints on components and their interactions, and a set of benefits that derive from those constraints [368]. To identify the development framework for component-based software, the framework or infrastructure for components should be identified first, as components are the basic units in component-based software systems.

Visual Basic Controls (VBX), ActiveX controls, class libraries, JavaBeans, etc., make it possible for their corresponding programming languages, i.e., Visual Basic, C++, and Java, and supporting tools to share and distribute application fragments. But all these approaches rely on certain underlying services to provide communication and coordination. The infrastructure of components (sometimes called a component model) acts as the "plumbing" that allows communication between components [47]. Among the component infrastructure technologies that have been developed, there are three de facto industrial standards: OMG's CORBA, Microsoft Corporation's Component Object Model (COM) and Distributed COM (DCOM), and Sun Microsystem's JavaBeans and Enterprise JavaBeans [234].

2.1 Common Object Request Broker Architecture (CORBA)

CORBA is an open standard for interoperability. It is defined and supported by the Object Management Group (OMG), an organization of over 400 software vendors and object technology user companies [310]. CORBA manages details of component interoperability, and allows applications to communicate with one another despite their different locations and designs. Interfaces are the only way in which applications or components communicate.

The most important part of a CORBA system is the Object Request Broker (ORB). ORB is the middleware that establishes a client/server relationship between components. Using an ORB, a client can invoke a method on a server object, whose location is completely transparent. ORB is responsible for intercepting a call and finding an object, which can implement the request, pass its parameters, invoke its method, and return the results. The client does not need to know where the object is located, its programming language, its operating system, or any other system aspects that are not related to the interface. In this way, ORB supports interoperability among applications on different machines in heterogeneous distributed environments, and can seamlessly interconnect multiple object systems.

CORBA is widely used in object-oriented distributed systems [431], including component-based software systems, because it offers a consistent distributed programming and runtime environment for common programming languages, operating systems, and distributed networks.

2.2 Component Object Model (COM) and Distributed COM (DCOM)

Component Object Model (COM) is a general architecture for component software [284]. It supports Windows- and Windows NT-based platform-dependent and language-independent component-based applications.

COM defines how components and their clients interact. As such, a client and a component can be connected without the support of an intermediate system component. In particular, COM provides a binary standard that components and their clients must follow to ensure dynamic interoperability. This enables online software update and cross-language software reuse [417].

Distributed COM (DCOM) is an extension of the Component Object Model (COM). It is a protocol that enables software components to communicate directly over a network in a reliable, secure, and efficient manner. DCOM supports multiple network protocols, including Internet protocols such as HTTP. When a client and its component reside on different machines, DCOM simply replaces the local interprocess communication with a network protocol. Neither the client nor the component is aware of changes in physical connections.

2.3 Sun Microsystems's JavaBeans and Enterprise JavaBeans

Sun Microsystem's Java-based component model consists of two parts: the JavaBeans for client-side component development and the Enterprise JavaBeans (EJB) for the server-side component development. The JavaBeans component architecture supports multiple platforms, as well as reusable, client-side and server-side components [381].

The Java platform offers an efficient solution to the portability and security problems through the use of portable Java bytecode and the concept of trusted and untrusted Java applets. Java provides a universal integration and enabling technology for enterprise application integration (EAI). The technology enables 1) interoperation across multi-vendor servers; 2) propagation of transaction and security contexts; 3) multilingual clients; and 4) supporting ActiveX via DCOM/CORBA bridges.

JavaBeans and EJBs extend the native strength of Java incorporating portability and security into component-based development. The portability, security, and reliability of Java are well suited for developing robust server objects independent of operating systems, Web servers, and database management servers.

2.4 Comparison among Different Architectures

Comparisons between development technologies for component-based software systems can be found in [47, 337, 385]. Table 1 summarizes their different features.

Table 1. Comparison of development technologies for component-based software systems.

	CORBA	EJB	COM/DCOM
Development environment	Underdeveloped	Emerging	Supported by a wide range of strong development environments
Binary interfacing standard	Not binary standards	Based on COM; Java-specific	A binary standard for component interaction is the heart of COM
Compatibility and portability	Particularly strong in standardizing language bindings; but not so portable	Portable by Java language specification; but not very compatible	Not having any concept of source-level standard of standard language binding
Modification and maintenance	CORBA IDL for defining component interfaces, need extra modification and maintenance	Not involving IDL files, defining interfaces between component and container; easier modification and maintenance	Microsoft IDL for defining component interfaces, need extra modification and maintenance
Services provided	A full set of standardized services; lack of implementations	Neither standardized nor implemented	Recently supplemented by a number of key services
Platform dependency	Platform-independent	Platform-independent	Platform-dependent
Language dependency	Language-independent	Language-dependent	Language-independent
Implementation	Strongest for traditional enterprise computing	Strongest in general Web clients	Strongest in traditional desktop applications

3 Quality Assurance for Component-Based Software Systems

3.1 The Development Life Cycle of Component-Based Software Systems

A component-based software system (CBS) is developed by assembling different components rather than programming from scratch. Thus, the life cycle of a component-based software system is different from that of a traditional software system. The cycle can be summarized as follows [335]: 1) Requirements analysis; 2) Software architecture selection, construction, analysis, and evaluation; 3) Component identification and customization; 4) System integration; 5) System testing; and 6) Software maintenance.

The architecture of CBS defines a system in terms of computational components and interactions among components. The focus is on composing and assembling components. Composition and assembly mostly take place separately, and even independently. Component identification, customization and integration are crucial activities in the development life cycle of CBS. It includes two main parts: 1) evaluation of candidate COTS based on the functional and quality requirements provided by the user; and 2) customization of suitable candidate COTS prior to integration. Integration involves communication and coordination among the selected components.

Quality assurance (QA) for CBS targets every stage of the development life cycle. QA technologies for CBS are currently premature, as specific characteristics of component systems are not accounted for. Although some QA techniques, such as the reliability analysis model for distributed software systems [429, 430] and the component-based approach to Software Engineering [308], have been studied, there are still no clear and well defined standards or guidelines for CBS. The identification of the QA characteristics, along with the models, tools, and metrics, have urgent need for standardization.

3.2 Quality Characteristics of Components

QA technologies for component-based software development have to address two inseparable questions: 1) How do we ensure the quality of a component? and 2) How do we ensure the quality of the target component-based software system? To answer these questions, models should be defined for quality control of individual components and the target CBS; metrics should be defined to measure the size, complexity, reusability, and reliability of individual components and the target CBS; and tools should be designed to evaluate existing components and CBS.

To evaluate a component, we must determine how to assess the quality of the component [150, 433]. Here, we propose a list of component features for the assessment: 1) Functionality; 2) Interface; 3) Usability; 4) Testability; 5) Maintainability; and 6) Reliability.

Software metrics can be proposed to measure software complexity [339, 340]. Such metrics are often used to classify components [211]. They include:

1) Size. This affects both reuse cost and quality. If it is too small, the benefits will not exceed the cost of managing it. If it is too large, it is hard to ensure high quality.

2) Complexity. This also affects reuse cost and quality. It is not cost-effective to modularize a component that is too trivial. But, on the other hand, for a component that is too complex, it is hard to ensure high quality.

3) Reuse frequency. The number of times and different domains in which a component has been used previously is an indicator of its usefulness.

4) Reliability. This is the probability of failure-free operations of a component under certain operational scenarios [252].

4 A Quality Assurance Model for Component-Based Software Systems

Since component-based software systems are developed on an underlying process different from that for traditional software, their quality assurance model should address both the process of componentization and the process of the overall system development. Figure 3 illustrates this view.

Many standards and guidelines, such as ISO9001 and CMM model [376], are used to control the quality activities of a traditional software development

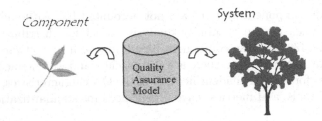

Fig. 3. Quality assurance model for both components and systems.

process. In particular, Hong Kong Productivity Council has developed the HKSQA model to localize the general SQA models [184]. In this section, we propose a quality assurance model for component-based software development.

In our model, the main practices relating to components and software systems contain the following phases: 1) Component requirement analysis; 2) Component development; 3) Component certification; 4) Component customization; 5) System architecture design; 6) System integration; 7) System testing; and 8) System maintenance.

4.1 Component Requirement Analysis

Component requirement analysis is the process of discovering, understanding, documenting, validating, and managing the requirements of a component. The objectives of component requirement analysis are to produce complete, consistent, and relevant requirements that a component should realize, as well as the programming language, platform, and interfaces related to the component.

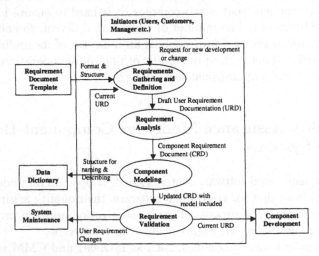

Fig. 4. Component requirement analysis process overview.

The component requirement process overview diagram is shown in Fig. 4. Initiated by the users or customers for new development or for changes to an old system, component requirement analysis consists of four main steps: requirements gathering and definition, requirement analysis, component modeling, and requirement validation. The output of this phase is the current user requirement documentation, which should be transferred to the next component development phase, the user requirement changes for the system maintenance phase, and data dictionary for all the latter phases.

4.2 Component Development

Component development is the process of implementing the requirements for a well functioning, high quality component with multiple interfaces. The objective of component development is the development of the final component products, their interfaces, and their corresponding development documents. Component development should lead to the final components satisfying the requirements with correct and expected results, well defined behaviors, and flexible interfaces.

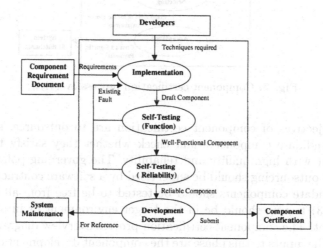

Fig. 5. Component development process overview.

The component development process overview diagram is shown in Fig. 5. Component development consists of four procedures: implementation, function testing, reliability testing, and development documentation. The input to this phase is the component requirement document. The output should be the developed component and its documents, ready for the following phases of component certification and system maintenance.

4.3 Component Certification

Component certification is the process which involves: 1) component outsourcing, or managing a component outsourcing contract and auditing the contractor performance; 2) component selection, or selecting the right components in accordance with the requirements for both functionality and reliability; and 3) component testing, or confirming that the component satisfies the requirements with acceptable quality and reliability.

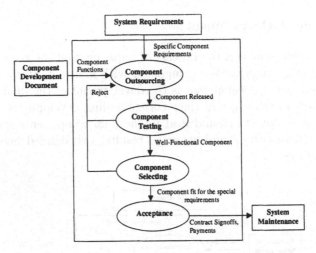

Fig. 6. Component certification process overview.

The objectives of component certification are to outsource, select, and test the candidate components and check whether they satisfy the system requirement with high quality and reliability. The governing policies are: 1) component outsourcing should be supervised by a software contract manager; 2) all candidate components should be tested to be free from all known defects; and 3) testing should be in the target environment or in a simulated environment. The component certification process overview diagram is shown in Fig. 6. The inputs to this phase are the component development documents, and the output is the testing documentation for system maintenance.

4.4 Component Customization

Component customization is the process which involves 1) modifying the component for specific requirements; 2) making necessary changes to the component for running on local platforms; and 3) upgrading the specific component to get better performance or higher quality. The objective of component customization is to make necessary changes to a developed component so that it can be used in a specific environment or cooperate well with other components.

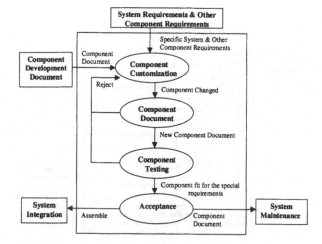

Fig. 7. Component customization process overview.

All components must be customized according to the operational system requirements or the interface requirements. The component customization process overview diagram is shown in Fig. 7. The inputs to component customization are the system requirements, the component requirements, and the component development documents. The outputs are the customized components, and documents for system integration and system maintenance.

4.5 System Architecture Design

System architecture design is the process of evaluating, selecting, and creating the software architecture of a component-based software system. The objectives of system architecture design are to collect the user requirements, determine the system specification, select an appropriate system architecture, and determine the implementation details such as platform, programming languages, and so on.

System architecture design should compare the pros and cons of different system architectures and select the one most suitable for the target CBS. The process overview diagram is shown in Fig. 8. This phase consists of system requirement gathering, analysis, system architecture design, and system specification. The output of this phase comprises the system specification document for system integration, and the system requirements for the system testing and system maintenance phases.

4.6 System Integration

System integration is the process of properly assembling the components selected to produce the target CBS under the system architecture designed. The process overview diagram is shown in Fig. 9. The inputs are the system

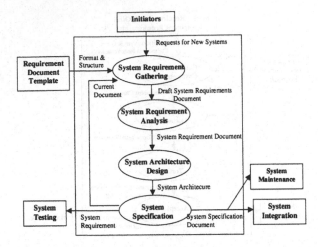

Fig. 8. System architecture design process overview.

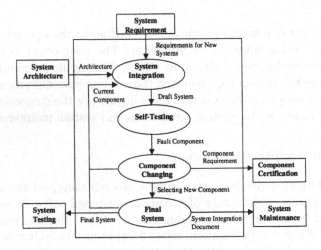

Fig. 9. System integration process overview.

requirement documentation and the specific architecture. There are four steps in this phase: integration, testing, changing components, and reintegration (if necessary). At the end of this phase, the final target system will be ready for system testing, with the appropriate document for the system maintenance phase.

4.7 System Testing

System testing is the process of evaluating a system to: 1) confirm that the system satisfies the specified requirements; and 2) identify and correct defects. System testing includes function testing and reliability testing. The process overview diagram is shown in Fig. 10. This phase consists of selecting a testing

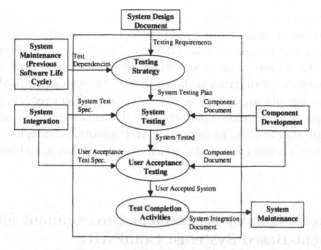

Fig. 10. System testing process overview.

strategy, system testing, user acceptance testing, and completion activities. The input comprises the documents from the component development and system integration phases. And the output includes the testing documentation for system maintenance. Note that this procedure must cater to interaction testing between multiple components, and includes coordination issues and deadlocks.

4.8 System Maintenance

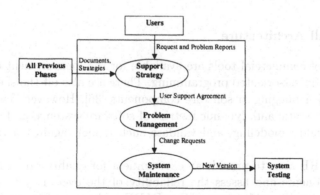

Fig. 11. System maintenance process overview.

System maintenance is the process of providing service and maintenance activities required to use the software effectively after it has been delivered. The objectives of system maintenance are to provide an effective product or service to the end users while repairing faults, improving software performance or other attributes, and adapting the system to a changed environment.

A maintenance organization should be available for every CBS product. All changes for the delivered system should be reflected in the related documents. The process overview diagram is shown in Fig. 11. According to the outputs from all previous phases, as well as requests and problem reports from users, system maintenance should be performed to determine the setup support and problem management (e.g., identification and approval) strategies. This phase produces a new version of the CBS, which may be subjected to further system testing.

5 A Generic Quality Assessment Environment for Component-Based Systems: ComPARE

We propose Component-based Program Analysis and Reliability Evaluation (ComPARE) to evaluate the quality of software systems in component-based software development. ComPARE automates the collection of different metrics, the selection of different prediction models, the formulation of user-defined models, and the validation of the established models according to faulty data collected in the development process. Different from other existing tools [253], ComPARE takes dynamic metrics into account (such as code coverage and performance metrics), integrates them with process metrics and other static code metrics (such as complexity metrics, coupling and cohesion metrics, and inheritance metrics) that are adopted from object-oriented software engineering, and provides different estimation models for overall system assessment.

5.1 Overall Architecture

A number of commercial tools are available for the measurement of software metrics for object-oriented programming. There are also off-the-shelf tools for testing and debugging of software components [36]. However, few tools can measure the static and dynamic metrics of software systems, perform various types of quality modeling, and validate such models against actual quality data.

ComPARE aims to provide an environment for quality prediction of software components and assess the reliability of the overall system based on them. The overall architecture of ComPARE is shown in Fig. 12. First of all, various metrics are computed for the candidate components; then the users can select and weigh the metrics deemed important to quality assessment. After the models have been constructed and executed (e.g., "case base" is used in the BBN model), the users can validate the selected models with previous failure data collections. If the users are not satisfied with the prediction result,

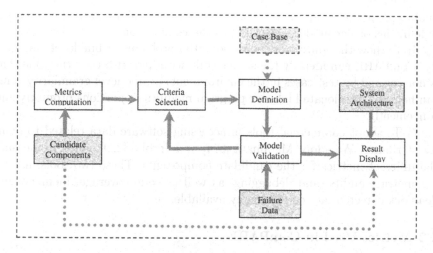

Fig. 12. Architecture of ComPARE.

they can go back to the previous step, redefine the criteria, and construct a revised model. Finally, the overall quality prediction can be displayed based on the architecture of the candidate system. Results from individual components can also be displayed for sensitivity analysis and system redesign.

The objectives of ComPARE are summarized as follows:

1) To predict the overall quality by using process metrics and static code metrics, as well as dynamic metrics. In addition to complexity metrics, we use process metrics, cohesion metrics and inheritance metrics, as well as dynamic metrics (such as code coverage and call graph metrics) as inputs to the quality prediction models. Thus, the prediction is more accurate, as it is based on data from every aspect of the candidate software components.

2) To integrate several quality prediction models into one environment and compare the prediction results of different models. ComPARE integrates several existing quality models into one environment. In addition to selecting or defining these different models, the user can also compare the prediction results of the models on the candidate component and see how good the predictions are if the failure data of the particular component is available.

3) To define the quality prediction models interactively. In ComPARE, the user can select from several quality prediction models and select the one most suitable for the prediction task at hand. Moreover, the user can also define his or her own models and validate them in the evaluation stage.

4) To classify components using different quality categories. Once the metrics are computed and the models selected, the overall quality of the component can be displayed according to the category it belongs to. Program modules with problems can also be identified.

5) To validate reliability models defined by the user against real failure data (e.g., change report). Using the validation criteria, the result of the selected

quality prediction model can be compared with real failure data. The user can redefine his or her models according to the comparison.

6) To show the source code with potential problems at line-level granularity. ComPARE can identify the source code with high risk (i.e., the code that is not covered by test cases in the environment) at line-level granularity. This can help the user locate high risk program modules or portions promptly and conveniently.

7) To adopt commercial tools in accessing software data related to quality attributes. We adopt Metamata [274] and Jprobe [229] suites to measure the different metrics for the candidate components. These two tools, involving metrics, audits, and debugging, as well as code coverage, memory, and deadlock detected, are commercially available.

5.2 Metrics Used in ComPARE

Table 2. Process Metrics.

Metric	Description
Time	Time spent from design to delivery (months)
Effort	Total human resources used (man*month)
Change Report	Number of faults found in development

Three different categories of metrics, namely process, static, and dynamic, are analyzed in CompARE to give the overall quality prediction. We have chosen proven metrics, i.e., those that are widely adopted by previous software quality prediction tools in the software engineering research community [218,362]. The process metrics we selected are listed in Table 2 [224]. Since we perceive that object-oriented (OO) techniques are essential in component-based software development, we select static code metrics according to the most important features in OO programs, i.e., complexity, coupling, inheritance, and cohesion. They are listed in Table 3 [251,274,384,411]. The dynamic metrics measure component features when they are executed. Table 4 shows the detailed description of the dynamic metrics.

Sets of process, static, and dynamic metrics can be collected from commercial tools, e.g., Metamata Suite [274] and Jprobe Testing Suite [229]. We adopt these metrics in ComPARE.

5.3 Models Definition

In order to predict the quality of software systems, several techniques have been developed to classify software components according to their reliability [144]. These techniques include discriminant analysis [297], classification trees [334], pattern recognition [45], Bayesian network [121], case-based reasoning (CBR) [216], and regression tree model [224].

Table 3. Static Code Metrics.

Abbreviation	Description
Lines of Code FF(LOC)	Number of lines in the components including statements, blank lines, lines of commentary, and lines consisting only of syntax such as block delimiters.
Cyclomatic Complexity (CC)	A measure of the control flow complexity of a method or constructor. It counts the number of branches in the body of the method, defined by the number of WHILE statements, IF statements, FOR statements, and CASE statements.
Number of Attri-butes (NA)	Number of fields declared in the class or interface.
Number Of Classes (NOC)	Number of classes or interfaces, which are declared. This is usually 1, but nested class declarations will increase this number.
Depth of Inheritance Tree (DIT)	Length of inheritance path between the current class and the base class.
Depth of Interface Extension Tree (DIET)	The path between the current interface and the base interface.
Data Abstraction Coupling (DAC)	Number of reference types, which are used in the field declarations of the class or interface.
Fan Out (FANOUT)	Number of reference types, which are used in field declarations, formal parameters, return types, throws declarations, and local variables.
Coupling between Objects (CO)	Number of reference types, which are used in field declarations, formal parameters, return types, throws declarations, local variables and also types from which field and method selections are made.
Method Calls Input/Output (MCI/MCO)	Number of calls to/from a method. It helps analyze the coupling between methods.
Lack of Cohesion of Methods (LCOM)	For each pair of methods in the class, the set of fields each of them accesses is determined. If they have disjoint sets of field then increase the count P by one. If they share at least one field then increase Q by one. After considering each pair of methods, $$LCOM = (P - Q) \quad if \quad P > Q$$ $$= 0 \qquad otherwise$$

Table 4. Dynamic Metrics.

Metric	Description
Test Case Coverage	The coverage of the source code when the given test cases are executed.
Call Graph metrics	Statistics about a method, including method time (the amount of time the method spent in execution), method object count (the number of objects created during the method execution) and number of calls (how many times each method is called in you application).
Heap metrics	Number of live instances of a particular class/package, and the memory used by each live instance.

Up to now, there is no good quality prediction model for CBS. Here, we set some evaluation criteria for good quality prediction models [298]: 1) Useful quantities, i.e., the model can make predictions of quantities reflecting software quality; 2) Prediction accuracy, i.e., the model can make predictions of quality which can be accurately observed later; 3) Ease of measuring parameters, i.e., the parameters in the model are easily measured or simulated; 4) Quality of assumptions, i.e., the assumptions should be reasonable, rather than too narrow or limited; 5) Applicability, i.e., the model should be widely used in various projects or experiments; and 6) Simplicity, i.e., the model should not be too hard to implement or realize.

In ComPARE, we combine existing quality prediction models according to the above criteria. Initially, one employs an existing prediction model, e.g., classification tree model or BBN model, customizes it, and compares the prediction results with different tailor-made models. In particular, we have investigated the following prediction models and studied their applicability to ComPARE in our research.

Summation Model

This model gives a prediction by simply adding all the metrics selected and weighted by the user. The user can validate the result by real failure data, and then benchmark the result. Later, when new components are included, the user can predict their quality according to their differences with the benchmarks. The concept of the summation model is formulated as follows:

$$Q = \sum_{i=1}^{n} \alpha_i m_i, \tag{1}$$

where m_i is the value of one particular metric, α_i is its corresponding weighting factor, n is the number of metrics, and Q is the overall quality mark.

Product Model

Similar to the summation model, the product model multiplies all the metrics selected and weighted by the user. The resulting value indicates the level of quality of a given component. Similarly, the user can validate the result by real failure data, and then determine the benchmark for later usage. The concept of product model is shown as follows:

$$Q = \prod_{i=1}^{n} m_i, \tag{2}$$

where m_i is the value of one particular metric, n is the number of metrics, and Q is the overall quality mark. Note that the m_i's are normalized to a value close to 1 so that no single metric can dominate the result.

Classification Tree Model

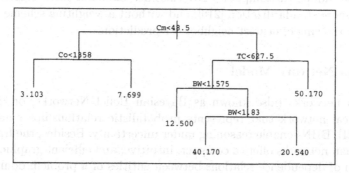

Fig. 13. An example of the classification tree model.

Classification tree model [334] classifies candidate components into different quality categories by constructing a tree structure. All candidate components (with a certain failure rate) form the leaves of the tree. Each node of the tree represents a metric (or a composed metric calculated from other metrics) with a certain value. All children of the left sub-tree of a node represent those components whose values of the same metrics are smaller than the value of the node. Similarly, all children of the right sub-tree of a node are those components whose values of the same metric are equal to or larger than the value of the node. Figure 13 gives an example of the classification tree model.

In ComPARE, a user can define the metrics and their values at each node from the root to the leaves. Once the tree is constructed, a candidate component can be directly classified by following the threshold of each node in the tree until it reaches a leaf node. Again, the user can validate and evaluate the final tree model after its definition. Figure 13 is an example of the outcome of a tree model, where Cm (number of comments), Co (code characters), Tc (total line of code), and BW (Belady's bandwidth metric) are sample metrics [144]. At each node of the tree are metrics and values, and the leaves represent the components with a certain number of predicted faults in the classification result.

Case-Based Reasoning Model

Case-based reasoning (CBR) has been proposed for predicting quality of software components [216]. A CBR classifier uses previous "similar" cases as the basis for prediction. Previous cases are stored in a case base. Similarity is defined in terms of a set of metrics. The major conjecture behind this model is that a candidate component which has a similar structure as a component in the case base will be assigned to a similar quality level.

A CBR classifier can be instantiated in different ways by varying its parameters. But according to previous research, there is no significant difference in prediction validity with any combination of parameters in CBR. For this reason, we adopt the simplest CBR classifier modeling with Euclidean distance, z-score standardization [216], and without a weighting scheme. Finally, we select the single, nearest neighbor for prediction.

Bayesian Network Model

Bayesian networks (also known as Bayesian Belief Networks, or BBNs) is a graphical network that represents probabilistic relationships among variables [121]. BBNs enable reasoning under uncertainty. Besides, the framework of Bayesian networks offers a compact, intuitive, and efficient graphical representation of dependence relations between entities of a problem domain. The graphical structure reflects properties of the problem domain directly, and provides a tangible visual representation of, as well as a sound mathematical basis for Bayesian probability [118]. The foundation of Bayesian networks is based on the following theorem, which is known as Bayes' Lemma:

$$(H|E, c) = \frac{P(H|c)P(E|H, c)}{P(E|c)}, \qquad (3)$$

where H, E, and c are independent events and P is the probability of such an event under certain circumstances.

With BBNs, it is possible to integrate expert beliefs about the dependencies between different variables and to propagate consistently the impact of evidence on the probabilities of uncertain outcomes, such as "unknown component quality." Details of the BBN model for quality prediction can be found in [121]. Users can also define their own BBN models in ComPARE, and compare the results with other models.

5.4 Operations in ComPARE

ComPARE suggests eight functions: File Operations, Metrics Selection, Criteria Selection and Weighting, Model Selection and Definition, Model Validation, Display Result, Windows Switch, and Help. The details of some of these key functions are described in the following:

Metrics Selection

Users can select the metrics they want to collect for the component-based software systems. Three categories of metrics are available: process metrics, static metrics, and dynamic metrics. The details of these metrics are shown in Section 5.2.

Criteria Selection and Weighting

After computing different metrics, the users will select and weigh the criteria associated with these metrics before using them. Each metric can be assigned a weight between 0 and 1.

Model Selection and Definition

This operation allows the users to select or define the model they would like to use in the evaluation. The users are required to provide the probability of each metric that affects the quality of the candidate component.

Model Validation

Model validation enables comparison between different models with respect to actual software failure data. It helps users compare different results based on a subset of the software failure data chosen under certain validation criteria. Comparison between different models in their predictive capability are summarized in a summary table. Model validation operations are employed only when software failure data are available.

5.5 Prototype

We have developed a ComPARE prototype for QA of Java-based components and CBS. Java is one of the most popular languages used in off-the-shelf components development today. It is a common language binding the three standard architectures of component-based software development, namely, CORBA, DCOM, and Java/RMI.

Figures 14 and 15 show screen dumps of the ComPARE prototype. The computation of various metrics for software components and the application of

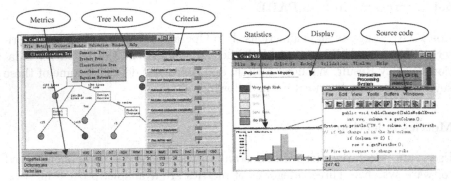

Fig. 14. GUI of ComPARE for metrics, criteria and tree model.

Fig. 15. GUI of ComPARE for prediction display, risky source code and result statistics.

quality prediction models can be seen as a straightforward process. Users also have flexible choices in selecting and defining different models. The combination of simple operations and a variety of quality models makes it easy for the users to identify an appropriate prediction model for a given component-based software system.

6 Experiment and Discussion

6.1 Objective

ComPARE provides a systematic procedure for predicting the quality of software components and for assessing their reliability in the final target system. As there is no existing QA model for CBS, ComPARE adopts existing quality prediction models.

In this section, we investigate the effectiveness of different existing quality prediction models and their applicability to CBS. In our experiment, we use the five models selected in Section 5.3 to predict and evaluate the relationship between the number of faults and the software metrics of some CORBA programs obtained in a component-based software engineering experiment. In this experiment, all programs were designed according to the same specification. The programming teams could choose their own programming languages. The test cases were designed to assess the functionalities of the final programs according to the specification. The details of the testing and evaluation of this experiment is shown in [427]. We applied the selected prediction models to the final CORBA programs and investigated how well they behave. This information is useful to the users for determining the appropriate quality prediction models.

6.2 Data Description and Experiment Procedure

In the fall of 1998, we engaged 19 programming teams to design, implement, test, and demonstrate a Soccer Team Management System using CORBA. This was a class project for students majoring in computer science. The duration of the project was four weeks. The programming teams (two or three students for each team) participating in this project were required to independently design and develop a distributed system. The system had to allow multiple clients to access a Soccer Team Management Server for 10 different operations. The teams were free to choose different CORBA vendors (VisiBroker or Iona Orbix) and use different programming languages (Java or C++) for the client and server programs. These programs had to pass an acceptance test, in which programs were subjected to two types of test cases for each of the 10 operations: one for normal operation and the other for operations which would raise exceptions. In total, 57 test cases were used in the experiment.

Among these 19 programs, 12 used VisiBroker and seven used Iona Orbix. For the 12 VisiBroker programs, nine used Java and two used C++ for both client and server implementations, and one used Java and C++ for client and server, respectively. Because Team 1 did not pass the acceptance test, we will not include it in our evaluations. The metrics collected and the test results for the 18 different program versions are shown in Table 5. The meaning of the metrics and testing results are listed below:

- Total Lines of Code (TLOC): the total length of the whole program, including lines of codes in the client and server programs;
- Client LOC (CLOC): lines of codes in the client program;
- Server LOC (SLOC): lines of codes in the server program;
- Client Class (CClass): number of classes in the client program;
- Client Method (CMethod): number of methods in the client program;
- Server Class (SClass): number of classes in the server program;
- Server Method (SMethod): number of methods in the server program;
- Fail: the number of test cases that the program failed on;
- Maybe: the number of test cases designed to raise exceptions that failed to work because the client-side of the program forbade it. In this situation, we were not sure whether the server was designed to properly raise the expected exceptions. Thus, we put down "maybe" as the result.
- R: pass rate, defined by $R_j = \frac{P_j}{C}$, where C is the total number of test cases applied to the programs (i.e., 57); P_j is the number of "Pass" cases for program j, and $P_j = C - Fail - Maybe$.
- R1: pass rate 2, defined by $R1_j = \frac{P_j + M_j}{C}$, where C is the total number of test cases applied to the programs (i.e., 57); P_j is the number of "Pass" cases for program j, $P_j = C - Fail - Maybe$; and M_j is the number of "Maybe" cases for program j.

Table 5. General Metrics of Different Teams.

Team	TLOC	CLOC	SLOC	CClass	CMethod	SClass	SMethod	Fail	Maybe	R	R1
P2	1129	613	516	3	15	5	26	7	6	0.77	0.88
P3	1874	1023	851	3	23	5	62	3	6	0.84	095
P4	1309	409	900	3	12	1	23	3	12	0.74	0.95
P5	2843	1344	1499	4	26	1	25	2	1	0.95	0.96
P6	1315	420	895	3	3	1	39	13	10	0.60	0.77
P7	2674	1827	847	3	17	5	35	3	14	0.70	0.95
P8	1520	734	786	3	24	4	30	1	6	0.88	0.98
P9	2121	1181	940	4	22	3	43	4	2	0.89	0.93
P10	1352	498	854	3	12	5	41	2	2	0.93	0.96
P11	563	190	373	3	12	3	20	6	3	0.84	0.89
P12	5695	4641	1054	14	166	5	32	1	4	0.91	0.98
P13	2602	1587	1015	3	27	3	32	17	19	0.37	0.70
P14	1994	873	1121	4	12	5	39	4	6	0.82	0.93
P15	714	348	366	4	11	4	33	2	5	0.88	0.96
P16	1676	925	751	3	3	23	44	30	0	0.47	0.47
P17	1288	933	355	6	25	5	35	3	3	0.89	0.95
P18	1731	814	917	3	12	3	20	4	9	0.77	0.93
P19	1900	930	970	3	3	2	20	35	1	0.37	0.39

To evaluate the quality of these CORBA programs, we applied the test cases to the programs and assessed their quality and reliability based on the test results. We describe our procedure below.

First of all, we collected the different metrics of all the programs. Metamata [274] and JProbe Suite [229] were used for this purpose. We designed test cases for these CORBA programs according to the specification. We used black-box testing methods, i.e., testing was on system functions only. Each operation defined in the system specification was tested. We defined some test cases for each operation. The test cases selected were from two categories: normal cases and cases that caused exceptions in the system. For each operation in the system, at least one normal test case was conducted in testing. In the other cases, all the exceptions were covered. But, in order to reduce the workload, we tried to use as few test cases as possible as long as all the exceptions had been accounted for.

We used the test results as indicators of quality. We applied different quality prediction models, i.e., the classification tree model and Bayesian Network model, to the metrics and test results. We then validated the prediction results of these models against the test results. We divided the programs into two groups: training data and testing set, and adopted cross evaluation. This was done during or after the prediction process, according to the prediction models. After applying the metrics to the different models, we analyzed the accuracy of their predicting results and identified their advantages and disadvantages. Also, based on the results, we adjusted the coefficients and weights of different metrics in the final models.

6.3 Experiment Results

Summation Model

The summation model gives a prediction by simply adding all the metrics selected and weighted by the user. For simplicity, we give equal weighting to all the metrics, e.g., the weights of all metrics equal 1. Also, we normalize the values of the metrics by using the ratio of the actual value to the maximum value of that particular metric, i.e., $m_1 = \frac{TLOC}{max(TLOC)}$, $m_2 = \frac{CLOC}{max(CLOC)}$, and so on, for every program. The overall quality mark, then, is $Q = m_1 + m_2 + \cdots$ for the 18 programs. The result of the summation model is listed in Table 6.

Product Model

The product model multiplies all the metrics selected and weighted by the user. The values of the metrics are also normalized to values close to 1, using the same method as above. The final result is the product of these normalized values. It is listed in Table 6.

Classification Tree Results Using CART

We adopted the commercial tool CART [118] in our classification tree modeling. The CART methodology is technically known as binary recursive partitioning. The process is binary because parent nodes are always split into exactly two child nodes, and recursive because the process can be repeated by treating each child node as a parent. The key element of a CART analysis is a set of rules for: 1) splitting each node in a tree; 2) deciding when a tree is complete; and 3) assigning each terminal node to a class outcome (or predicted value for regression).

We applied the metrics and testing results in Table 5 to the CART tool, and collected the classification tree results for predicting the quality variable "Fail". Table 7 is the option setting of the classification tree. The tree constructed is shown in Fig. 16, and the relative importance of each metric is listed in Table 8. From Fig. 16, we can see that the 18 learning samples are classified into nine groups (terminal nodes), whose information is listed in Table 9. The most important vector was the number of methods in the client program ($CMethod$), and the next three most important vectors were $TLOC$, $SCLASS$, and $CLOC$. From the node information, we observe that the most non fault-prone nodes are those programs with $638.5 < TLOC < 921.5$ and $7 < CMETHOD < 26$ and $SLOC < 908.5$, or $CEMTHOD > 7$ and $TLOC < 638.5$. The relationship between classification results and the three main metrics was analyzed, and the results are listed in Table 10.

Table 6. Results of Summation Model and Product Model.

Team	Summation Modeling	Product Model	Fail	Maybe	R	R1
P2	7.00	0.0000159	7	6	0.77	0.88
P3	1.62	0.0002658	3	6	0.84	095
P4	2.69	0.0000030	3	12	0.74	0.95
P5	1.62	0.0001134	2	1	0.95	0.96
P6	2.68	0.0000013	13	10	0.60	0.77
P7	1.82	0.0002813	3	14	0.70	0.95
P8	2.53	0.0000577	1	6	0.88	0.98
P9	1.97	0.0002036	4	2	0.89	0.93
P10	2.50	0.0000323	2	2	0.93	0.96
P11	2.08	0.0000007	6	3	0.84	0.89
P12	1.13	0.0788932	1	4	0.91	0.98
P13	5.44	0.0002482	17	19	0.37	0.70
P14	2.50	0.0001391	4	6	0.82	0.93
P15	2.49	0.0000040	2	5	0.88	0.96
P16	1.50	0.0000808	30	0	0.47	0.47
P17	2.94	0.0000853	3	3	0.89	0.95
P18	2.03	0.0000213	4	9	0.77	0.93
P19	1.83	0.0000047	35	1	0.37	0.39

Table 7. Option Setting of the classification tree.

Construction Rule	Least Absolute Deviation
Estimation Method	Exploratory - Resubstitution
Tree Selection	0.000 se rule
Linear Combinations	No
Initial value of the complexity parameter	= 0.000
Minimum size below which node will not be split	= 2
Node size above which sub-sampling will be used	= 18
Maximum number of surrogates used for missing values	= 1
Number of surrogate splits printed	= 1
Number of competing splits printed	= 5
Maximum number of trees printed in the tree sequence	= 10
Max. number of cases allowed in the learning sample	= 18
Maximum number of cases allowed in the test sample	= 0
Max # of nonterminal nodes in the largest tree grown	= 38
(Actual # of nonterminal nodes in largest tree grown	= 10)
Max. no. of categorical splits including surrogates	= 1
Max. number of linear combination splits in a tree	= 0
(Actual number cat. + linear combination splits	= 0)
Maximum depth of largest tree grown	= 13
(Actual depth of largest tree grown	= 7)
Maximum size of memory available	= 9000000
(Actual size of memory used in run	= 5356)

Table 8. Importance of different variables in the classification tree.

Metrics	Relative Importance	Number of Categories	Minimum Category
CMETHOD	100.000		
TLOC	45.161		
SCLASS	43.548		
CLOC	33.871		
SLOC	4.839		
SMETHOD	0.000		
CCLASS	0.000		
N of the learning sample = 18			

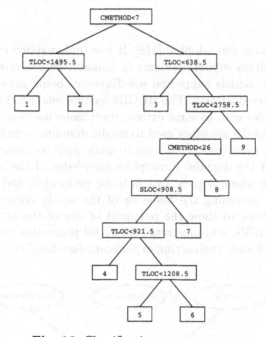

Fig. 16. Classification tree structure.

Table 9. Terminal node information in the classification tree.

Parent Node	Wgt Count	Count	Median	MeanAbsDev	Complexity
1	1.00	1	13.000	0.000	17.000
2	2.00	2	35.000	2.500	17.000
3	1.00	1	6.000	0.000	6.333
4	1.00	1	2.000	0.000	2.500
5	1.00	1	7.000	0.000	4.000
6	6.00	6	3.000	0.500	4.000
7	3.00	3	4.000	0.000	3.000
8	1.00	1	17.000	0.000	14.000
9	2.00	2	2.000	0.500	8.000

Table 10. Relationship between the classification results and 3 main metrics.

Terminal Node	Mean Faults	CMethod	TLOC	SLOC
4	2	7̃26	638.5~921.5	≤908.5
9	2	>7	≤638.5	-
6	3	7̃26	1208.5~2758.5	≤908.5
7	4	7̃26	638.5~921.5	>908.5
3	6	>7	≤638.5	-
5	7	7̃26	638.5~921.5	≤908.5
1	13	≤7	≤1495.5	-
8	17	>26	638.5~921.5	-
2	35	≤7	>1495.5	-

BBN Results

The HUGIN System was adopted [118]. It is a tool enabling one to construct model-based decision support systems in domains characterized by inherent uncertainty. The models supported are Bayesian belief networks and their extension influence diagrams. The HUGIN System enables the user to define both discrete nodes and, to some extent, continuous nodes in the models.

Bayesian networks are often used to model domains, which are characterized by inherent uncertainty. This uncertainty may be caused by imperfect understanding of the domain, incomplete knowledge of the state of the domain at the time where a given task is to be performed, and randomness in the mechanisms governing the behavior of the whole system. We have developed a prototype to show the potential of one of the quality prediction models, namely BBN, and illustrated its useful properties using real metrics data from the software engineering experiment (see Section 6.2).

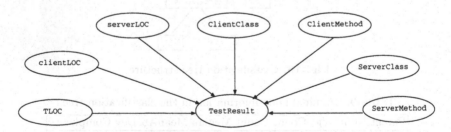

Fig. 17. The Influence Diagram of the BBN model.

We constructed an influence diagram for the CORBA programs according to the metrics and testing results collected in the testing procedure, as shown in Fig. 17. However, due to interactions between these metrics, some of the metrics are redundant. We assumed the worst scenario and considered every metrics. Each of these metrics shown in Fig. 17 had its own impact on the

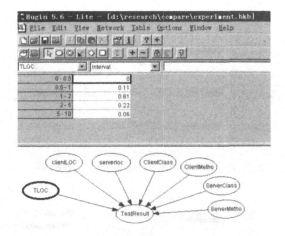

Fig. 18. The probability description of nodes in BBN model.

testing result. Once the influence diagram is constructed, we input the probability of the metrics and testing results collected in our test procedures, as shown in Fig. 18.

The result of the HUGIN tool are shown in Fig. 19 and Fig. 20, where (a) is the original probability distribution of different metrics and testing results; (b) is the probability distribution of the metrics when the number of faults is less than 5; and (c) is the probability distribution of the metrics when the number of faults is between five and 10. Figure 19 shows the results of summation propagation, and Fig. 20 shows the results of maximum propagation.

Summation propagation shows the true probability of the states of the nodes with the total summation equal to 1. For maximum propagation, if a state of a node belongs to the most probable configuration, it is given the value 100. All other states are given the value of the probability of the most probable configuration they found relative to the most probable configuration. That is, assume node N has two states, a and b, and b belongs to the most probable configuration of the entire BBN, which has probability 0.002; then, b is given the value 100. Now, assume that the most probable configuration which a belongs to has probability 0.0012; then, a is given the value 60.

Using maximum propagation instead of sum propagation, we can find the probability of the most likely combination of states under the assumption that the evidence holds. In each node, a state having the value 100 belongs to the most likely combination of states. From Fig. 20(b), we can find the best combination of the metrics with respect to the corresponding testing results, as listed in Table 11. For test results between 0 and 5, the ranges of $CMethod$, $TLOC$, and $SLOC$ are very close to the results of the classification tree in Table 10.

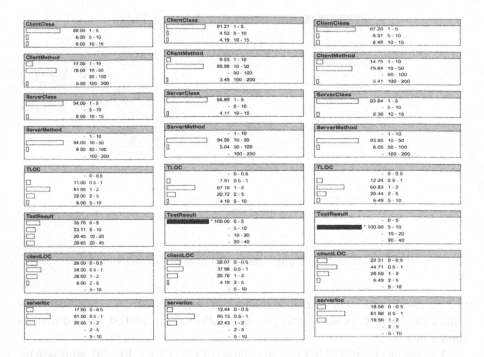

Fig. 19. The different probability distribution of metrics according to the quality indicator (sum propagation).

Table 11. Relationship between test result and metrics in BBN.

TestResult	CCLASS	CMethod	SCLASS	SMethod	TLOC	CLOC	SLOC
0-5	1-5	10-50	1-5	10-50	1-2K	0-0.5K	0.5-1K
5-10	1-5	10-50	1-5	10-50	1-2K	0.5-1K	0.5-1K

Case-Based Reasoning Model

To use case-based reasoning model, a case base containing a number of components with various metric values and quality levels should be established. When a new component is developed, the component most similar to it in the case base should be identified. The quality data of the case is then used for the new component. Case base is unavailable for CBS at present. Thus, we simply illustrate how the CBR model works with our own synthetic data set.

Assume we already have a case base containing 17 programs, i.e., P3 through P19. To predict the quality of a new program P2, we would find the most similar program in the case base (using, for example, Euclidean distance without weighting; see Table 12). We would then predict that program P2 had a quality level similar to that of the selected program, e.g., P17, with three faults, under a reliability indicator of 89%.

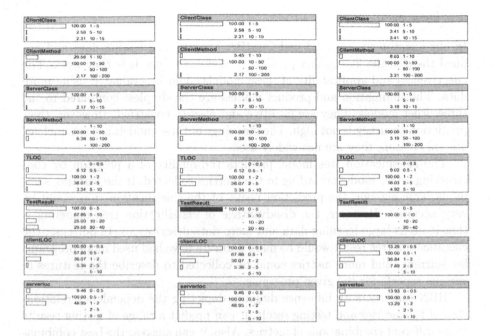

Fig. 20. The different probability distribution of metrics according to the quality indicator (max propagation).

Table 12. Result of Case-Based Reasoning Model.

Team	Distance with P2	Fail	Maybe	R	R1
P3	914.7185	3	6	0.84	095
P4	470.6442	3	12	0.74	0.95
P5	2106.7950	2	1	0.95	0.96
P6	464.5589	13	10	0.60	0.77
P7	1992.6031	3	14	0.70	0.95
P8	490.4284	1	6	0.88	0.98
P9	1219.3470	4	2	0.89	0.93
P10	421.2268	2	2	0.93	0.96
P11	720.9598	6	3	0.84	0.89
P12	6114.3718	1	4	0.91	0.98
P13	1835.0995	17	19	0.37	0.70
P14	1087.2116	4	6	0.82	0.93
P15	514.7980	2	5	0.88	0.96
P16	672.7332	30	0	0.47	0.47
P17	392.1632	3	3	0.89	0.95
P18	750.7696	4	9	0.77	0.93
P19	949.3340	35	1	0.37	0.39

6.4 Discussion

In our experiment, we used real CORBA programs as testing data and applied them to the five quality prediction models to show how they work. The effectiveness and applicability of these models could be evaluated using more data. The summation and product models are the simplest compared to the three other models. They are intuitive and easy to construct. However, their prediction accuracy is not high. The meanings of these models are yet unclear. For this reason, they are not widely used.

The classification tree model predicts the quality of a program by constructing a tree model according to the metrics collected. If the learning sample is large enough, the prediction result of the classification tree would be very accurate. However, the disadvantage of classification tree modeling is that it needs large learning data and more data descriptions. In our case, the classification tree result would be more accurate if we had used more programs for learning, and more metrics could be collected to describe the features of various aspects for the given programs.

BBN constructs an influence diagram depicting the dependency relationship of the metrics and testing result. It can predict a range of testing results using different combinations of metrics. Also, it can suggest the best combination of metrics. This is more clear in BBN than in the classification tree. The obvious disadvantage of the BBN model is that the user is required to know well the dependency relationship in his or her specific domain before an effective influence diagram can be constructed. But such knowledge is available only after several runs.

The case-based reasoning model requires an established and sizable case base. Due to the lack of such data, the effectiveness of the CBR model for CBSD awaits further investigation.

The testing data used in our experiment is limited, i.e., only 18 programs were used to construct the models and to validate the prediction. To make the comparison more accurate, we will use more programs as test data in our future work. Also, if we could collect data from real component-based systems, we would apply these models to individual components as well as to entire systems in order to obtain a relationship of their qualities.

7 Conclusion

In this chapter, we introduce a component-based software development framework. We propose a QA model for component-based software development, which covers both the component QA and the system QA, as well as their interactions. As far as we know, this is the first effort to formulate a QA model for developing software systems based on component technologies. We further propose a generic quality assessment environment for component-based software systems: ComPARE. ComPARE is new in that it collects more metrics for software systems, including process metrics, static code metrics, and dynamic metrics for software components, integrates reliability assessment models from different techniques currently used in quality prediction field, and validates these models against real failure data. ComPARE can be used to assess live off-the-shelf components and to evaluate and validate the models selected for their evaluation. The overall component-based software system can then be composed and analyzed seamlessly. ComPARE can be an effective environment to promote component-based software system construction with higher reliability evaluation and proper quality assurance.

Acknowledgment

The work described in this book chapter was supported by the following projects:

- "Open Component Foundation," an Industry Support Fund project supported by the Hong Kong Industry Department (Project No. AF94/99).
- a grant from the Research Grants Council of the Hong Kong Special Administrative Region (Project No. CUHK4360/02E).
- a strategic grant supported by the Chinese University of Hong Kong (Project No. 4410001).

Automatic Testing for Robustness Violations

Christof Fetzer[1] and Zhen Xiao[2]

[1] Dresden University of Technology
Dresden, Germany
christof.fetzer@inf.tu-dresden.de
[2] AT&T Labs—Research
Florham Park, NJ, USA
xiao@research.att.com

Summary. Detecting programming errors in component-based systems can be difficult and very expensive. Due to the trend in outsourcing the development of software, companies are deploying more third-party software for mission critical systems. Hence, there is an increased need to assess the robustness and security of software. The traditional way of supporting component-oriented programming is to provide components in the form of shared libraries. In this chapter we describe a tool called HEALERS that can detect programming errors and security vulnerabilities in third-party libraries without source code access. A major advantage of our approach is that it is highly automated and could be used by component users who have little knowledge about the internals of a library.

1 Introduction

The scale and complexity of computer software have increased significantly during the last decade. Developing a large piece of software is a difficult task. A classical solution to this problem is to develop the software from a set of components instead of as a large, monolithic system. In this approach, the high-level functionality requirements of the system are decomposed into a set of orthogonal properties that are implemented by software components. This allows a new application type to be created easily by composing a set of components to suit the specific needs of the application. Since each component implements only a single property, it is easy to optimize and reuse. A software developer can add new components to support new features, which can then be combined with existing components to implement a large variety of software types. Such a component-based architecture is similar to previous work in microkernel designs and group communication systems. x-Kernel, for example, defines a modular structure for implementing network software [317]. Horus [398] and Ensemble [174] are two examples of modular group communication systems where protocol layers can be stacked on top of each other in a variety of ways.

While a component-based approach facilitates software development, it also imposes stringent requirements on the reliability and security of those components. A programming error in a software component may cause the failure of the overall system built with that component. The consequences can be costly due to the increasing reliance on computer technology in our society. For example, many financial transactions nowadays are conducted using computers on the Internet. Many companies utilize virtual office technology to allow their employees to work comfortably at home. This trend is expected to continue in the years to come. If a computer server crashes, hangs, or gives erroneous output, it may lead to severe disruption of service or loss of productivity. Moreover, sometimes a subtle programming error in a commonly used component can become a serious security hole if exploited by malicious users. For example, the incorrect handling of the `glob` command in WU-FTPD was exploited by attackers to gain unauthorized access to the victim's machine [63]. Hence, an effective testing method to detect programming errors and vulnerabilities in software components is essential to the correctness of the overall system.

Traditionally, manual inspection of the source code is a commonly used method for detecting programming errors. Although effective, this method can be expensive (in terms of human cost) and time consuming. Moreover, the quality of manual inspections can be erratic and depends largely on the level of expertise of the software engineers involved. For systems with a large number of components, even the best software engineers may not detect all the errors.

One way to enhance the correctness of computer programs is through formal methods. In this approach, the properties of a software module are described by a set of specifications. An example of a specification for a distributed service can be that all messages received must be delivered in FIFO order. The correctness of an implementation is checked against its specification through formal analysis. This can give strong guarantees regarding the behaviors of the program in various execution contexts. The advantage of formal methods is that they can check global properties of a system and may find deep, logical errors. Such kinds of errors are difficult to catch using other methods.

However, formal methods cannot address all problems related to software robustness. The specifications of a program usually abstract away many implementation details that need to be considered in practice. Unfortunately, many security vulnerabilities are due to low-level programming errors, such as incorrect error handling for memory or I/O operations. Catching these kinds of errors is beyond of the state of the art of formal methods. In fact, formal verification usually requires that a program be written in some special, *safe* language amenable to formal analysis and manipulation. The Ensemble project, for example, was developed using Objective Caml, a dialect of ML [242]. A nice property of this language is that it has a precise mathematical semantics that can be used for formal reasoning. However, the majority of software written today is in imperative languages like C or C++ that practically cannot be verified using formal methods.

Recently, considerable research has been done on the use of static analyses to check for programming errors. The authors of [112] use meta-level compilation to write compiler extensions that automatically check the source code of a program for violations of certain *rules*. An example of such a rule is that spin_lock and spin_unlock must be paired. Later, in [113], the authors propose an innovative approach to infer such rules automatically based on the programmer's *beliefs*. It then detects any violation of such beliefs as potential programming errors. For example, the dereference of a pointer in a program implies the belief that the pointer must not be NULL at that point. If this belief contradicts an early belief (i.e., the pointer might be NULL), then it indicates a potential bug in the code. It was shown that this approach successfully detected hundreds of bugs in Linux and OpenBSD with substantially less effort than manual inspection [113].

Static analyses require access to the source code of the program. However, many component-based systems are built using Commercial-Off-The-Shelf (COTS) components in order to reduce development cost. The source code of COTS software is seldom available to component users. Therefore, when a security vulnerability is found, users of such components have to wait until a patch is released by the software vendor. Another problem with static analyses is that its results still need manual examination. Although automated techniques (such as those in [113]) can substantially reduce the amount of efforts required for checking errors in large systems, every piece of the suspicious code still needs to be verified manually in order to remove "false positive", a nontrivial task in a large system.

In this chapter, we describe the HEALERS project that uses automated fault injection experiments to discover vulnerabilities in shared libraries without source code access. A major advantage of this approach is that it is highly automated and could be used by system administrators with little domain-specific knowledge. The rest of the chapter is organized as follows. In Sect. 2 we introduce the goals and objectives of HEALERS and in Sect. 3 we discuss its underlying methodology. In Sect. 5 we review related work, and conclude the chapter with Sect. 6.

2 Goals and Objectives

While many software testing methods have been proposed in the past, not all of them are suitable for COTS components. To achieve wide applicability, the HEALERS project was designed with the following goals and objectives:

- **Transparency:** COTS components are usually developed by third-party vendors, and their source code is seldom available. Hence, any method that requires modification or recompilation of source code is in this context undesirable. Our tool is designed to work transparently with existing applications without source code access.

- **Automation:** With the exponential increase in processing power during the past several decades, the cost of a computer programmer is nowadays usually much higher than the cost of a group of high-end PCs. Any testing method that is labor-intensive will not scale well due to its high operational cost. Another design goal of our tool is to achieve a high degree of automation: robustness testing for COTS components should be mostly a "push-button" process.

- **Flexibility:** Applications built on COTS components may have different reliability and security requirements and need different degrees of testing. A "one size fits all" approach would not work. Flexibility is a design objective of our tool: the tool should be highly configurable so that it can suit the needs of various applications.

- **Profiling:** A key to achieving reliability of COTS components is to understand why these components fail. What is needed is an extensive analysis of the common errors and faults that arise in practice. This would provide valuable insights to both component users and component developers. A final goal of our project is to facilitate statistics collection and analysis during runtime.

Our current focus is on errors related to library functions written in C or C++. C and C++ are two of the most efficient languages, and give programmers extensive control over system resources, in particular, over memory. Compared with languages that support automatic memory management (e.g., garbage collection), C and C++ permit savvy programmers to optimize resource usage based on application knowledge. This explicit control over memory also supports memory-mapped I/O, which is important for system-level programming.

Unfortunately, the high performance of C libraries comes at the expense of system robustness. Previous studies have found that many functions in the POSIX C library are brittle with respect to invalid inputs [231]. This is because they make implicit assumptions about their arguments and often omit validity checks for efficiency. For example, the strcpy(char *dst, const char *src) function copies a string pointed to by src to the location pointed to by dst. If the destination buffer does not have sufficient memory space to accommodate the source string, a segmentation fault may be generated if the buffer overflows into an unmapped page, as shown in Fig. 1.

In C, it is up to the programmer to check buffer boundaries for potential overflows. Missing boundary checks are commonly exploited by attackers to get unauthorized access to a computer (so-called buffer overflow attacks) [16]. Such a design prevents correct programs from being penalized by unnecessary checks, but it makes building robust and secure programs more difficult.

strcpy(dst, src)

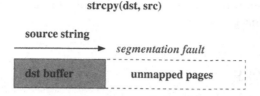

Fig. 1. A segmentation fault may be generated due to a buffer overflow in strcpy.

The fundamental solution to this kind of problem is to maintain a good coding style: a program should avoid unsafe C library functions like strcpy (and use strncpy instead) and perform careful argument checks before calling a function. Although effective, this approach requires manual inspection of the source code of a program to detect and fix programming errors or security loopholes. Given the huge volume of existing C and C++ programs, it is not possible to inspect and rewrite all of them. Moreover, whenever there is a new software release or update, the software has to be examined again. As shown in [231], new library releases are sometimes more robust than previous versions due to bug fixes, but sometimes less robust due to bugs introduced in new features. Inspecting each new release of a library manually will be time consuming and error-prone. The contribution of our work is to show that we can detect a specific class of errors in a highly automated manner. These are errors that result in externally observable behaviors, such as a program crash. We call such behaviors *robustness violations*. We do not aim to detect logical errors. Examples of robustness violations include:

- Reading or writing beyond the boundaries of allocated blocks on the heap.
- Overwriting return addresses on the stack.
- An error from a library function call or other parts of the application leading to a segmentation fault.
- A function call from the application violating the robust argument types of the function (defined later in the chapter).

A robustness violation is not only a programming error, but also a potential security hole. For example, previous studies have shown that buffer overflows on the stack or on the heap is a favored technique by many hackers to break into a victim's computer [16, 125]. Of course, not all robustness violations are exploitable security bugs, but the line between them is fairly thin. As an example, when the memory allocation bug in WU-FTPD was first discovered, it was considered a programming error that would cause the server to crash when processing file names with special characters. The maintainers of the program believed the bug could not be exploited. Then, about half a year later, it was found that careful manipulation of the bug could give a hacker root access to the remote computer [303].

In the following section, we will describe our methodology for achieving our goals and objectives.

3 Methodology

We detect robustness violations in shared libraries through automated fault injection experiments. Our methodology falls into the category of dynamic testing, but with an emphasis on the behavior of the software under exceptional or stressful situations. Field experience indicates that the error handling paths in the software typically contain the most bugs [75]. This is not surprising because the normal execution paths are usually adequately tested during the software development process. For example, a Web server may work perfectly well until a flash crowd of requests consumes all the file descriptors in the system. Such kinds of bugs are difficult to detect or reproduce because they happen rarely (i.e., only when resources in the system are depleted). Moreover, certain errors in a program may have a delayed effect. For example, a buffer overflow may lead to heap corruption and cause a system crash much later.

We detect potential robustness violations by computing *robust argument types* for each function in the COTS component. The robust argument types of a function restrict the set of values the arguments can take so that the function will not exhibit robustness violations. For example, the first argument of the `strcpy` function has a C type of `char *`. However, it is not sufficient to enforce the value of the first argument to be of the type specified in its prototype if we want to prevent robustness violations (recall Fig. 1). In HEALERS, we use automated fault injection experiments to discover that its robust type should be `warray(strlen(a2)+1)`, a writable array at least as large as the length of the string in the second argument.

We need to conduct fault injection experiments on each function to derive its robust argument types, error return codes, and `errno`. A challenge here is doing so in an efficient manner. One may think that it is sufficient to focus on the most commonly used libraries in a system. As an example, Fig. 2 shows the 10 most popular libraries and the percentage of applications linked with them in SuSE Linux 8.2. The figure indicates that almost all applications are linked with the first two libraries.

However, we observed that in practice a system may contain a large number of applications, each of which is linked with many library functions. Figure 3 shows the distribution of the number of libraries an application is linked with. As can be seen from the figure, only 20.69% of applications are linked with just two libraries. The majority of applications are linked with many more. Table 1 shows the number of libraries, functions, and executables in the above system. It indicates that there are more than 3,000 libraries in the system and that on average each executable is linked with 16.6 libraries and

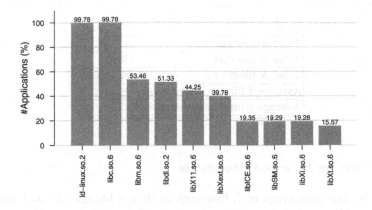

Fig. 2. The top 10 most popular libraries and the percentage of applications linked with them in SuSE Linux 8.2.

contains 122 undefined functions (which are defined in the libraries). Clearly, it will be prohibitive to test them manually.

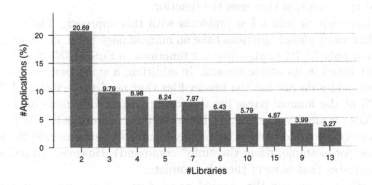

Fig. 3. Distribution of the number of libraries an application is linked with. Only the top 10 bars are shown.

Our solution to this problem is to use an automated approach to extract the prototypes of these functions and then conduct adaptive fault injection experiments based on their prototypes. The prototype of a function contains the C types of all the arguments and the return value of the function. For example, the prototype for `malloc` contains an argument of type `size_t` and a return value of type `void *`. In the following subsection, we will describe how to extract function prototypes automatically.

Table 1. Number of libraries, functions, and executables in SuSE Linux 8.2.

Type	Number
Total # executables	1102
Total # libraries	3083
Total # functions	824380
Average #library/executable	16.6
Average #functions/executable	122

3.1 Extracting Function Prototypes

Extracting the prototypes of C functions in shared libraries is nontrivial because typically such information is not stored in the shared libraries. We address this problem by parsing header files that contain the prototypes of global functions. However, it turns out that there typically does not exist a well defined set of header files that describe the interface of a shared library. In addition, some functions are defined multiple times in different header files while the definitions of other functions are spread across multiple header files. To determine the proper set of header files that contain the full definition of a function type, we parse the manual page that describes the function. By convention, manual pages contain a list of all header files that need to be included by a program that uses the function.

We have experienced a few problems with this approach. The first problem is that many global functions have no manual page [126]. For example, we found that only 51.1% of the glibc 2.2 functions in SuSE LINUX 7.2 Professional are listed in its online manual. In addition, a small percentage (1.2%) of manual pages do not list the header files that need to be included. Worse yet, 7.7% of the manual pages list the wrong header files: none of the listed header files (or any files included by them) define a prototype for the function. Alternatively, we could parse other online documents that describe the library functions (for example, using the "info" command). However, empirical evidence indicates that none of them is complete.

Nevertheless, we use the manual pages first because we have a higher chance of success in case the function is defined across multiple header files. If a function has no manual page or its manual page does not include the proper header files, we search through all header files (below a given path) to locate the prototype of the function. Using this approach, we were able to find header files for 96.0% of the glibc 2.2 functions. Note that if a function is not found in any header file, it most likely means that the function is intended only for internal use or that the function is deprecated.

After locating the header files for a function, we parse them to extract the prototype of the function. Currently, this is achieved using the CINT C/C++ interpreter [149]. The advantage of CINT is that it provides an easy interface to query extended runtime type information of all functions that are declared.

3.2 Adaptive Fault Injection Experiments

After the prototypes of the library functions have been extracted, our system conducts a set of fault injection experiments to determine their robust argument types. The system generates a fault injector program for each function. The fault injector calls the function with a sequence of test cases that contain normal and exceptional values. The test cases are generated by a set of test case generators based on the argument types of the function. For functions with multiple arguments, the set of test cases is the cross product of the test cases for each argument. Previous studies indicated that the number of data types in C libraries is significantly smaller than the number of functions [231]. Hence, our approach scales well for libraries with a large number of functions: after paying a fixed cost to construct the test case generators for the data types in a library, our system can automatically generate test cases for any function based on its prototype.

It is possible for a test case generator to be used to test multiple C types, as long as they can be casted to the same basic type. For example, the arguments for function `asctime` and function `ctime` are `const struct tm *` and `const time_t *`, respectively. Both of them can be casted to the generic pointer type (i.e., `void *`) and are handled by the test case generator for fixed size arrays. On the other hand, it is also possible for multiple test case generators to be used to test a single argument type. This is the case if we want to use specific information about the argument type to discover more robustness violations. For example, we have a specific test case generator for `FILE *`. An argument of this type will be tested by two test case generators: one for the generic pointer type and the other for the file pointer type.

The generated fault injector iterates over all test cases and computes a robust type for each argument when it is done. The fault injector itself is robust. To perform a call of the tested function, the fault injector spawns a child process to execute the call. The child process sets up a signal handler for segmentation faults before calling the function. In most cases, the signal handler will intercept segmentation faults caused by the tested function. However, some segmentation faults cannot be intercepted (e.g., some caused by `longjmp`). This is why the fault injector spawns a child process to execute the actual call.

The test case generation in our system is adaptive: if a tested function call crashes, the fault injector determines which argument caused the crash based on the address where the segmentation fault occurred. It then tries a finite number of times to change the input value for the argument until the robustness violation disappears or another argument causes the violation. This adaptive testing behavior is particularly useful to determine the exact amount of memory needed for an argument without using a massive number of static test cases. In the following exposition, we will describe some examples of test case generators.

Example: Test Case Generator for Fixed Size Arrays

Fixed size arrays are often used to represent pointers to structures. For example, the argument for the `asctime` function described above is an array of bytes that contains the `tm` structure. The function exhibits robust violations if the array pointed to by its argument is not readable or does not have enough space. At first glance, it seems that we can derive the required size of the array based on the size of the `tm` structure from its header file. However, we experienced two major problems in doing so. The first problem was that some structures are opaque: the structure is declared but not completely defined in the header files. This means that while the name of an opaque structure is known, its size is not. For example, the `DIR` structure used by directory-related functions is opaque in glibc 2.2. This is a good engineering practice, and may be used in other libraries as well. The second problem was that sometimes a structure was defined in the header file with a certain size, but the size allocated for the structure by the library functions was different. For example, the `FILE` structure is defined in the header file. However, the library (e.g., calls to `fopen`) allocates less space than what is needed by the definition of the `FILE` structure. This is possible because there are some "unused" fields in the structure. This is not good engineering practice, but it can actually be handy (since it consumes less memory).

Therefore, it is necessary for us to determine the size of the structure dynamically using fault injection experiments. The test case generator for `void*` allocates an array of a specific size at a page boundary. It places an unmapped page (i.e., a read and write protected memory page) after the array. This ensures that any access beyond the boundary of the allocated array generates a segmentation fault, a technique previously used in ElectricFence [328]. As an example, Fig. 4 illustrates the testing of a read-only array with five bytes.

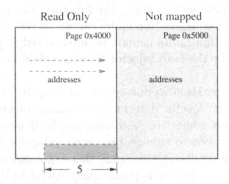

Fig. 4. Example of testing RONLY_FIXED[5].

The test case generator can also allocate arrays with different memory protection mechanisms, as shown in Table 2. (Note that we consider a null terminated string as a "fixed" size array since its size does not depend on other arguments of the function.) If a segmentation fault occurs, the test case generator checks the address of the segmentation fault to see how it should adjust its test case to prevent this fault. It may change the type of the array (e.g. from a readable array to a writable array), null-terminate the array, or increase the size of the array. For example, in order to determine the robust argument type for asctime(const struct tm *tm), our test case generator first allocates an array of zero size. This generates a segmentation fault during the test. The test case generator iteratively enlarges the array until no more segmentation faults occur or until a maximum size is reached. This way, we determine that the size of the tm structure is 44 bytes in our system.

Table 2. Types of Fixed Size Arrays.

Type	Description
NULL	the NULL pointer
RONLY_FIXED[s]	readable array of s bytes
WONLY_FIXED[s]	writable array of s bytes
RW_FIXED[s]	readable/writable array of s bytes

3.3 Determining Error Return Code

There are two ways in which we can determine the error return code of a function. The first way is to parse the manual page of the function. Most manual pages have a RETURN VALUE section that describes the return values of the function under various conditions and an ERRORS section that describes the list of possible errors. Due to the uniform format of manual pages, it is straightforward to parse them to get the information we need. One problem we encountered is that sometimes a manual page defines multiple functions. In this case, our script needs to carefully analyze the sentences in the manual page to make sure it extracts information for the right function. Unfortunately, as we described in Sect. 3.1, many functions have no manual page. In addition, sometimes the manual page of a function does not describe its error return code even if the function can fail.

The second approach we used to determine the error return code of a function is through the adaptive fault injection experiments described previously. If a test case does not result in a crash, and the function sets errno, we record the error return code. Our experience indicates that this approach is more applicable than parsing manual pages. The only problem we encountered was that a small number of functions did not set errno when tested with invalid input values, even though they correctly returned the error code specified in their manuals. Hence, we use a combination of the two approaches to achieve the best results.

4 Example: Fault-containment Wrapper

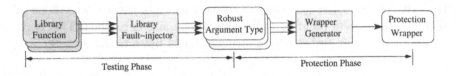

Fig. 5. Architecture of HEALERS.

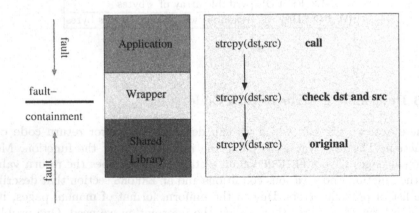

Fig. 6. A wrapper intercepts library function calls from the application and performs error checking.

In this section, we describe a usage example of our testing methology: a fault-containment wrapper that protects the application software from the vulnerabilities of its COTS components discovered in the testing phase [127]. Figure 5 illustrates this process, which consists of two phases: the testing phase and the protection phase. We have discussed the testing phase. The goal of the protection phase is to increase the robustness of applications even if the source code is not available. This is achieved by implementing our tool as a dynamically loadable *wrapper*, as shown in Fig. 6.

The wrapper sits between an application and the shared library. It intercepts library function calls from the application. When a program executes the strcpy function, it invokes the version of the function in our wrapper which checks if the dst buffer has enough space before invoking the original function. A nice feature of wrapping dynamic link libraries is that it can protect existing software without source code access [128]. Previous studies indicate that a major category of software failures related to C library functions are API failures: function calls with invalid arguments may cause the calling process to terminate abnormally [231]. Intercepting such function calls gives us a convenient way of checking the validity of their arguments, and hence avoiding such failures. Note that it only works for applications that are dynamically linked. In practice, we found that this is not a problem because an overwhelming majority of applications are dynamically linked.

5 Related Work

Various techniques have been proposed for reducing programming errors of software components. One approach to is to use safe languages like Java or ML. Both of them have support for automatic memory management and hence eliminate a large class of memory related errors. However, most software today are still using unsafe languages like C and C++.

Another way to enhance the correctness of software components is through static analyses. As described in Sect. 1, previous work by Engler et al. checks programming errors by extracting a set of correctness *rules* from the source code automatically [113]. The major advantage of this approach is that it can be applied to all flow paths in the source code, including those that cannot be executed (such as the code in certain device drivers). Hence, it can provide valuable help to component developers in checking and diagnosing the source code and in enforcing good, consistent programming practices. In contrast, our approach can be used by component users to evaluate the behavior of COTS components from third-party vendors. We believe the two approaches are complementary and should be used together to enhance the correctness of component-based systems.

Eraser is a debugging tool for detecting race conditions in lock-based multithreaded programs [358]. It uses binary rewriting techniques to verify that all shared memory accesses follow a consistent locking discipline. Like HEALERS, Eraser uses a dynamic testing technique and does not require source code access. It detects a different (albeit equally important) category of errors and can be used side-by-side with our approach.

Previously, software wrappers have been used for fault tolerance [356] and exception handling [404]. Xept is a software instrumentation tool that can be used to handle exceptions from library functions [404]. It provides a language to write exception specifications for certain C functions, as well as a convenient framework for incorporating such specifications into application code.

The authors of [356] used fault containment wrappers to improve the robustness of COTS microkernels. By verifying certain predicates when a system call is performed, the wrapper detects errors due to corrupt parameters, and may optionally perform some corrective actions to restore the system into a consistent state.

Fault injection experiments were previously used in the Ballista project to evaluate the robustness and diversity of POSIX operating systems [94, 231]. For each POSIX function, the Ballista tests generate various combinations of valid and invalid input values and feed them into the function to see whether or not error conditions are handled correctly. Our system is different from Ballista in that we use adaptive fault injection experiments to compute the robust argument types for library functions. Our system can inject faults into almost all library functions linked to an application, not to just POSIX functions.

6 Conclusion

Errors and vulnerabilities in software components can compromise the dependability and security of component-based systems. This chapter has described HEALERS, a flexible toolkit that detects programming errors and software vulnerabilities in third-party libraries without source code access. The main feature of HEALERS is the use of automated fault injection experiments to determine what types of arguments lead a function to crash. The robust argument types computed for a function can be used to generate protection wrappers to prevent crash failures: arguments that would lead to a crash are detected and an error code is returned, or, alternatively, the application is terminated in a clean way.

Testing Component-Based Systems Using FSMs

Sami Beydeda[1] and Volker Gruhn[2]

[1] Federal Finance Office (Bundesamt für Finanzen)
   Friedhofstr. 1
   53225 Bonn, Germany
   sami.beydeda@bff.bund.de
[2] University of Leipzig
   Chair of Applied Telematics / e-Business
   Klostergasse 3
   04109 Leipzig, Germany
   gruhn@ebus.informatik.uni-leipzig.de

Summary. No matter which tools, techniques, and methodologies are used for software development, it remains an error-prone process. Nevertheless, changing such important constituents of the software process surely has an effect on the types of faults inherent in the developed software. For instance, some types of faults are typical for structured development, whereas others are typical for object-oriented development.

This chapter explores the question of whether component-based software requires new testing techniques, and proposes an integrated testing technique. This technique integrates various tasks during testing component-based software: white- and black-box testing of the main component (i.e., the top level component controlling the other components), black-box testing of components, black-box testing of the middleware and integration testing of the main component with other components.

Benefits of this technique are shown using a real-world example: the technique is automatable and applicable to existing component-based software.

1 Introduction

In the last few years, component-based software development has received much attention from both researchers and practitioners. Components seemed to be the *silver bullet* software engineers have sought for decades. Researchers have developed component models together with the necessary technologies, which have been applied by practitioners in their daily work.

Unfortunately, testing of such software systems has not gained enough interest. In the opinion of both practitioners and researchers, a component once sufficiently tested does not require testing when reused. But experience shows that this belief to be wrong, because components are often initially tested with respect to a certain application domain, thus failing in new environments [423].

The first subsection identifies the properties of components in order to understand components and component-based software. Furthermore, this subsection gives the reasons why traditional testing techniques cannot be used for testing this kind of software. The second subsection outlines several requirements for testing techniques for component-based software.

1.1 Properties of Components Affecting Testing

Although components and development of software based on components were discussed by computer scientists more than 30 years ago [262], there is no common definition of these terms available to date. Different authors define the term *component* differently, although all have roughly the same concepts in mind [48, 49]. Another reason for this is that developers of component models like Sun Microsystems with its JavaBeans[3] and Enterprise JavaBeans models[4], and Microsoft Corporation with COM[5], have a diverse technical understanding of the notion of a component. However, we do not try to define these terms. Rather, we establish a list of properties most components have in common. Although this list cannot be complete, it is sufficient to investigate the implications of component-based development on testing. Components typically share the following properties:

- Components are (nearly) independent and replaceable parts of a system. A component conforms to and provides a set of interfaces [48].
- Usually, a component possesses an internal state which affects results delivered by its methods and its dynamic behavior.
- Special components, called *commercial-off-the-shelf* (COTS), can be purchased on a component market. Often, these types of components are delivered without their source code.
- Since components may be distributed over several computers, communication among components requires middleware technologies like CORBA[6] and DCOM[7].

Obviously, software development will remain an error-prone process even if component-based development contributes to an improvement of software quality. However, an important question at this point is *do the above properties of a typical component affect testing?*

Predictably, component-based software requires techniques for testing other than those for traditional software. There are several reasons for this:

---

[3]http://www.javasoft.com/beans/
[4]http://java.sun.com/products/ejb/
[5]http://www.microsoft.com/com/
[6]http://www.omg.org/corba/
[7]http://www.microsoft.com/com/

- In contrast with in-house developed software, white-box testing cannot be conducted for COTS, since their source code is usually not available.
- Traditional testing techniques do not consider middleware technologies. But the middleware of component-based software is an integral part of it, and has also to be tested.

1.2 Requirements for Testing Techniques

Having identified the reasons as to why traditional testing techniques cannot be applied to component-based software, the next question is *what requirements do a testing techniques have for component-based software?*

With respect to the reasons explained above, such testing techniques have to fulfill the following requirements:

White- and black-box testing of the main component. Generally, software has to be tested using several techniques. Specifically, these techniques have to include both white- and black-box techniques [24]. Since few techniques combine the white- and black-box approach [38,65], the main component has to typically be tested first using test cases generated on the basis of the source code, and then using test cases generated on the basis of its specification.

Black-box testing of components. Since source code may not be available for some components, they can only be black-box tested. In fact, black-box testing of components is usually sufficient, because at this level there is often no need for low-level testing techniques based on source code. Harrold et al. [170] distinguish two different perspectives during testing in component-based development. One of these perspectives is called the *component-provider perspective* and refers to the testing of components by their developers on the basis of the source code. Since developers have detailed knowledge about the internal structure of their components, they can test their components more effectively than users. The other perspective, called the *component-user perspective*, refers to the testing of components by their users, without access to their source code. Even if source code is available, components should be only black-box tested, because of the missing knowledge about the internal structure of the component and the danger of losing oneself in too much detail. In this article, we assume that components, except for the main component, are tested by their users. Thus, testing is performed with the component-user perspective.

Testing only the required component functionality. Often the main component requires only a subset of the functionality a component provides. Thus, testing techniques for component-based software have only to test these required subsets [170,350,422]. Experience shows that these subsets have to actually be tested, because components are often tested with respect to a special application domain, and thus subsequently fail in new environments [423].

Testing the middleware. Test cases have to be provided for testing the middleware used. It is obvious that failures of middleware are likely to influence the behavior of the entire system. Therefore, testing of component-based software has also to aim at ensuring the absence of faults in the middleware layer.

Testing the interaction of the main component. Another important issue for such testing techniques concerns integration testing. Integration testing consists of testing the interaction of the main component with other components. Even if all components are free of faults, a system consisting of them may fail due to wrong interactions.

The requirements explained above make clear that component-based software cannot be sufficiently tested with existing techniques. Therefore, research in this area has to aim at developing new techniques suited for these requirements.

2 Demonstrative Example

In this section, an example from the banking area, used in the remainder of this article, is introduced. The example used to demonstrate our testing technique is a system called BankApp, used for making deposits and withdrawals on bank accounts. The BankApp system consists of the main component, a component called account, and a middleware component, required for interaction of the main component with the account component. Each of these constituents is described in detail below.

2.1 The account Component

As its name suggests, the account component simulates the bank customers' account. It encapsulates ID and account balance and provides suitable methods to check and alter the balance. Figure 1 shows the specification of this component. In our approach, the specification for each component is given as a special finite state machine, called *component state machine* (CSM), which corresponds to *class state machines* described by Hong et al. [183]. In fact, the component state machines used in our technique originate from their class state machines. The main difference between a class state machine and a component state machine is that transitions within a component state machine are augmented with Java code in order to allow automatic generation of an executable frames for event types and executable *oracle* for testing. An oracle determines the result a program should compute for a particular input, with respect to the specification, and compares this result with that obtained by actually executing the program for the same input. Executable oracles have been used, for instance, by Hoffman and Strooper [179, 180]. However, automatic generation of executable oracles is left for further study.

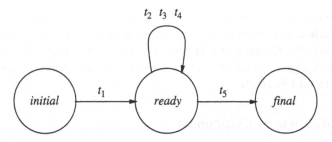

source	target	event	guard	action
t_1	initial	ready	Account(accountId,initialBalance)	true	Id=accountId; balance=initialBalance;
t_2	ready	ready	deposit(amount)	true	balance+=amount;
t_3	ready	ready	withdraw(amount)	amount<=balance	balance-=amount;
t_4	ready	ready	balance()	true	return balance;
t_5	ready	final	remove()	true	home.remove(accountId);

Fig. 1. Specification of the account component as a component state machine.

In Fig. 1, abstract states of the component are represented by circles, while each transition is depicted as an arrow leading from its source state to its target state. These transitions are formally specified through 5-tuples (*source, target, event, guard, action*). A transition consists also – in addition to a *source* and a *target* state – of an *event* causing the transition, a predicate *guard* which has to be fulfilled before the transition can occur, and the *action* defining the operations on the component variables during the transition. As explained above, the *guard* and the *action* of a transition are defined using Java statements for automation purposes.

As depicted in Fig. 1, a CSM includes two special circles, labeled *initial* and *final*. These two circles represent the state of a component before its creation and after its destruction, respectively. Thus, they represent states in which the component variables and their values are not defined, meaning that these two states are abstract states of a component. Furthermore, Hong et al. [183] have proposed introducing an *error* state representing the state of a class after an error has occurred. In the following figures, the *error* state has been omitted for the sake of clarity. However, components are supposed to enter the *error* state after the occurrence of an event that is either not specified for a particular state or does not fulfill one of the guards.

After initialization, the account component enters the *ready* state. The *ready* state indicates that the account has been initialized and is ready to receive deposit and withdrawal requests. After each deposit request, the account component remains in the *ready* state. However, withdrawal requests can imply a change to the *error* state. The *error* state is entered when clients of the account component try to overdraw from the account. The account component also provides an observer method, called balance(), for checking the account balance. A change to the *final* state is triggered by invoking the

remove() method. This method does not correspond to a finalize (destructor) method. Rather, it invokes the appropriate method of the middleware which then destroys the **account** component. In the specification of the **account** component in Fig. 1, an account is modeled by a Java object having the two attributes **Id** and **balance**.

2.2 The Middleware Component

The **BankApp** system is implemented using the Enterprise JavaBeans technology[8] of Sun Microsystems. The Enterprise JavaBeans specification defines a component architecture for building distributed, object-oriented applications in Java. Each component in the Enterprise JavaBeans technology, called *bean*, is encapsulated in a server which addresses multithreading, resource pooling, clustering, distributed naming, automatic persistence, remote invocation, transaction boundary management, and distributed transaction management. More information can be found on the Internet[9].

For testing the **BankApp** system, a CSM is used that specifies only a small subset of features an Enterprise JavaBeans server provides. The CSM depicted in Fig. 2 models only the resource pooling functionality of an Enterprise JavaBeans server. To keep the example simple, other important features such as automatic persistence and remote invocation have not been addressed.

The simple server used in the example possesses two main states, namely, *capacityAvailable* and *capacityLimit*. Assuming that this simple server does not provide an automatic persistence functionality, it enters, after its invocation and initialization, the *capacityAvailable* state. The server maintains a pool that can store several **account** beans. Since this pool has a limited capacity, the state of the server changes to the *capacityLimit* state after the creation of a certain number of beans[10]. The server also provides a method which does not change its state. The **findByPrimaryKey()** selects a particular account, identified by its ID, from the pool. The specification in Fig. 2 uses a **Hashtable** object as a pool defined in the **java.util** package.

2.3 The Main Component

Figure 3 contains the specification of the main component. Assuming that persistence is not addressed, the main component enters the *accountNotAvailable* state after its initialization . The *accountNotAvailable* state indicates that a certain account referred by **ac** does not exist. This state can be changed by creating a new account using

---

[8]http://java.sun.com/products/ejb/

[9]http://www.javasoft.com/

[10]Note that in the simple example used, *activation* and *passivation* of beans are not considered.

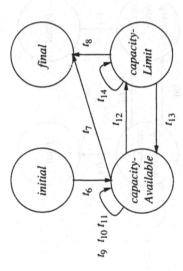

	source	target	event	guard	action
t_6	initial	capacityAvailable	AccountHome()	true	int capacity=3; p=new Hashtable(capacity);
t_7	capacityAvailable	final	finalize()	true	
t_8	capacityLimit	final	finalize()	true	
t_9	capacityAvailable	capacityAvailable	create(id,balance)	!p.containsKey(id) && p.size()<capacity-1	ac=new Account(id,balance); p.put(id,ac);
t_{10}	capacityAvailable	capacityAvailable	remove(id)	p.containsKey(id)	p.remove(id);
t_{11}	capacityAvailable	capacityAvailable	findByPrimaryKey(id)	p.containsKey(id)	return p.get(id);
t_{12}	capacityAvailable	capacityLimit	create(id,balance)	!p.containsKey(id) && p.size()==capacity-1	ac=new Account(id,balance); p.put(id,ac);
t_{13}	capacityLimit	capacityAvailable	remove(id)	p.containsKey(id)	p.remove(id);
t_{14}	capacityLimit	capacityLimit	findByPrimaryKey(id)	p.containsKey(id)	return p.get(id);

Fig. 2. Component state machine of a simple Enterprise JavaBeans server.

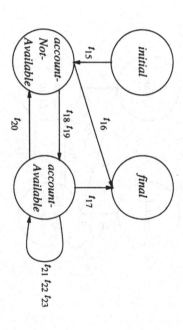

	source	target	event	guard	action
t_{15}	initial	accountNotAvailable	main()	true	home=new AccountHome();
t_{16}	accountNotAvailable	final	exit()	true	ac=null;
t_{17}	accountAvailable	final	exit()	true	
t_{18}	accountNotAvailable	accountAvailable	createAccount(id,balance)	true	ac=home.create(id,balance);
t_{19}	accountNotAvailable	accountAvailable	lookUpAccount(id)	true	ac=home.findbyPrimaryKey(id);
t_{20}	accountAvailable	accountNotAvailable	removeAccount()	ac.balance()==0.0	ac.remove(); ac=null;
t_{21}	accountAvailable	accountAvailable	lookUpAccount(id)	true	ac=home.findbyPrimaryKey(id);
t_{22}	accountAvailable	accountAvailable	depositAccount(amount)	true	ac.deposit(amount);
t_{23}	accountAvailable	accountAvailable	withdrawAccount(amount)	true	ac.withdraw(amount);

Fig. 3. Specification of the main component as a component state machine.

createAccount(). In this case, the *accountAvailable* state is entered. Similarly, the *accountNotAvailable* state is entered again when the account referred to as ac is removed using the removeAccount() method. Moreover, the main component provides the lookUpAccount() method for selecting accounts from the pool maintained by the Enterprise JavaBeans server. After the invocation of this method, the state of the main component either changes from the *accountNotAvailable* state to the *accountAvailable* state, if the account considered before has been removed, or remains in the *accountAvailable* state. Although the state does not change in the latter case, the considered account changes. Other methods provided by the BankApp component do not change its state. depositAccount() and withdrawAccount() can be used to change the balance of an existing account. Since the balance of the referenced account does not influence the state, these two methods do not affect the state. The *error* state can be entered in various situations. These situations can be distinguished into two groups. An error can occur either when trying to operate on an account which does not exist or when trying to remove an account which is not empty.

2.4 Implementation of the BankApp System

The account component is implemented as a *stateful session bean*[11]. The persistence of the component is ensured by the Enterprise JavaBeans server using a database via JDBC[12]. The Enterprise JavaBeans server used in the example is the BEA WebLogic Server 4.0.3, available as a trial version on the Internet[13]. However, the proposed technique is not tailored to a special technology. In the first section of this article, we have described the notion of a component only by a set of properties; no technology or existing component model has been referred to for defining the notion of a component. The only information required is the specification of the middleware.

The source code of the account component is available together with other necessary files on Websites of the BEA WebLogic Server[14].

3 Description of the Testing Technique

This section contains a detailed description of the testing technique. The first subsection explains a graphical representation of component-based software, which facilitates test case generation. The following subsections demonstrate the generation of test cases for the various constituents of the BankApp system.

---

[11]http://java.sun.com/products/ejb/
[12]http://java.sun.com/products/jdbc/
[13]http://www.beasys.com/download/weblogic.html
[14]http://www.weblogic.com/docs/examples/ejb/basic/containerManaged/index.html

3.1 Component-Based Software Flow Graph (CBSFG)

The basis of the proposed technique is a graphical representation of component-based software, called *component-based software flow graph* (CB-SFG), visualizing information gathered from both specification and source code. After having generated this graphical representation, well known techniques for structural testing [24] can be applied on this representation to identify test cases. Thus, test cases for white- and black-box testing are determined simultaneously, without considering these strategies separately.

In our approach, test cases for black-box testing are generated according to the ideas of Hong et al. [183]. Their technique for black-box testing of classes requires a specification of the class in the form of a finite state machine, which they call *class state machine*. Hong et al. have proposed determining test cases for black-box testing of classes by associating definitions and uses of class variables according to a data flow criterion, and identifying those test cases that cover these def-use pairs. The important idea is to determine test cases for black-box testing by techniques for white-box testing.

Our first idea was to build a control flow graph on the basis of the source code and then to identify the definitions and uses of the class variables within this control flow graph. After the identification of definitions and uses, they can be associated with each other, and test cases can be generated to cover the associated def-use pairs – in exactly the same way as in the handling of conventional definitions and uses. Although this approach is feasible in theory, the identification of definitions, and especially of uses of the attributes, might be impossible. For instance, assume the guard of a transition looks like $a \leq b$. In the best case, this guard would appear in the source code as 'if a<=b ...;'. But a programmer who is not restricted in his style of programming could transform this expression into 'if a<b { ...; if a==b ...; }'. Even in this simple case, it is almost impossible to identify the guard. Of course, this problem could be solved by constraining the programmer to a certain style. But this solution has two shortcomings: the technique would not be applicable to existing software, and constraining programmers to a certain programming style would hinder acceptance of the technique.

To tackle this problem, we have elaborated the following solution:

1. A frame is generated for each event type occurring within transitions of CSMs of the component-based software,
2. the action part of each frame is marked with a label indicating the method implementing the action.

These steps are explained using the CSM of the main component in Fig. 3. During the first step, each transition $t = (source, target, event, guard, action)$ is transformed to a nested if-then-else construct:

```
if (predicate(source)) {   // state
    if (guard) {   // guard
        action;   // action
```

```
    }
    else throw new ErrorStateException();
}
else throw new ErrorStateException();
```

`predicate(source)` refers to the predicate of the source state, i.e., the predicate on component variables defining the occurrence of state *source*. For instance, `predicate(accountNotAvailable)` is `ac==null`.

After transforming each transition to a frame, frames of transitions having the same event type are combined. For instance, transition t_9 and transition t_{12} in Fig. 2 share the event `create()`. Their frames can be merged to the following frame:

```
createSpec(id, balance) {
  if (predicate(capacityAvailable)) {
    if (!p.containsKey(id) && p.size()<capacity-1) {
      ac=new Account(id, balance);
      p.put(id, ac);
    }
    else
      if (!p.containsKey(id) && p.size()==capacity-1) {
        ac=new Account(id, balance);
        p.put(id, ac);
      }
      else throw new ErrorStateException();
  }
  else throw new ErrorStateException();
}
```

Having represented each event type in this way, the identification of definitions and uses during a transition is trivial due to the simple and predefined structure of a frame. After the identification, test cases covering the identified def-use pairs can be generated. Note that we do not validate the frame. Test cases determined in this way also cover statements within the source code representing the definition and the use identified within the frame. The reason is that the predicate statements 'if (predicate(source)) ...' and 'if (guard) ...' act as a filter. They filter exactly those inputs which execute only the corresponding statements in the source code. Generally, a definition is tested by a use by executing first the definition and then the use. It is not necessary to know which statements represent the definition and the use. It is only important to ensure that both the definition and the use are executed in a certain order and that the variable is not redefined before the use occurs.

The second step consists of adding a label to the action parts of the frames, indicating the method implementing the event type. Note that this is where the integration of the white- and the black-box approach takes place. For instance, during the second step, the action parts of the frame of method create() are augmented with a label 'implementing method: create()' which refers to the appropriate method:

```
ac=new Account(id, balance);
p.put(id, ac);
// implementing method: create()
```

A frame can be generated for the entire component-based software under test by repeating this procedure for every event type, including also those of the components. After generating the frames for each event type, a control flow graph showing the overall structure of the component-based software can be generated. The CBSFG of the BankApp system is shown in Fig. 4.

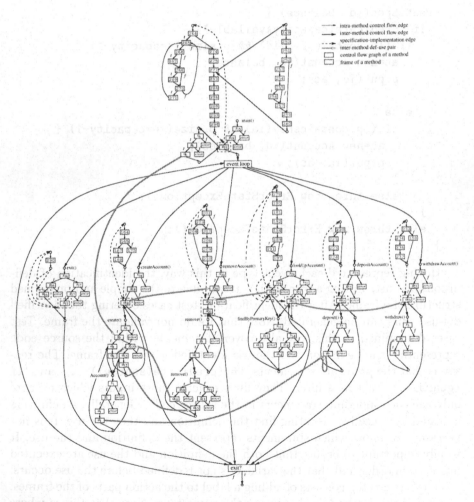

Fig. 4. Component-based software flow graph of BankApp.

As explained before, a CBSFG is a directed graph visualizing both control and data flow within component-based software. Each method of the main component is represented by two subgraphs. One of these subgraphs represents control flow of the frame generated on the basis of the specification, whereas the other represents control flow determined using the source code of the method. Contrary to a method within the main application, a method in another component is represented by a flow graph visualizing only its frame. The reason is obvious: a control flow graph of a method can only be built if its source code is available.

These subgraphs are interlinked with each other by control and data flow edges. Three types of control and data flow edges can be distinguished:

Intra-method control and data flow edges. Intra-method control and data flow edges visualize control and data dependencies within a single subgraph. For instance, an intra-method data flow edge connects a node representing a definition of a variable with another node representing a use in the same method. Intra-method control flow edges are drawn as thin arrows, whereas intra-method data flow edges have been omitted in Fig. 4.

Inter-method control and data flow edges. Edges of this type model control and data flow between subgraphs of the same type. For instance, an invocation of a method within another is modeled by an inter-method control flow edge leading from the node representing the invoking statement in the first method to the node representing the entry statement of the second method. Similarly, an inter-method control flow edge also models triggering an event of a CSM within the action part of a transition of another CSM. Inter-method control flow edges connect both control flow graphs of methods with each other and control flow graphs of frames with each other. Contrary to inter-method control flow edges, inter-method data flow edges connect only nodes within control flow graphs of frames. As stated above, the objective of frames is to ease identifying and associating definitions and uses of component variables. Thus, inter-method data flow edges are not required for method control flow graphs. Inter-method edges are shown by bold gray arrows in Fig. 4. Note that inter-method data flow edges which do not represent def-use pairs are omitted.

Specification-implementation edges. These type of edges visualize the connection between specification and source code by connecting the two subgraphs of the main component methods. Thus, a specification-implementation edge leads from the node representing the action within a frame to the node representing the entry node of the method referred to by the label added during the second step of the frame generation. Specification-implementation edges are drawn as dashed arrows in Fig. 4.

In Fig. 4, statements are represented by rectangles which are interlinked to each other by control and data flow edges. The number of outgoing control flow edges can be either one or two, depending on the statement represented by a node. A node representing a predicate statement has two outgoing edges, labeled *t(rue)* and *f(alse)*, to indicate the path which is to be taken, whereas all other nodes representing other statements have only one outgoing control flow edge[15]. The number of outgoing data flow edges can vary according to the number of references to the variable defined in the node.

The graph in Fig. 4 also possesses two special nodes, labeled *event loop* and *exit?*. These two nodes take into account the event-driven nature of the example used.

3.2 Generating Test Cases for the Main Component

Our approach combines white- and black-box strategies by using a single technique for test case generation. White-box testing is conducted to test source code of individual methods, whereas black-box testing aims at testing the state-dependent behavior of a component that is tested by validating data flow among methods. Thus, test cases for black-box testing consist of a sequence of method invocations, whereas test cases for white-box testing consist of only one method invocation[16].

In the remainder of this chapter, only a data flow criterion is used for simplicity. However, the proposed technique is not restricted to a data flow criterion. Several criteria, including control flow criteria, can be used. As a first step for test case generation, definitions and uses of variables have to be identified and associated with each other. Associating definitions and uses of local variables within methods can be carried out only by considering their source code. In contrast with associating local definitions and uses, associating definitions and uses of component variables has to take into account the possible method sequences defined by the appropriate CSM. A definition and a use can be associated with each other only if the method including the use can be invoked after an invocation of the method including the definition. It is important to ensure that the component variable is not redefined.

For instance, the definition of variable ac within the action a_{19} of transition t_{19} cannot be associated with the use of the variable within guard g_{19}, since this would imply invoking removeAccount() two times to ensure the correct order of definition and use. But removeAccount() is not defined for state *accountNotAvailable*; thus, the main component would enter the *error* state after the second invocation. However, the definition within action a_{18} can be tested by the use in guard g_{19} by invoking (createAccount(), removeAccount()).

Figure 4 shows the def-use pairs within the main component induced by the *all-definitions* criterion [24]. These def-use pairs are (a_{18}, g_{20}),

---

[15]Note that a switch statement in C or Java can be transformed into a nested if-then-else construct.

[16]In some cases, initialization of the state might require invocation of a sequence prior to the invocation of the specific method.

(a_{19}, a_{20}), and (a_{21}, a_{23}). These def-use pairs can be covered by the following test cases: (main(), createAccount(), removeAccount(), exit()), (main(), createAccount(), lookUpAccount(), removeAccount(), exit()) and (main(), createAccount(), lookUpAccount(), withdrawAccount(), exit()).

3.3 Generating Test Cases for the account Component

Since source code for the account component is not available, white-box testing cannot be carried out. Black-box testing is performed in exactly the same way as in the case of the main component. Definitions and uses within control flow graphs of frames are associated with each other according to the all-definitions criterion, and test cases are generated covering those def-use pairs.

However, there is one significant difference in test case generation between the main component and the account component. Since the account component is used in the context of the main component, some of its valid method sequences cannot be tested. The account component is invoked through the main component, which uses a subset of the functionality the account component provides. Thus, some def-use pairs cannot be covered in this context, although such a data flow might occur in another context. However, we do not need to test functionality which is not required in a specific context [350, 422, 423].

For instance, although (deposit(), balance()) is a valid test case for testing the definition of component variable balance within action a_2, this test case is not valid in the current context because the BankApp system does not provide a functionality to check account balances. Thus, we do not need to test the interaction of methods deposit() and balance(). However, since balance() is invoked by the main component within guard g_{19}, we cannot completely omit this method.

Taking into account the possible method sequences within the BankApp system, the following def-use pairs have to be covered in order to fulfill the *all-definitions* criterion: (a_1, a_2), (a_2, a_2), and (a_3, g_3). These def-use pairs can be tested by the following test case sequences: (main(), createAccount(), depositAccount(), exit()), (main(), createAccount(), depositAccount(), depositAccount(), exit()) and (main(), createAccount(), depositAccount(), withdrawAccount(), withdrawAccount(), exit()).

3.4 Generating Test Cases for the Middleware

Test case generation for the middleware component is carried out in exactly the same way as in the case of the account component. Test cases have to fulfill the *all-definitions* criterion, have to be valid method sequences of the middleware component and have to be possible in the context of the BankApp system.

In order to test the middleware appropriately, the following def-use pairs have to be covered by test cases: (a_6, a_{18}), (a_9, g_{12}), (a_{12}, a_{13}), (a_{13}, a_{10}), and (a_{10}, g_{12}). Test case sequences executing these def-use pairs are (main(), createAccount(), exit()), (main(), createAccount(), createAccount(), exit()), (main(), createAccount(), removeAccount(), exit()), (main(), createAccount(), removeAccount(), createAccount(), exit()) and (main(), createAccount(), createAccount(), removeAccount(), removeAccount(), exit()).

3.5 Generating Test Cases for the Integration Test

Another important task is testing the interaction of the main component with the account component and the middleware component. The main component is tested with the same test cases that have been generated for its black-box testing. The main difference between black-box testing of the main component and integration testing is that in the latter the same test cases are repeated for every possible state of the components [55].

The integration test of the main component with the account component does not require new test cases because the account component possesses only one abstract state. This state is entered after initializing the component, done in each test case by invoking createAccount().

In contrast with the account component, the middleware component requires generating new test cases. The middleware component can enter two abstract states, namely *capacityAvailable* and *capacityLimit*. The integration test can be performed with the test cases used for testing the main component; the only difference is in the parameters passed. To test the *capacityAvailable* state, the capacity parameter has to be higher than 1. For the other cases, the capacity parameter has to be set exactly to 1 in order to enter the *capacityLimit* state by creating one account.

3.6 Regression Test based on CBSTDs

CBSFGs can also be used for identifying test cases for regression testing on the basis of the technique of Rothermel and Harrold [351, 352]. They have proposed comparing two successive versions of an object-oriented program with respect to their graphical representations called *class control flow graph* (CCFG). This comparison identifies those statements which have to be tested due to modifications made during the last correction, or due to modified control and data dependencies from modified statements. Using the same approach, a CBSFG is generated after a modification, and is compared with the CBSFG of the prior version of the component-based software. By comparing these two graphs, those statements and def-use pairs can be identified that have been modified or that are affected by modifications made to other statements. The modified version needs to be tested only with respect to these changed or affected statements or def-use pairs. Since CCFG and CBSFG have a similar structure, their algorithms can also be used, with some adjustments, for selecting test cases for component-based software on the basis of CBSFGs. Note that CBSFGs also permit selection of test cases for black-box testing and integration testing, whereas CCFGs do not.

4 Conclusions

In this chapter, we outlined requirements that have to be addressed by testing techniques for component-based software. After discussing these requirements, we have described a graphical representation of component-based software called *component-based software flow graph* (CBSFG) facilitating test case generation. The generated test cases cover the important features of component-based software to be tested: white- and black-box testing of the main component, black-box testing of other components (including the middleware component), and integration testing.

The applicability of this approach has been demonstrated with an example, a system for conducting deposits and withdrawals a bank account. Enterprise JavaBean technology has been used as middleware.

Our aim during the development of this technique was its automatability. Every step during testing, except test case generation, which is in fact a very hard problem, can be carried out automatically.

References

1. JUnit - Testing Resource for eXtreme Programming. http://www.junit.org. Access date April 5th, 2004.
2. *IEEE Computer*, volume 32. July 1999.
3. J. Aagedal and E. Ecklund. Modelling QoS: Towards a UML profile. In *Proceedings of UML 2002*, Dresden, Germany, Oct. 2002.
4. A. Abdurazik and J. Offutt. Using UML collaboration diagrams for static checking and test generation. In *UML'00*, pages 383–395, York, UK, Oct. 2000.
5. Exception handling for a 21st century programming language proceedings. *ACM SIGAda Ada Letters*, XXI(3), 2001.
6. H. Agrawal, J. R. Horgan, E. W. Krauser, and S. A. London. Incremental regression testing. In *Proceedings of the Conference on Software Maintenance*, pages 348–357, Washington, Sept. 1993.
7. J. Aidemark, J. Vinter, P. Folkesson, and J. Karlsson. GOOFI: Generic object-oriented fault injection tool. In *Proceedings of the International Conference on Dependable Systems and Networks (DSN 2001)*, Gothenburg, Sweden, 2001.
8. R. Alexander and J. Offutt. Criteria for testing polymorphic relationships. In *Int. Symp. on Softw. Reliability Eng.*, pages 15–23, 2000.
9. R. Allen and D. Garlan. A formal basis for architectural connection. *ACM Trans. on Software Engineering and Methodology*, 6(3), April 1997.
10. P. America, H. Obbink, R. van Ommering, and F. van der Linden. Copam: A component-oriented platform architecting method family for product family engineering. In *Proceedings of the First Software Product Lines Conference, Software Product Lines, Experience and Research Directions*, pages 167 – 180, Boston, 2000. Kluwer Academic Publishers.
11. Apple Computer. *MacAppII Programmer's Guide*. Apple Computer, 1989.
12. J. Arlat, M. Aguera, L. Amat, Y. Crouzet, J.-C. Fabre, J.-C. Laprie, E. Martin, and D. Powell. Fault injection for dependability validation: A methodology and some applications. *IEEE Transactions on Software Engineering*, 16(2):166–182, 1990.
13. C. Atkinson and H.-G. Groß. Built-in contract testing in model-driven, component-based development. In *Proceedings of Workshop on Component-Based Development Processes*, April 2002.

14. F. Bachman, L. Bass, C. Buhman, S. Cornella-Dorda, F. Long, J. Robert, R. Seacord, and K. Wallnau. Volume II: Technical concepts of component-based software engineering. Technical Report CMU/SEI-2000-TR-008, Carnegie Mellon University, Software Engineering Institute, 2000.

15. S. Balsamo, P. Inverardi, and C. Mangano. An approach to performance evaluation of software architectures. In *Proceedings of the First International Workshop on Software and Performance*, pages 178–190, 1998.

16. A. Baratloo, N. Singh, and T. Tsai. Transparent run-time defense against stack smashing attacks. In *Proceedings of USENIX Annual Technical Conference*, June 2000.

17. F. Barbier. Composability for software components: An approach based on the whole-part theory. In *Proceedings of The 8th IEEE International Conference on Engineering of Complex Computer Systems, Greenbelt, USA, IEEE*, pages 101–106. Computer Society Press, 2002.

18. F. Barbier, N. Belloir, and J.-M. Bruel. Incorporation of test functionality into software components. In *Proceedings of The 2nd International Conference on COTS-Based Software Systems, Ottawa, Canada, Lecture Notes in Computer Science 2580*, pages 25–35. Springer, 2003.

19. M. Barnett, W. Grieskamp, W. Schulte, N. Tillmann, and M. Veanes. Validating use-cases with the asml test tool. In *QSIC'03*, pages 238–246, Dallas, USA, Oct. 2003.

20. V. R. Basili and B. Boehm. COTS-based systems top 10 list. *IEEE Computer*, 34(5):91–93, 2001.

21. L. Bass, C. Buhman, S. Comella-Dorda, F. Long, J. Robert, R. Seacord, and W. K. Volume i: Market assessment of component-based software engineering. Technical Report CMU/SEI-2000-TR-008, ESC-TR-2000-007, Carnegie Mellon University, Software Engineering Institute, 2000.

22. L. Bass, P. Clements, and R. Kazman. *Software Architecture in Practice*. Addison-Wesley, Massachusetts, Reading, 1998.

23. K. Beck and E. Gamma. Test infected: Programmers love writing tests. *Java Report*, 3(7):37–50, 1998.

24. B. Beizer. *Software Testing Techniques*. Van Nostrand Reinhold, New York, 2nd edition, 1990.

25. S. Bernardi, S. Donatelli, and J. Merseguer. From UML sequence diagrams and statecharts to analysable Petri Nets models. In *Proceedings of the 3rd International Workshop on Software and Performance(WOSP02)*, pages 35–45, 2002.

26. M. Bertoa and A. Vallecillo. Quality attributes for cots components. In *ECOOP Workshop on Quantitative Approaches in Object-Oriented Software Engineering, Malaga, Spain*, 2002.

27. A. Bertolino, F. Corradini, P. Inverardi, and H. Muccini. Deriving test plans from architectural descriptions. In *Proceedings of the 22nd international conference on Software engineering*, pages 220–229. ACM Press, 2000.

28. A. Bertolino, E. Marchetti, and R. Mirandola. Real-time UML-based performance engineering to aid manager's decisions in multi-project planning. In *Proceedings of the 3rd International Workshop on Software and Performance (WOSP-02)*, pages 251–261, New York, July 24–26 2002. ACM Press.

29. A. Bertolino, E. Marchetti, and A. Polini. Integrating "components" to test software components. In *Proceedings of 1st International Workshop on Testing*

and Analysis of Component Software at ETAPS 2003, April 13th 2003. Warsaw - Poland.

30. A. Bertolino and R. Mirandola. Modeling and analysis of non-functional properties in component-based systems. In *Proceedings of 1st International Workshop on Testing and Analysis of Component Software at ETAPS 2003*, April 13th 2003. Warsaw - Poland.

31. A. Bertolino and A. Polini. Re-thinking the development process of component-based software. In *Procediings ECBS 2002 Workshop On CBSE, Composing Systems From Components*, April 2002.

32. A. Bertolino and A. Polini. WCT: a wrapper for component testing. In *Proceedings of International Workshop Fidji'2002*, volume 2604 of *LNCS*, pages 141–151, Luxembourg, November 28-29 2002.

33. A. Bertolino and A. Polini. A framework for component deployment testing. In *Proceedings of 25th International Conference on Software Engineering*, pages 221–231, May 2003.

34. S. Beydeda and V. Gruhn. Integrating white- and black-box techniques for class-level testing object-oriented prototypes. In *Proceedings of the Software Engineering and Applications Conference*, pages 23–28, Nov. 2000.

35. S. Beydeda and V. Gruhn. An integrated testing technique for component-based software. In *Proceedings of the AICCSA ACS/IEEE International Conference on Computer Systems and Applications*, June 2001.

36. S. Beydeda and V. Gruhn. Merging components and testing tools: The self-testing cots components (stecc) strategy. In *Proceedings of the 29th EUROMICRO Conference (EUROMICRO'03)*, pages 107–114, Belek-Antalya, Turkey, Sept. 2003.

37. S. Beydeda and V. Gruhn. State of art in testing components. In *QSIC'03*, pages 146–153, Dallas, USA, Oct. 2003. IEEE Computer Society.

38. S. Beydeda, V. Gruhn, and M. Stachorski. A graphical representation of classes for integrated black- and white-box testing. In *International Conference on Software Maintenance (ICSM)*, pages 706–715. IEEE Computer Society Press, 2001.

39. R. V. Binder. *Testing Object-Oriented Systems: Models, Patterns, and Tools.* Addison-Wesley, 2000.

40. D. Binkley. Semantics guided regression test cost reduction. *IEEE Transactions on Software Engineering*, 23(8):498–516, Aug. 1997.

41. G. Booch, J. Rumbaugh, and I. Jacobson. *The Unified Modeling Language User Guide*. Addison-Wesley, 1999.

42. G. Booch, J. Rumbaugh, and I. Jacobson. *The Unified Software Development Process*. Addison-Wesley, 1999.

43. J. Bosch. *Design and use of software architectures: adopting and evolving a product-line approach*. Addison-Wesley, Harlow, 2000.

44. J. Bosch, P. Molin, M. Mattsson, P. Bengtsson, and M. Fayad. Framework problems and experiences. In M. Fayad, D. Schmidt, and R. Johnson, editors, *Object-Oriented Application Frameworks*, pages 55–82. John-Wiley, 1999.

45. L. C. Briand, V. R. Basili, and C. Hetmanski. Developing interpretable models for optimized set reduction for identifying high-risk software components. *IEEE Transactions on Software Engineering*, 19(11):1028–1034, 1993.

46. P. Broadwell, N. Sastry, and J. Traupman. FIG: A prototype tool for online verification of recovery mechanisms. In *ACM ICS SHAMAN Workshop*, Ney York, NY, June 2002.

384   References

47. A. W. Brown and K. C. Wallnau. The current state of cbse. *IEEE Software*, 15(5):37–46, 1998.

48. A. W. Brown and K. C. Wallnau. The current state of CBSE. *IEEE Software*, 15(5):37–46, 1998.

49. M. Broy, A. Deimel, J. Henn, K. Koskimies, F. Plasil, G. Pomberger, W. Pree, M. Stal, and C. Szyperski. What characterizes a (software) component? *Software – Concepts and Tools*, pages 49–56, 1998.

50. A. Brucker and B. Wolff. Checking OCL Constraints in Distributed Systems Using J2EE/EJB. Technical Report 157, Albert-Ludwigs-Universität Freiburg, http://www.brucker.ch/bibliography/download/2001/tr01.pdf, July 2001.

51. M. Buchi and W. Weck. The greybox approach: When blackbox specifications hide too much. Technical Report TUCS TR No. 297, Turku Centre for Computer Science, 1999. http://www.tucs.abo.fi/.

52. T. A. Budd. *Mutation Analysis: Ideas, Examples, Problems and Prospects*, pages 129–149. Computer Program Testing. North Holland, 1981. Chandrasekaran and Radicchi (eds.).

53. T. A. Budd and D. Angluin. Two notions of correctness and their relation to testing. *Acta Informatica*, 18:31–45, 1982.

54. G. A. Bundell, G. Lee, J. Morris, K. Parker, and P. Lam. A software component verification tool. In *Proceedings of International Conference on Software Methods and Tools (SMT2000)*, pages 137–146, Wollongong, Australia, November 6-10 2000.

55. U. Buy, C. Ghezzi, A. Orso, M. Pezze, and M. Valsasna. A framework for testing object-oriented components. In *International ICSE Workshop Testing Distributed Component-Based Systems (Los Angeles, USA)*, 1999.

56. C. Atkinson et al. *Component-based Product Line Engineering with UML*. Addison-Wesley, 2001.

57. C. Atkinson et al. *Component-based Product Line Engineering with UML*. Addison-Wesley, London, 2002.

58. D. Carney and F. Long. What do you mean by COTS? – finally, a useful answer. *IEEE Software*, 17(2), 2000.

59. J. Carreira, H. Madeira, and J. Silva. Xception: A technique for the experimental evaluation of dependability in modern computers. *Software Engineering*, 24(2):125–136, 1998.

60. A. Carzaniga, D. S. Rosenblum, and A. L. Wolf. Design and evaluation of a wide-area event notification service. *ACM Transactions on Computer Systems*, 19(3):332–383, Aug 2001.

61. A. Cechich and M. Polo. Black-box Evaluation of COTS Components using Aspects and Metadata. In *Proceedings of the 4th International Conference on Product Focused Software Process Improvement, Springer-Verlag LNCS 2559*, pages 494–508, 2002.

62. A. Cechich and M. Prieto. Comparing Visual Component Composition Environments. In *Proceedings of the XXII International Conference of the Chilean Computer Science Society, IEEE Computer Society Press*, pages 217–225, 2002.

63. CERT. CERT Advisory. CA-2001-33, multiple vulnerabilities in wu-ftpd. http://ftp.wu-ftpd.org/pub/wu-ftpd-attic/cert.org/CA-2001-33.

64. J. Cheesman and J. Daniels. *UML Components - a Simple Process for Specifying Component-Based Software*. Addison-Wesley, 2000.

65. H. Y. Chen, T. H. Tse, F. T. Chan, and T. Y. Chen. In black and white: an integrated approach to class-level testing of object-oriented programs. *ACM Transactions on Software Engineering and Methodology*, 7(3):250–295, 1998.

66. H. Y. Chen, T. H. Tse, and T. Y. Chen. Taccle: a methodology for object-oriented software testing at the class and cluster levels. *ACM Transactions on Software Engineering and Methodology*, 10(1), 2001.

67. J. C. Cherniavsky and C. H. Smith. A recursion theoretic approach to program testing. *IEEE Transaction on Software Engineering*, 13(7):777–784, July 1987.

68. J. Choi. Aspect-Oriented Programming with Enterprise JavaBeans. In *Proceedings of the Fourth International Enterprise Distributed Object Computing Conference*, pages 252–262, 2000.

69. P. Clements, R. Kazman, and M. Klein. *Evaluating Software Architecture: Methods and Case Studies*. Addison-Wesley, 2002.

70. P. Clements and L. Northrop. *Software Product Lines: Practices and Patterns*. Addison-Wesley, Massachusetts, Boston, 2002.

71. Component+ Consortium. Built-in testing for component-based development, technical report d.3. http://www.component-plus.org, 2001.

72. K. Compton, Y. Gurevich, J. Huggins, and W. Shen. An automatic verification tool for UML, 2000.

73. J. C. Corbett, M. B. Dwyer, J. Hatcliff, and Robby. A language framework for expressing checkable properties of dynamic software. In *Proceedings of the 7th SPIN Workshop*, volume 1885 of *LNCS*, August 2000.

74. V. Cortellessa and R. Mirandola. PRIMA-UML: a performance validation incremental methodology on early UML diagrams. *Science of Computer Programming*, 44:101–129, 2002.

75. F. Cristian. Exception handling and tolerance of software faults. In M. Lyu, editor, *Software Fault Tolerance*, pages 81–107. Wiley, 1995.

76. I. Crnkovic, B. Hnich, T. Jonsson, and Z. Kiziltan. Specification, implementation, and deployment of components. *Communications of the ACM*, 45(10):35–40, 2002.

77. I. Crnkovic and M. Larsson. A case study: demands on component-based development. In *ICSE'2000*, pages 22–30, Limerick, Ireland, June 2000.

78. I. Crnkovic and M. Larsson. Component-based software engineering – new paradigm of software development. 2001.

79. I. Crnkovic and M. Larsson, editors. *Building Reliable Component-Based Software System*. Artech House Publisher, 2002.

80. I. Crnkovic, H. Schmidt, J. Stafford, and K. Wallnau, editors. *The Journal of Systems and Software - Special issue on CBSE*, volume 65. 2003.

81. I. Crnkovic, H. Schmidt, J. Stafford, and K. C. Wallnau, editors. *6th ICSE workshop on CBSE: Automated Reasoning and Prediction*. May 2002. Orlando, Florida - USA.

82. D. Crocker. The verified design-by-contract paradigm. In *Safety-Critical Systems Symposium*, Meriden, Warwickshire, UK, February 2004.

83. G. Cugola, E. D. Nitto, and A. Fuggetta. The JEDI event-based infrastructure and its application to the development of the OPSS WFMS. *IEEE Transactions on Software Engineerings*, 27(9):827–850, Sept. 2001.

84. D. Garlan and S.Khersonsky and J.S. Kim. Model checking publish-subscribe systems. In *Proceedings of the 10th SPIN Workshop*, volume 2648 of *LNCS*, May 2003.

85. W. Damm and D. Harel. LSCs: Breathing life into message sequence charts. *Formal Methods in System Design*, 19(1):45–80, 2001.

86. L. Davis, R. Gamble, and J. Payton. The impact of component architectures on interoperability. *The Journal of Systems and Software*, 61:31–45, 2002.

87. M. Davis and W. E. Metric space-based test-data adequacy criteria. *The Computer Journal*, 13(1):17–24, Feb. 1988.

88. S. Dawson, F. Jahanian, T. Mitton, and T.-L. Tung. Testing of fault-tolerant and real-time distributed systems via protocol fault injektion. In *Symposium on Fault-Tolerant Computing*, pages 404–414, 1996.

89. M. de Miguel, J. Ruiz, and M. Garcia. QoS-aware component frameworks. In *Proceedings of Tenth International Workshop on Quality of Service*, 2002.

90. J. C. Dean. Timing the testing of COTS software products. In *International ICSE Workshop Testing Distributed Component-Based Systems*, 1999.

91. M. E. Delamaro, J. C. Maldonado, and A. P. Mathur. Interface mutation: an approach to integration testing. *IEEE Transactions on Software Engineering*, 27(3):228–247, March 2001.

92. L. G. DeMichiel. Enterprise javabeans specification, version 2.1. Technical report, Sun Microsystems, 2002.

93. R. A. DeMillo, R. J. Lipton, and F. G. Sayward. Hints on test data selection: Help for the practising programmer. *IEEE Computer*, 11(4):34–41, April 1978.

94. J. P. DeVale and P. Koopman. Robust software – no more excuses. In *Proceedings of the International Conference on Dependable Systems and Networks*, June 2002.

95. L. K. Dillon and Y. S. Ramakrishna. Generating oracles from your favorite temporal logic specifications. In *Proceedings of the Fourth ACM SIGSOFT Symposium on the Foundations of Software Engineering*, volume 21 of *ACM Software Engineering Notes*, pages 106–117, New York, Oct.16–18 1996. ACM Press.

96. L. K. Dillon and Q. Yu. Oracles for checking temporal properties of concurrent systems. In *Proceedings of the ACM SIGSOFT '94 Symposium on the Foundations of Software Engineering*, pages 140–153, Dec. 1994.

97. L. Dobrica and E. Niemelä. A strategy for analyzing product line software architectures. Technical report, VTT Publications 427, VTT Technical Research Centre of Finland, Espoo, 2000.

98. L. Dobrica and E. Niemelä. Using uml notation extensions to model variability in product line architectures. In *ICSE, International workshop on Software Variability Management, Portland, USA*, pages 8–13, 2003.

99. F. Doucet, S. Shukla, and R. Gupta. Typing abstractions and management in a component framework. In *Proceedings of the Design Automation Conference, Asia-South Pacific*, January 2003.

100. D. D'Souza and A. C. Wills. *Objects, Components and Frameworks with UML: The Catalysis Approach*. Addison Wesley, Reading, MA, 1999.

101. J. Duran and S. Ntafos. An evaluation of random testing. *IEEE Trans. on Software Eng.*, 10:438–444, 1984.

102. EC. IST-1999-20162, Component+. http://www.component-plus.org, 2002.

103. H. Edler and J. Hörnstein. BIT in software components, european component+, 2001.

104. A. Egyed and C. Gacek. Automatically detecting mismatches during component-based and model-based development. In *14th IEEE International*

Conference on Automated Software Engineering, Florida, USA, pages 191–198, 1999.

105. N. S. Eickelmann and D. J. Richardson. An evaluation of software test environment architectures. In *Proceedings of the 18th international conference on Software engineering*, pages 353–364. IEEE Computer Society, 1996.

106. S. Elbaum, D. Gable, and G. Rothermel. Understanding and measuring the sources of variation in the prioritization of regression test suites. In *Proceedings of the Seventh International Software Metrics Symposium (METRICS 2001)*, pages 169–179, Apr. 2001.

107. S. Elbaum, A. Malishevsky, and G. Rothermel. Prioritizing test cases for regression testing. In *Proceedings of the ACM International Symposium on Software Testing and Analysis*, pages 102–112, Aug. 2000.

108. W. Emmerich. *Engineering Distributed Objects*. John-Wiley & Sons, 2000.

109. W. Emmerich. Software engineering and middleware. In *Proceedings of the 22th International Conference on Software Engineering (ICSE-00)*, pages 117–132. ACM Press, 2000.

110. W. Emmerich. Distributed component technologies and their software engineering implications. In *Proceedings of the 24th International Conference on Software Engineering (ICSE-02)*, pages 537–546. ACM Press, 2002.

111. W. Emmerich and J. Skene. Model driven performance analysis of enterprise information systems. In *Proceedings of the International Workshop on Testing and Analysis of Component-Based Systems(TACOS'03)*, 2003.

112. D. Engler, B. Chelf, A. Chou, and S. Hallem. Checking system rules using system-specific, programmer-written compiler extensions. In *Proceedings of the Fourth Symposium on Operating Systems Design and Implementation*, San Diego, CA, Oct. 2000.

113. D. Engler, D. Y. Chen, S. Hallem, A. Chou, and B. Chelf. Bugs as deviant behavior: a general approach to inferring errors in systems code. In *Proceedings of the eighteenth ACM symposium on Operating systems principles*, pages 57–72. ACM Press, 2001.

114. ETSI - Telecom Standards. The testing and test control notation: Core language, es 201 873-1, v.2.2.1, Oct. 2002.

115. ETSI - Telecom Standards. The ttcn-3 control interfaces (tci), es 201 873-6, v.1.0, Mar. 2002.

116. ETSI - Telecom Standards. The ttcn-3 run-time interface (tri), es 201 873-5, v.1.0, Oct. 2002.

117. P. T. Eugster, P. A. Felber, R. Guerraoui, and A. Kermarrec. The many faces of publish/subscribe. *ACM Computing Surveys*, 35(2):114–131, 2003.

118. H. Expert. http://www.hugin.com, 2001.

119. J.-C. Fabre, M. Rodriguez, J. Arlat, and J.-M. Sizun. Building dependable cots microkernel-based systems using mafalda. In *Proceedings of the Pacific Rim International Symposium on Dependable Computing (PRDC'00)*, pages 85–94, Los Angeles, California, Dec. 2000.

120. P. Felber. Transparent parallelization of java applications. In *Proceedings of the International Symposium on Distributed Objects and Applications (DOA'03)*, Nov. 2003.

121. N. E. Fenton and M. Neil. A critique of software defect prediction models. *IEEE Transactions on Software Engineering*, 25(5):675–689, 1999.

122. N. E. Fenton and N. Ohlsson. Quantitative analysis of faults and failures in a complex software system. *IEEE Transactions on Software Engineering*, 26(8):797–814, 2000.

123. C. Fetzer and K. Högstedt. Self*: A component based data-flow oriented framework for pervasive dependability. In *Eighth IEEE International Workshop on Object-oriented Real-time Dependable Systems (WORDS 2003)*, Jan. 2003.

124. C. Fetzer, K. Högstedt, and P. Felber. Automatic detection and masking of non-atomic exception handling. In *Proceedings of the International Conference on Dependable Systems and Networks (DSN'03)*, June 2003.

125. C. Fetzer and Z. Xiao. Detecting heap smashing attacks through fault containment wrappers. In *Proceedings of the 20th IEEE Symposium on Reliable Distributed Systems*, Oct. 2001.

126. C. Fetzer and Z. Xiao. An automated approach to increasing the robustness of C libraries. In *Proceedings of the International Conference on Dependable Systems and Networks*, June 2002.

127. C. Fetzer and Z. Xiao. A flexible generator architecture for improving software dependability. In *Proceedings of the International Symposium on Software Reliability Engineering*, Nov. 2002.

128. C. Fetzer and Z. Xiao. Healers: A toolkit for enhancing the robustness and security of existing applications. In *Proceedings of the International Conference on Dependable Systems and Networks*, June 2003.

129. C. Floyd. A systematic look at prototyping. In R. Budde, K. Kuhlenkamp, L. Mathiassen, and H. Züllighoven, editors, *Approaches to Prototyping*, pages 1–18. Springer Verlag, 1984.

130. P. Frankl and J. Weyuker. An applicable family of data flow testing criteria. *IEEE Transactions on Software Engineering*, 14(10):1483–1498, Oct. 1988.

131. P. G. Frankl, R. G. Hamlet, B. Littlewood, and L. Strigini. Evaluating testing methods by delivered reliability. *IEEE Transactions on Software Engineering*, 24(8):586–601, 1998.

132. P. G. Frankl and J. E. Weyuker. A formal analysis of the fault-detecting ability of testing methods. *IEEE Transactions on Software Engineering*, 19(3):202–213, March 1993.

133. G. Froehlich, H. Hoover, L. Liu, and P. Sorenson. Hooking into object-oriented application frameworks. In *Proc. of 1997 Int. Conf. on Software Engineering*, pages 141–151. ACM, 1997.

134. S. Fujiwara, G. v. Bochmann, F. Khendek, M. Amalou, and A. Ghedamsi. Test selection based on finite state models. *IEEE Transactions on Software Engineering*, 17(6):591–603, June 1991.

135. E. Gamma, R. Helm, R. Johnson, and J. Vlissides. *Design Patterns Elements of Reusable Object-Oriented Software*. Addison Wesley, 1995.

136. J. Gao, K. Gupta, S. Gupta, and S. Shim. On building testable software components. In *COTS-Based Software Systems (ICCBCC)*, volume 2255 of *LNCS*, pages 108–121. Springer Verlag, 2002.

137. J. Gao, E. Y. Zhu, and S. Shim. Monitoring software components and component-based software. In *Computer Software and Applications Conference (COMPSAC)*, pages 403–412. IEEE Computer Society Press, 2000.

138. J. Gao, E. Y. Zhu, and S. Shim. Tracking software components. *Journal of Object-Oriented Programming*, 14(4):13–22, 2001.

139. D. Garlan, R. Allen, and J. Ockerbloom. Architectural mismatch or why it's hard to build systems out of existing parts. In *17th International Conference on Software Engineering*, pages 179–185. ACM Press, Washington, Seatle, 1995.

140. D. Garlan, R. Allen, and J. Ockerbloom. Architectural mismatch: Why reuse is so hard. *IEEE Software*, 12(6), November 1995.

141. D. Garlan and M. Shaw. *Software Architecture: Perspective on an Emerging Discipline*. Prentice-Hall, 1996.

142. S. Ghosh and A. P. Mathur. Issues in testing distributed component-based systems. In *International ICSE Workshop Testing Distributed Component-Based Systems*, 1999.

143. S. Gnesi, D. Latella, and M. Massink. Model checking UML statecharts diagrams using JACK. In *Proceedings of the 4th IEEE International Symposium on High Assuarance Systems Enginering (HASE)*, pages 46–55. IEEE Press, 1999.

144. S. S. Gokhale and M. R. Lyu. Regression tree modeling for the prediction of software quality. In *Proceedings of the Third ISSAT International Conference on Reliability and Quality in Design*, pages 31–36, Anaheim, California, Mar. 1997.

145. O. Goldreich, S. Goldwasser, and D. Ron. Property testing and its connection to learning and approximation. *J. ACM*, 45(4):653–750, 1998.

146. J. Goodenough. Exception handling: issues and a proposed notation. *Communications of the ACM*, 18(12):683–696, 1975.

147. J. B. Goodenough and S. L. Gerhart. Toward a theory of test data selection. *IEEE Transactions on Software Engineering*, 3, June 1975.

148. I. Gorton and A. Liu. Software component quality assessment in practice: successes and practical impediments. In *Proceedings of the 24th International Conference on Software Engineering (ICSE-02)*, pages 555–558, New York, 2002. ACM Press.

149. M. Goto. CINT C/C++ interpreter. http://root.cern.ch/root/Cint.html.

150. M. Goulao and F. B. e Abreu. The quest for software components quality. In *Proceedings of the 26th Annual International Computer Software and Applications Conference (COMPSAC'02)*, pages 313–318, Oxford,England, Aug. 2002.

151. F. Griffel. *Componentware: Konzepte und Techniken eines Softwareparadigmas*. dpunkt Verlag, 1998.

152. M. L. Griss. Software reuse architecture, process, and organization for business success. In *Proceedings of the Eighth Israeli Conference on Computer Systems and Software Engineering*, pages 86–98, Dan Accadia, Herzliya, June 1997.

153. H. Gross, C. Atkinson, and F. Barbier. Component integration through built-in contract testing. In *Component-Based Software Quality: Methods and Techniques*, volume LNCS 2693, pages 159–183, 2003.

154. H.-G. Gross. Testing and the UML – a perfect fit. Technical Report 110.03/E, Fraunhofer Institute for Experimental Software Engineering, Oct. 2003.

155. H.-G. Gross, C. Atkinson, and F. Barbier. Component integration through built-in contract testing. In Cechich, Piattini, and Vallcillo, editors, *Component-based Software Quality, Lecture Notes in Computer Science, Vol 2693*, Heidelberg, 2003. Springer.

156. H.-G. Gross, C. Atkinson, F. Barbier, N. Belloir, and M. Bruel. Built-in contract testing for component-based development. In Barbier, editor, *Business Component-Based Software Engineering*. Kluwer, 2003.

157. H.-G. Gross and N. Mayer. Built-in contract testing in component integration testing. *Electronic Notes in Theoretical Computer Science*, 82(6), 2003.

158. V. Gruhn and A. Thiel. *Komponentenmodelle: DCOM, JavaBeans, Enterprise JavaBeans, CORBA.* Addison-Wesley, 2000.

159. J. Grundy. Aspect-Oriented requirement Engineering for Component-Based Software Systems. In *Proceedings of the 4th IEEE International Symposium on Requirements Engineering*, pages 84–91, 1999.

160. J. Grundy. Multi-Perspective Specification, Design, and Implementation of Software Components using Aspects. *International Journal of Software Engineering and Knowledge Engineering*, 10(6):713–734, 2000.

161. C. A. Gunter and D. S. Scott. *Semantic domains*, volume B: Formal Models and Semantics of *Handbook of Theoretical Computer Science*, pages 633–674. The MIT Press/Elsevier, 1990. (Ed.) J. van Leeuwen.

162. D. Hamlet, D. Mason, and D. Woit. Theory of software reliability based on components. In *Proceedings of the 23rd international conference on Software engineering*, pages 361–370. IEEE Computer Society, 2001.

163. D. Hamlet and R. Taylor. Partition testing does not inspire confidence. *IEEE Trans. on Software Eng.*, 16(12):1402–1411, 1990.

164. S. Han, K. Shin, and H. Rosenberg. DOCTOR: An integrated software fault injection environment for distributed real-time systems. In *Proceedings of the International Computer Performance and Dependability Symposium (IPDS'95)*, pages 204–213, Erlangen, Germany, Apr. 1995.

165. R. A. Haraty, N. Mansour, and B. Daou. Regression testing of database applications. In *Proceedings of the 2001 ACM symposium on Applied computing*, pages 285–289. ACM Press, 2001.

166. M. Hardy. Cots components in software development. In *Computer Science Discipline Seminar Conference (CSCI 3901), University of Minnesota, Minnesota, USA*, 2000.

167. D. Harel. Statecharts: A visual formalism for complex systems. *Science of Computer Programming*, 8:231–274, 1987.

168. D. Harel and E. Gery. Executable object modeling with statecharts. *IEEE Computer*, 30(7):31–42, 1997.

169. M. J. Harrold. Testing: A roadmap. In *The Future of Software Engineering (special volume of the proceedings of the International Conference on Software Engineering (ICSE))*, pages 63–72. ACM Press, 2000.

170. M. J. Harrold, D. Liang, and S. Sinha. An approach to analyzing and testing component-based systems. In *International ICSE Workshop Testing Distributed Component-Based Systems*, 1999.

171. M. J. Harrold, A. Orso, D. Rosenblum, G. R. G., M. L. Soff, and H. Do. Using Component Metadata to Support the Regression Testing of Component-Based Software. Technical Report GIT-CC-01-38, College of Computing, Georgia Institute of Technology, 2001.

172. M. J. Harrold and M. L. Soffa. Selecting and using data for integration testing. *IEEE Software*, pages 58–65, March 1991.

173. J. Hatcliff, W. Deng, M. Dwyer, G. Jung, and V. Ranganath. Cadena: An integrated development, analysys, and verification environment for component-based systems. In *Proceedings of the 25th International Conference on Software Engineering*, pages 160–172, May 2003.

174. M. Hayden. *The Ensemble System*. PhD thesis, cornell, Jan. 1998.

175. S. Heiler. Semantic interoperability. *ACM Computing Surveys*, 27(2):271–279, 1995.

176. G. T. Heineman and W. T. C. (ed.). *Component-Based Software Engineering: Putting the Pieces Together*. Addison-Wesley, Reading, MA, 2001.

177. R. Helm, I. Holland, and D. Gangopadhyay. Contracts: Specifying behavioral compositions in object-oriented systems. In *OOPSLA-ECOOP*, pages 169–180, 1990.

178. D. Hemer and P. Lindsay. Supporting component-based reuse in CARE. In *Proceedings of the 25th Australasian conference on Computer science - Volume 4*, Melbourne, Victoria, Australia, 2002.

179. D. Hoffman and P. Strooper. Graph-based class testing. *The Australian Computer Journal*, 26(4):158–163, 1994.

180. D. Hoffman and P. Strooper. The testgraph methodology: Automated testing collection classes. *Journal of Object Oriented Programming*, 8(7):35–41, 1995.

181. G. Holzmann. *Design and Validation of Network Protocols*. Prentice Hall, 1991.

182. G. Holzmann. The model checker SPIN. *IEEE Transactions on Software Engineering*, 23(5):279–295, May 1997.

183. H. S. Hong, Y. R. Kwon, and S. D. Cha. Testing of object-oriented programs based on finite state machines. In *Second Asia-Pacific Software Engineering Conference (Brisbane, Australia)*, pages 234–241. IEEE Computer Society Press, 1995.

184. Hong Kong Productivity Council. http://www.hkpc.org/itd/servic11.htm, 2000.

185. J. Hopkins. Component primer. *C. ACM*, 43(10):27–30, Oct. 2000.

186. J. Hörnestein and H. Edler. Test reuse in cbse using built-in tests. In *Proceedings of the 9th IEEE Conference and Workshops on Engineering of Computer-Based Systems. Workshop on Component-based Software Engineering*, 2002.

187. C. Horstmann. *Mastering Object-Oriented Design in C++*. Wiley, 1995.

188. W. E. Howden. Reliability of the path analysis testing strategy. *IEEE Transaction on Software Engineering*, 2(9):208–215, Sept. 1976.

189. Y.-W. Huang, S.-K. Huang, T.-P. Lin, and C.-H. Tsai. Web application security assessment by fault injection and behavior monitoring. In *Proceedings of the twelfth international conference on World Wide Web*, pages 148–159. ACM Press, 2003.

190. D. Hybertson. A uniform component modeling space. *Informatica*, 25(4), November 2001.

191. D. Hybertson. Strengthening the modeling foundation of the mda. In *Workshop in Software Model Engineering at UML 2002*, http://www.metamodel.com/wisme-2002/papers/hybertson.pdf, October 2002.

192. IBM. http://www4.ibm.com/software/ad/sanfrancisco, 2000.

193. F. IGD. Rin system specification. Technical report, Fraunhofer Institut für Graphische Datenverarbeitung, Darmstadt, Germany, 2004.

194. Institute of Electrical and Electronics Engineers. *IEEE 610.12-1990: IEEE Standard Glossary of Software Engineering Terminology*, 1990.

195. Institution of Electrical and Electronics Engineers. Ieee std 1063-1987, ieee standard for software user documentation, 1987.

196. Institution of Electrical and Electronics Engineers. Ieee std 1016.1-1993, ieee guide to software design descriptions, 1993.

392   References

197. Institution of Electrical and Electronics Engineers. Ieee std 829-1998, ieee standard for software test documentation, 1998.

198. Institution of Electrical and Electronics Engineers. Ieee std 829-1998, ieee standard for software test documentation, 2002.

199. International Organization for Standardadization. ISO/IEC (1991) information technology - software product evaluation - quality characteristics and guidelines for their use.

200. International Organization for Standardization. *ISO 8402: Quality management and quality assurance - Vocabulary*, 1994.

201. International Organization for Standardization. Basic reference model of open distributed processing, 1995.

202. International Organization for Standardization. *ISO/IEC 14598-5: Information technology – Software product evaluation – Part 5: Process for evaluators*, 1998.

203. International Organization for Standardization. *ISO/IEC 14598-1: Information technology – Software product evaluation – Part 1: General overview*, 1999.

204. International Organization for Standardization. *ISO/IEC 14598-4: Software engineering – Product evaluation – Part 4: Process for acquirers*, 1999.

205. International Organization for Standardization. *ISO/IEC 14598-2: Software engineering – Product evaluation – Part 2: Planning and management*, 2000.

206. International Organization for Standardization. *ISO/IEC 14598-3: Software engineering – Product evaluation – Part 3: Process for developers*, 2000.

207. International Organization for Standardization. *ISO/IEC 14598-5: Software engineering – Product evaluation – Part 6: Documentation of evaluation modules*, 2001.

208. International Organization for Standardization. *ISO/IEC 9126-1: Software engineering – Product quality – Part 1: Quality model*, 2001.

209. P. Inverardi, H. Muccini, and P. Pelliccione. Automated check of architectural models consistency using SPIN. In *Proceedings of the 16th IEEE International Conference on Automated Software Engineering conference (ASE)*, pages 349–349, 2001.

210. H. Ishikawa, Y. Ogata, K. Adachi, and T. Nakajima. Requirements for a component framework of future ubiquitous computing. In *Proceedings of the IEEE Workshop on Software Technologies for Future Embedded Systems (WSTFES'03)*, 2003.

211. I. Jacobson, M. Christerson, P. Jonsson, and G. Overgaard. *Object-Oriented Software Engineering: A Use Case Driven Approach*. Addison-Wesley, Reading, MA, 1992.

212. M. Jazayeri, A. Ran, and F. van der Linden. *Software Architecture for Product Families*. Addison-Wesley, Boston, 2000.

213. T. Jeon, H. W. Seung, and S. Lee. Embedding built-in tests in hot spots of an object-oriented framework. *SIGPLAN Not.*, 37(8):25–34, 2002.

214. Z. Jin and J. Offutt. Integration testing based on software couplings. In *COMPSAC'95*, pages 13–23, Gaithersburg, Maryland, June 1995.

215. R. Johnson and B. Foote. Designing reusable classes. *Journal of OOP*, 1:26–49, 1988.

216. N. G. K. E. Emam, S. Benlarbi and S. N. Rai. Comparing case-based reasoning classifiers for predicting high risk software components. *The Journal of Systems and Software*, 55(3):301–320, 2001.

217. P. Kallio and T. Ihme. Evolution of the use and risks of the commercial software components. In *28th Euromicro Conference, Dortmund, DE*, pages 55 – 61, 2002.

218. S. H. Kan. *Metrics and Models in Software Quality Engineering (Second Edition)*. Addison-Wesley, Reading, MA, 2003.

219. G. Kanawati, N. Kanawati, and J. Abraham. FERRARI: A tool for the validation of system dependability properties. In *Proceedings of the 22nd International Symposium on Fault Tolerant Computing (FTCS-22)*, pages 336–344, Boston, Massachusetts, 1992. IEEE.

220. W. Kao and R. Iyer. A user-oriented synthetic workload generator. In *12th International Conference on Distributed Computing Systems (ICDCS '92)*, pages 270–277. IEEE Computer Society Press, June 1992.

221. N. Kaveh and W. Emmerich. Deadlock detection in distributed object systems. In *Proceedings of the joint 8th European Software Engineering Conference (ESEC) and 9th ACM SIGSOFT Symposium on the Foundations of Software Engineering (FSE)*, pages 44–51, 2001.

222. A. Kelkar and R. Gamble. Understanding the architectural characteristics behind middleware choices. In *1st Conference on Information Reuse and Integration, Georgia, Atlanta*, 1999.

223. R. Keshav and R. Gamble. Towards a taxonomy of architecture integration strategies. In *3rd International Software Architecture Workshop, Florida, Orlando*, 1998.

224. A. A. Keshlaf and K. Hashim. A model and prototype tool to manage software risks. In *Proceedings of the First Asia-Pacific Conference on Quality Software*, pages 297–305, Kowloon, Hong Kong, Oct. 2000.

225. G. Kiczales and J. des Rivières. *The Art of the Metaobject Protocol*. MIT Press, 1991.

226. G. Kiczales, J. Lamping, A. Menhdhekar, C. Maeda, C. Lopes, J.-M. Loingtier, and J. Irwin. Aspect-oriented programming. In M. Akşit and S. Matsuoka, editors, *Proceedings European Conference on Object-Oriented Programming*, volume 1241, pages 220–242. Springer-Verlag, Berlin, Heidelberg, and New York, 1997.

227. K. N. King and A. J. Offutt. A fortran language system for mutation-based software testing. *Software–Practice and Experience*, 21(7):685–718, July 1991.

228. S. Kirani and W. Tsai. Method sequence specification and verification of classes. *Journal of Object-Oriented Programming*, pages 28–38, Oct. 1994.

229. KLGroup. http://www.klgroup.com, 2001.

230. J. Kontio. A case study in applying a systematic method for cots selection. In *18th International Conference on Software Engineering, Berlin, Germany*, pages 201 – 209. IEEE Computer Society Press, 1996.

231. P. Koopman and J. DeVale. The exception handling effectiveness of POSIX operating systems. *IEEE Transactions on Software Engineering*, 26(9):837–848, Sep 2000.

232. B. Korel. Black-box understanding of COTS components. In *Proceedings: Seventh International Workshop on Program Comprehension*, pages 92–99. IEEE Computer Society Press, 1999.

233. M. Koutlis, P. Kourouniotis, K. Kyrimis, and N. Renieri. Inter-component communication as a vehicle towards end-user modeling. In *ICSE Workshop on Component-Based Software Engineering*, 1998.

234. W. Kozaczynski and G. Booch. Component-based software engineering. *IEEE Software*, 15(5):34–36, 1998.
235. R. Kramer. iContract - The Java Design by Contract Tool. In *Proceedings of Technology of Object-Oriented Languages and Systems*, pages 295–307, Santa Barbara, California, August 03-07 1998.
236. N. Kranitis, A. Paschalis, D. Gizopoulos, and Y. Zorian. Effective software self-test methodology for processor cores. In *Proceedings of the conference on Design, automation and test in Europe*, page 592. IEEE Computer Society, 2002.
237. N. Kropp, P. K. Jr., and D. Siewiorek. Automated robustness testing of off-the-shelf software components. In *Proceedings of the Symposium on Fault-Tolerant Computing (FTCS)*, pages 230–239, 1998.
238. A. Krstic, W. C. Lai, K. T. Cheng, L. Chen, and S. Dey. Embedded software-based self-testing for soc design. In *Proceedings of the 39th conference on Design automation*, pages 355–360. ACM Press, 2002.
239. P. Kruchten. *The Rational Unified Process: An Introduction*. Addison Wesley Longman, 2000.
240. P. Lago and M. Matinlassi. The wise approach to architect wireless services. In *Proceedings of the 4th International Conference in Product Focused Software Process Improvement, PROFES2002*, pages 367 – 382, Berlin, Heidelberg, 2002. Springer.
241. D. Lea. Collections. http://gee.cs.oswego.edu/dl/classes/collections.
242. X. Leroy. The Objective Caml system release 2.03, June 2001.
243. J. Lilius and I. Paltor. vUML: a tool for verifying UML models. In *Proceedings of the 14th IEEE International Conference on Automated Software Engineering (ASE)*, pages 255–258, October 1999.
244. C. Lin, A. Avritzer, E. Weyuker, and L. Sai-Lai. Issues in interoperability and performance verification in a multi-orb telecommunications environment. In *Proceedings of the International Conference on Dependable Systems and Networks (DSN 2000)*, pages 567–575, 2000.
245. J.-L. Lions. Ariane 5, flight 501 failure, report by the inquiry board. http://java.sun.com/people/jag/Ariane5.html, 1996.
246. M. Lippert and C. V. Lopes. A study on exception detection and handling using aspect-oriented programming. In *Proceedings of the 22nd international conference on Software engineering*, pages 418–427. ACM Press, 2000.
247. Y. Liu, I. Gorton, A. Liu, N. Jiang, and S. Chen. Designing a test suite for empirically-based middleware performance prediction. In *Fortieth International Conference on Technology of Object-Oriented Languages and Systems (TOOLS Pacific 2002)*, Sydney, Australia, 2002. ACS.
248. D. Luckham, J. Vera, and S. Meldal. Three concepts of system architecture. Technical Report CSL–TR–95–67, Computer Systems Lab, Stanford University, July 1995.
249. C. Lüer and D. Rosenblum. WREN - An Environment for Component-Based Development. In *Proceedings of the Joint 8th European Software Engineering Conference and 9th ACM Sigsoft International Symposium on the Foundations of Software Engineering (FSE-9)*, pages 207–217, 2001.
250. R. Lutz and G. Gannod. Analysis of a software product line architecture: an experience report. *Journal of Systems and Software*, 66(3):253 – 267, 2003.
251. M. R. Lyu, editor. *Handbook of Software Reliability Engineering*. McGraw-Hill, New York, 1996.

252. M. R. Lyu. Software reliability theory. In J. J. Marciniak, editor, *Encyclopedia of Software Engineering*. Wiley, New York, 2001.

253. M. R. Lyu, J. S. Yu, E. Keramidas, and S. R. Dalal. Armor: Analyzer for reducing module operational risk. In *Proceedings of Twenty-Fifth International Symposium on Fault-Tolerant Computing (FTCS-25)*, pages 137–142, Pasadena, California, June 1995.

254. J. Magee, N. Dulay, S. Eisenbach, and J. Kramer. Specifying distributed software architectures. In *Proceedings 5th European Software Engineering Conference (ESEC 95)*, pages 137–153, Sitges, Spain, 1995.

255. E. Martins, C. Toyota, and R. Yanagawa. Constructing Self-Testable Software Components. In *Proceedings of the 2001 International Conference on Dependable Systems and Networks*, pages 151–160, 2001.

256. M. Matinlassi and E. Niemelä. The impact of maintainability on component-based software systems. In *Proceedings of the 29th Euromicro Conference*, Antalya, Turkey, 2003.

257. M. Matinlassi, E. Niemelä, and L. Dobrica. Quality-driven architecture design and quality analysis method, a revolutionary initiation approach to a product line architecture. Technical report, VTT Technical Research Centre of Finland, Espoo, 2002.

258. P. M. Maurer. Components: What if they gave a revolution and nobody came? *IEEE Computer*, 33(6):28–34, June 2000.

259. R. Maxion and R. Olszewski. Eliminating exception handling errors with dependability cases: a comparative, empirical study. *IEEE Transactions on Software Engineering*, 26(9):888–906, 2000.

260. T. McCabe, L. Dreyer, A. Dunn, and A. Watson. Testing an object-oriented application. *J. of the Quality Assurance Institute*, 8(4):21–27, 1994.

261. D. McIllroy. Mass produced software components. In P. Naur and B. Randall, editors, *Software Engineering: Report on a Conference by the NATO Science Committee*, pages 138–155, 1969.

262. M. D. McIlroy. Mass produced software components. In *NATO Software Engineering Conference*, pages 138–155, 1968.

263. K. McMillan. *Symbolic Model Checking*. Kluwer Academic, 1993.

264. N. Medvidovic, E. Dashofy, and R. Taylor. On the role of middleware in architecture-based software development. *International Journal of Software Engineering and Knowledge Engineering*, 13(4), 2003.

265. N. Medvidovic, P. Oreizy, J. E. Robbins, and R. N. Taylor. Using object-oriented typing to support architectural design in the c2 style. In *Proceedings of 4th Symposium on the Fundation of Software Engineering (FSE4)*, pages 24–32. ACM Press, October 1996. San Francisco, California (USA).

266. N. Medvidovic, D. Rosenblum, D. Redmiles, and J. Robbins. Modeling software architectures in the unified modeling language. *ACM Transcations on Software Engineering and Methodology*, 11(1):2–57, January 2002.

267. N. Mehta, N. Medvidovic, and S. Phadke. Towards a taxonomy of software connectors. In *Proceedings of the 22nd International Conference on Software Engineering (ICSE-00)*, pages 178–187. ACM Press, 2000.

268. P. Melliar-Smith and B. Randell. Software reliability: The role of programmed exception handling. In *Proceedings of the ACM conference on Language Design for Reliable Software*, pages 95–100, 1977.

269. S. Mellor and S. Balcer. *Executable UML - A Foundation for Model-Driven Architecture*. Addison-Wesley, 2002.

270. A. M. Memon, M. E. Pollack, and M. L. Soffa. Automated test oracles for GUIs. In *Proceedings of the ACM SIGSOFT 8th International Symposium on the Foundations of Software Engineering (FSE-8)*, pages 30–39, NY, Nov. 8–10 2000.

271. A. M. Memon and M. L. Soffa. Regression testing of GUIs. In *Proceedings of the 9th European software engineering conference held jointly with 10th ACM SIGSOFT international symposium on Foundations of software engineering*, pages 118–127. ACM Press, 2003.

272. A. M. Memon, M. L. Soffa, and M. E. Pollack. Coverage criteria for GUI testing. In *Proceedings of the 8th European Software Engineering Conference (ESEC) and 9th ACM SIGSOFT International Symposium on the Foundations of Software Engineering (FSE-9)*, pages 256–267, Sept. 2001.

273. P. Merle. CORBA 3.0 new components chapters. Technical report, TC Document ptc/2001-11-03, Object Management Group, 2001.

274. Metamata. http://www.metamata.com, 2001.

275. B. Meyer. Applying design by contract. *IEEE Computer*, 25(10):40–51, October 1992.

276. B. Meyer. *Object-Oriented Software Construction*. Prentice Hall, second edition edition, 1997.

277. B. Meyer. *Object-oriented Software Construction*. Prentice-Hall, Upper Saddle River, 1999.

278. B. Meyer. The grand challenge of trusted components. In *Proceedings of the 25th International Conf. on Software engineering*, May 2003.

279. B. Meyer, C. Mingins, and H. Schmidt. Trusted components for the software industry. http://trusted-components.org/documents/tc_original_paper.html.

280. B. Meyers and P. Oberndorf. *Managing Software Acquisition: Open Systems and COTS Products*. Addison-Wesley, New York, 2001.

281. Microsoft Corporation. Microsoft .NET framework. http://www.microsoft.com/net/.

282. Microsoft Corporation. .Net resources. http://www.microsoft.com/net/. Access date April 5th, 2004.

283. Microsoft Corporation. The component object model specification. http://www.microsoft.com/COM/resources/COM1598D.ZIP, 1995.

284. Microsoft Corporation. http://www.microsoft.com/isapi, 2000.

285. H. D. Mills. Top-Down Programming in Large Systems. In R. Ruskin, editor, *Debugging Techniques in Large Systems*. Prentice Hall, 1971.

286. S. Mitchell, A. Burns, and A. Wellings. Mopping up exceptions. *ACM SIGAda Ada Letters*, XXI(3):80–92, 2001.

287. R. T. Mittermeir, A. Bollin, H. Pozewaunig, and D. Rauner-Reithmayer. Goal-driven combination of software comprehension approaches for component based development. In *Proceedings of the 2001 symposium on Software reusability*, pages 95–102. ACM Press, 2001.

288. L. J. Morell. *A Theory of Error-based Testing*. PhD thesis, University of Maryland, Department of Computer Science, 1984.

289. M. Morisio, C. Seaman, A. Parra, V. Basili, S. Kraft, and S. Condon. Investigating and improving a COTS-based software development process. In *International Conference on Software Engineering (ICSE)*, pages 32–41. ACM Press, 2000.

290. M. Morisio, C. B. Seaman, V. R. Basili, A. T. Parra, S. E. Kraft, and S. E. Condon. COTS-based software development: Processes and open issues. *The Journal of Systems and Software*, 61(3):189–199, 2002.

291. M. Morisio and M. Torchiano. Definition and classification of COTS: A proposal. In *COTS-Based Software Systems (ICCBSS)*, volume 2255 of *LNCS*, pages 165–175. Springer Verlag, 2002.

292. J. Morris, P. Lam, G. Lee, K. Parker, and G. A. Bundell. Determining component reliability using a testing index. In *Proceedings of the twenty-fifth Australasian conference on Computer science*, pages 167–176. Australian Computer Society, Inc., 2002.

293. J. Morris, G. Lee, K. Parker, G. A. Bundell, and C. P. Lam. Software component certification. *IEEE Computer*, 34(9):30–36, September 2001.

294. M. Morrison. *Presenting JavaBeans: SunSITE India*. Virtual Library, 1997.

295. C. J. Mueller and B. Korel. Automated evaluation of COTS components. In *International Workshop on Automated Program Analysis, Testing and Verification (Limerick, Ireland)*, 2000.

296. R. Mukherjee, J. Jain, K. Takayama, and M. Fujita. Automatic partitioning for efficient combinatorial verification. In *Proceedings of the 2000 conference on Asia South Pacific design automation*, pages 67–72. ACM Press, 2000.

297. J. Munson and T. Khoshgoftaar. The detection of fault-prone programs. *IEEE Transactions on Software Engineering*, 18(5):423–433, 1992.

298. J. D. Musa. *Software Reliability Engineering*. McGraw-Hill, New York, 1998.

299. G. J. Myers. *The Art of Software Testing*. John Wiley and Sons, New York, 1979.

300. National Coordination Office for Information Technology Research and Development. January: High confidence software and systems research needs. http://www.ccic.gov/iwg/hcss.html, 2001.

301. National Product Line Asset Center. Nplace, 2002.

302. C. Ncube and N. Maiden. Cots software selection: The need to make tradeoffs between system requirements, architectures and cots/components. In *ICSE 2000 Workshop on Continuing Collaborations for successful COTS Development, Limerick, Ireland*, 2000.

303. S. H. News. Oops! Linux bug escapes early. http://www.securityfocus.com/news/293.

304. E. Niemelä and M. Holappa. Experiences with the use of corba. In *Proceedings of the 24th EUROMICRO Conference, Västerås, SE*, pages 989 – 996. IEEE Computer Society, 1998.

305. E. Niemelä and T. Ihme. Product line software engineering of embedded systems. *ACM SIGSOFT Software Engineering Notes*, 26:118 – 125, 2001.

306. E. Niemelä, M. Matinlassi, and P. Lago. Architecture-centric approach to wireless service engineering. *IEC, Annual Review of Communications*, 56:875 – 889, 2003.

307. E. Niemelä, H. Perunka, and T. Korpipää. A software bus as a platform for a family of distributed embedded system products. In F. Linden, editor, *Development and Evolution of Software Architectures for Product Families*, pages 14–23. Springer, 1998.

308. J. Q. Ning, K. Miriyala, and W. Kozaczynski. An architecture-driven, business-specific, and component-based approach to software engineering. In *Proceedings of Third International Conference on Software Reuse: Advances in Software Reusability*, pages 84–93, Rio De Janeiro, Brazil, Nov. 1994.

309. Object Management Group. CORBA Component Model specifications. `http://www.omg.org/technology/documents/formal/components.htm`. Access date April 5th, 2004.
310. Object Management Group. `http://www.omg.org/corba/whatiscorba.html`, 2000.
311. Object Management Group. CORBA component model v3, formal/2002-06-65. `http://www.omg.org/technology/documents/formal/components.htm`, 2002.
312. Object Management Group. Corba components. `http://www.omg.org/cgi-bin/doc?formal/02-06-65.pdf`, 2002.
313. Object Management Group. XMI: XML metadata interchange v.1.2. `http://www.omg.org/`, 2002.
314. Object Management Group. Adtf, 2nd revised submission on unified modeling language: Superstructure. version 2.0, 2003.
315. Object Management Group. Adtf: The uml 2.0 testing profile, July 2003.
316. Object Management Group. Omg unified modeling language specification, version 1.5. `http://www.omg.org/technology/documents/formal/uml.htm`, 2003.
317. S. W. O'Malley and L. L. Peterson. A dynamic network architecture. *ACM Transactions on Computer Systems*, 10(2):110–143, May 1992.
318. A. K. Onoma, W.-T. Tsai, M. Poonawala, and H. Suganuma. Regression testing in an industrial environment. *Commun. ACM*, 41(5):81–86, 1998.
319. A. Orso. Component Metadata for Software Engineering Tasks. In *Proceedings of the Second International Workshop on Engineering Dsitributed Objects, Springer-Verlag LNCS 1999*, pages 126–140, 2000.
320. A. Orso, M. J. Harrold, and D. Rosenblum. Component metadata for software engineering tasks. In W. Emmerich and S. Tai, editors, *Proceeedings of International Conference on Engineering Distributed Objects 2000*, LNCS 1999, pages 129–144, 2000.
321. A. Orso, M. J. Harrold, D. Rosenblum, G. Rothermel, M. L. Soffa, and H. Doo. Using component metadata to support the regression testing of component-based software. In *Proceedings of the International Conference on Software Maintenance (ICSM2001)*, pages 716–725, Florence, Italy, November 6-10 2001.
322. A. Orso, M. J. Harrold, and D. S. Rosenblum. Component metadata for software engineering tasks. In *Revised Papers from the Second International Workshop on Engineering Distributed Objects*, pages 129–144. Springer-Verlag, 2001.
323. T. J. Ostrand and M. J. Balcer. The category-partition method for specifying and generating functional tests. *Communications of the ACM, CACM*, 31(6):676–686, June 1988.
324. R. Paige and J. Ostroff. A proposal for a lightweight rigorous uml-based development method for reliable systems. In *Proceedings of Workshop on Practical UML-Based Rigorous Development Methods 2001 (co-located with UML 2001)*, Toronto, Canada, October 2001.
325. H. D. Pandi, B. G. Ryder, and W. Landi. Interprocedural def-use associations in c programs. In *Proc. of TAV4*, pages 139–153, Oct. 1991.
326. A. S. Parrish and S. H. Zweben. Analysis and refinement of software test data adequacy properties. *IEEE Transactions on Software Engineering*, 17(6):565–581, June 1991.
327. A. S. Parrish and S. H. Zweben. Clarifying some fundamental concepts in software testing. *IEEE Transactions on Software Engineering*, 19(7):742–746, July 1993.

328. B. Perens. Electricfence. ftp://ftp.perens.com/pub/ElectricFence/.

329. D. Petriu, C. Shousha, and A. Jalnapurkar. Architecture-based performance analysis applied to a telecommunication system. *IEEE Transactions on Software Engineering*, 26(11):1049–1065, 2000.

330. M. Pezzè and M. Young. *Software Testing and Analysis: Process, Principles, and Techniques*. John Wiley, 2004.

331. A. Pnueli. The temporal logic of programs. In *Proceedings of 18th IEEE Symposium Foundations of Computer Science(FOCS)*, pages 46–57, October 1977.

332. M. Polo. Automating Testing of Java Programs using Reflection. In *Proceedings of the ICSE 2nd International Workshop on Automated Program Analysis, Testing, and Verification, WAPATV*, 2001.

333. R. Pooley. Using UML to derive stocastic process algebra models. In *Proceedings of the 15th UK Performance Engineering Workshop (UKPEW)*, pages 23–34, 1999.

334. A. A. Porter and R. W. Selby. Empirically guided software development using metric-based classification trees. *IEEE Software*, 7(2):46–53, 1990.

335. G. Pour. Component-based software development approach: New opportunities and challenges. In *Proceedings of Technology of Object-Oriented Languages Tools 26*, pages 375–383, Santa Barbara, California, Aug. 1998.

336. G. Pour. Enterprise javabeans, javabeans & xml expanding the possibilities for web-based enterprise application development. In *Proceedings of Technology of Object-Oriented Languages and Systems*, pages 282–291, Nancy, France, June 1999.

337. G. Pour, M. Griss, and J. Favaro. Making the transition to component-based enterprise software development: Overcoming the obstacles - patterns for success. In *Proceedings of Technology of Object-Oriented Languages and systems*, pages 419–419, Nancy, France, June 1999.

338. A. Purhonen, E. Niemelä, and M. Matinlassi. Viewpoints of dsp software and service architectures. *Journal of Systems and Software*, 69(1–2):57–73, 2004.

339. C. Rajaraman and M. R. Lyu. Reliability and maintainability related software coupling metrics in C++ programs. In *Proceedings 3rd IEEE International Symposium on Software Reliability Engineering (ISSRE'92)*, pages 303–311, North Carolina, USA, Oct. 1992.

340. C. Rajaraman and M. R. Lyu. Some coupling measures for C++ programs. In *Proceedings of TOOLS USA 92 Conference*, pages 225–234, Santa Barbara, California, Aug. 1992.

341. B. Randell and J. Xu. The evolution of the recovery block concept. In M. Lyu, editor, *Software Fault Tolerance*, pages 1–21. Wiley, 1995.

342. T. Ravichandran and M. A. Rothenberger. Software reuse strategies and component markets. *Communications of the ACM*, 46(8):109–114, 2003.

343. D. Richardson and A. Wolf. Software testing at the architectural level. In *Proc. of 2nd International Software Architecture Workshop*, pages 68–71, San Francisco, California, Oct. 1996. ACM Press.

344. D. J. Richardson. Taos: Testing with analysis and oracle support. In *Proceedings of the 1994 international symposium on Software testing and analysis*, pages 138–153. ACM Press, 1994.

345. D. J. Richardson, S. Leif-Aha, and T. O. OMalley. Specification-based Test Oracles for Reactive Systems. In *Proceedings of the 14th International Conference on Software Engineering*, pages 105–118, May 1992.

400   References

346. E. H. Riedemann. *Testmethoden für sequentiell und nebenläufige Software-Systeme.* B. G. Teubner, 1997.

347. Robby, M. B. Dwyer, and J. Hatcliff. Bogor: an extensible and highly-modular software model checking framework. In *Proceedings of the joint 9th European Software Engineering Conference (ESEC) and 10th ACM SIGSOFT Symposium on the Foundations of Software Engineering (FSE)*, pages 267–276, 2003.

348. A. Romanovsky, C. Dony, J. L. Knudsen, and A. Tripathi, editors. *Advances in Exception Handling Techniques.* Springer Verlag, 2001.

349. D. Rosenblum. Challenges in exploiting architectural models for software testing. In *Proceedings of the International Workshop on the Role of Software Architecture in Testing and Analysis (ROSATEA)*, 1998.

350. D. S. Rosenblum. Adequate testing of component-based software. Technical Report 97-34, University of California, Department of Information and Computer Science, 1997.

351. G. Rothermel and M. J. Harrold. A safe, efficient regression test selection technique. *ACM Transactions on Software Engineering and Methodology*, 6(2):173–210, 1997.

352. G. Rothermel, M. J. Harrold, and J. Dedhia. Regression test selection for C++ software. *Software Testing, Verification and Reliability*, 10(2):77–109, 2000.

353. A. Rountev, A. Milanova, and B. Ryder. Fragment class analysis for testing of polymorphism in java software. In *Int. Conf. on Softw. Eng.*, pages 210–220, 2003.

354. J. Rumbaugh, I. Jacobson, and G. Booch. *The Unified Modeling Language Reference Manual.* Addison Wesley Lognman, 1999.

355. S. Bodoff et al. *The J2EE Tutorial.* Addison-Wesley, 2002.

356. F. Salles, M. Rodriguez, J.-C. Fabre, and J. Arlat. Metakernels and fault containment wrappers. In *Proceedings of the 29th International Symposium on Fault-Tolerant Computing*, June 1999.

357. P. Santos, T. Ritter, and M. Born. Rapid engineering of collaborative and adaptive multimedia systems on top of corba components. In K. Irmscher, editor, *Kommunikation in Verteilten Systemen.* VDE, Offenbach, 2003.

358. S. Savage, M. Burrows, G. Nelson, P. Sobalvarro, and T. Anderson. Eraser: a dynamic data race detector for multi-threaded programs. In *Proceedings of the sixteenth ACM symposium on Operating systems principles*, pages 27–37. ACM Press, 1997.

359. T. Schäfer, A. Knapp, and S. Merz. Model checking UML state machines and collaborations. *Electronic Notes in Theoretical Computer Science*, 55(3):13 pages, 2001.

360. C. H. Schmauch. *ISO9000 for Software Developers.* ASQC Quality Press, Milwaukee, Wisconsin, 1994.

361. R. Seacord and L. Wrage. Replaceable components and the service provider interface. Technical report, Software Engineering Institute, 2002.

362. S. Sedigh-Ali, A. Ghafoor, and R. A. Paul. Metrics and models for cost and quality of component-based software. In *Proceedings of the Sixth IEEE International Symposium on Object-Oriented Real-Time Distributed Computing (ISORC'03)*, pages 149–155, Hokkaido, Japan, May 2003.

363. Z. Segall, D. Vrsalovic, D. Siewiorek, D. Yaskin, J. Kownacki, J. Barton, D. Rancey, A. Robinson, and T. Lin. FIAT — fault injection based automated testing environment. In *Proceedings of the 18th International Sympo-*

sium on Fault-Tolerant Computing (FTCS-18), pages 102–107, Tokyo, Japan, June 1988.

364. B. Selic, G. Gullekson, and P. Ward. *Real-Time Object-Oriented Modeling.* John Wiley, 1994.

365. B. Shannon. Java 2 platform enterprise edition specification, 1.4 - proposed final draft 2. Technical report, Sun Microsystems, 2002.

366. M. Shaw and D. Garlan. *Software Architecture. Perspectives on an Emerging Discipline.* Prentice-Hall, 1996.

367. J. Skene and W. Emmerich. A model-driven approach to non-functional analysis of software architectures. In *Proceedings of 18th IEEE International Conference on Automated Software Engineering (ASE2003)*, pages 236–239, Montreal, Canada, October 6-10 2003.

368. D. J. Smith. *Achieving Quality Software (Third Edition).* Chapman & Hall, 1995.

369. I. Sommerville. *Software Engineering.* Addison-Wesley, sixth edition, 2001.

370. N. Soundarajan and S. Fridella. Understanding OO frameworks and applications. *Informatica*, 25:297–308, 2001.

371. M. Sparling. Lessons learned through six years of component-based development. *Communications of the ACM*, 43(10):47–53, 2000.

372. O. Spinczyk, A. Gal, and W. Schrder-Preikschat. AspectC++: an aspect-oriented extension to C++. In *Proceedings of the 40th International Conference on Technology of Object-Oriented Languages and Systems (TOOLS Pacific 2002)*, Sydney, Australia, Feb. 2002.

373. K. Sreenivasan and A. Kleinman. On the construction of a representative synthetic workload. *Communications of the ACM*, 17(3):127–133, Mar. 1974.

374. J. Stafford and L. Wolf. Annotating Components to Support Component-Based Static Analyses of Software Systems. Technical Report CU-CS-896-99, University of Colorado at Boulder, 1999.

375. J. A. Stafford and A. L. Wolf. Annotating components to support component-based static analyses of software systems. In *Proceedings of the Grace Hopper Celebration of Women in Computing*, 2001.

376. F. Stallinger, A. Dorling, T. Rout, B. Henderson-Sellers, and B. Lefever. Software process improvement for component-based software engineering: An introduction to the oospice project. In *Proceedings of the 28th EUROMICRO Conference (EUROMICRO'02)*, pages 318–323, Dortmund, Germany, Sept. 2002.

377. B. Subraya and S. Subrahmanya. Object driven performance testing of Web applications. In *Proceedings of the First Asia-Pacific Conference on Quality Software (APAQS'00)*, 2000.

378. G. Sullivan. Aspect-Oriented Programming using Reflection and Metaobject Protocols. *Communications of the ACM*, 44(10):95–97, 2001.

379. Sun Microsystem. Java message service specification. Technical report, Sun Microsystem Technical Report.

380. Sun Microsystems. Enterprise JavaBean Technology. http://java.sun.com/products/ejb/. Access date April 5th, 2004.

381. Sun Microsystems. http://developer.java.sun.com/developer, 2000.

382. Sun Microsystems. Java management extensions, instrumentation and agent specification, version 1.2. http://java.sun.com/products/JavaManagement, 2002.

383. Sun Microsystems. Java 2 platform, enterprise edition (J2EE). http://java.sun.com/j2ee/, 2003.

384. T. Systa, Y. Ping, and H. Muller. Analyzing java software by combining metrics and program visualization. In *Proceedings of the Fourth European Software Maintenance and Reengineering*, pages 199–208, Zurich, Switzerland, Mar. 2000.

385. C. Szyperski. *Component Software: Beyond Object-Oriented Programming.* Addison-Wesley, New York, 1998.

386. C. Szyperski, D. Gruntz, and S. Murer. *Component Software - Beyond Object-Oriented Programming.* Addison-Wesley, second edition edition, 2002.

387. A. Taulavuori. Component documentation in the context of software product lines. Technical report, VTT Publications 484, VTT Technical Research Centre of Finland, Espoo, 2002.

388. A. Taulavuori, E. Niemelä, and P. Kallio. Component documentation - a key issue in software product lines. *Journal Information and Software Technology*, 2004.

389. R. N. Taylor, D. L. Levine, and C. D. Kelly. Structural testing of concurrent programs. *IEEE Transaction on Software Engineering*, 18(3):206–215, 1992.

390. Testing Technologies. Ttcn-3 tool series. http://www.testing-technologies.de/products, 2004.

391. The Apache Software Foundation. BCEL: Byte Code Engineering Library. http://jakarta.apache.org/bcel.

392. The Apache Software Foundation. Regexp. http://jakarta.apache.org/regexp.

393. TIBCO. The power of now. TIBCO hawk. www.tibco.com/solutions/.

394. A. Tikkala and M. Matinlassi. Platform services for wireless multimedia applications: case studies. In *1st International Conference on Mobile and Ubiquitous Multimedia, Oulu, Finland*, pages 76 – 81, 2002.

395. A. Ulrich and G. Chrobok-Diening. International workshop on testing distributed component-based systems. *SIGSOFT Softw. Eng. Notes*, 24(4):43–46, 1999.

396. H. Ural and B. Yang. Modeling software for accurate data flow representation. In *ICSE'93*, pages 277–286, May 1993.

397. D. Urting, Y. Berbers, S. V. Baelen, T. Holvoet, Y. Vandewoude, and P. Rigole. A tool for component based design of embedded software. In *Proceedings of the 40th International Conf. on Tools Pacific: Objects for internet, mobile and embedded applications - Volume 10*, February 2002.

398. R. van Renesse, K. P. Birman, and S. Maffeis. Horus: A flexible group communication system. In *Commnications of the ACM*, Apr. 1996.

399. M. Vidger and J. Dean. An architectural approach to building systems from cots software components. In *Proceedings of the 22nd Annual Software Engineering Workshop*, pages 99 – 131, Greenbelt, Maryland, 1997. National Research Council.

400. M. Vigder. An architecture for cots based software systems. Technical Report NRC Report No. 41603, National Research Council of Canada, 1998.

401. M. Vigder, T. McClean, and F. Bordeleau. Evaluating cots based architectures. In *Proceedings of the Second International Conference on COTS-Based Software Systems*, pages 240 – 250, 2003.

402. J. Vincent. Built-in test vade mecum part i - a common bit architecture, version 2.0. http://www.component-plus.org, 2002.

403. P. Vitharana. Risks and challenges of component-based software development. *Communications of the ACM*, 46(8):67–72, 2003.

404. K.-P. Vo, Y.-M. Wang, P. Chung, and Y. Huang. Xept: a software instrumentation method for exception handling. In *Proceedings of the Eighth International Symposium on Software Reliability Engineering*, pages 60–69, Albuquerque, NM, USA, Nov 1997.

405. J. Voas. Certifying off-the-shelf software components. *IEEE Computer*, 31(6):53–59, June 1998.

406. J. Voas. COTS software: The economical choice? *IEEE Software*, 15(2):16–19, 1998.

407. J. Voas. Maintaining component-based systems. *IEEE Software*, pages 22 – 27, 1998.

408. J. Voas. Developing a usage-based software certification process. *IEEE Computer*, 33(8):32–37, August 2000.

409. J. Voas, F. Charron, G. McGraw, K. Miller, and M. Friedman. Predicting how badly "good" software can behave. *IEEE Software*, 14(4):73–83, /1997.

410. J. Voas and J. Payne. Cots software failures: Can anything be done? In *Proceedings of the First IEEE Workshop on Application Specific Software Engineering and Technology (ASSET'98)*, pages 140–145. IEEE Press, Mar. 1998.

411. J. Voas and J. Payne. Dependability certification of software components. *The Journal of Systems and Software*, 52(2-3):165–172, 2000.

412. M. Volter, A. Schmid, and E. Wolff. *Server Component Patterns: Component Infrastructures Illustrated with EJB*. John Wiley, 2002.

413. K. Wallnau. Volume iii: A technology for predictable assembly from certifiable components. Technical Report CMU/SEI-2003-TR-009, Carnegie Mellon University, Pittsburgh, PA, 2003.

414. K. Wallnau, S. Hissam, and R. Seacord. *Building Systems from Commercial Components*. Addison-Wesley, 2002.

415. Y. Wang and G. King. A European COTS Architecture with Built-in Tests. In *Proceedings of the 8th International Conference on Object-Oriented Information Systems, Springer-Verlag LNCS 2425*, pages 336–347, 2002.

416. Y. Wang, G. King, and H. Wickburg. A method for built-in tests in component-based software maintenance. In *Proceedings of the IEEE International Conference on Software Maintenance and Reengineering*, pages 186–189, 1999.

417. Y. M. Wang, O. P. Damani, and W. J. Lee. Reliability and availability issues in distributed component object model (DCOM). In *Fourth International Workshop on Community Networking Proceedings*, pages 59–63, Atlanta,Georgia, Sept. 1997.

418. C. Warner. *Evaluation of Program Testing*. IBM Data Systems Division Development Laboratories, Poughkeepsie, N.Y., 1964.

419. E. Weyuker. The evaluation of program-based software test data adequacy criteria. *Communications of the ACM*, 31(6):668–675, June 1988.

420. E. Weyuker. Testing component-based software: A cautionary tale. *IEEE Software*, 15(5):54–59, 1998.

421. E. Weyuker and F. Vokolos. Experience with performance testing of software systems: issues, an approach, and case study. *IEEE Transactions on Software Engineering*, 26(12):1147–1156, 2000.

422. E. J. Weyuker. Axiomatizing software test data adequacy. *IEEE Transactions on Software Engineering*, 12(12):1128–1138, 1986.

423. E. J. Weyuker. Testing component-based software: A cautionary tale. *IEEE Software*, 15(5):54–59, 1998.

424. J. Whaley, M. C. Martin, and M. S. Lam. Automatic extraction of object-oriented component interfaces. In *Proceedings of ISSTA 2002*, pages 218–228, July 22-24 2002. Roma, Italy.

425. C. H. Wittenberg. Progress in testing component-based software (abstract only). In *Proceedings of the International Symposium on Software Testing and Analysis*, page 178. ACM Press, 2000.

426. Y. Wu, M. Chen, and J. Offutt. UML-based integration testing for component-based software. In *Int. Conf. on COTS-Based Software Sys.*, 2003.

427. G. Xing and M. R. Lyu. Testing, reliability, and interoperability issues in the corba programming paradigm. In *Proceedings of 1999 Asia-Pacific Software Engineering Conference (APSEC'99)*, pages 530–536, Takamatsu, Japan, Dec. 1999.

428. S. Yacoub, A. Mili, C. Kaveri, and M. Dehlin. Hierarchy of cots certification criteria. In P. Donohoe, editor, *Proceedings of the First Software Product Lines Conference*, pages 397 – 411, Boston, 2000. Kluwer Academic Publishers.

429. S. M. Yacoub, B. Cukic, and H. H. Ammar. A component-based approach to reliability analysis of distributed systems. In *Proceedings of the 18th IEEE Symposium on Reliable Distributed Systems*, pages 158–167, Lausanne, Switzerland, Oct. 1999.

430. S. M. Yacoub, B. Cukic, and H. H. Ammar. Scenario-based reliability analysis of component-based software. In *Proceedings of 10th International Symposium on Software Reliability Engineering*, pages 22–31, Boca Raton,Florida, Nov. 1999.

431. S. S. Yau and B. Xia. Object-oriented distributed component software development based on corba. In *Proceedings of COMPSAC'98*, pages 246–251, Vienna, Austria, Aug. 1998.

432. M. Young and R. N. Taylor. Rethinking the taxonomy of fault detection techniques. In *Proceedings of the 11th International Conference on Software Engineering*, pages 53–62, May 1989.

433. Y. Yu and B. W. Johnson. A bbn approach to certifying the reliability of cots software systems. In *Proceedings of Annual Reliability and Maintainability Symposium*, pages 19–24, Tampa, Florida, Jan. 2003.

434. A. Zaremski and J. Wing. Specification matching of software components. *ACM Trans. on Software Engineering and Methodology*, 6(4), October 1997.

435. W. Zhao and C. Papachristou. Testing dsp cores based on self-test programs. In *Proceedings of the conference on Design, automation and test in Europe*, pages 166–172. IEEE Computer Society, 1998.

436. H. Zhu. Axiomatic assessment of control flow based software test adequacy criteria. *Software Engineering Journal*, Sept. 1995.

437. H. Zhu. A formal analysis of the subsume relation between software test adequacy criteria. *IEEE Transactions on Software Engineering*, 22(4):248–255, April 1996.

438. H. Zhu. A note on test oracles and semantics of algebraic specifications. In *QSIC'03*, pages 91–98, Dallas, USA, Oct. 2003.

439. H. Zhu and P. Hall. Test data adequacy measurement. *Software Engineering Journal*, 8(1):21–30, Jan. 1993.

440. H. Zhu, P. A. V. Hall, and J. H. R. May. Software unit test coverage and adequacy. *ACM Computing Surveys*, 29(4):366–427, 1997.

441. H. Zhu and X. He. A theory of behaviour observation in software testing. Technical Report CMS-TR-99-05, School of Computing and Mathematical Sciences, Oxford Brookes University, Oxford, UK, Sept. 1999.
442. H. Zhu and X. He. Constructions of behaviour observation schemes in software testing. In *HASE'00*, pages 2–12, New Mexico, Nov. 2000.
443. H. Zhu and X. He. A theory of testing high-level petri nets. In *Proc. of the IFIP 16th World Computer Congress*, pages 443–450, Beijing, China, Aug. 2000.
444. H. Zhu and X. He. An observational theory of integration testing for component-based software development. In *COMPSAC'2001*, pages 363–368, Chicago, Illinois, USA, Oct. 2001.
445. H. Zhu and X. He. A methodology of testing high-level petri nets. *Information and Software Technology*, 44(8):473–489, June 2002.
446. H. Zhu, L. Jin, and D. Diaper. Application of task analysis to the validation of software requirements. In *SEKE'99*, pages 239–245, Kaiserslautern, Germany, June 1999.
447. H. Zhu, L. Jin, D. Diaper, and G. Bai. Software requirements validation via task analysis. *Journal of System and Software*, 61(2):145–169, March 2002.

Index

Abstraction, 3, 216
Abstraction level, 3
Adequacy criterion, 27
Adequacy measurement, 246
Analysis, 274, 277, 284, 288, 289, 291
Architectural mismatch, 21
Architecture, 273–276, 278, 281, 284, 287, 289–291
Aspects, 74
Attachment, 215
Automatic code generation, 195
Automation, 349
Axioms of Behavioral Observations, 246

BIT component, 198
Branch testing, 241
Built-in contract testing, 196, 197
Built-in test, 55, 59

CDT framework, 179
Class state machine, 366
COM, 10, 319
Commercial-off-the-shelf, 14, 57, 315, 364
Complete partially ordered sets (CPO sets), 242
Component, 364
Component analysis, 17
Component container, 10
Component context, 197
Component contract, 197
Component definition, 5
Component deployment testing, 172
Component framework, 9

Component from external sources, 14, 18
Component instance, 5
Component interface, 364
Component model, 8
Component Object Model, 10
Component persistence, 5
Component produced by contract, 14, 18
Component produced in-house, 14, 18
Component provider perspective, 19, 365
Component specification variation, 227
Component state machine, 366
Component stub, 265
Component type, 5
Component user perspective, 19, 365
Component-based software development, 239, 315
Component-based software system, 320
Composability, 56, 70
Configuration, 197
Contract, 197
Contract checking, 191
Contract testing, 55, 56
Controllability, 28
CORBA, 318, 364
CORBA Component Model, 10
Cost-effectiveness, 1
COTS, 364
COTS component, 14
COTS Components familiarization, 21
CSM, 366

DCOM, 319, 364
Dependability, 349
Design by Contract, 34
Design pattern, 3
Distributed Objects, 314
Distributed systems, 314

Enterprise JavaBeans, 10, 319, 368
Entity bean, 11
Exception injection, 91
Exceptions, 89
Explicit server, 199
External quality, 24
Extraction Relation Between Schemes,
    248

Failure atomicity, 89
Fault detection ability, 249
Fault injection, 92, 349
Fault propagation, 29
Fault-tolerance, 349
Functional specification, 34

Glueware, 17

Hook methods, 34

Implicit server, 199
Incremental testing, 247
Independent commercial item, 14, 18
Infection, 30
Infinite test, 243
Information flow testing, 261
Input inconsistency, 27
Integration strategy, 265
    bottom-up, 265
    Top-down, 266
Integration testing, 239, 366
    Generalization of WIT methods, 263
    Heterogeneous WIT testing, 264
    Hierarchical, 261
    Higher order WIT methods, 263
    Incremental, 265
    White-box (WIT), 255
Interaction parameter testing, 258
Interaction sequence testing, 260
Interaction specification, 34
Interaction statement testing, 257
Interface probing, 27

Internal quality, 24
Introspection, 7

JavaBeans, 319
JUnit, 203

Limited exchange of information, 16
Live sequence charts, 274, 276, 281, 291
Logical state, 198

Message-driven bean, 11
Meta-data, 72, 75
Meta-information, 7, 17
Meta-object, 83
Middleware, 314, 349, 365
Model checker, 274, 284, 287, 289–291
Model coverage, 200
Model Driven Architecture, 196
Mutation score, 253
Mutation testing, 241, 245

Object-oriented framework, 33
Observation scheme, 243
Oracle, 366

Paragraph, 219
Path testing, 241
Polymorphism, 34
Prediction, 58, 60, 70
Product line, 2
Prototyping, 21, 26
Publish/subscribe, 273–277, 282, 289,
    290

Quality, 23
Quality assurance, 320
Quality attribute, 25
Quality characteristic, 23
Quality in use, 25
Quality indicator, 25
Quality metric, 25
Quality prediction model, 338

Reflection, 7, 85
Reliability, 349
Reuse, 1
Reverse engineering, 27
Risk management, 26
Robustness, 349

Security, 349
Session bean, 10
Software architecture, 314
Software metrics, 328
Software performance, 314
Software performance evaluation, 314
Software performance testing, 314
Software testing, 349
Special version of a commercial item, 14, 18
SPIN, 273–275, 284, 285, 288–291
Statement coverage, 253
Statement testing, 241
Subsumption relation, 249
System configuration, 197
System under test, 201

Template methods, 33
Test adequacy criteria, 245
Test architecture, 201
Test behavior, 201
Test case, 202
Test data, 201
Test driver, 265
Test models, 200
Test specification, 201
Test validation, 202
Test verdict, 202
Tester component, 197
Testing, 23
Testing communication protocols, 241

Testing component, 199
Testing concurrent systems, 241
Testing criteria, 200
Testing interface, 197
Testing methods, 246
    Design based, 240
    Design patterns, 250
    High order WIT, 263
    Program based, 240
    Specification based, 240
Testing profile, 196
Trace, 34
Tracing, 29
TTCN-3, 196, 203, 209

UML, 58, 60, 61, 70
UML testing profile, 196, 201
UML-based testing, 200
Universe of phenomena, 242
    Case-wise statistical construction, 254
    Design patterns, 250
    Partially ordered set (poset) construction, 251
    Product construction, 252
    Set construction, 250
    Statistical construction, 253

Validation, 273–278, 281, 287–289, 291
Virtual component, 180

Wrapper, 349